SYNTHESIZER PERFORMANCE
and Real-Time Techniques

THE COMPUTER MUSIC AND DIGITAL AUDIO SERIES
John Strawn, *Series Editor*

DIGITAL AUDIO SIGNAL PROCESSING
Edited by John Strawn

COMPOSERS AND THE COMPUTER
Edited by Curtis Roads

DIGITAL AUDIO ENGINEERING
Edited by John Strawn

COMPUTER APPLICATIONS IN MUSIC: A BIBLIOGRAPHY
COMPUTER APPLICATIONS IN MUSIC: A BIBLIOGRAPHY,
 SUPPLEMENT I
Deta S. Davis

THE COMPACT DISC HANDBOOK (2nd Edition)
Ken C. Pohlmann

COMPUTERS AND MUSICAL STYLE
David Cope

MIDI: A COMPREHENSIVE INTRODUCTION
Joseph Rothstein
William Eldridge, *Volume Editor*

SYNTHESIZER PERFORMANCE AND REAL-TIME TECHNIQUES
Jeff Pressing
Chris Meyer, *Volume Editor*

VOLUME 8   THE COMPUTER MUSIC AND DIGITAL AUDIO SERIES

SYNTHESIZER PERFORMANCE
and Real-Time Techniques

Jeff Pressing

A-R Editions, Inc.

Madison, Wisconsin

Library of Congress
Cataloging-in-Publication Data

Pressing, Jeff.
    Synthesizer performance and real-time techniques / Jeff Pressing.
        p.   cm. — (The Computer music and digital audio series ; v.
    8)
    Includes bibliographical references and index.
    ISBN 0-89579-257-5 : $49.95
    1. Synthesizer (Musical instrument)   I. Title.   II. Series.
ML1092.P68   1992
786.7′4—dc20   91-39700
                                                                        CIP
                                                                        MN

A-R Editions, Inc.
801 Deming Way
Madison, Wisconsin 53717-1903
(608) 836-9000

CONTENTS

· ·

v

PREFACE

· ·

The changes wrought by the MIDI and microcomputer revolution in the 1980s have dramatically transformed the world's music—some would say not for the better. Composers and listeners have grown to expect much more from electronic music than ever before, not only in audio quality, but in stylistic compass, reliability of hardware and software, and skill and versatility of its performers. Yet the synthesizer performer still finds it difficult to get up-to-date and accurate information about the details of the field. Periodicals are inevitably limited in detail and space; synthesizer and software manuals are often obscure or incomplete. Texts covering recent developments in these areas, with few exceptions, are often not current, focus only on specific instruments, or betray fundamental misconceptions about the musical and technological aspects of synthesis and synthesizer performance. Some adopt a cheerful attitude of condescension towards the reader that can be educationally counterproductive.

Along with these problems, great traditions of separatism have grown up between composer, performer, and technologist, a separation exacerbated by the ongoing stylistic segregation between jazz, classical, popular, contemporary art, and various "ethnic" musics in our culture. For many, musical preference acts as a litmus test for membership in this or that social group. As a result, the technologically knowledgeable often have very naive playing and composing skills, while many very musical performers may throw up their hands in despair at the first programming difficulty. Compounding all this is a remarkable confusion and misuse of terminology, resulting from manufacturers and researchers with NIH (Not

Invented Here) syndrome, daunting deadlines set for technical writers due to the rapid pace of technological change, a rapid obsolescence rate that means that most users only begin to explore the programming potentials of their instruments before they are tempted to buy another, and a commercial marketplace that leaps from one aural fad to the next.

This book tries to avoid these failings and bridge the gap between these separatist stances. Music of all styles is discussed. Musical issues and detailed performance techniques are consistently related to existing technological resources. Terminology has been consolidated and systematized whenever possible, hopefully not at the expense of creating new jargon. Each new term appears in italics when it is defined or first discussed. To avoid the problem of the rapid obsolescence of particular synthesizers and related devices, the book has been written as generically as possible, and mention of specific devices kept to a minimum.

The overall plan of the text is as follows. Chapter 1 begins with an exploration of the history and identity of the synthesizer. Chapter 2 examines the technological and conceptual resources needed by the synthesist for effective synthesizer programming and playing. These resources include the basic elements of synthesis, sampling, and computer software, a limited amount of acoustic and psychoacoustic terminology, and the theory of tuning systems. The emphasis throughout is on how this knowledge can be applied to performance. Chapter 3 explains MIDI—the method now used to control most synthesizers—in practical terms.

Chapter 4 examines the keyboard technique required of the synthesist, looking at its relations to other keyboard precedents as well as contemporary practice. A comprehensive set of exercises for performance techniques unique to the synthesizer is given. Chapter 5 focuses on single line (or "lead") performance. The point of view taken is that all synthesizer performers should be able to play an expressively shaped single line. Chapter 6 extends this point of view to polyphonic performance, focusing again on those techniques unique to the synthesizer. Extended performance techniques (such as keyboard remapping and real-time transformation of MIDI data) are also treated here, and numerous musical examples given.

Chapter 7 discusses a number of practical issues in synthesizer performance, whether on stage, in the studio, with tape, with a sequencer, or with other instruments. Chapter 8 examines procedures used to imitate sounds, primarily those of acoustic instruments. The emphasis is on how sounds should be performed to enhance realism. Chapter 9 looks at the increasingly important role played by nonkeyboard controllers.

Chapter 10 considers the current and future role of the synthesizer in ensembles and discusses possible repertoire for synthesizer "orchestras." It also includes a brief review of discographical sources for electronic music. Chapter 11 investigates new concepts in musical performance available through computer assistance, including such notions as intelligent instruments and interactive music systems.

Each chapter has its own set of references. In addition, a general bibliography at the end of the book lists important source materials (books and journals) in certain related areas, including tuning systems, acoustics, and electronic composition. Two appendices contain information on the history of synthesis and a number-system conversion table.

I have not found a novel way of acknowledging the vital assistance given by many friends and colleagues in the preparation of this book. But to the following persons my heartfelt thanks for valuable criticism and advice: David Mash, Tom Rhea, Jim Sosnin, John O'Donnell, John McCaughey, Darryl Pratt, Michael Spicer, Tony Falla, Chris Lai, David Ward-Steinman, Barton McClean, Neil Rolnick, Simon Emmerson, Roger Dean, Simone De Haan, Cathy Falk, and John Stinson. For the guiding editorial hand of John Strawn and especially the mammothly detailed improvements of editors Chris Meyer and David Severtson I am especially indebted. They have put up with my stubbornness and made it a much better book. I am also grateful to various institutions that have supported me during this writing process: La Trobe University, Berklee College of Music, and the Media Laboratory of the Massachusetts Institute of Technology. For invaluable personal support and patience I thank Jill and Adam and Rebecca.

Jeff Pressing
Melbourne, Australia
February 1, 1992

THE SYNTHESIZER AS INSTRUMENT

· ·

We also have sound-houses, where we practice and demonstrate all sounds, and their generation. We have harmonies which you have not, of quarter sounds and the lesser slides of sounds. Diverse Instruments of Musick likewise to you unknown, some sweeter than you have; together with Bells and Rings that are dainty and sweet. We represent small sounds as well as Great and Deep.... We make diverse Tremblings and Warblings of sounds.... We have certain helps, which set to the ears doe further hearing greatly. We have strange and artificial echos, reflecting the voice many times, as if it were tossing it.... We have also means to convey sounds in trunks and pipes, in strange lines and distances.

▪ Sir Francis Bacon, *New Atlantis* (1624)

To understand performance issues on the synthesizer, it is helpful to begin by asking a single question: Is the synthesizer a musical instrument? The answer to this might seem to be an obvious yes. After all, the synthesizer is a device—a tool—that can produce sound when manipulated by a performer. This is certainly one basic definition of a musical instrument.

This affirmative answer may well be correct, but it leaves much unsaid. The problem is that the given definition is very broad; it includes "instruments" as diverse as the oboe, African drums, voice, electric guitar, washboard, a pair of tin cans whacked with spoons, the tape recorder, a mixing desk, the computer, even a radio or an electric blender. So let us supplement our first question with another: What kind of musical animal is the synthesizer?

To answer this question, we must look at what we expect a musical instrument to be able to do and what causes musicians to play it and compose music for it. There are perhaps three ideas of central importance here: the versatility, identity, and degree of development of an instrument. An instrument should be versatile if it is to be widely usable; it should have a sense of identity if it is to attract performers and composers alike; and it must be developed technically and cybernetically to the point where it can be truly musically expressive if it is to be more than a novelty item. *Cybernetics* means the science of control and communication, referring here to the human/machine interface. *Expression* refers to the vividness of musical experience that can be obtained by optimal placement, design, and articulation of musical statements in performance. It is fostered by integrated musicality and attention to fine detail. (Expression may also refer to other qualities such as emotion and symbolism.)

When an instrument comes to be highly developed, these three ideas take root in many practicalities. A highly developed instrument acquires highly developed special playing techniques, along with a dependable relationship between characteristic performance gestures and the sound produced. It tends to have a characteristic sound (timbral palette) and *sound ideal*. It has an associated repertoire and constellation of cultural baggage. It has a more or less standard shape and construction, and associated approaches to tuning and articulation. Well-developed instruments have a strong sense of individual identity, one that is reinforced by a number of further factors like shared terminology, teaching traditions, and conventions of use in standard ensembles. Many such instruments have a depth or power of expression that makes them capable of successful extended solo performance, like the violin or electric guitar. Others without this potential are nonetheless effective in their contribution to expressive ensemble performances.

Unfortunately for our earlier answer, the synthesizer fails nearly every one of these tests. It is so versatile that its identity is compromised. It can make almost any sound; therefore it has in principle no characteristic sound and in practice a set of widely differing sound ideals. Because of the synthesizer's youth, the rapid rate of technological change, and other factors, there is virtually no standard repertoire; the closest to it is the recurrence of certain popular or academic market approaches that use the currently fashionable sound engines or conceptual designs. The synthesizer's terminology is confused and inconsistent due to the market-driven naming practices of the major manufacturers, and the users of commercial software are divided into largely noncommunicating camps by the professional dominance of different computers in different geographical areas (Macintosh in the United States, Atari in Europe, and NEC in Japan, with Amiga and especially IBM users also quite visible internationally).

Playing techniques are showing some signs of standardization, but there is still great diversity and downright inconsistency. Pitch bend, for example, is accomplished by wheels on some instruments, by joysticks on others, and even by ribbon controllers on a few others. Such controllers have different sizes and shapes and frequently display different response curves. Nearly all have programmable ranges of response. Keyboard velocity output curves are widely inconsistent, even between products made by the same manufacturer in some cases. The relation between technique and sound is almost arbitrarily reconfigurable; this is a tremendous resource, but it makes technical standardization very difficult. Many synthesizers can be retuned, in principle, to any tuning; but the fingering patterns for one tuning system may not transfer to the next. Many synthesizer performers, often through naiveté, completely disregard the idea of expressive control.

If this isn't bad enough, synthesizers may have any shape or size, even though keyboards are still far and away the most widespread type of control interface. Increasingly, we find controllers based on traditional techniques of other instruments, like guitar, trumpet, sax, recorder, violin, and mallet or kit percussion, as well as some others that propose completely novel techniques, like the Theremin and Airdrums. Furthermore, pitch trackers allow, in principle, any sound source to act as a control interface, including the voice. Certainly, the synthesizer is history's least standardized instrument in physical appearance.

It is the dramatic and grass roots growth of the synthesizer that has been largely responsible for this—it is a victim of its own success. Like every rapidly changing movement whose time has come, it is messy, unplanned, and full of rough edges; it is stimulating, causes trouble, forces us to rethink, and sets trends.

Put another way, the synthesizer's potentials are still far from fully developed, despite the unifying influence of MIDI; it is a nascent, immature instrument. But it has come far in a short time, even if users and designers continue to forget much that was known before. The synthesizer *is* an instrument, simply one unlike any that has come before it. It is very young, but offers a range of sonic possibilities without historical precedent. A child of the computer age in its current incarnation, it demands an unprecedented degree of sound-shaping skill and performance versatility, both physically and conceptually. This may partly explain why synthesizer performance still relies so heavily on earlier modes of music design and technique.

The rapid obsolescence of commercial synthesizers poses unique problems for the synthesizer performer. Sounds or recorded performance data programmed in one synthesis environment may need to be transferred later (or, more likely, soon) to another such environment, requiring a great expenditure of time without guaranteed success. As discussed above, technique may not be portable from one environment to another without considerable modification and relearning.

One can dream of a level of standardization where the performer simply brings disks or other storage media containing sounds, programs, and sequencer data to a standard concert hall performance configuration, plugs them in, and starts playing. It may be a long time before that happens; it may well never happen. Until then, physical and mental versatility will be part of synthesizer performance skills.

Because of these issues, it is not possible to study synthesizer performance in isolation from the detailed technical design of the instrument, as is customary on many traditional Western instruments. Even so, this varies. Pianists very often know next to nothing about piano action and couldn't begin to revoice their instrument or tune it properly. On the other hand, oboists and bassoonists regularly cut their own reeds. But because the synthesizer's palette of sound is so broad, and because the function of the synthesizer controller actions can be so drastically reprogrammed, a synthesist who does not understand how to fine-tune ("tweak") the sounds to fit the occasion will be a limited performer. Yet while it is clear that the synthesist must understand his or her particular synthesizers well, any book focusing on the details of specific instrumental models will be out of date very rapidly.

The approach taken here is therefore a generic one. Specific synthesizer models are mentioned in the text as little as possible and only as examples of more general ideas. The resources and processing procedures of synthesis are described generically and illustrated by examples and exercises. On the other hand, general playing procedures are described in detail. The aesthetic and technical issues involved in mapping sound resources onto the playing interface are thoroughly discussed. It is left for readers to interpret this in full detail on their own performance devices.

THE SYNTHESIZER AND ELECTRONIC MUSIC PERFORMANCE: SOME HISTORICAL HIGHLIGHTS

Before looking further at the contemporary synthesizer, it will be useful to examine a little of its history. In making our survey, we will emphasize the distinction beween the use of the synthesizer as a performing instrument and its use as a composing instrument, since it is the first use that forms the primary subject of this book.

The history of the development of electronic instruments for performance is a fascinating story, part quixotic and idiosyncratic, part rigorously scientific, part intuitive and musical. It is full of dead ends, missed opportunities, and tales of researchers imaginatively marrying science and music. Of course, its full details are far too vast for this book. Instead, I highlight instruments that were especially ambitious, successful, or conceptually novel. A detailed outline of developments in and related to electronic music may be found in Appendix A.

One point of terminology must first be cleared up. In this survey we include both electric and electronic instruments. These terms are different, though in common parlance they are often interchanged. Strictly, *electric* means using electricity, although it is often used today to mean "not electronic." *Electronic* means using tubes or semiconductors. Thus a doorbell is electric, but a radio is electronic.

As outlined in Appendix A, electric instruments go back at least as far as 1759, to the static electricity-driven electric harpsichord of Jean-Benjamin de La Borde. Other electric instruments, using such sound sources as electrically driven bells, or whistles from electric arc lamps, found persistent if sporadic development in the nineteenth century. But the first synthesizer, in the sense of an instrument that could not only generate but shape sound using electricity, is arguably the Telharmonium (also sometimes called the Dynamophone) of Thaddeus Cahill (1867–1934).

The instrument's first patent was lodged in 1896, but its first finished form dates from 1900, and it only emerged in a fully developed model at its public debut in early 1906 in Holyoke, Massachusetts. It was essentially a large modified electrical dynamo, able to produce a form of additive synthesis. Although its general synthesis facilities were quite limited, it had two velocity-sensitive keyboards and envelope shaping, was multitimbral, and required one or two keyboard players for live performance. Cahill's Telharmonium project was nothing if not ambitious; one version of it weighed over 200 tons, occupied an entire city block in New York, and was to be broadcast over the telephone transmission lines in a national network of "Telharmony." Yet the Telharmonium failed to catch on. Its high voltages interfered with other users of the telephone system, it was very expensive, and it was built on a technology that rapidly became obsolete (courageously, it had predated the thermionic tube). For full details see Weidenaar (1988).

With the patenting of the vacuum tube diode (by Ambrose Fleming in 1904) and triode amplifier (by Lee De Forest in 1906), the foundations of electronic musical instruments were laid. On the one hand amplification techniques were applied to traditional instruments, ultimately producing the electric guitar and devices such as the neo-Bechstein piano. On the other hand electronic sources and shaping procedures were progressively refined and incorporated into the production of new musical instruments that were often synthesizers in all but name. Most of these machines continued to use traditional instrument-type performance interfaces, with the keyboard far and away the favorite. One that did not was the proximity-controlled monophonic Thérémin (1919) of Leon Thérémin—often written without its accents as "Theremin"—which probably qualifies as the first successful electronic musical instrument. It used two detectors, one controlling volume and one controlling frequency of sound, that sensed the spatial positions of the hands of the performer. The Theremin gave the world its first electrical musical virtuoso, Clara Rockmore, and is still played today. Many contemporary listeners first heard it in the Beach Boys' pop masterpiece, "Good Vibrations."

Another significant instrumental success was the Ondes Martenot (1928) of Maurice Martenot. Although its synthesis facilities are very limited (far more than on the Telharmonium, for example), this low-note priority monophonic instrument rapidly achieved a developed performance status in the hands of virtuosi like Jeanne Loriod. It is played with a keyboard and also has a portamento-based ribbon technique that involves slipping a ring over the finger of one hand. Vibrato is produced using lateral motion of the key depressed by the right hand, while the left hand controls dynamics and basic filtering at a small console. Many composers (e.g., Maurice Ravel, Paul Hindemith, Olivier Messiaen, Arthur Honegger, Charles Koechlin, Edgard Varèse, Darius Milhaud) have written works for ensembles that include this instrument or consist entirely of Ondes Martenots. Though rarely seen in standard concert fare, it is still played today and may be studied as a bona fide instrumental major, primarily in France, notably at the Paris Conservatoire. The most commonly performed pieces today include Messiaen's *Turangalîla-symphonie* (1948) and his *Trois petites liturgies* (1944).

Also in 1928 the Trautonium of Friedrich Trautwein emerged. This was a performance machine incorporating subtractive synthesis and the use of formants (peaked filters that emphasize certain frequencies). It attracted a number of composers to write for it, including Richard Strauss and Paul Hindemith, the latter becoming a proficient performer. This was not a keyboard machine; it used foot pedals and a linear band for control. The Trautonium, though rare, is still played today and has evolved to have an expressive control interface matched by few contemporary synthesizers. Oskar Sala, a notable early virtuoso on the instrument, made numerous changes and improvements resulting ultimately in the Mixtur-Trautonium (1949–1952).

Another significant development was the Coupleux-Givelet synthesizer, developed by Edouard Coupleux and Joseph Givelet. Premiered at the 1929 Paris Exposition, it was the first extensively programmable synthesizer. Although its official name was "Automatically Operating Musical Instrument of the Electric Oscillation Type," its inventors also used the term *synthesizer,* and were probably the first to do so. This machine allowed dynamic variation, modulation, envelope shaping, and filtering but was basically a device designed to realize compositions automatically—it was not a performance instrument.

The Coupleux-Givelet was fairly short-lived and was overshadowed by events such as the commercial success of the Hammond organ, introduced in 1935 by Laurens Hammond. The conception of this instrument moved away from the synthesis model, although other less well-known machines by Hammond, like the Novachord (1939), allowed considerable sound shaping.

Harald Bode was another important early researcher and instrument builder. His Warbo Formant-Orgel (1937) was an early polyphonic polytimbral electronic keyboard, his Melodium (1938) a sophisticated monophonic touch-sensitive keyboard. Bode's later Melochord (1947) was an early electronic split-keyboard instrument.

A new level of real-time expressive electronic performance was ushered in by the advent of Canadian Hugh Le Caine's instrumental constructions, notably the electronic sackbut (1948). The name, a term for a medieval ancestor of the trombone, was chosen by Le Caine to avoid well-known historical associations. Le Caine's sackbut was monophonic, with pitch (key selector and lateral pressure) and volume (vertical pressure) finely controllable by the right hand at the keyboard. In the original forms of the instrument three dimensions of timbre control were available for the left hand: waveform selection, frequency modulation, and formant frequency. Later on Le Caine expanded the left-hand design to control six aspects of timbre, which, from remaining documentation, seem to correspond to six independent dimensions. Work on this later model stopped in 1960 and the instrument disappeared, but apparently a total of eight dimensions of control were eventually possible. Existing recordings show that Le Caine had developed synthesis and real-time control techniques to a level rarely matched since.

The later 1940s saw the beginning of a nearly twenty-year period when the synthesizer was largely used in the studio with multitrack tape recording. The orientation was compositional, and the studio techniques of tape manipulation and audio processing of recordings of both acoustic sounds (*musique concrète*) and electronic sources (*elektronische musik*) date from this period. These different orientations soon merged to become simply "electronic music"; the studio methods became known as "classical studio technique." Composers and music researchers were excited about the possibilities for precise sonic realization that the newly perfected multitrack recording supplied, and the role of the performing artist in interpretation was glossed over or assumed to be supplantable by equivalent studio techniques. Symptomatic of this orientation was the development of the RCA Mark II Electronic Music Synthesizer, which was installed at the Columbia-Princeton Electronic Music Center (formally founded in 1959). The synthesizer's growth as a live performance instrument was also stymied by certain persistent technical problems and the lack of standardized instruments usable by performers.

But other technological changes were favoring opposite tendencies. In particular, the development of the transistor in 1947–48 allowed, among other things, a miniaturization and ruggedness of construction compatible with the musician's idea of a small and portable instrument. It came to be realized by engineers like Harald Bode that these advances also made possible a modular design based on voltage control. *Voltage control* is the shaping of some parameter of a synthesis module (for example, oscillator frequency) by an applied voltage. Devices such as VCOs (voltage-controlled oscillators), VCFs (voltage-controlled filters), and VCAs (voltage-controlled amplifiers) proliferated. This meant that not only could sound modules arbitrarily control each other in complicated patch configurations, but live performance could be readily driven by all sorts of devices — not just the commonly available knobs and dials that were far from being optimal for producing musical expression.

Such changes began to be reflected in the formation of a number of live electronic music ensembles in the later 1950s and particularly throughout the 1960s, including the ONCE Group, the Sonic Arts Union, Intermodulation, Mother Mallard's Portable Masterpiece Company, Nuovo Consonanza,

FLUXUS, Musica Elettronica Viva, AMM, Teleopa, and others. For a comprehensive review of these early live avant-garde groups, see Mumma (1975).

Eventually, electronic refinements in transistors and other semiconductor devices made possible affordable voltage-controlled synthesizers that could be reliably played in the public forum. While the first commercial synthesizers may be safely attributed to Robert Moog (1964), other workers were also active in this period and made significant contributions in the development of these early voltage-controlled machines. Don Buchla was building his Electronic Music Machines on the West coast of the United States at the same time Moog was active on the East coast. Paul Ketoff contributed his portable triple manual Synket in 1964–65, built at the behest of composer/performer John Eaton.

According to electronic music historian Tom Rhea, Moog was the first to use exponential envelopes for control, which allowed the synthesizer both to play familiar tunings and create time shapes that were "natural"—that is, they took into account the basically logarithmic processing of human perception. Others involved in the design of these early modern synthesizers included Herb Deutsch and Vladimir Ussachevsky.

Beginning in the middle 1960s computers began to be seriously applied to music, work that was ultimately to bring about new synthesis methods and a change from analog to digital circuitry. The main method used here is *direct digital synthesis,* which simply means that the computer directly outputs sound via a *digital-to-analog converter* (DAC or D/A converter). The DAC takes a series of numbers from the computer and converts them to a smoothly varying voltage that can drive a loudspeaker. A series of music languages were developed, initially by Max Mathews, to control musical information. These were called Music 1, Music 2, and so forth, with particularly viable results being found with Music 4, Music 11, Csound, and others. (Generically, we shall refer to them as *Music N.*) Direct digital synthesis remains the favored research tool of workers in the field of synthesis, but it is not potentially a real-time technique on any but the largest computers, which are seldom available for music use. As such, it does not feature prominently in our history of synthesizer performance. (Continuing advances in computer and digital signal processing design are expected to soon change this.) However, computers may be linked with synthesizers for real-time effects, and this collaboration began in this period as well, being called *hybrid synthesis* (a now largely obsolete term in this meaning), where digital computers controlled analog synthesizers (at that time all that was available).

For well over a decade after their introduction, voltage-controlled machines held exclusive public sway. Wendy Carlos's album *Switched-On*

Bach (1968) brought this type of synthesizer to public awareness in a way that few could ignore, whether or not they approved. Commercial monophonic performance synthesizers proliferated in the early 1970s, supplemented by the introduction of polyphonic machines beginning around 1975. The first synthesizer festival was held in 1974. Controlling devices, predominantly keyboards, started to become separated from the sound sources they drove, often being strapped on the body in a standing position.

Then, beginning in the early 1970s, the next technical change occurred: The synthesizers themselves began to become digital rather than analog. As part of this, the microprocessor came to electronic music systems. A *microprocessor* is just the central processing unit (CPU) of a computer, built from a small number of integrated circuits (chips)—often just one. The use of this device allows the functions of various synthesis modules to be duplicated by software rather than being located in physically separate circuits. It also allows for improved stability, reliability, and control of synthesis components. Just as important, synthesizers, like the computers making them up, soon became *programmable:* A group of settings corresponding to a certain sound can be stored and recalled quickly as needed. Synthesizer performance became increasingly practical with this development. The Synclavier (1976, New England Digital Corporation) was the first commercially marketed digital synthesizer, one that has grown to be the undisputed top-end professional system for studio work, with a price to match. In 1977, the Prophet 5 (designed by Dave Smith of Sequential Circuits) became the first microprocessor-based fully programmable polyphonic synthesizer.

New sources of sound entered the digital world by the advent of *sampling,* or digital recording. The *analog-to-digital converter* (ADC or A/D converter) made this possible by converting continuous acoustic sound into discrete numerical representation. Samplers could take natural sounds and process them digitally in a way that had only previously been feasible with the studio techniques of *musique concrète.* The Australian Fairlight CMI (Computer Music Instrument), released in 1979, alerted many people's attention to the musical possibilities of this procedure for the first time. Also new to commercial machines was practical FM-based synthesis, exemplified by Yamaha's DX7 (1983) and subsequent products, based upon innovative research by John Chowning at Stanford University a decade or more earlier. These techniques were the first real departures from the instruments of Buchla and Moog, created over a decade before.

Around this same time some synthesizers became *multitimbral,* allowing more than one sound color to sound at once. *Composite synthesis* techniques soon proliferated, this term being used here to refer to machines that incorporate both electronic waveforms and samples of acoustics instruments as sound sources, as is now common in machines made by Roland (D series, L/A synthesis), Korg (M and T series), Ensoniq, E-mu, Kurzweil, Yamaha, and Kawai.

This explosion of different devices gave rise to an encouraging example of cooperation among musicians: MIDI, the Musical Instrument Digital Interface. This is a universal serial communication protocol between electronic music devices of any kind. Proposed in 1981 by Sequential Circuits and refined by a number of companies in the years 1981–82, it was first used to connect two musical devices from different manufacturers (Sequential and Roland) in January 1983 at a meeting of the U.S. National Association of Music Merchants convention ("NAMM show"). This simple protocol has now been adapted to control virtually every possible electronic musical device, and a flotilla of new products has sprung into being on the back of its versatility and universality, including special performance devices like master controllers.

By the early 1980s microcomputers were having an increasing impact on synthesizer performance. A *microcomputer* is just a small computer made up of a microprocessor, memory for programs and data storage, and information input and output devices. Their low price and increasing ease of use have brought about their wide adoption in the world of electronic music. Although the first microcomputers date back to 1975, it was not until the 1980s that enough standardization and speed became available to make them practical for any serious musical purposes, and many potentials have only become either apparent or practical since 1985 or so. Today their use is widespread for a variety of purposes including direct digital synthesis, composition, synthesizer programming, scoring, and *sequencing* (the recording, editing, and playback of digital data).

The combination of MIDI and microcomputers has led to the development of many so-called *intelligent instruments,* or *interactive music systems,* in the second half of the 1980s. Here the performer interacts with the computer as a partner in improvisational performance. Many workers have been active here, as discussed in chapter 11. One of the earliest developed composing systems that showed interactive intelligence was the Electronium of Raymond Scott (ca. 1965). In 1970, Max Mathews's GROOVE system appeared, extensively used by composer/performer Emmanual Ghent. William Buxton and the SSSP group developed a system that incorporated conducting and a complex system of real-time control. Interactive performers active into the MIDI era include Salvatore Martirano, Joel Chadabe, Tod Machover, Morton Subotnick, Michel Waiswicz, keyboardist Richard Teitelbaum, and trombonist George Lewis.

Late in the 1980s the digital workstation concept—a synthesizer (possibly also sampler) with built-in sequencer, audio effects, and, often, disk drive—became popular. This term can be used with better justification to refer to multisynthesis hardware and software environments that support both real-time digital signal processing and MIDI, such as the Kyma/Capybara system or the NeXT computer with IRCAM Signal Processing Workstation board.

By 1990, the standard synthesizer was digital, programmable, multitimbral, MIDI-based, and included both synthesized and sampled sound sources. Increasingly, it had its own built-in audio effects unit, and one or more software companies somewhere had written a computer editor for it. Although the keyboard remained the standard controller, an increasing number of alternatives, based on traditional instruments or completely novel designs, were being produced and used by musicians.

SYNTHESIZERS AND SYNTHESISTS

In the above catalog of possibilities we have avoided actually defining what a synthesizer is. This is not an arbitrary omission; its great variety and mutability make it hard to pin down. One sense of it is given by Hubert Howe in *The New Grove Dictionary of Music and Musicians:* "a machine which generates and modifies sounds electronically." This definition is useful, but not sufficiently specific. For example, it means that things like a stereo playback system or the traditional Hammond organ might be called synthesizers—a worrisome position. It also does not distinguish a synthesizer from a sampler, as is commonly done today, even though some machines exist with both functions, and even though the term *synthesizer* is sometimes used to encompass all electronic sound modules, including samplers. We will therefore use the following: A synthesizer is a musical instrument that produces sound by combining, shaping, and processing constituent electronic sound sources. Its central features involve electricity, the ability to combine and modify basic sonic elements, and some degree of programmability. Sometimes we will use the term to include samplers, and sometimes we will distinguish the two types of machines. Context should make clear which usage applies.

Some synthesizers are designed only for the automatic execution of compositions. These we will call *composition synthesizers.* They are not the main focus here. Synthesizers with a performance interface (e.g., built-in keyboard) or a potential connection to one (e.g., via MIDI) we will call *performance synthesizers.* All modern synthesizers fall into this second category.

Synthesizers can be either analog or digital, as described above. Here we will find it useful to define these terms more carefully. An *analog signal* is one that varies continuously (smoothly). A *digital signal* (or message) varies discretely, via a list of numbers; it jumps from one value to another, and is fundamentally discrete. Analog signals or processes are often more "natural" but are susceptible to errors, higher levels of noise, and circuit instabilities. Digital signals are far more reliable but must have sufficient resolution if they are to avoid inaccuracies in the representationof signals, such as sound, that are fundamentally continuously varying. Figure 1.1 shows an analog signal and a coarse digital representation of it. Conversion between analog and digital representations of sound (or other signals) is frequently necessary in synthesis.

Although the push towards complete digitalization of synthesizers is now well along, many current machines still contain some analog components yet are referred to as digital instruments. Moreover, the term *analog synthesizer* is still used anachronistically to describe some synthesizers that are based on additive and some subtractive synthesis, even when their design is actually predominantly or completely digital. We will avoid this terminology in this book, but it is still commonly encountered. Terms like *DCO*, used by Korg and Roland for digitally controlled oscillator, explicitly indicate the use of digital processing, in contrast to terms such as *VCO* (voltage-controlled oscillator), which might be pure analog or a mixture of analog and digital. Other terms for digital audio devices are also found, such as *TVA* and *TVF* for time variant amplifier and filter respectively.

Another problem in terminology is finding a suitable single word for a person who plays a synthesizer. If we try to form this word in the normal way, from the name of the instrument, we find that *synthesist* is already in use to describe the programmer, not the player, of the instrument. The logical possibility *synthesizist* is a phonetic disaster of the first order, and there seems to be no other generally accepted term. So in this book we will use the cumbersome phrases *synthesizer performer, synthesizer player,* and sometimes *synthesist.*

FIXED AND REAL-TIME SYNTHESIS

Synthesizer performance has three primary conceptual components: the fixed programming of the basic sounds (sound objects), the real-time programming that provides access to the expressive potentials needed in performance, and the gestures and techniques needed to play the music correctly and idiomatically. We distinguish in particular here between the first two components: *fixed synthesis,* the synthesis design components that create the basic sound objects serving as notes or distinct events, and *real-time synthesis,* the design components that specify

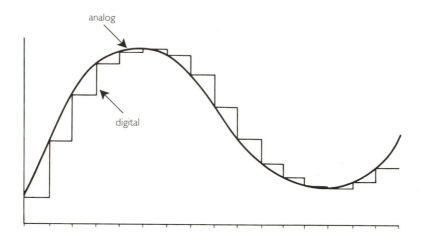

analog

digital

FIGURE 1.1   An analog signal and its digital representation.

how the basic sound objects can be changed in real time by the performer. For example, fixed synthesis will specify waveforms, fixed modulation routes, hard-wired frequency relations, envelopes, and so on. Real-time synthesis will specify such things as controllable pitch bend range, the function and range of response of controllers like wheels and footpedals, velocity response curves, system performance design issues, and so on. Real-time controls often alter otherwise fixed parameters.

In musical terms, fixed synthesis determines the repeatable nature of the sound objects triggered when a Note On command is sent by the instrument interface. Real-time synthesis determines how expression, articulation, and timbral change can be dynamically added to these sound objects by the performer. Both of these components are vital in making musically useful sounds. Older concepts of timbre have often emphasized the role of the fixed sound object in sound imitation; it is now recognized that the role of real-time shaping is at least as critical. This lesson has still to be absorbed by many synthesizer owners.

These two types of synthesis, though conceptually distinct, cannot always be completely untwined from each other. In so far as it is possible to do so, we will emphasize the issues of real-time synthesis, assuming that the reader has access to sound objects with something like an appropriate shape and timbre for their intended function. The repertoire of fixed synthesis techniques will be summarized in chapter 2.

Note that we use the term *sound object* here to generalize the concept of note. This term was first coined by Pierre Schaeffer (1952). The word *note* is perfectly usable when it refers to a sound that has a reasonably fixed pitch and a single attack in its amplitude envelope. It can become restrictive and distracting when the sound produced from a key depression is, for example, a continuous glissando, a rapid string of different pitches, or the looped sound of seals barking. Especially if such sonic conglomerations are heard as a unified event, the term *sound object* is far more appropriate.

THE GENERIC SYNTHESIZER, SYNTHESIZER MODULE, SAMPLER, AND MASTER CONTROLLER

Throughout this book we will sometimes refer to specific types of synthesizers and performance devices as examples of the issues under discussion. But to avoid the problem of rapid obsolescence, we will primarily address performance on an imaginary generalization of contemporary synthesizer models, called here the *generic synthesizer*, which has a common core of standard features. This is not the only generic performance device we shall need to discuss. We can similarly distinguish a *generic synthesizer module, generic sampler,* and *generic master controller*. These share many common features, to be described below, but the essential elements that distinguish these four categories of musical machines from one another are the performance interface, programming controls, and sound engine. Before we can investigate further, we will discuss these three elements.

By *performance interface* we mean all the things manipulated by the player in performance: pitch selector and ancillary controllers. The *pitch selector* allows the selection of pitch and is nearly always modeled after a traditional instrument: keyboard, wind instrument, mallet percussion, drum set, violin, and so on; but it can have any design in principle. The *ancillary controllers* are auxiliary devices that allow further real-time control of the sound. These devices may operate via MIDI (and are then called MIDI controllers), or they may operate directly on the internal sound engine, possibly in ways different from those allowed by MIDI.

Such controllers may be either continuous or discrete. *Continuous controllers* allow physically continuous motion and send out information at a rapid enough rate to give the effect of continuous change in the sonic variable they control. They include the wheel, joystick, slider, ribbon, knob, bar, breath controller, foot controller, channel pressure, and polyphonic pressure. The most common controllers of this type are two wheels or a joystick with two control directions, dedicated to pitch bend and modulation. Many such controllers may be programmed to have a variety of functions. *Discrete controllers* function as two-state switches, sending on- and off-values. They may take the form of foot switches (pedals or buttons) or switches operated by the hand (buttons and switches).

The programming controls are the controls that allow the device to be programmed, and there are three kinds: editing controls, mode selection-controls, and program selection controls. *Editing controls* allow the synthesizer to change the parameters that make up a program. Editing on most synthesizers is organized into a hierarchy of pages. Each *page* is a distinct screen on the display, accessed by one or more specific sequence of button pushes (or dial or slider movements). Most machines now have *mark* and *jump* features for convenience in editing. These allow one or more pages to be marked (singled out) so that editing may move directly between these few pages using the jump button rather than laboriously going up and down the predefined hierarchy of pages that constitutes the machine's editing architecture. Some synthesizers number all pages and allow direct access to any page via this numerical label.

On any particular page, a cursor is normally used to select from among the available parameters; the cursor may be moved about with the aid of cursor buttons or a special knob. Once a parameter is selected, its value may be adjusted by using the *data entry device*. Some parameters affect the synthesizer only in certain states or programs, whereas others may be global, applying to every state of the machine.

Mode selection controls select distinct modes of operation of the device. These include play mode, where the synthesizer is configured for performance; edit mode, where the synthesizer is configured for editing and programming, as just described; store mode, where data are stored and recalled; and often a utility mode, which contains miscellaneous functions. These modes are not necessarily all present in a specific synthesizer and sometimes are not delineated in precisely the way given, but the classification remains generally useful.

The *program selection controls* pick between the different programs stored in memory. A *program* is a set of stored parameter values and information routings on a synthesizer or other device, selectable by number from an ordered collection of such programs (often 1–32 or 1–64). Another term we will use for this is *patch,* a term that as a verb means "to connect together." Its synonymity with program comes from older analog machines that used patch cables to connect different electronic modules. A set of programs (thirty-two, sixty-four, and 100 are common sizes) stored as a unit is called a *bank.*

On equipment that has other functions, a program may have no associated sound. For example, a program on a MIDI patch bay just specifies what is connected to what. Where the instrument in question is a sound source, each program corresponds to a specific stored sound or, on a multitimbral machine, a set of sounds. Various manufacturers use such terms as *voice, keyboard, performance, instrument, setup, tone, partial,* and *timbre* to refer to sound programs or components of multitimbral setups. We will avoid all these, except in discussing multitimbral programming, since they have other well-established uses. These other meanings will be summarized below. Sometimes we will simply refer to the sound of a patch or program or its components (other constituent sounds).

The individual front panel controls are often used to perform more than one chore, such as to select programs and edit parameters. Which function is active is determined by the settings of other controls (normally the mode selection controls). This is done to minimize cost; yet while this overlap of function is economical it can also occasionally be confusing. Carried to the extreme of a very small total number of buttons, it can result in highly complex tree structures for editing. The general idea of multifunctional controls is not likely to be overturned since the separability of form and function is a prominent computer design principle.

The *sound engine* consists of the parts of the device that electronically generate the sound, whether by synthesis or sampling. Sound engines can be either monophonic or polyphonic: Those that are monophonic can produce only one note at a time; polyphonic sound engines can produce two or more simultaneous notes, each of which is assigned at least one *voice* (an independent sound generating unit). The most common numbers of available voices are four, six, eight, twelve, sixteen, twenty, twenty-one, twenty-four, thirty, thirty-one and thirty-two. A synthesizer capable of sounding up to sixteen voices at once would be called sixteen-voice polyphonic. Note that more than one voice may be assigned to each note; for example, if each note is assigned two voices, then a sixteen-voice polyphonic synthesizer could play at most eight notes at once. In musical parlance, the machine could play up to eight monophonic parts, each with a potentially different timbre (tone color).

Now we can distinguish the generic devices described above. The true self-contained synthesizer has all three essential elements: performance interface, programming controls, and sound engine. The synthesizer module denotes a synthesizer that has no performance interface. It consists of a sound engine and programming controls, and is played by remote control via MIDI. The master controller has a performance interface and programming controls but no sound engine. It is used to drive synthesizers, synthesizer modules, and other devices. Nonaudio controllers are sometimes called *remote keyboards*. (It should be noted that most contemporary synthesizers have a Local Off function, which disconnects the synthesizer keyboard from its sound engine, effectively making it a master keyboard.) Professional models of all these devices are always programmable.

The contemporary *sampler* is very similar to the categories of synthesizer and synthesizer module. It may or may not have a performance interface (keyboard) attached, but its central feature is the ability to record sound digitally and use these recorded samples as the basis for its sound engine. Samplers will also incorporate some synthesizer-like facilities for sound shaping, the amount and type depending on the particular model. *Sample players* are modules that have acoustic samples as the basis for their sound engine, limited editing facilities, and no ability to record new samples.

Other cases besides our four main categories exist. Some electronic sound devices lack both a performance interface and any significant programmability, such as the piano module; these consist of preset sounds externally playable via MIDI. There is no standard term for these machines, but we may call them *sound modules* where such a distinction is necessary. Other devices, like digital pianos or inexpensive preset organs, have a performance interface (keyboard) and a sound engine but are not programmable. There seems to be no standard term for these devices either, but we will not need to refer to them very often in this book.

There are also *MIDI-driven traditional instruments,* notably pianos controlled by solenoids, such as Yamaha's Disklavier. These are not sonically programmable, but they do normally have a performance interface and, of course, a nonelectronic sound engine. Some such devices, like the Yamaha MIDI Grand Piano, may not be MIDI controllable but build MIDI control facilities into the traditional instrument itself to allow sound modules to be driven from a normal grand piano. So-called *MIDI retrofits* are available; these convert a traditional instrument to a MIDI controller. These include devices such as the Forte MIDI Rail Modification for piano, Keyboard Systems' retrofit for Hammond organs, and numerous guitar retrofits. Many pre-MIDI synthesizers can likewise be converted to allow MIDI control by modification kits.

The four major devices of this section—the synthesizer, synthesizer module, sampler, and master controller—share a number of practical features. These include an operating system, internal memory, external data storage device, a display, program selection controls, audio connections and controls (not found on the master controller), and MIDI connections.

The terms *operating system* and *memory* have their standard meanings in the field of computing. The operating system is the part of the device or set of software instructions that coordinates its overall operation, tells the device how to respond to commands from the user, and performs other functions. It can either be in the form of hardware or software; software often has the advantage of being upgradable or rewritable by the computer-literate user.

Memory is the location where data are stored. It can be internal or external. A small area of internal memory used for quick and convenient temporary data storage is called a *buffer*. External storage devices in common use are the disk drive, which stores data on computer floppy disk, special manufacturer-specific RAM and ROM cartridges, PCM cards, and audio cassette. (CD-and optical-based storage of MIDI data also exists but is less common.) Some of these, such as ROM (read-only memory) cartridge and PCM (pulse code modulation) cards, are *read-only,* meaning that the user can access (read) the stored data but cannot store (write) new data. Others, such as floppy disk, RAM (random access memory) cartridge, and cassette, permit both reading and writing.

Most terms used to refer to memory on synthesizers are transferred directly from the terminology of computers. Thus, synthesizers use the term *save* to mean to transfer data from internal memory to external device and *load* to mean to transfer data from external storage device to internal memory. Volatile memory, which disappears when the synthesis device is turned off, is distinguished from nonvolatile memory, which is retained when the machine is shut down, usually by the use of a long-term battery. For example, ROM is always nonvolatile, as is synthesizer cartridge RAM, but microcomputer RAM is volatile. Storage media that allow both reading and writing must typically be formatted (or initialized) before use. This procedure sets up the disk or RAM cartridge for correct data storage and retrieval, much in the manner that the lines on a parking lot guide where automobiles should be placed.

Displays allow more convenient editing, and are commonly based on liquid crystal display (LCD) or light emitting diodes (LEDs). *Program selection controls* are the controls used to choose programs for performance. *Audio connections* are typically monophonic or a stereo pair. Contemporary multitimbral synthesizers and samplers tend to have as many audio outputs as they have capacity for simultaneous independent timbres: Six or eight is not uncommon. Samplers have one or two audio inputs as well; two inputs are only needed for stereo sampling. The physical audio controls are usually just master volume; relative volumes between different timbres on a multitimbral machine are typically programmed by the editing controls. *MIDI connections* usually include IN, OUT, and THRU; the master controller normally has four or even more OUTs.

Figure 1.2 shows the generic synthesizer, with a sixty-one-note keyboard. Figure 1.3 shows a generic synthesizer module. Samplers are

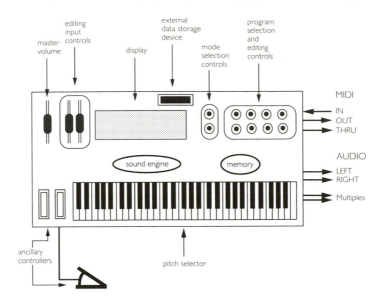

FIGURE 1.2   The generic synthesizer.

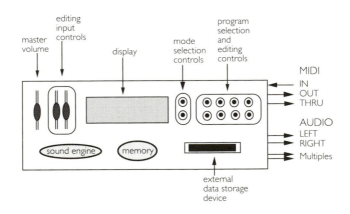

FIGURE 1.3   The generic synthesizer module.

schematically nearly identical to the given diagrams, depending on whether or not they include a built-in keyboard, the only external difference being the presence of audio inputs. In making such diagrams, one has to make visible assumptions about the nature of the playing interface. Here, a keyboard has been chosen since it remains the most common controlling device. However, nonkeyboard controllers are increasingly important, and so, in the following chapters, discussion of the type of interface will be kept generic whenever possible. In cases where keyboard terminology is used, the concepts will nearly always be transferable to other performance interfaces. Chapter 9 discusses these controllers in some depth.

KEYBOARD SYNTHESIZERS AND CONTROLLERS

There is a variety of keyboard sizes in the contemporary synthesizer marketplace. The most common key spans for synthesizers and master controllers are given in table 1.1. This list of sizes is not exhaustive, and other keyboards, like electric pianos and clavinets, come in still other sizes. The Wurlitzer electric piano has sixty-four keys (A to C), while the old Fender Rhodes had seventy-three; contemporary electronic grand pianos usually have the full eighty-eight note range. Figure 1.4 shows a schematic of an eighty-eight note master controller. Master controllers also exist with more than eighty-eight notes: The Bohm P92 has ninety-two keys, from F to C.

The main differences between master controllers and keyboard synthesizers are that master controllers lack audio outputs, have more sophisticated MIDI implementation, and have more front panel controls for the real-time control of synthesis. All professional keyboards now have some form of velocity sensitivity, which is also sometimes called touch sensitivity, though it is absent on some less expensive and home entertainment models. Further discussion of the resources of various synthesizer keyboards in comparison to traditional keyboards is found in chapter 4.

THE MULTITIMBRAL SYNTHESIZER

The multitimbral (polytimbral) synthesizer in many ways is just a collection of monotimbral synthesizers in one box. The maximum number of independent timbres in such machines normally varies from two up to a possible sixteen. Devices that allow only two timbres are bitimbral and can be said to operate in *dual* mode; more typically, four to eight separate timbres are available. Each timbre can be controlled separately by assigning it a distinct MIDI channel (numerical label), and each program is typically a global program that can reconfigure the entire set of sounds available from the machine. The limit of sixteen comes from the maximum number of MIDI channels, but it is in principle possible for a

SPAN	COMMENTS
3-octave C to C (37 keys)	strap-on keyboards; small, inexpensive synthesizers
4-octave C to C or F to F (49 keys)	strap-on keyboards; small, inexpensive synthesizers
5-octave C to C (61 keys)	standard professional synthesizer keyboard (organ concept)
6¼-octave E to G (76 keys)	light touch master controllers
7¼-octave A to C (88 keys)	heavy touch master controllers, digital piano controllers (piano concept)

TABLE 1.1   Common sizes for synthesizer keyboards and keyboard controllers.

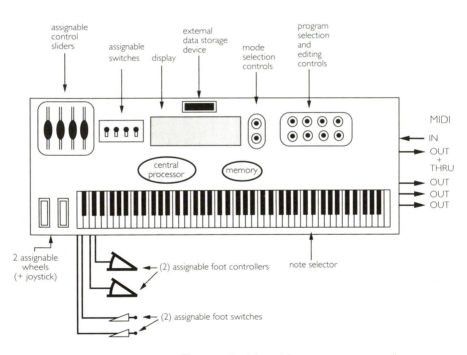

FIGURE 1.4   The generic eighty-eight-note master controller.

multitimbral synthesizer to play more than sixteen timbres, either by having two or more separately addressable MIDI inputs or by a programming design that allows the timbre within each channel to be chosen on a note-by-note basis, depending on such things as keyboard position (called *range limiting*) or velocity of keystroke (called *velocity switching*).

Multitimbral programming design is hierarchical, and terminology varies widely from company to company. One typical design runs as follows. At the top level are the multitimbral programs, each with a distinct number. Each program consists of a number (six, for example) of separately controllable *parts* (each possibly having a different timbre), to which specific single sounds (variously called *tones, partials, roots,* etc.) have been assigned from a set of stored possible sounds. MIDI control operates on a basic channel for certain global operations and on part-specific channels for note and controller performance data. Figure 1.5 shows the basic three-level architecture. Note that different parts may have the same MIDI channel and the same basic sound (here called *tone*), and that some parts may be set to be inactive if they are not required. The only limitations in layering will be the total number of voices available from the sound engine. Devices with more than three levels to their multitimbral design allow layering and more developed processing of basic sources in the extra levels, as is indicated in a basic form in program 3 (parts 4 and 6) in the figure. An alternative but somewhat less common organization of multitimbral synthesizers directly assigns one or more internally stored sounds (*layers, programs,* etc.) to each MIDI channel.

THE IMPROVISATION–COMPOSITION CONTINUUM

Music is produced in our culture, as in every other, under a continuum of procedures whose identifiable end points are usually labeled *composition* and *improvisation.* In the case of composition, the musical materials are substantially worked out by the composer before performance. It is well to remember here that music can be completely composed (fixed) without being set to paper. But even in the most exhaustively notated score or precisely imagined aural conception, gaps and ambiguities remain, and these must be filled in and resolved by the performer. Much unspecified performance detail is provided by relevant traditions of performance practice, some is provided by the performer's rehearsed interpretation, and some will be different every time due to the vagaries of human action.

Improvisation is the simultaneous design and execution of musical ideas. The devising and performance of the invented material are "synchronous" or, more realistically, occur without substantive introspection in a fraction of a second. Improvisations are either free or, more typically, use a referent. The *referent* is an underlying scheme or guiding image specific to the given piece. The referent may exist in time, either with a

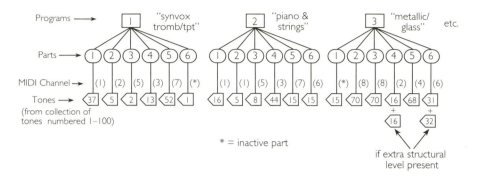

FIGURE 1.5   Architecture of a multitimbral synthesizer.

pulse (clocked referent) or without one (sequenced referent); it may make no specification of the order of events (out-of-time referent). Improvisation referents may include almost anything, such as the figured bass of baroque music, the jazz song form, a story, the theme and variations approach, the kinetic images of modern dance, or film and drama. Those who wish to look deeper into the general issues behind contemporary improvisation should consult Bailey (1980), Pressing (1984; 1987), and Dean (1989).

Typically, the style in which the synthesizer is played will determine the amount of improvisation appropriate: Jazz-like solos will feature improvisation; pieces in classical style will have fixed arrangements of notes; popular song solos may be improvised, newly composed, or slavishly copied from a previously recorded studio version, depending on the band. Even very free styles of improvisation are likely to use largely composed sounds. The integration of computers and sequencers in synthesizer performance has provided new possibilities in the range of options between freely improvised and completely scored music. "Interactive composition" and "intelligent instruments" are two such possibilities.

AESTHETICS, STYLE, AND FUNCTION

The production of electronic sound is not without its full share of aesthetic problems and considerations. What shall guide us in designing sound objects? What makes a sound or a collection of sounds good or bad (or, more to the point, contextually effective)? According to what models or orientations shall sounds be shaped in real time by performers? What shall we expect of electronic music in terms of style and innovation? The answers to these questions are crucial, yet will be incomplete and contradictory for the foreseeable future—such is the nature of art of any kind, particularly one in such an active stage of development. It is clear that electronic music is still in a stage of exploration and that electronic music composers, when they do not imitate traditional styles, are still grappling with the formation of an authentic language (or authentic languages). The stylistic pluralism of electronic music aptly mirrors our culture's own musical diversity.

In practical terms, we take the point of view here that the synthesizer should be able to play in any existing musical style—from popular to "avant-garde" to classical to African-American to various non-Western traditions—and also act in good faith with regard to its own electronic stylistic conventions and history. (The term *avant-garde* is given in quotation marks because it is used in different ways by different musicians. Its fundamental meaning is innovative or pioneering art, but it can be used among practicing MIDI musicians to mean a certain collection of freer styles associated with experimental music traditions that were widely influential in the 1950s through the 1970s. Furthermore, some postmodernist critics question whether the idea of an avant-garde even makes sense today, when virtually anything is possible. Other stylistic terms, like *contemporary music,* can also be unclear. Music of our time is contemporary, but the term is used by art music musicians and writers to mean "serious" concert music—another unfortunate piece of language—and by popular musicians and some of the lay public to mean popular and rock music.)

In structural terms, due to the synthesizer's wide timbral and dynamic palette and developing potential for real-time control, it can readily service almost any musical function: lead, accompaniment, doubling, call-and-response, obbligato, sound effect source, drone, harmonic pad, generator of textural smears, and so on. These potentials can be realized only when fixed and real-time programming are developed to a sufficient degree and when the performer has learned sufficient repertoire and cultural or historical context to understand something of the "essence" of the music in question—what its function is meant to be and how the performer must think and act to realize that function.

REFERENCES

Bailey, D. *Improvisation: Its Nature and Practice in Music.* London: Moorland Publishing, 1980.

Darter, T., compiler. ed. G. Armbruster, T. Rhea et. al. *The Art of Electronic Music.* New York: Quill, Keyboard, 1984.

Davies, H. "Electronic Instruments." In *The New Grove Dictionary of Musical Instruments,* ed. Stanley Sadie. London: Macmillan, 1984.

Dean, Roger. *Creative Improvisation.* London: Open University Press, 1989.

Mumma, G. "Live Electronic Music." In *The Development and Practice of Electronic Music,* ed. J. H. Appleton and R. C. Perera. Englewood Cliffs, N. J.: Prentice-Hall, 1975.

Pressing, J. "Cognitive Processes in Improvisation." In *Cognitive Processes in the Perception of Art,* ed. W. R. Crozier and A. J. Chapman. Amsterdam: North-Holland, 1984.

————. "Improvisation: Methods and Models." In *Generative Processes in Music,* ed. J. Sloboda. London: Oxford University Press 1987.

Rhea, T. L. "The Evolution of Electronic Musical Instruments in the United States." Ph. D. diss., George Peabody College, Nashville, Tennessee, 1972.

Schaeffer, Pierre. *À la recherche d'une musique concrète.* Paris: Éditions du Seuil, 1952.

Weidenaar, Reynold. "The Telharmonium: A History of the First Musical Synthesizer 1893–1918." Ph.D. diss., New York University, 1988.

SYNTHESIS, SAMPLING, AND SOFTWARE

. . . .

I'm just not excited by [synthesizers] at all. I'm not thrilled by something that does exactly the same thing over and over. Why people are is beyond me. I mean, they're not excited by assembly lines. . . . To me, synthesizers are a little bit like formica. If you see it from a distance, it looks great—this big panel of blue or pink or whatever that fits in well with your designer home. But when you get close to the surface of formica, it's not interesting; nothing's going on there. Contrast this with a . . . forest, for instance. You look at it from the air and it's rich, complex, and diverse. You come in closer and look at one tree and it's still rich, complex, and diverse. You look at one leaf, it's rich and complicated. You look at one molecule, it's different from any other molecule. . . . I want to make things that have that same quality . . . things that allow you to enter them as far as you can imagine going, yet don't suddenly reveal themselves to be composed of paper-thin, synthetic materials.

▪ Brian Eno, from an interview in *Downbeat* magazine, June 1983

In this chapter we look at a general overview of certain technological resources available to the synthesizer performer. These resources are not the performed music but the technological tools (and their supporting knowledge bases) with which such music can be created and refined. The primary resources fall in the areas of synthesis, sampling, and computer software, and this chapter looks at these three areas from both practical and conceptual viewpoints. The intention is not to treat these areas exhaustively, which would be in any case impossible in a single chapter, but to provide a core of common terminology and understanding and an overview of possibilities for the performer.

In the case of synthesis and sampling, we examine the kinds of sound sources and the kinds of sound modification and combination techniques that are available on commercially available synthesizers, samplers, and related sound engines. These resources vary from machine to machine, but they are based on a relatively small number of possibilities that have been developed by researchers in the field of electronic music. A good understanding of the principles behind synthesis is essential for getting the most out of any particular synthesis system and also in choosing which synthesizers may best complement each other in the construction of a multisynth setup.

The fundamental procedure of synthesis and sampling may be looked at as follows. Synthesis starts with some basic sound sources. These are then combined and modified in various ways by sound-processing modules to produce a complete synthesizer program. Each such program can be stored for recall and corresponds to a specific sound (or set of sounds) and a specific setup of the performance interface (keyboard, controllers) for performer manipulation of specific musical parameters. In other words, each program may contain both fixed and real-time synthesis components. In our survey of synthesis resources, therefore, the goal is to gain a sense of the spectrum of sonic and control possibilities available to the synthesizer performer and programmer.

ACOUSTIC AND PSYCHOACOUSTIC PRELIMINARIES

Before proceeding with the main material at hand, it will be essential to make a few comments about acoustics and psychoacoustics and define some terms to ensure that we are speaking a common language. Acoustics is the study of the physical properties of sound. Psychoacoustics may be defined as the study of the way humans perceive sound. We will treat neither of these topics rigorously or in depth in this book. However, certain facts and terms from these disciplines will have a direct effect on synthesizer performance and must therefore be examined briefly.

Physical and Perceptual Variables

First, it is important to keep in mind the difference between physical variables and perceptual variables. Physical variables are scientifically measurable quantities; perceptual variables are human interpretations or responses to them. Thus, frequency (e.g., 264 Hz, or Hertz, meaning cycles per second) is a physical variable; the corresponding pitch (close to middle C) is the corresponding perceptual variable. Clock time (e.g., 1.00 second) is a physical variable; a rhythm of equivalent duration (e.g., two beats of a certain rhythmic feel at M.M. = 120) is a possible corresponding perceptual variable. (M.M. means Maelzel's metronome and refers to the number of beats—usually quarter notes—per minute.) Amplitude is a physical variable that corresponds to the amount of atmospheric displacement of a sound or the voltage of an electrical signal; the corresponding perception is of loudness, which is usually indicated musically in only a relative fashion, by dynamic markings in a score. We will find several of these distinctions to be quite important in synthesizer performance.

Perceived variables often turn out naturally to have a roughly logarithmic (log) basis. In other words, if the physical variable varies linearly, our perception appears, approximately, to vary logarithmically. An equivalent way of saying the same thing is that if the physical variable varies exponentially (e.g., by multiplication by a constant), our perception of it varies roughly linearly (e.g., by addition of a constant). Thus, if we double the frequency, we add an octave to the perceived pitch. If we double it again, we add another octave, and so on. Other musical variables, including dynamics and envelope times, show similar effects. Figure 2.1 shows the three types of curves: logarithmic, linear, and exponential. The value of each function (here the perceptual variable) is read on the y axis (vertical axis); the value of the independent variable (here the physical variable) is read on the x axis (horizontal axis).

In the area of loudness or sound level, the relation between physics and perception normally relies on the unit called the *decibel* (a tenth of a bel—written dB). This variable measures the physical intensity of sound and is defined using a base 10 logarithmic scale. It allows a comparison of the intensities of a sound of intensity I and a reference sound of intensity (power) I_0, as follows: Relative intensity in dB = 10 log (I/I_0). If, instead of intensities, amplitudes A and A_0 are used, the formula becomes: Relative intensity in dB = 20 log (A/A_0), since $I \sim A^2$ (intensity is proportional to

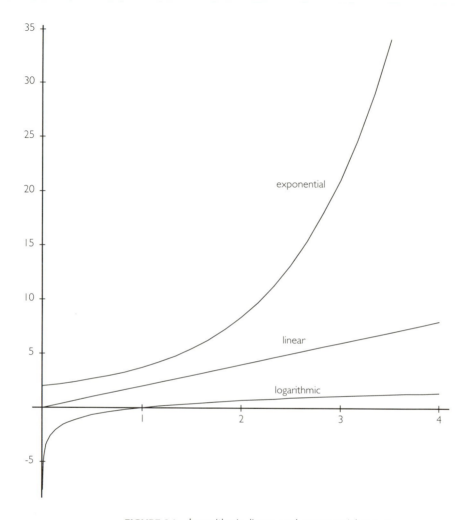

FIGURE 2.1   Logarithmic, linear, and exponential curves.

the square of amplitude). From this we can see that if one source has twice the amplitude (volume) of another, it will be $20 \, log_{10}2 = 20 \times 0.30103 \approx$ 6 dB higher in intensity.

The decibel can also be used as a measure of absolute sound level by adopting a standard reference level. A common reference level is called the threshold of audibility. If this threshold is set to 0 dB, then 60 dB corresponds to normal speech, 80 dB to shouting, and 120 dB to the threshold of pain.

Spectral and Temporal Qualities of Sound

The primary physical variables affecting the perceived quality or timbre of a sound are its spectrum and its behavior over time. A sound's spectrum is simply its frequency distribution—in other words, where its sound energy is localized over the full audible frequency range of approximately 20 to 20,000 Hz. Such a spectrum will in general be dynamic, meaning constantly changing in time. In any particular time interval we may plot the energy distribution of a sound as a function of frequency; this is called a *frequency domain* plot or representation. Alternatively, we may plot the actual instantaneous amplitude of the sound over time; this is called a *time domain* plot or representation. Figure 2.2 compares these two ways of representing sound. Conversion between time and frequency domains is achieved by a mathematical procedure known as the *Fourier transform.*

The spectra of many musical sounds consist of sharp peaks at a number of frequencies. The simplest spectrum of this kind is that of a pure single frequency: a sine wave. Its spectrum is shown in figure 2.3a. More generally, there will be a lowest frequency and additional tones heard above this, all called *partials*. These are numbered in order so that lowest frequency is the first partial, the next highest frequency the second partial, and so on. (The term *overtone* is sometimes used for any partial above the lowest, but this is a use we will not favor here.) If these partials are found at frequencies very close to small integer multiples of some *fundamental* frequency, the partials are said to be *harmonic,* and the partials themselves are often called *harmonics*. If the fundamental is actually the lowest frequency in the spectrum, with frequency f_0, then the harmonics will be found at $2f_0$, $3f_0$, $4f_0$, ... and so on. These idealized harmonics form what is called the *harmonic series*; a harmonic spectrum is shown in figure 2.3b. Instruments based on vibrating strings and tubes have partials that follow this series, and these have been dominant in our culture. With most harmonic sound sources, such as musical instruments, this sequence of simple ratios is preserved when different fundamental frequencies are used, allowing us to make sense of melodic progressions.

The psychoacoustic point is that when partials are in harmonic relation, we will hear an overall pitch for the sound in question that is at the fundamental frequency, sometimes even if that fundamental frequency is weak or not present. For example, if the frequencies making up a tone are 100 Hz, 200 Hz, and 300 Hz, we will hear 100 Hz as its fundamental pitch. If the frequencies in a tone are 200 Hz, 300 Hz, 400 Hz, and 500 Hz, we may still interpret 100 Hz as its fundamental pitch, depending on relative amplitudes of the partials and their time behavior; only the apparent timbre will be different. This effect, where the ear supplies an implied

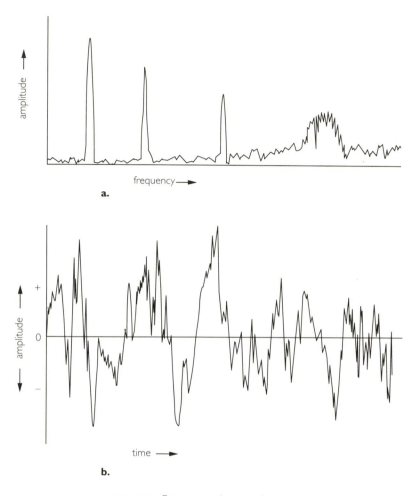

FIGURE 2.2 Frequency domain plot (a) and time domain plot (b).

fundamental, is strongest in the range 150 to 500 Hz. The issue of what we really hear is a complex one because the ear can also add significant amounts of higher harmonics when sounds are sufficiently loud.

If the spectrum of the sound consists of distinct peaks, but the corresponding partials do not coincide with small integer multiples of some fundamental frequency, the sound and its partials are said to be *inharmonic,* as illustrated schematically in figure 2.3c. Another word for such sounds is *clangorous.* Vibrating plates, bars, bells, drums, and membranes have such spectra. In this case there may or may not be a perceived fundamental pitch, and if there is one listeners may disagree about what it is.

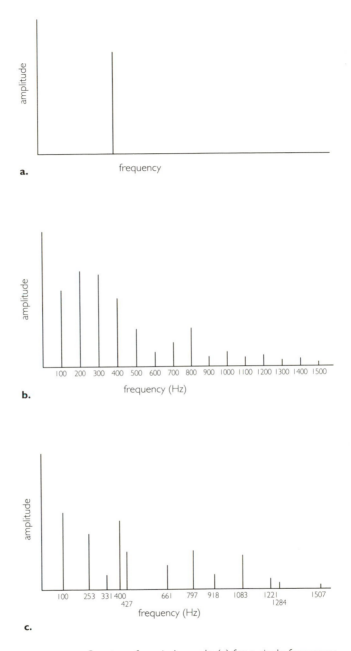

FIGURE 2.3 Spectra of musical sounds: (a) for a single frequency, or sine wave; (b) for a harmonic sound—with partials belonging to the harmonic series; (c) for a sound composed of inharmonic partials.

When the spectrum is without significant peaks or bands it is characterized as *noise,* as shown in figure 2.4a. Noise can be shaped, however, to
emphasize high or low frequencies. Overall, spectral purity decreases as
follows: sine wave, harmonic spectrum, inharmonic spectrum, noise.

Another phenomenon found in sound spectra is the *formant*. This is a
spectral envelope—usually a broad peak—that accentuates whatever portion of an input sound source falls within its range, as shown in figure 2.4b.
In the figure, the lower-pitched formant is shaping a harmonic source (the
most common case), while the upper one shapes a noise source. Formants
usually correspond to resonances in a sound-producing system. Hence
they do not transpose as the underlying input spectrum changes and have
no predictable relation to fundamental pitch; instead, they provide timbral
coloration. Many traditional instruments have formant bands in their spectra that help define their fundamental sound. The vowels of the spoken
(and to a lesser extent the sung) voice form a notable example of a sound
dominated by formants.

The temporal qualities of sound have been shown to have an effect at
least as powerful as that of spectrum on perceived timbre. The attack
characteristics have been found to be particularly important. However,
since there are fewer specialized terms in this area, we will cover only the
topic of envelopes below, deferring until chapter 7 a general discussion of
time shapes in connection with the use of layering.

Beating, Masking, and Critical Band

Beating is a familiar effect that occurs when two tones
have very nearly the same fundamental frequency, say f_1 and f_2. An auxiliary frequency (the beat frequency) is produced, with a value equal to the
difference in frequencies of the two tones ($f_1 - f_2$, presuming $f_1 > f_2$). The
resulting effect is that of a tone with a frequency halfway between the two
component tones and whose amplitude varies with the beat frequency.
Second-order beating occurs when some of the partials of two tones beat
but the fundamentals do not—for example, when the two tones are separated by a slightly mistuned octave or a twelfth. This is often considered
a source of dissonance. *Binaural beats* are produced when two tones
capable of beating are routed individually to the separate ears, normally
with headphones. This distinctive effect produces apparent side-to-side
motion of the sound.

When the frequency difference between such tones enters the 10–15
Hz range, a characteristic *roughness* or *tonal roughness* appears. As the
frequency difference is increased further, this roughness eventually disappears, allowing the separate tones to be heard distinctly, forming an
audible interval with each other. The range over which the roughness is

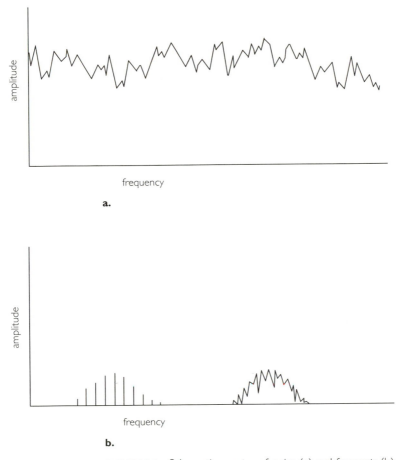

FIGURE 2.4   Schematic spectra of noise (a) and formants (b).

heard is called the *critical band*. Above about 440 Hz, the critical band stays roughly constant, at about a minor third in size. At lower frequencies the critical band becomes a larger interval, which partly explains the typical tendency for many diverse kinds of music to use larger intervals in the bass register.

The additional concept of *masking* will be of use to us. This term refers to a louder sound completely blocking the perception of another, softer sound. This effect is more pronounced at high volume and depends strongly on the frequency difference of the two sounds as well as on their spectral differences. It is particularly noticeable when the two sounds fall within a critical bandwidth of each other.

Coherence, Fission, and the Composite Sound

The concepts of *coherence* and *fission* have at their base the idea of how we hear a group of sounds. The central questions are under what conditions such a group is heard as a single unit and under what conditions it is heard as a collection of different sounds (e.g., as separate notes or separate subgroups of notes). For example, a rapid tremolo at the interval of a minor third will be heard by all listeners as a single coherent process. In contrast, a slow tremolo at the interval of three octaves will usually be heard as two interleaved streams of repeated notes — this is fission. In between these two extremes, musical context and listener orientation can play significant roles in the interpretation of musical events. The boundary between fissioned and coherent perception of a group of notes may operate similarly, based on the timbres, dynamics, registers, starting times, envelopes, and other variables of the individual notes. For example, the slight arpeggiation of block chords will heighten the perception that the chords are collections of individual notes; a *f* pitch in a *pp* diatonic cluster will stand out; the top note of a chord may be the easiest to discern; noticeably different attack envelopes or spectra on sounds nominally struck together will enhance their perceptual separateness. If a musical event has perceptually identifiable components (whether layered or in succession), we shall call it a *composite* sound. Pierre Schaeffer referred to layered sounds as *mixages* and successions of juxtaposed sounds as *montages*.

A related issue is the degree of *internal detail* in a synthesized sound. Even a sound heard as a single sound object will often have audible internal structure. How much this internal structure is discernable or musically significant will in general depend on both context and listener orientation. For example, a slow line will allow the unfolding of the internal structure of sounds that are heard only as timbrally equivalent entities in fast lines. In some intervening tempo range both perceptions may be possible, depending on the listener's focus of attention. This is an active area of psychoacoustic research (Bregman and McAdams 1979; McAdams 1984).

TUNING AND TEMPERAMENT

The synthesizer allows one major theoretical resource to be practically explored in a way no previous performing instrument has: the idea of tuning systems. A *tuning system* is a system for deciding on the frequencies to be assigned to musical notes. Some instruments can readily play a continuous range of frequencies, like the violin or trombone, and variably tune each note, constantly making small variations to give optimal intonation. Other instruments, like the guitar or flute, have standard, physically fixed frequency positions for notes but can alter them in performance within certain limits. Still other instruments, like the piano and xylophone, have completely fixed pitches; they must be *tempered,* meaning adjusted, to some sort of compromise tuning so that they fit with other instruments that use variable intonation. Hence, another common word for a fixed tuning is *temperament.* Instruments in this last category are inevitably slightly out of tune on some notes in any key.

The vast majority of Western tuning systems in historical and contemporary use has been designed to be as concordant as possible with the harmonic series described above. The acoustic foundation for this is that many of the most widely used Western instruments have partials that are harmonic or very nearly harmonic; in other words, they form small ratios with the fundamental frequency. If, then, a tuning system is set so that the partials of a tone coincide closely with the fundamentals (and partials) of notes commonly played above it at the more consonant intervals— typically thirds, fourths, fifths, and sixths—beating and resultant dissonance will be minimized.

The use of the intervals of the harmonic series allows specification of the frequency ratios of the "pure" intervals (see figure 2.5; note that they provide more than one value—large and small—for some intervals). These intervals are, in principle, maximally "in tune" with a given keynote when the sound source is harmonic. However, it is not generally possible to use these ratios to construct a tuning system in which all the notes in the octave are in such excellent tune with each other as they are with the keynote. Except for special limited musical circumstances, we have to make compromises—deviations from these ratios—so that bad tuning does not appear elsewhere in the panoply of intervals. The most essential intervals to get in tune, after the octaves and unisons, are the fifths and thirds. If these are in tune, then so will be their inversions, the fourths and sixths, and the ear is more forgiving of out-of-tune seconds and sevenths. As it so happens, there is usually a trade-off between having major thirds or fifths in tune.

Where we need to be very specific about pitch, we will use the term *cent*, which means $\frac{1}{100}$ of a semitone. Specifically, this is a ratio of $2^{1/1200}$ = 1.000576, a frequency change of roughly 0.06 percent. Hence, an octave contains 1200 cents. Those readers who wish to convert ratios to cents may consult Blackwood (1985), which contains conversion tables. The number of cents contained in any interval may also be calculated from the formula *cents* = $1200 \log_2 (f_2/f_1)$, where f_2 and f_1 are the frequencies of the two tones making up the interval.

RATIO	MUSICAL INTERVAL
1:1	unison
2:1	octave
3:2	perfect fifth
4:3	perfect fourth
5:4	major third
6:5	minor third
5:3	major sixth
8:5	minor sixth
9:8	large major second
10:9	small major second
16:9	small minor seventh
9:5	large minor seventh
16:15	large semitone
25:24	small semitone
48:25	large major seventh
15:8	small major seventh

FIGURE 2.5   Frequency ratios for the "pure" (harmonic) intervals.

In general, tuning systems are of two types: irregular (or unequal) and regular (or equal). *Irregular tuning systems* are asymmetrical and therefore produce different sets of pitches from key to key and must be labeled by their tonics. In contrast, *regular tuning systems* are tuning systems that are equally tempered, have no particular associated key, and produce only one set of chromatic pitches when transposed to a common starting point (Lloyd and Boyle 1978).

The best-known historical tunings that are based on the purity of intonation of the small ratio system of harmonic intervals include just, Pythagorean, mean-tone, and the various equal-tempered systems (twelve, nineteen, twenty-four, thirty-one, thirty-six, forty-eight, and fifty-three notes to the octave being most commonly mentioned). The first three of these, the twenty-four- and forty-eight-note tempered systems, as well as tunings by Werckmeister, Kirnberger, and Vallotti and Young, have been made readily accessible to the synthesist by Yamaha, a pioneer in this area.

Just tuning is, in simple diatonic settings, often the most consonant. It proceeds by setting the thirds and fifths in the tonic, subdominant, and dominant chords to the exact harmonic ratios of 3:2 and 5:4. These three chords are therefore in perfect tune, and a major scale is unambiguously defined. Other notes may be tuned by a variety of procedures based on these same intervals, so that the result is not a single just tuning but actually a family of them, including just tunings of more than twelve notes per octave. (Yamaha and Korg call just tuning *pure*; this terminology can hardly be recommended. Both also distinguish pure [just] major and minor forms, which are simply the same scale with a different modal starting point, related as relative major and minor. Thus, C "pure major" equals A "pure minor.")

The faults with this system when it ventures away from simple diatonicism can be heard easily at a number of spots, most dramatically if an A♭ triad is played with C just intonation: the G♯–E♭ interval is noticeably out of tune. These markedly out-of-tune intervals produce so-called *wolf tones,* so named because of the howling of the beating dissonances. Hence, this system can normally be the tuning system of choice only when there is a fixed tonal center without modulation; it works especially well if the piece is strictly diatonic. La Monte Young's *The Well-Tuned Piano,* a work in progress, provides one contemporary perspective on such tunings; some of Terry Riley's and Ben Johnson's recent work provide two others. However, in other musical circumstances involving modulation or chromaticism, it will not be practical unless more than twelve notes are used per octave or unless more instruments—such as synthesizers—allow tunings to be switched instantly.

The *Pythagorean tuning* preserves the purity of all but one perfect fifth in the chromatic scale by using the pure fifth repeatedly to generate all twelve notes. The gap from the last fifth to the first will be out of tune by a small interval known as the *Pythagorean comma,* producing one "wolf fifth" somewhere. Such purity of fifths comes, of course, at the expense of the thirds: Some of them have pronounced beating. This is the tuning system closest to that used by classical string players, and it was common on Renaissance keyboard instruments, where only occasional and limited chromaticism occurred. If the cycle of fifths is continued past twelve, the additional notes provide better overall intonation.

The basic *mean-tone tuning* provides true major thirds, though it slightly flattens all the fifths as well as the minor thirds. The mean-tone idea provides a family of possible variants, with the basic form known as *quarter-comma mean-tone,* taking its name from the interval used to flatten the fifths—$5\frac{1}{2}$ cents, one-quarter of the so-called *syntonic comma.* (The syntonic comma is a small interval, 81:80, that expresses the difference between the large and small just whole-tone intervals, 9:8 and 10:9 respectively.) Mean-tone temperaments were used widely on organs until the later nineteenth century. Like the Pythagorean, they display one or more wolf tones, easily noticeable in the G♯–E♭ "fifth" or the B–E♭ "major third" in the key of C. These tuning problems are also largely removed if the mean-tone system is extended to more than twelve notes per octave—for example, nineteen.

Various interpolations and modifications of these systems were proposed by many authors, including Andreas Werckmeister, Johann Kirnberger (both of these systems being part of the mean-tone family of tuning), and

Francescantonio Vallotti and Thomas Young, who independently devised a modification of Pythagorean intonation. In Renaissance and baroque times it was common to retune harpsichords and clavichords for different pieces to reflect the tonal areas they emphasized. J. S. Bach probably used a system different from any of those mentioned (Barnes 1979) and certainly did not use equal temperament.

As most readers will be aware, our dominant keyboard tuning system is equal tempered, meaning that it is a bastardized compromise between the demands of various musical usages to which a tuning can be put. Each octave is divided into twelve logarithmically equal parts, and the ratio of the frequencies of adjacent semitones is the twelfth root of 2, written $2^{1/12} = 1.0594631\ldots$. This is the system used by all fixed-pitch Western instruments, like the piano—with some small practical modifications, as we shall see below. Its main advantages are that its intervals are, in many people's opinions, tolerably in tune with the intonation of the pure intervals, and it permits modulation to any key with equality of all interval relationships. Nevertheless, all intervals except the octave are out of tune to various degrees, and the synthesist should be under no illusion that this is universally used, even today. Orchestras, for example, do not play in tempered tuning. Problems can occur when synthesizers are combined with traditional instruments for this reason.

Equal-tempered systems do not by any means have to be based on the number 12. The others that exist seem to have several rationales. Those based on nineteen, thirty-one, and fifty-three tones to the octave are based on the closer approximation to the harmonic series that they offer over the twelve-note system. Instruments with these tuning systems are in use today and have their advocates. The nineteen-tone equal-tempered system is found on some harpsichords and was employed by many late Renaissance and early baroque musicians; Yasser (1975) discusses the advantages of this system. The thirty-one-tone system is found on a number of pipe organs in the Netherlands; Adrian Fokker (1949) has had a large role in promoting this system.

Equal temperaments with twenty-four (quartertone), thirty-six (sixth tone), and forty-eight (eighth tone) tones to the octave allow further subdivisions of the whole tone, while preserving the traditional twelve chromatic tempered tones per octave. Pieces using all these tunings have been composed by such composers as Julián Carrillo, Alois Hába, Ivan Vishnegradsky, Charles Ives, and Pierre Boulez. Easley Blackwood has written a series of pieces for all tempered tunings of size N with $13 \le N \le 24$ (his *Twelve Microtonal Etudes*). Other suggestions for equal-tempered systems based on twenty, thirty, or forty-two tones per octave have been constructed by reference to the structural underpinnings of the number 12 (Balzano 1980).

When we consider the tuning systems of other cultures, we find a great diversity of possibilities that can be investigated by the synthesizer user. Our own twelve-tone tempered system is mentioned in China as early as the twenty-seventh century B.C. by a certain Ling Lun (Yasser 1975). Equal five-note-per-octave systems exist, both in East Africa and Indonesia, and an approximately equal seven-tone-per-octave system is found in traditional Thai music. In the stratified orchestras of Asia, tuning systems are predominantly not equal tempered and vary from locale to locale and ensemble to ensemble. Great diversity of tuning systems is found likewise in India, other parts of the Orient, the Middle East, and in the traditional musics of aboriginal peoples of the Americas, Australia, Oceania, and elsewhere. The possibilities are truly vast.

Some twentieth-century composers have created their own synthetic scales and then designed instruments to play them, either acoustic or electronic. Such efforts have been made by Lou Harrison and Ivor Darreg. Visionary composer Harry Partch proposed an unequal just forty-three notes to the octave system and built a flotilla of special instruments to play music in it. His *Genesis of a Music* (1974) is an engaging summary of historical developments up to the early 1970s. In electronic music there have been many new ventures such as those of Jon Appleton, John Chowning, and Wendy Carlos. Chowning used the golden mean ratio (approximately 1.618) to generate pseudo octaves in his piece *Stria* (Dodge and Jerse 1985). Carlos's album *Beauty in the Beast* features α, β, and γ scales, which divide the octave into nonintegral numbers of parts, abandoning the purity of the octave to achieve heightened purity of other intervals, including higher ones such as 7:4 and 11:8. The α scale divides the octave into 15.385 equal steps, the β scale divides it into 18.809 steps, and the γ scale has 34.188 equal steps per octave (Carlos 1987; Wilkinson 1988). The reader who would like to implement many of these special scales is advised to consult Wilkinson (1988), which includes tables of implementation for all these scales and others as well. Some of these scales (both ethnic and invented) are available as presets in recent Kurzweil synthesizers.

Complicating the intonation issue still further is a practical consideration. We, like most peoples in the world, use a *stretched* tuning system. This means that octaves (and hence other intervals) sound in some way "best" when they are stretched to be some 0.2 to 1.5 percent larger than the exact 2:1 ratio that is used to define them. (This range can vary with type of timbre, register, and other musical considerations.) This means that the treble of all pianos, for example, is normally tuned slightly sharp relative to its midrange, while the bass is tuned slightly flat. The reason for this is that the actual partials of any given note are usually slightly sharp from their ideal harmonic values (usually due to the mechanical stiffness in the vibrating material), and a stretched tuning minimizes, though does not eliminate, beating between upper partials and higher notes. However, most synthesizers do not use stretched tuning as of this writing. Hence, there is a potential problem when they are played with other instruments; one or the other may have to compromise.

Although the ear can hear a remarkable degree of pitch nuance in musical situations with drones and slow moving voices, in most situations the ear is usually quite forgiving with tuning, due to a principle called *categorical perception*. This principle states that, if possible, we will perceive notes "in between the cracks" as familiar notes plus deviations rather than as completely new things. It reflects the essential conservatism of the auditory perceptual system.

SYNTHESIS AND SAMPLING

Before plunging into the details of synthesis techniques, it will be useful to present a simplified schematic diagram that shows the common features found in synthesizers and samplers. Figure 2.6 shows such a device. Synthesis begins with the sound sources, which may be shaped by fixed synthesis or by real-time control using the note selection interface and real-time controllers, either directly or indirectly. The available processing includes LFOs (low frequency oscillators) to produce modulation, envelope generators to shape the sound in time, mixing (basic additive synthesis), and audio processing of various kinds. These first three types of processing seem to be the minimum requirement for synthesizers and samplers (but not preset sound modules) that aim to be more than toys, and we will sometimes call this *standard processing*.

We are now in a position to be able to begin our examination of the resources of synthesis and sampling. We look first at sound sources, the starting point of synthesis, the basic sonic building blocks used in constructing a final synthesizer program.

Sound Sources

There are four primary types of sound sources for synthesizer performance: oscillators, samples, noise, and live performance. While all these sources can be shaped by many kinds of audio processes, they have in each case "natural" parameters associated with them that characterize how they can most readily be controlled in synthesis programming. The parameters associated naturally with these sources are shown in table 2.1.

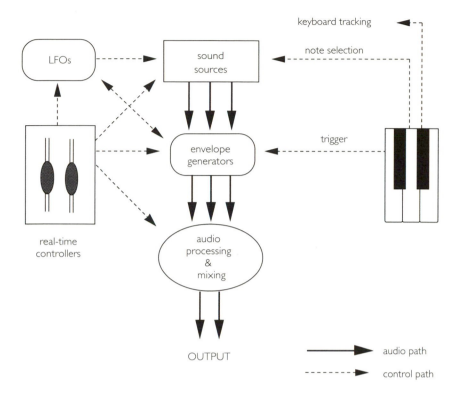

FIGURE 2.6 Functional schematic of a synthesizer or sampler.

SOURCES	ASSOCIATED CONTROL PARAMETERS
Oscillators	Frequency, amplitude, phase, special waveform parameters
Samples	Playback speed, amplitude, starting point, loop parameters
Noise	Amplitude, noise distribution parameter
Live Performance	Amplitude

TABLE 2.1 Types of sound sources for synthesizer performance and their associated control parameters.

This control relation can be fixed so that whenever the program is called up and played with a certain MIDI note number, an identical sound is produced. This is non-real-time programming and is a fascinating topic in itself, but it is not the focus of this book. The alternative, and our main emphasis here, is real-time performance synthesis, where the design of the program ensures that the parameters can be controlled in real time by a performer operating controllers and keyboard or other note-selection interface. Depending on the nature of the controller, such changes may be either continuous or discrete.

Real-time control of these parameters can be either direct or indirect. *Direct control* is when the controller directly controls the parameter. In *indirect control,* the performer controls a modification process (such as modulation, filtering, etc.) that itself controls the parameter. Indirect control can be nested and operate in parallel: Both a wheel and a given envelope might control the rate of an envelope that determined the frequency of an oscillator that controlled the frequency cut-off of a filter that shaped a sound source (and so forth). Complex control routings can be set up, and it is impossible to give a comprehensive description of every possibility. We therefore first survey the four types of sources, emphasizing the effects of direct control. Indirect control will be discussed in the later section on processing techniques.

Oscillators produce relatively simple repeating waveforms that can be used to cause periodic fluctuations of pressure in the air. We hear these fluctuations as sound. Oscillators were traditionally generated from specific electronic circuits as continuous mathematical functions of time, but now they are commonly stored as wavetables in computers and synthesizers to save processing time. Such tables are simply lists of function values at representative points along one cycle of the waveform. Values are read out from the table using different rates and selection procedures to create frequency variation and other effects.

The most common waveforms are sine, triangle, sawtooth (or ramp, up or down), square, pulse, and S/H (sample-and-hold). These are shown in figure 2.7. The sine (and cosine) are pure tones, consisting of a single frequency (harmonic), while the others have richer structures. The triangle wave and square wave contain only odd harmonics; with the others, all higher harmonics are normally present, with amplitudes decreasing with harmonic number. The sample-and-hold wave is a special case, produced by sampling some process (normally a random one) at regular intervals and using the sampled value to set the wave's output level until the next sample time. Its most common use is for modulation, as discussed below.

The pulse wave is the most common waveform that has special associated control parameters. This parameter is the duration of the positive portion of the wave cycle in relation to the overall cycle duration and is called either *duty cycle* or *pulse width*. It is expressible as either a fraction or a percentage. For example, a square wave has a duty cycle of $\frac{1}{2}$ and a pulse width of 50 percent. Because of the pulse wave's symmetry, a wave of x percent duty cycle will sound identical to one of $100-x$ percent. A

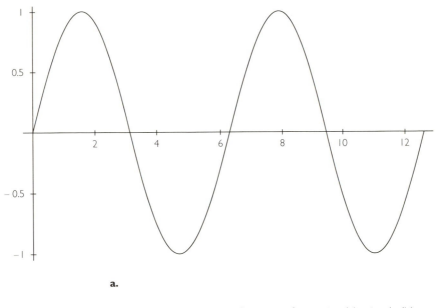

a.

FIGURE 2.7 Common oscillator waveforms: sine (a); triangle (b); sawtooth up, or ramp up (c); sawtooth down, or ramp down (d); square (e); 25% pulse (f); and S/H, or sample-and-hold (g).

pulse wave of duty cycle $1/n$ is missing every nth harmonic from its spectrum.

The pitch of oscillators is usually indicated by the MIDI note controlling them, their physical frequency, or footage ($2'$, $4'$, $8'$, $16'$, etc.—the length of a pipe that would sound that note). This last method has become less common, except with instruments based on an organ design. Some manufacturers use special terms for combinations of oscillators and other synthesis functions. For example, Roland uses *WG* (*wave generator*) for an oscillator plus pitch envelope and LFO, and Yamaha uses *operator* for an oscillator plus amplifier and envelope generator. Hard-wired configurations of oscillators or such aggregate synthesis objects as those just mentioned are often given special names such as *structures* (Roland) or *algorithms* (Yamaha, Kurzweil).

The effects of real-time frequency control of oscillators will be examined first. Direct programming of frequency control is usually broken up into several modes or sensitivities, using terms like *coarse, fine,* and *detune* (meaning very fine). Coarse control usually moves in frequency multiples or semitone steps, while fine control moves quasi-continuously. Coarse control provides a much greater frequency range of effect than

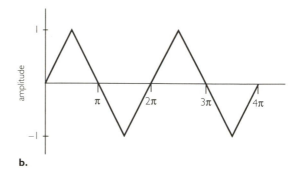

b.

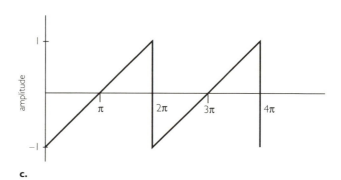

c.

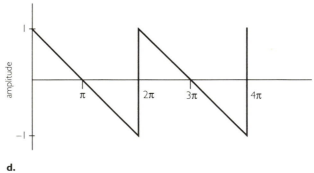

d.

FIGURE 2.7.   continued.

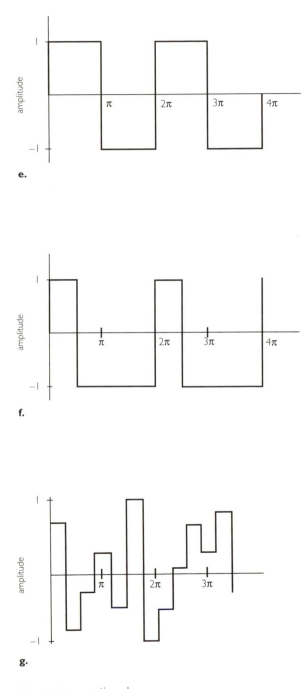

FIGURE 2.7. continued.

fine. Detuning usually operates over a very restricted range, such as 3 Hz or several hundred cents. Such direct frequency control is typically a fixed programming technique, but it can also be accessed via real-time controllers on many synthesizers.

Real-time controlled coarse pitch produces a sweep through the harmonics of the tone if coarse pitch controls frequency multiples, a sweep along the chromatic scale (glissando) if coarse control moves in semitones. Real-time controlled fine pitch produces a portamento glide similar to pitch bend. Real-time detuning change causes only a barely noticeable effect unless the oscillator in question is tuned in unison with another such source, when an effect like chorusing (see "Processing Techniques" below) will be produced.

The other common alternative for direct frequency control is via the synthesizer's pitch bend device, which is capable of continuous pitch bend effects (portamento), typically over a range up and down of at least an octave. This device is sometimes capable of quantized bending as well, typically quantizing to semitones or multiples thereof, producing glissandi of various kinds. For example, if the pitch bend range is set to an octave, and the interval of quantization is set to two semitones, bending will produce a whole tone scale. Pitch bend will be discussed in depth in chapters 5 and 6.

Amplitude is the next most important control parameter for oscillators. This is an important component of what we call *dynamics,* one of the fundamental dimensions of expression in music. Direct control simply affects the volume of the sound. Programming to allow real-time dynamic control is an essential skill for the synthesizer performer. If this sort of control is not built in, the types of music the sounds can service will be very limited. See chapter 5 for a full discussion.

Phase can be an important parameter when the oscillator is used as a modulation source or acts in concert with other oscillators (see "Processing Techniques" below) or if subtle room acoustics effects are at issue. Used directly, however, it often has no significant sonic effects. In many situations the ear is truly "phase-deaf." In other words, the ear is insensitive to phase relations between the components of a complex periodic sound; this is fortunate, since such effects are very dependent on their acoustic environment and are smeared by reverberation (Risset 1985). Most synthesizers allow only basic forms of phase control, based on synchronization. The traditional form of such synchronization is called *oscillator sync* and refers to the synchronization of two oscillators, where the onset of each cycle of one, the master, consistently retriggers the other, the slave, giving a dependable phase relation. Today such phase control as exists is often based on key synchronization, where the relation of the phase of the waveform to the note onset can be defined. Usually there is only a simple choice between starting the waveform at a preset phase position and starting it at its current ongoing value.

Some oscillators have built-in special parametric controls. The pulse wave is the traditional synthesis waveform for which this is true. If pulse width is changed in real time, a spectral sweep-like effect will occur. A related type of control possible on some synthesizers allows the waveform type or shape itself to be chosen in real time. Changing the corresponding waveform parameter in real time can cause both continuous and discontinuous changes in spectrum and sound. Some synthesizers are able to cross-fade between or sweep through a series of related waveforms (usually present as wavetables or samples), producing everything from animation of the overtones (e.g., Ensoniq VFX) to loops of rhythmic patterns (Roland D series), depending on the similarity of the different waves.

Samples are digital recordings of (usually acoustic) sounds. They are found in samplers, sample players, and also widely in synthesizers. Most of the same parameters and control considerations apply as in the case of oscillators; it is mainly terminology that is different. Playback speed effectively determines frequency of the sample, and hence the considerations above apply directly. The above discussion on amplitude is also directly applicable. The idea of phase is similarly replaced by the starting point chosen for sample playback.

The primary differences are that dedicated sampling environments usually have less extensive processing facilities than synthesizers, and there is generally less possibility of real-time modification of samples than there is of synthesized sounds. The reason for both of these is that a sample is a self-contained audio product without obvious component parts and hence does not have special waveform parameters naturally adaptable for control, whereas a final synthesized sound can be a combination of a number of oscillators and types of processing and has all the parametric controls available from each of its components. Of course, samples can be likewise overlaid and separately controlled, but as a general rule this difference is true both of samplers and synthesizers that contain samples. Improved real-time control of samples requires that some sort of parametric control over the samples be established beyond such global procedures as envelopes and filtering. For this to work, some sort of analysis and resynthesis of the musically significant components of a sound must have been made. Such schemes (for example, linear predictive coding) are slowly filtering into the commercial synthesizer market.

Some types of real-time control are (or have been) more common on samplers than on synthesizers, however. Primary among these are the switch and cross-fade between sounds; looping also has unique control potential, though it remains a largely fixed-synthesis procedure as of this writing. These techniques will be discussed shortly.

Noise can be produced in several ways. One common way is by the use of dedicated noise generators that produce random or weighted random pitches over the entire frequency spectrum. (By *weighted random* we mean that processes are used that allow parametric control over the randomness, allowing it to be shaped in certain ways.) Noise can also be generated by certain types of modulation, feedback, distortion, controlled chaos, and other nonlinear signal processing, enabling better parametric control.

The most common uses of noise are as a backdrop, in the creation of special effects, and in the addition of noisy transients that imitate instrumental bow or breath attacks. Real-time direct control is therefore normally confined to volume, either by key velocity or controllers. Indirect control, notably filtering effects, will be discussed in more detail.

Several types of noise spectra have acquired special names. White noise, for example, is random noise distributed to contain equal energy per unit bandwidth over the entire frequency spectrum. In other words, the band between 1,000 and 2,000 Hz will have the same white noise energy as the band between 2,000 and 3,000 Hz. The total energy per octave increases with frequency at the rate of 6 dB per octave. Pink noise is random noise biased towards low frequencies. Specifically, it has an equal amount of energy in each octave. For example, the band between 1,000 and 2,000 Hz will contain the same amount of energy as the band between 2,000 and 4,000 Hz.

Exactly where noise ends and music begins is a matter for personal preference. Over seventy years ago Futurist Luigi Russolo said

> Musical sound is too limited in its variety of timbre. The most complicated of orchestras reduce themselves to four or five classes of instruments differing in timbre: instruments played with the bow, plucked instruments, brass-winds, wood-winds and percussion.... We must break out of this narrow circle of pure musical sounds and conquer the infinite variety of noise sounds. (Russolo 1913, pp. 24–25)

Live performance sounds can be monitored and used as an audio source. Since such sounds must be picked up by some sort of electrical input device to be usable in synthesis, amplitude is listed as a natural control parameter. MIDI volume control of mixers is now widely available; hence, this is a viable real-time control technique. Dynamically controlled filtering of live sources is also widespread, as described below. Live audio sources can also be used with pitch-to-MIDI converters and pitch-to-voltage converters to exert real-time control over other sound sources. This is defined below and treated in more depth in chapter 9.

PROCESSING TECHNIQUE	ASSOCIATED CONTROL PARAMETERS
Amplification	Gain or level
Mixing	Gains or levels
Filtering	
High pass/Low pass	Cutoff frequency, Q (resonance), rolloff (slope)
Band pass/Band reject	Center frequency + bandwidth *or* upper and lower cutoff frequencies, Q (resonance), center attenuation (band reject only)
Envelope shaping	Times, rates, levels
Modulation (LFO, FM)	Depth and source-specific control parameters; e.g., for oscillators: frequency, waveform, delay, depth, phase, modulation index (FM)
Switching and layering	Key velocity, controller values, note number
Cross-fade	Key velocity, controller values, note number
Panning	Stereo amplitudes
Ring modulation	Parameters of the two input signals
Vocoding	Parameters of the two input signals
Phase distortion	Distortion index or phase angle
Delay	Delay time, amplitude
Echo	Delay time, echo attenuation/amplification (re-generation or feedback), number of echoes
Reverberation	Pre-delay, reverberation time (decay), reverberation density, first reflection prominence, first reflection time, equalization
Pitch-to-MIDI conversion	Frequency
Pitch-to-voltage conversion	Frequency
Flanging	LFO frequency, modulation depth, delay time, feedback level (strength), mix
Phasing	LFO frequency, modulation depth, delay time, mix
Chorusing	LFO frequencies, modulation depths, delay time, feedback level (strength)
Pitch shifting	Shift interval
Frequency shifting	Frequency shift
Excitation	Excitation parameters
Fuzz	Distortion parameters
Timbral interpolation	Synthesis parameters
Compression	Compression ratio, threshold, attack and release times
Limiting	Compression ratio, threshold, attack and release times

TABLE 2.2 Electronic processing techniques and their associated control parameters.

Processing Techniques

The next step in synthesis is the processing of the sources listed above. By processing we mean shaping, modification, and interaction. Each such processing technique has one or more associated parameters, which, as above, may be used (in principle) for both fixed synthesis and real-time control. The most significant processing techniques used in commercial synthesizers are given in table 2.2 (the listing in some cases is more representative than comprehensive).

The potential control sources for all these parameters are various physical controllers, key velocity, and note number. Note number control is also called *keyboard tracking, key follow,* or *keyboard scaling.* For example, on the Yamaha X series, keyboard control of volume is called keyboard level scaling, and keyboard control of rate is called keyboard rate scaling. The term *envelope tracking* is sometimes used to refer to note number variation of envelope times. Some control sources are of the so-called *one-shot* type—they produce a single value for a given action. Examples are key velocity and note number. Other controllers, called *continuous controllers,* are scanned many times per second, and changes in the controller position or applied force will continue to be transmitted. (These controllers are strictly speaking not really generating continuous output but rather a very rapid approximation to it.)

Some of these processing techniques—such as amplification, envelope shaping, and modulation—are available on all synthesizers. Others are widely found but missing from certain important synthesis procedures— for example, Yamaha's FM-based X series machines have no filtering. Other processes are almost always found external to the synthesizer, as for example fuzz tone and vocoder. The current trend is to bring increasing amounts of processing into the synthesizer to allow the synthesizer to act more as a self-contained device. This also usually increases the real-time controllability of such processing.

Some modifications are special techniques that can apply to a single sound source, while others are formed by the interaction of two or more sources. The following discussion will focus on the primary sonic effects of each process, and mention will be made of any special uses in real-time programming.

Amplification boosts the sound level of a signal. The amount of amplification, or gain, may be controlled in real time by a physical gain control, or via MIDI (controller 7).

Mixing is the adding together of two or more signals. In music production, it refers to setting the level of amplification of a number of sources relative to each other. Mixing may be performed in real time by using various controllers to affect the volumes of the different signals being mixed. One common setup is to use a continuous controller to bring in additional components of a sound in real time. Another is to use separate controllers for each contributing sound source. More complex real-time mixing effects are facilitated by the use of automated MIDI mixers—mixer control can be given to a sequencer using a stored body of mix data or determined interactively from performer and software control.

Filtering refers to the attenuation of sound in particular regions of the frequency spectrum. There are a number of ways this can occur, but four types of filters are most common in synthesizers and samplers: high pass, low pass, band pass, and band reject (also called notch), shown schematically in figure 2.8. *High pass filters* pass all frequencies above the cutoff frequency (f_c), and attenuate those below it. *Low pass filters* pass all frequencies below the cutoff frequency and attenuate those above it. This attenuation is not perfect, and the sharpness of the cutoff is measured by the filter's *rolloff* or *slope*. This rolloff can be measured in dB per octave. It is common to classify the rolloff in dB by the number of *poles* in the filter. Each 6 dB rolloff per octave constitutes one pole. Hence a two-pole filter has 12 dB rolloff per octave, a four-pole filter has 24 dB rolloff per octave, and so forth. As shown in the figures, f_c is customarily taken to be the frequency 3dB below the plateau regions.

A *band pass filter* passes all frequencies in the band and attenuates those outside it. Its characteristic parameters can be either center frequency (f_0) and bandwidth or upper and lower cutoff frequencies (f_u and f_l respectively). As before, the attenuation outside the band is not perfect, and rolloff is used to quantify the degree of sharpness of the filter.

These three types of filters also have another control parameter: Q. Other names for this parameter are *emphasis, resonance, regeneration,* and *feedback,* which suggest how it works: The output of the filter is fed back to its input, with emphasis on the cutoff frequency. This feedback boosts the volume of frequencies near the cutoff frequency relative to the others, creating a resonant or "vocalish" effect. If the feedback is increased high enough (very high Q), the filter puts out only one frequency so that it essentially becomes a sine wave oscillator. This can be a useful special effect.

The *band reject filter,* sometimes called a *notch filter,* is just the opposite of the band pass. Its natural control parameters are the same as for the band pass filter, with the addition of the level of attenuation of the central band.

The effects that occur with real-time control of these parameters are as follows. If the cutoff frequency is varied smoothly, the filter attenuates different parts of the audio spectrum accordingly, producing a well-known

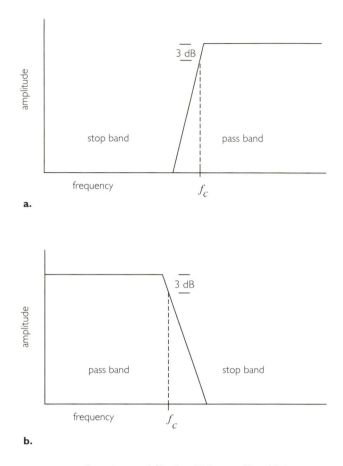

FIGURE 2.8   Four types of filtering: high pass filter (a); low pass filter (b); band pass filter (c); band reject, or notch, filter (d).

filter sweep effect. If the sound is pitched, this will change its spectrum but not its perceived pitch. If the sound is a broad band noise, the apparent registral emphasis of the sound will change.

If the Q (resonance) is varied in real time, the strength of harmonics around the cutoff frequency are variably boosted until Q approaches its maximum value. Near this maximum value resonance sets in, and the filter turns rapidly into a sine wave oscillator, one whose pitch may be controlled by the keyboard or other source.

Equalization is a term closely related to filtering, and so it has not been given a separate heading above. It differs in that both boosting and attenuation can be achieved, not just attenuation. It has many forms. It may consist of a number of dovetailed band pass filters that span the frequency

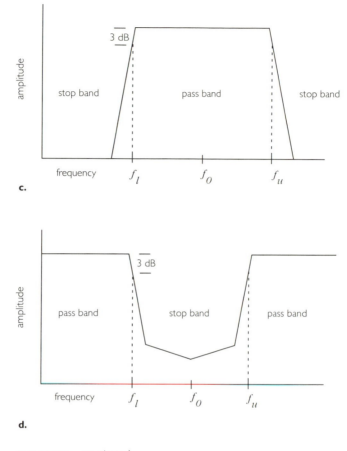

FIGURE 2.8. continued.

spectrum and whose outputs may be separately boosted or cut (graphic equalization). It may consist of a number of filters having a continuously variable center frequency and Q (parametric equalization). Although it is increasingly found as a real-time control technique in synthesis (particularly to further shape the overall sound or simulate formants), its most typical use is to fine tune the frequency spectrum of a sound system via a mixing desk.

Envelope shaping refers to the construction of shapes (envelopes) in time. These may be fixed in the synthesis programming, triggered by performer actions, or parametrically changed by real-time control. Names for the synthesis unit producing time shaping include *envelope generator* (preferred in this book), *contour generator*, and *transient generator*. Such an envelope can control almost any variable, but dynamics, filtering, volume, pitch, panning, and timbre are most commonly controlled. The sonic effect varies greatly with the nature of the particular controlled parameter, and sometimes envelopes dedicated to special uses have different names. For example, envelopes applied to pitch may be called *pitch envelope generators, pitch warp,* or *autobend.*

Any envelope begins by being triggered by some external signal, usually a short electronic pulse. On the keyboard synthesizer, this trigger is sent by the depression of a key. Nearly all synthesizer envelopes are made by joining a number of distinct pieces or segments, which are characterized by their end points or levels, and either times or rates (occasionally called slopes). Such envelopes can be called *multistage* or *multisegment envelopes.* These segments are often drawn schematically as straight lines, which is the approach we shall use in the following figures.

The choice of whether to use rates or times varies from manufacturer to manufacturer, and the synthesist must be comfortable with either. The rate and time are related by inversion. In other words, rate = 1/ time: A large rate means a short time and a small rate means a long time.

The simplest of all common envelopes is the *AD envelope,* which has only two parameters: *attack time (rate)* and *decay time (rate).* The attack begins when the key is depressed ("attacked"), rising to a maximum in the attack time (or at the attack rate), and then falling to zero in the decay time (or at the decay rate). From the initial keystroke, this type of envelope runs its course completely unaffected by any further key actions. The *AR* (attack/release) *envelope* begins identically but remains at its maximum level at the end of the attack segment, beginning its descent only when the key is released. The descent is governed by the *release time* or *release rate* (see figure 2.9). The *ADSR envelope* has an attack time (rate), a decay time (rate), a *sustain level,* and a release time (rate), as indicated in figure 2.10. Key onset starts the envelope, which goes through its attack and decay portions and holds at its sustain level until key release initiates the release portion of the envelope. Other envelope types include *DADSR* (ADSR with initial delay), *AHDSR* (a "hold" time is inserted before the decay begins), and *DAHDSR* (ADSR with both initial delay and hold before decay).

More complex envelopes are often based on sticking a number of segments together, with two parameters per segment. These parameters are level and either time or rate. The Yamaha X series uses four segments, hence eight parameters, based on rates and levels: rate 1/level 1/rate 2/level 2/rate 3/level 3/rate 4/level 4, as indicated in figure 2.11. In such an envelope, rate 4 is triggered by key release, and level 4 represents the starting level of the envelope—even before the note is attacked. This far from exhausts the possibilities. Many Casio products use a sixteen-parameter, eight-segment envelope. The Kurzweil 250 uses a 256-parameter envelope. Some synthesizers (such as the Buchla 400 and the Prophet 5) allow some of the segments to be looped—repeated over and over. Some allow looping in both directions and multiple release segments (e.g., recent Kurzweil synthesizers).

Although the envelope shapes in figures 2.9–2.11 are drawn, as is customary in most synthesizer manuals, as straight lines, implying a linear shape, it is well to remember that the actual shape used may vary from instrument to instrument. Several forms are most common: linear, exponential, and logarithmic. Exponential envelopes mimic the roughly exponentially decaying envelopes of most natural instruments and seem to correspond better to the musical perceptions of most musicians. However, such envelopes have become less common with the switch to digital instruments since the exponential shape requires more precision power to compute.

It is useful to discuss the way nearly all synthesizers treat their envelopes when the key is released—namely, they jump immediately to the release portion of the envelope, skipping any intervening sections. This may be called a *conditional envelope protocol*. There are a few that insist on going through some other portion of the envelope first, using an *unconditional* protocol, but this is increasingly uncommon. A few synthesizers, and quite a few samplers, offer a choice of envelope style in this regard.

Real-time control can in principle be set up for any of the envelope parameters. Effects are most noticeable on the attack and release portions of envelopes that control volume. When other synthesis variables are controlled (timbre, pitch, etc.), this simple rule will often fail to hold. Envelopes may have quite startling effects when they operate at fast rates or control unusual variables. For example, a short sound with wildly varying pitch envelope may only create a noise or click effect—the pitch detail may not be audible as such.

Modulation means using one signal to affect another. This is very widely available as a fixed synthesis design and as a routing for controller activity. There are many possible ways this can occur. Most commonly, the frequency or amplitude of a sound is controlled (modulated) by the amplitude of the source of the modulation. However, any parameter can be used in principle as a basis for control. Let us call the modulating source the modulator and the target of the modulation the carrier, in line with usual FM (frequency modulation) terminology.

The sonic effects that result from modulation depend on the character of the modulating and modulated sources, and the control parameter(s) used. Synthesizers differ markedly in the versatility of modulation routings they allow. Since it is impossible to list every possible kind of modulation effect (when one takes into account multiple modulation effects—

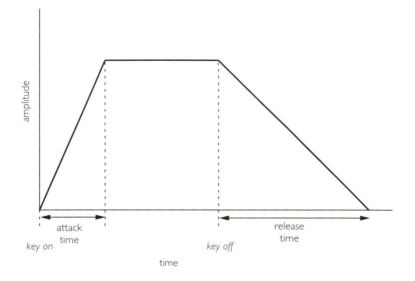

FIGURE 2.9   AR (attack/release) envelope.

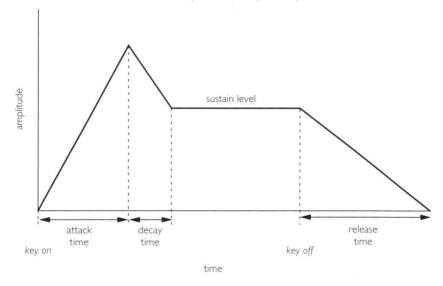

FIGURE 2.10   ADSR (attack/decay/sustain/release) envelope.

modulators modulating modulators modulating . . . etc.), we will have to content ourselves here with a description of typical uses. Extensions beyond this will be up to the creative skills of the reader.

If one oscillator modulates another (the most common case), the nature of the results depends critically on the frequencies of the two oscillators.

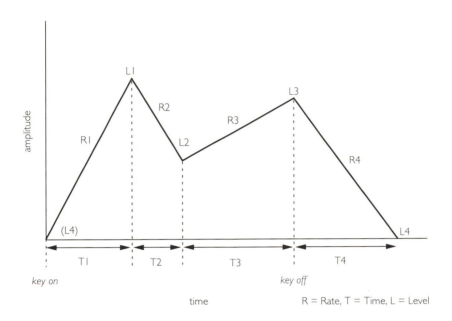

FIGURE 2.11   Four-segment eight-parameter envelope.

Let us first consider modulating oscillators operating in the subaudio or very low audio range, which are called low frequency oscillators (LFOs). If the modulator is an LFO, we get the familiar effects of vibrato or tremolo, depending on whether control is routed to frequency or amplitude respectively: Vibrato is low-frequency frequency modulation, and tremolo is low-frequency amplitude modulation. The effect is actually broader than this simple rule, since modulator waveforms with quickly rising or falling shapes will effectively act as triggers, producing the effect of a stream of notes with different musical implications. This is noticeable, for example, with sawtooth, pulse, or S/H waves. (The words *vibrato* and *tremolo* must be used with some caution because their meanings differ from those for the traditional musical terms. For example, bowed tremolo on a violin is a series of repeated notes; motorized "vibrato" on the vibraphone is actually amplitude modulation, and so forth. Where necessary, we will distinguish *synthesis* vibrato and tremolo from *musical* vibrato and tremolo.)

LFOs have the same control parameters as any other oscillators. The terminology is sometimes different, however. The LFO frequency is often called rate or speed. Amplitude of the modulator corresponds to what is called depth or amount or modulation index. Delay and sync parameters are often available. The variety of real-time effects here is considerable. Controllers can commonly change waveform parameters, onset point, depth, frequency, and type of waveform. A certain amount of randomness in modulating oscillator speed or depth may be programmable on some synthesizers as a way to enliven the sound by avoiding literal repetition.

If, on the other hand, both oscillators are in the audio range, modulation produces audio "sidebands" of considerable harmonic complexity. The technique of audio range frequency modulation is a powerful synthesis method and has been applied to the construction of Yamaha's FM synthesizers. The internal parameters of this synthesis method can be controlled in real time with considerable versatility. The result is to change the amount of sonic energy in these sidebands in real time. For background on the FM method, the reader should consult Chowning (1973) and Chowning and Bristow (1986).

Sound sources may also be modulated by such things as samples and noise, producing useful and characteristic sounds. Such features have been rare in comparison to oscillator-based modulation but are now increasingly common.

When a signal modulates itself, or in other words its output is in some way fed back into its input, *feedback* occurs. Feedback is responsible for the familiar squeal that can occur when the speakers of a PA system are too close to a microphone connected to the same system. It also occurs, in a different form, as a synthesis option in some machines; for example, in FM, an audio oscillator's output may be used directly to frequency modulate the same oscillator. Feedback is also the essential feature of filter resonance.

Switching and layering are effects based most commonly on velocity, in which case they are called velocity switching and layering. They allow more than one sound (most commonly a sample) to be accessed from the same MIDI note number. A velocity switch chooses between two (or more) sound sources on the basis of whether the key velocity falls in the range assigned to one source or another. In the simplest case, if velocity is less than the switch point velocity v_s, source 1 is heard, and if it is $\geq v_s$, source 2 is heard. With n switched sources, there will be $n-1$ switch points and a different sound in each velocity range. See figure 2.12a for an example of a three-way switch. The velocity switch has become a standard option on samplers and many synthesizers. It is also a feature of MIDI mappers and some patch bays.

The standard switching effect can also be based on continuous controllers (e.g., modulation wheel) rather than on velocity, although this is not as common. This allows continuously variable control rather than one-shot control. This option can be achieved using MIDI mappers where it is not built into a sampler or synthesizer.

Switching usually has an *Xor* (*exclusive or*) logic: Only one sound is selected at a time. However, if the various sounds sum, using *and* logic, we get what can be termed *switch layering,* as in figure 2.12b. This has its uses as well. Where such layering is specifically velocity-based, the term *velocity layering* is encountered.

Cross-fade is in some ways similar to the switch. It is commonly found on samplers and typically based on velocity. A velocity cross-fade, in its simplest case (two samples), is characterized by two end points $v_1 < v_2$. At velocity v_1 or less only sample 1 sounds; for velocity $v \geq v_2$ only sample 2 sounds. In the middle range of $v_1 < v < v_2$ there is an audio mixing of the two samples in proportion to the distance from the two end points of the range. With n sample cross-fading, there will be cross-fading across each of $n-1$ velocity ranges. Figure 2.13a shows a three-way velocity cross-fade, with cross-fading across the ranges v_1 to v_2 and v_3 to v_4.

Cross-fading normally involves sounding only one or a mixture of two sounds at a time. A related alternative begins with only one sound at lowest velocity and fades in those in higher velocity zones in order, but without fading out those sounds already present. This layering approach essentially yields a kind of real-time mixing, as illustrated in figure 2.13b: sound S_1 fades in from 0 to v_1, sound S_2 fades in from v_2 to v_3, and sound S_3 fades in from v_4 to v_5.

These same effects can be based on controllers rather than on velocity. This allows continuously monitored control rather than one-shot control. Increasingly, this option is being built into some samplers and synthesizers. As we shall see later, this sort of design is very useful in fostering expressivity in sustaining synthetic sounds. Cross-fading can also be controlled by keyboard position on some instruments.

Panning refers to the spatial placement of a sound. This is achieved by allocating different amounts of the sound signal to two or more speakers that have appreciable spatial separation from each other. The relative volumes sent to the outputs will affect the perceived spatial location of the sound in relation to the listener. Specifically, it affects the direction from which the sound is heard; the sound is said to be panned in a certain direction. This is not the only parameter affecting perceived spatial location. Perceived distance is determined largely by reverberation, which is an independent but complementary parameter. Other variables, often beyond the control of the synthesist, intervene here. It has been shown that perceived direction is strongly affected not only by the difference in volumes reaching the two ears but by the difference between the times the signals reach the two ears. This will depend on the listener's position relative to the speakers and any asynchrony between signal presentation to the speakers occasioned by different amplitude envelopes in the sounds. See chapter 7 for more discussion of sound localization.

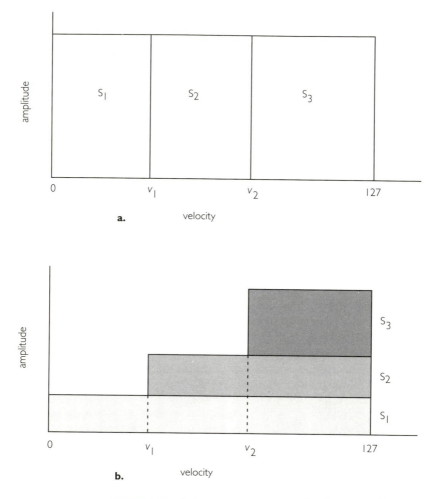

FIGURE 2.12   A three-way velocity switch (a); an example of switch layering (b).

Real-time control of panning is built into the programming functions of some synthesizers and can be achieved in a synthesizer setup that does not have it built in by routing the same sound to two (or more) speakers, with a separate volume control for each speaker. Foot pedals are often effective controllers when used this way.

Ring modulation, a kind of amplitude modulation, takes two audio input signals and multiplies them together. The effect of this is to produce an output signal that has frequencies corresponding to the sum and difference of all the input frequencies (so-called sum and difference tones).

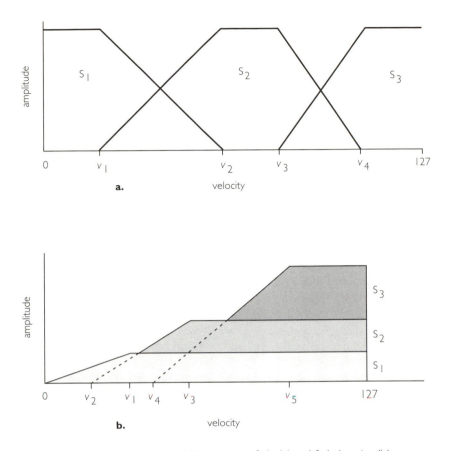

FIGURE 2.13   Velocity cross-fade (a) and fade layering (b).

Traditionally, the original frequencies are suppressed. For example, if input 1 has frequency f_1, while input 2 has frequencies f_2 and f_3, then the output will contain frequencies $f_1 + f_2$, $|f_1 - f_2|$, $f_1 + f_3$, and $|f_1 - f_3|$, where $|\ |$ means absolute value. The ring modulation features on some synthesizers do not produce true ring modulation but rather combine the two input signals to produce some other useful set of overtones that have a comparable aural effect. Sometimes a distinction between the two inputs is made, with one labeled the carrier and the other the modulator. Traditionally this distinction was fairly arbitrary, but in some modern synthesizers this is taken to mean that the carrier also makes a direct audio contribution to the output while the modulator does not. The natural performance parameters here are the control and spectral shaping parameters on each of the input signals.

Vocoding takes two audio inputs and uses the spectral shape of one to filter the other. This is normally a real-time technique using live performance as input. It is currently nearly always found as an outboard audio device, but its incorporation in synthesizers is becoming more common.

Phase distortion forms the basis for one type of audio synthesis and is not normally available as a separate processing technique on synthesizers not using this technique. It is therefore discussed in the following section on generic synthesis techniques.

Delays and *echos* are simply delayed copies of the original input signal. The copies may be attenuated or boosted in volume ("regeneration" or "feedback") and the delay times and number of echoes set. This effect is one of the most widely used for real-time control. The control possibilities commonly include a foot pedal switch allowing the digital delay effect to be turned on or off; continuous controllers can offer more subtle control. With such devices soloists commonly create canonical textures. A useful survey of delay effects has been given by Hall (1990).

Reverberation is the increase in a sound's ambience that occurs naturally due to the multiple and blended sound reflections from the surfaces of a room. It helps to allow the perceiver to infer the distance to the sound source. Historically, many studio forms have existed, typically based upon the excitation of metal plates, a small sealed chamber, or springs. These specific types of reverberation, as well as many others, are now routinely simulated and enhanced electronically. Real-time control of the various reverberation parameters is becoming increasingly common. These parameters include: *pre-delay* (a short delay before the onset of the reverberated signal); *reverberation time* (the time it takes for the signal to die away "completely"); *reverberation density* (number of echoes per unit time); *first reflection prominence* (the time between the prominent first reflection and the bulk of the reverberation); and various possibilities of equalization. (Note that in live performance, the term *first reflection time* refers to the time between the direct signal and the first sound heard from the walls of the room.) The significance of reverberation in performance is discussed in more depth in chapter 7.

Pitch-to-MIDI conversion and *pitch-to-voltage conversion* are similar processes: Both convert pitches from a (usually) monophonic audio source into other formats—MIDI messages and control voltages (CV) respectively. Both do this by analyzing the spectrum of the signal in some way in real time and computing a fundamental pitch and amplitude. In the conversion to MIDI, the fundamental pitch and amplitude are used to construct MIDI Note On and Note Off messages, and possibly MIDI controller 7 messages (volume) and pitch bend. In the conversion to CV the input sound is converted to control voltages. Other spectral characteristics, like brightness, may also be computed and converted into additional MIDI or CV control messages if the processors involved can act with sufficient speed. Although pitch-to-MIDI converters are steadily improving, such devices may have quirks in behavior and are capable of quicker response with higher frequencies. This is necessarily so since the number of cycles available for analysis in a given unit of time will be directly proportional to frequency. In particular, the performer should not expect fast bass register runs to be converted accurately. Control voltage devices are in principle capable of greater transmission speed than MIDI devices, and this may prove a significant factor in realizing precise percussive music.

Flanging, phasing, and *chorusing* are closely related effects that add a "broadened" or diffused quality to a sound. Flanging achieves this by adding to the input audio signal a copy of itself, delayed by a short, varying time interval. Very commonly, this delay time variation is controlled by an LFO. The technique was first discovered and originally executed by the fine manipulation of two tape recorders playing the same music. First one machine was slowed down slightly by applying pressure to the flange (the external surface near the rim) of the supply reel wheel, then the other was so treated, and so on. The aural effect of the resultant slight detuning and dephasing is similar to that obtained from what is called a comb filter.

Phasing is a technique, similar to flanging, that produces a copy of its input signal and sweeps its phase relation relative to the original signal. It normally does not include signal feedback. Chorusing is also similar to flanging. The main difference is that it produces several independently varying delayed copies of the incoming signal for an even more pronounced detuning and dephasing effect.

For all three processes, real-time control of variables such as LFO frequency, modulation depth, delay time, feedback level (strength), and mix can produce delicately expressive effects. Flanging, phasing, and chorusing are widely available both in outboard devices and as built-in features on increasing numbers of synthesizers.

In implementing these effects electronically, manufacturers have used a variety of techniques. Figure 2.14 shows one implementation of the three effects. The direct signal is split into two parts, and one part is processed with LFO-controlled delay while the other remains unaltered. The two parts are then mixed into a final composite signal. A more common implementation of chorusing is shown in figure 2.15, which shows more explicitly how it results from a number of slightly different copies of the original sound (each copy is produced by a separate line and independent LFO/delay pair). The effect occurs widely in acoustic music, as in the massed unisons of choirs and orchestral string sections.

Pitch shifting is a technique that transposes the audio signal by a controllable interval (frequency ratio). The harmonic spectrum of the sound is therefore preserved. Pitch shifters are commonly called harmonizers.

Pitch shifting is a valuable studio resource, and real-time control of this effect is becoming more common. Current harmonizers usually feature various intelligent modes of operation that do such things as add harmonies to the input signal in accordance with the prevailing chord, change the input signal's pitch to that of a currently held MIDI note, or add vibrato.

Frequency shifting is a related but distinct technique. This shifts all frequencies in the signal by a constant amount so that harmonic relationships are not preserved. Typically, sounds become more dissonant under this process. Real-time control of this effect is not common in the MIDI environment, and frequency shifting does not appear to form part of any current synthesizers.

Excitation, or enhancing, is used to boost upper harmonics of a sound to add "presence." This is not usually used with real-time control.

Fuzz is a distortion technique typically associated with the electric guitar. It also increases the sustain time of a sound. This is normally an outboard technique and one capable of real-time adjustment.

Timbral interpolation is often a computer-based non-real-time technique. It allows one sound to change smoothly into another by finding a common synthesis model for them and smoothly varying the synthesis parameters that make them up. Hence, interpolation between timbres is achieved. A form of it can be effected on any synthesizer that allows editing in real time by varying synthesis parameters with controllers. Interpolation should not be confused with simple cross-fading, although the latter can approximate this effect.

Compression and the related process of *limiting* regulate the audio level of a signal. A compressor increases a signal's volume during soft passages and decreases it in loud passages. In other words, it compresses its dynamic range. The extent of this increase or decrease is characterized by a *compression ratio.* A limiter keeps a signal from exceeding a certain peak level and has an adjustable *threshold* below which the signal is unaffected. Many compressors can be set to act as limiters. Compression and limiting inevitably affect the attack and decay times of sounds. Both these devices are typically used to obtain proper audio balance by assisting in the process of mixing rather than as real-time performance effects.

Approaches to Synthesis

The sources and processing techniques discussed above form the basis of a number of generic approaches to synthesis. These include the following: additive synthesis, subtractive synthesis, frequency modulation synthesis, sampling, composite synthesis, phase distortion, waveshaping, resynthesis, granular synthesis, linear predictive coding,

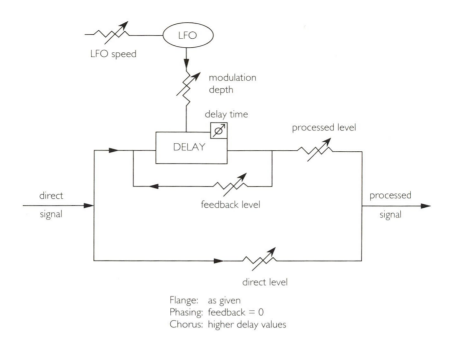

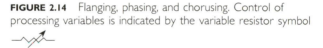

Flange: as given
Phasing: feedback = 0
Chorus: higher delay values

FIGURE 2.14   Flanging, phasing, and chorusing. Control of processing variables is indicated by the variable resistor symbol

direct digital synthesis, wave sequencing, vector synthesis, and physical modeling.

Each commercially available synthesizer uses at least one, and typically several, of these approaches. The choice of approaches and the details of their implementation determine what sorts of sounds and real-time control will be possible on the given machine. All contemporary synthesizers provide standard processing, as described earlier: signal combination (additive synthesis), modulation, and envelope shaping.

Additive synthesis can mean simply that two or more audio signals are added together to produce a new sound. The "classical" form of additive synthesis, still used on some synthesizers, may be called harmonic synthesis; here the sources added together are all simple waves (sines or cosines) and are in the simple frequency ratios of the harmonic series. This is potentially a very powerful technique, as it was shown well over 100 years ago by the Frenchman Jean Baptiste Fourier that any periodic sound can be so represented. In practice, the approach can be extremely time-consuming since hundreds of harmonics may need to be used.

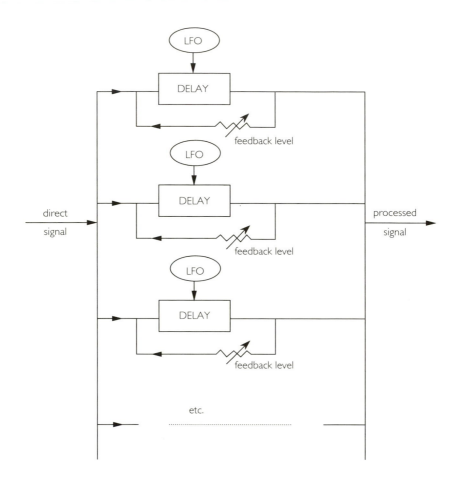

FIGURE 2.15   Chorusing (alternative implementation).

An alternative type of additive synthesis adds together a smaller number of harmonic or inharmonic components, or groups of such components, each with its own envelope. This forms the basis for many of the synthesizers produced by Kawai, for example. The real-time control potentials of this method are via the natural parameters of the components being added together. Similar principles operate when the components being added together are complex sources. The real-time effects available through this approach are discussed under "Layering" in chapter 7.

Subtractive synthesis refers to the use of filtering. Usually, spectrally rich sources are used: noise, pulse waves, certain types of samples, and so forth. Analog synthesis, in the meaning of this term now outdated by the rise of digital technology, refers to systems that provide subtractive capabilities along with standard processing.

Frequency modulation synthesis, as mentioned above, is often abbreviated FM. In its basic form it consists of one audio oscillator, the modulator (frequency *m*), modulating another audio oscillator, the carrier (frequency *c*). Complex "algorithms" can be built up by having more than one modulator modulate a given carrier and by having chains of modulators. The technique produces sidebands whose distribution is governed by the *c/m ratio*, and whose intensity is governed by the so-called *modulation index, I,* which is in essence the depth of modulation. The basic FM process may be described by the formula $e(t) = A \sin[ct + I\sin(mt)]$, where $e(t)$ is the FM output, A is the amplitude of the wave, c is the carrier wave frequency, m is the modulating wave frequency, and I is the modulation index. The sidebands are produced at frequencies given by the expression $|c \pm km|$, where $k = 0, 1, 2 \ldots$; in other words, at frequencies $c, c + m, |c-m|, c + 2m, |c-2m|, c + 3m$, and so on. The method can be extended to allow arbitrary waveforms and samples to act as carriers and modulators. Yamaha has pioneered the commercial potential of FM in its X and SY series.

Sampling refers to the digital storage of short samples of recorded sound and its subsequent processing using envelopes, filters, digital splicing, fading, looping, and other techniques. The processing possibilities basically combine traditional synthesis processing techniques, procedures from audio tape splicing (*musique concrète*), and specific new techniques of convenience such as the switch and cross-fade. Samples of acoustic sounds are commonly featured as sound sources in synthesizers themselves. The practical use of samplers is described in the next section.

Composite synthesis is a term used here to mean the use of both synthetic sources (oscillators and noise) and stored acoustic samples in one synthesizer. The stored samples may be complete sounds or truncated portions of such sounds. One typical implementation grafts attack samples onto the front of synthesized steady-state sounds, or cross-fades from the initial sample to a simpler steady state. For example, this approach has been used by Roland in their linear additive (L/A) synthesis and by Korg with their integrated M- and T-series machines. Composite synthesis is now very common, and machines with this design are made by virtually every synthesizer manufacturer. The tendency is for such machines to have significant on-board audio processing devices that offer reverb, digital delay, and other possibilities, as well as filtering and standard processing.

Phase distortion is a technique that is based on the phase alteration of simple waveforms stored as wavetables. The sound of the basic wave is distorted by altering the speed at which it is played back during a cycle. This speed can be parametrically controlled, for example by an envelope or a live performance device. This approach, used prominently by Casio, is sometimes termed *nonlinear distortion*. For a more in-depth look, see Roads (1985). Technically, FM is a kind of phase distortion (or nonlinear) synthesis.

Waveshaping is a closely related nonlinear technique that distorts the amplitude of a sound to produce spectral alterations. The process is based on the idea of a *transfer function*, a function used to alter an input wave-form to produce an output waveform. The typical nonlinearities of this function have the effect of adding sidebands to the input signal (some-times called the carrier). The method is described in detail by Le Brun (1979) and Dodge and Jerse (1985).

Resynthesis is an important synthesis technique in which sounds are digitally sampled, displayed in a representation for analysis (using com-puters), analyzed parametrically to form a special model, altered according to the possibilities in the parametric representation, and then resynthe-sized. Although not a real-time technique, it is finding increasing use in sound modules emphasizing instrument imitation (e.g., Roland's struc-tured adaptive—S/A—method).

Granular synthesis is a technique that creates sound by combining many small packets of sound, called grains, into composite sounds. These packets can be of any sound type but are typically of 20 milliseconds (msec) or less in duration. The characteristic resultant sound is shimmer-ing or animated (Moog 1988). This is a developing technology not implemented in any currently available commercial synthesizers, although this may soon change. For a more in-depth tutorial, see Roads (1988).

Linear predictive coding is a type of resynthesis technique that has proved particularly useful in synthesizing speech and singing. An excita-tion source (periodic pulse or noise) is fed into a suitably constructed all-pole filter, which allows the reconstitution of the waveform of the analyzed voice. It does not appear to be currently implemented in com-mercially available synthesizers.

Direct digital synthesis uses computers to generate waveforms directly and shape them. Because of the great computing power needed if such a procedure is to produce high fidelity results, this is normally not a real-time technique and hence is not directly relevant to the subject of this book. Every reader should realize, however, that this is a powerful re-search tool and is the method by which almost all current commercial synthesis methods were developed and shown viable. For this we are indebted to a number of people, but most deeply to Max Mathews of Bell

Laboratories, who pioneered construction of the Music N Languages (see Moore 1990).

Wave sequencing refers to the construction of sounds by stringing together a sequence of waveforms or samples—perhaps as many as several hundred—to make a composite wave. The sequence may be repeating or have random reordering. The waveforms are normally joined by cross-fading to make changes smooth rather than abrupt. Wave sequencing is related to the general technique of wavetable synthesis, where waveforms or samples are stored digitally in tables and then read out in various ways to produce sound.

Vector synthesis is a term used here to refer to the controllable cross-fading between four (in principle, any number) different sounds via a "vector control system"—normally a joystick that allows cross-fading along both x (horizontal) and y (vertical) axes. The four sounds are typically arranged at the vertices of a diamond shape. The cross-fading may be real-time controlled or preprogrammed—that is, affected by other synthesis functions like LFOs and envelopes. This technique is found implemented in some synthesizers by Prophet, Korg, and Yamaha. Vector synthesis machines often include the possibility of rapid circulation between different waveforms (wave sequencing). Note that the vector control system could readily be applied to other synthesis parameters acting on the four sounds, such as detuning or attack time. The term *vector synthesis* can likewise be used to describe similarly controllable timbral interpolation; these possibilities await further commercial development.

Physical modeling refers to the creation of sound by solving the mathematical equations that describe the acoustical properties of vibrating objects like instruments and resonators. Typically it is necessary to reduce the complexity of the mathematics by modeling the acoustical properties of the vibrating object, especially if anything approaching real-time computation is to be achieved. The Karplus-Strong algorithm, a procedure for string synthesis, is one of the best-known examples of this approach. Waveguide synthesis, used to model breath-based instruments and the voice, is another (Smith 1987). Physical modeling is expected to have a significant impact in commercial synthesis engines.

USING SAMPLERS

Samplers form such an important part of the synthesist's sonic resources that a special discussion on their use seems warranted. A sampler is a device that samples (digitally records) sounds and allows their processing, rearrangement, and control. Its maximum sampling time will be determined by the amount of on-board memory (usually RAM), and its fidelity of reproduction by both its resolution in bits and its sample rate. Professional standards in this regard are 16-bit resolution and 44.1 kHz maximum sample rate. Samplers are further characterized by the number of voices they can play. Top-end samplers have optional hard or optical disk attachments, which can store large amounts of sampled sound.

The basic digital sampling process is as follows, using the above numbers as examples. If the sample rate is s samples per second, then the machine makes a snapshot of the sound amplitude to 16-bit accuracy s times per second. Accuracy to 16 bits means a resolution of one part in 2^{16} (65,536). This corresponds to an optimal signal to noise ratio of $6 \times 16 = 96$ dB, equivalent to that of a CD player. In sampling a sound, it is best to use the maximum rate whenever possible; if memory is running out, plan to use the slower rate when it will make the least impairment of fidelity—for example, with dull or low-pitched sounds. When sampling rate is variable, the optimum rate depends on the use intended for the sound and a calculation of total required sample time.

In sampling there is a fundamental theorem that defines the resolution of the process. This relates the sampling rate s and the sample time t to N, the number of samples (words) produced in the digital recording. In our example, a word is a 16-bit sample. The fundamental equation describing this is $N = st$. In words, the number of samples (words) is equal to the sampling rate (in samples per second) times the sample length (in seconds).

Another important concept is the *Nyquist limit*. According to the Nyquist theorem, a sample rate s means that only sounds of frequency up to a maximum of $s/2$ Hz can be recorded faithfully, even in principle. This value ($s/2$) is the Nyquist limit. In practice, samplers only approach this limit since other components in the sampling system (e.g., input filters) introduce limitations in their quest to eliminate undesired side effects. Sounds in the sample above the Nyquist frequency will be reflected back into the range below it by the process of sampling, creating undesired frequencies, usually heard as high frequency static or "grunge." This is called *aliasing,* or *foldover.* Therefore, these components must be filtered out before sampling. In practice, frequencies up to 80 or perhaps 90 percent of $s/2$ will be accurately handled. Hence, a 44 kHz sampling rate just covers the full audio spectrum, and a 22 kHz rate yields a bandwidth under 10 kHz.

The process of sampling can be considered to consist of five steps:

1. preparation: selecting the source, making audio connections, minimizing background noise, deciding on sound processing and ambient conditions, the use of vibrato, etc.;

2. digital recording (sampling): setting input level, trigger level, sampling rate, and sample length and deciding on pitch to be recorded;

3. sample editing: making the sample musically usable by truncating dead spots, using time reversal, looping (forward, alternating, cross-fade), splicing (butt or cross-fade), etc. (visual waveform display can greatly clarify this process);

4. processing: samples or groups of them are treated with familiar electronic processing: filtering, envelope shaping, LFOs, pitch warp, etc.;

5. program building: a composite "instrument" is built by programming the samples for performance (this can be called *mapping*).

There are several types of mapping relevant in sampling: key mapping, velocity mapping, channel mapping, and controller mapping. *Key mapping* is the assignment of samples to different ranges of the keyboard. These ranges can be split or layered (on separate keys or overlapping). In constructing a program, the user must sample frequently enough so that samples are musically viable when assigned to cover their intended range of note numbers. This may require samples at the interval of a third, fourth, fifth, or so, depending very much on the nature of the sound and the use to which it is to be put. Some sounds, like the voice, cannot be transposed very far without sounding gimmicky; others are more forgiving. In other situations the point of the whole process may be to transform the sound drastically, casting aside any notions of naturalness.

Velocity mapping is when the playing of samples is velocity-dependent. Any variable may be velocity controllable in principle. Common variables include volume, filter cutoff, pitch modulation, and attack time. Velocity can also be used to switch between different samples (velocity switching) or to fade between them (velocity cross-fading).

Channel mapping refers to the assignment of different MIDI channels to different programs or samples. This allows multitimbral use of the sampler.

Controller mapping refers to the real-time control of sample processing by MIDI controllers like pressure, wheels, and sliders. This has the familiar advantage over velocity of continuous rather than one-shot control.

Looping requires a few special comments. There are two kinds of loops: short and normal. Short loops are those less than about 50 msec in duration. They require special treatment because they are perceived as having a separate pitch produced by the loop. This occurs because $\frac{1}{50 \text{ msec}} = 20$ Hz, the lower frequency threshold of hearing. To avoid introducing spurious pitches with short loops, it is necessary to pick a loop length corresponding to a frequency that will blend with the sampled sound; this means that the loop-produced frequency should most likely be at the fundamental pitch of the sample, or some multiple or submultiple of it. In practice, this works as follows: After recording, vary the length of short loops by trial and error, using your ear to match the loop generated pitch to the sample pitch. On samplers that have a continuously variable sample rate, one can choose a sampling rate ahead of time to make this relation work out naturally.

The primary issue with normal loops is that loops should be smooth, unless glitches are called for by the musical demands of the situation. This requires a precise and smooth matching of the start and end points of the loop. Variations in loudness, pitch, and modulation must be dovetailed smoothly. For this (and other) reasons it is often better to record sounds without processing like vibrato, tremolo, or reverberation; these can be added later. For example, if room resonance effects are included in the sound, the size of the room will appear to change as the sample is transposed to different pitch levels. This is often undesirable.

Contemporary samplers now normally have an autoloop function, which is often very successful. With stereo samples, both channels must be looped in synchronization. Nearly all samplers also allow the loop ends to be dovetailed (cross-faded), and either to play in one direction always or alternate back and forth.

Loops can also be used to create rhythms. The time duration of a loop can be computed from the fundamental equation above. Simply divide the loop length in samples by s. For example, an eighth note at a tempo of quarter note = 108, with a sampling rate of 44 kHz, would require a loop length of $(60/108) \times (4/8) \times 44,000 = 12,222$ samples.

Sampling is the best way to imitate natural sounds; its main limitations are that there is limited sample time available and that real-time control and modulation options are often not as developed as on synthesizers.

MUSICAL QUALITIES AND SYNTHESIS

This great list of resources for synthesis and sampling does not necessarily have very much to do with music. It is this point—the connection between sound and music—that we must now examine. The approach we will use will be to "translate" between the language of synthesis and the language of music. The relations here are difficult to systematize since we are drawing correlations between artistic expression and scientific representation, and the two areas have different world views behind them: the first ultimately personal and subjective, emphasizing intuition, the second rigorous and objective, emphasizing method—caricatures, perhaps, but they do have some validity. The problem is a central one for the synthesist, who is forced to work in both worlds continually.

One natural approach to this is to try to classify the world of electronic sound—both its objects and processes—on the basis of the musical effects they produce. Most workers in this field today would probably agree that this approach is too difficult and convoluted, especially given the pluralistic nature of contemporary musical thought, to admit of any definitive or unique classification scheme. But there have been several noteworthy attempts that raise essential issues for the practicing synthesist.

This classification can occur from several points of view. Most commonly, there are parameters or classifications referring to sound quality (bright, dark, shrill, etc.) and others referring to concepts of note organization (e.g. monophony, heterophony, imitation). Of course, in many situations in electronic music, there is often no hard line between synthesis and composition. Nevertheless, we must draw some practical line between the two if this book is not to drift into becoming a composition text. Other bases for systematic classification of electronic sound have been used, including time shapes, motion types, gesture, and texture.

In addition, special effects occur with the use of *natural language* (for example, English) due to its invocation of specific meanings and associations, *quotations*, references to previously composed (and typically well-known) music, and synthesis designs that invoke *mimesis*, the imitation of other sources (such as animal sounds, the heartbeat, etc.).

A significant early attempt at systematic classification of electronic sound was made by Pierre Schaeffer, in his classic books *À la recherche d'une musique concrète* (1952), and *Traité des objets musicaux* (1966). In these works he proposes the idea of the sound object (*objet sonore*), which we have already defined in chapter 1 as a bundle of sound heard as a related whole. Schaeffer classified these sound objects on the basis of their time envelopes, their degree of internal complexity, and the processes being applied to them. He further proposed that there were three important *reference plans*, which described the interactions between the important musical parameters of pitch, intensity, and duration, which shaped the characteristic qualities of any sound object. These he labeled "plan mélodique ou des tessitures"(the relation between pitch and time), "plan dynamique ou des formes" (the relation between dynamics and time), and "plan harmonique ou des timbres" (the relation between pitch and intensity). He also specified techniques for combining sounds. Although he had in mind primarily the techniques of *musique concrète*, these techniques are perfectly applicable to contemporary synthesizer performance. Manning (1985) aptly summarizes these classifications and manipulations.

A number of the details of Schaeffer's classification system are open to dispute, and they go beyond the scope of this book. But he gave a crucial impetus to now widely used terminology used to describe sound quality and musical timbre. This terminology can take the form of descriptive polarities, aspects, or descriptive/perceptual/musical dimensions. Starting from the traditional parameters of music analysis, these aspects can be expanded to a considerable list. We will detail the best known of these here, drawing from Schaeffer and a number of later workers (Risset 1985; Wessel 1985; Smalley 1986). These particular terms aim for some measure of objectivity and attempt to be neutral in terms of emotional or personally evaluative response.

We will take the point of view that where such terms aim for objectivity, they can be organized along musical aspects or dimensions, like pitch or brightness, and that, depending on how developed the English language of music is, there may be a number of useful terms that describe reference points along these musical dimensions, like low/medium/high (for pitch) and shrill/buzzy/bright/mellow/dull (for brightness). Table 2.3 gives a number of examples of this.

Such terms can include traditional music parameters like dynamics, timbre, and articulation and can progress to finer and more specific kinds of control, the nature of which depends on the chosen process and synthesis procedures. Other aspects of sound that may not possess clear adjectival reference points, such as naturalness, liveliness, identity, personality, suppleness, and presence, also occur. These descriptions can be useful in conceptualizing sounds in terms of their possible uses, either by combination or by the assignment of controllers to the aspect in question.

These musical aspects or dimensions can also be characterized in terms of the common synthesis parameters that can control them, as shown in table 2.4. This list attempts to be more complete than table 2.3, but it is clearly impossible to be comprehensive. As always, these corresponding synthesis parameters may be fixed, or controllable in real time.

For those who wish to delve more deeply in the relations between music, synthesis, sound structuring, and psychoacoustics, there is very little of a coherent theory of timbre or electronic composition available. Deutsch (1982) provides a psychoacoustic starting point. An insightful discussion of the general possibilities in sound structuring is given by Smalley (1986). He develops the idea of *spectro-morphology,* meaning the design of music based on the full spectrum of available pitches and the general temporal processes that can shape them, not confined to notes or traditional musical processes. The interested reader should also consult Robert Erickson's book *Sound Structure in Music* (1975), which gives perspectives on the organization of timbre. Wayne Slawson, in his book *Sound Color* (1985), gives a theory of timbre based on phonetics and the

ASPECT	DESCRIPTIVE TERMS
Register	High/low
Volume	Loud/soft
Attack	Fast/slow
Overall envelope shape	Decaying/swelling/sustaining/evolving
	single trigger/multiple attacks
Duration	Long/short
Spectral content	Dull/mellow/bright/buzzy/shrill
	pure/rich/noisy/distorted
	harmonic/nonharmonic
"Naturalness"	Natural/imitative/synthetic
Ambience	Wet/dry/resonant
	degree of reverb and echo
Modulation depth	Zero/maximum
	fixed/varying
Modulation speed	Zero/maximum
	fixed/varying
Coherence	Fission/fusion (both sequential and vertical)

TABLE 2.3 Musical dimensions (aspects) and some corresponding descriptive terms.

ASPECT	SYNTHESIS PARAMETERS AND PROCESSES
Pitch + register (macrovariation)	Frequency, playback speed (samples), pitch envelope, pitch bend, portamento time
Pitch (microvariation)	Fine frequency, detune, pitch bend, retuning
Volume	Gain or level
Dynamics	Volume + timbral change: via gain, envelope parameters (most importantly attack time), brightness
Timbre	Rapid portions of volume envelopes (particularly attack and decay), spectrum
Attack	First and possibly subsequent volume envelope segments, amplitude of high frequencies in note attack
Envelope shape	Segment levels, rates (times)—affecting volume, brightness, frequency, timbre, etc.
Duration	Decay, release times of volume envelope(s)
Vibrato	LFO frequency modulation: depth, speed, waveform, onset point
Tremolo	LFO volume modulation: depth, speed, waveform, onset point

TABLE 2.4 Aspects of sound and synthesis parameters used to control them.

ASPECT	SYNTHESIS PARAMETERS AND PROCESSES
Brightness/richness	Filter parameters (cutoff frequency, resonance), volume of brighter components (via gain), FM modulation index
Noisiness	Volume of noise generator, filter control of noise generator, volume of noisy components, distortion or feedback level, frequency of audio modulation (nonintegral or real c/m ratio)
Perceived definite pitch	Harmonicity of partials, volume of pitched components, integer c/m ratio (FM)
Pureness/purity	Absence of noise and upper partials: sine wave, absence of processing other than reverberation
Ambience/reverberation	Send and return gains on reverberation unit or digital delay, time (rate) of release (or possibly decay) envelope segments
Spatial location	Panning, reverberation, speaker placement
Naturalness/imitation /realism	Synthetic imitation of natural spectra and envelopes, resynthesis variables, presence of appropriate formants, use of samples with crossfades and switches, fine tuning across register of scaling and rates, absence of processing, realtime expressive control parameters: microtuning (pitch bend, random detuning), dynamics, vibrato, articulation, timbre
Coherence (spatial, temporal or timbral)	Spectral and envelope similarity of components, synchronicity of components' attacks, similar modulation on harmonics or components, isorhythm of parts, integrated rhythmic design, shared register and pitch frames, Gestalt ideas (Deutsch 1982)
Fission	Lack of coherence (see above), independence of parts
Granularity/graininess	Depth of fast LFO modulation, quantization
Identity/personality ("life," "luster")	Consistency of sound and control over register, integration of fixed and real-time synthesis with performance and compositional design
Presence/edge/bite (being "up front")	Brightness (filtering) and attack component of envelope, limiting of echo and reverb, relative prominence of frequencies in roughly the 2–5 kHz range, use of exciters or distortion
Resonance	Reinforcement in specific frequency bands

TABLE 2.4   continued.

voice. John Grey (1975) has attempted to quantify the idea of timbre space. He grouped instrument sounds into a timbre space and found that timbral relatedness could be boiled down to three basic dimensions. These dimensions are:

1. onset synchrony of sound components;
2. spectral energy distribution;
3. amplitudes of high frequencies in note attacks.

Although timbre depends on the attack portion of the envelope more than anything, the overall spectrum is also important, particularly whether the sound is based on overtones or formants or both. Release characteristics are also critical for some sounds like the guitar or harpsichord (where the spectrum changes dramatically on release, due to the string release mechanism).

Metaphoric Sound Description

It is often the task of the practicing synthesist in studio, film, and band work to go from word descriptions to produce sounds. Objective or quasi-objective terms, as above, are helpfully concrete in this translation process.

Other kinds of musical descriptions occur in practical playing situations, and these have a different, more subjective character. The practicing synthesist will need to be able to deal with this class of sound descriptions as well. These descriptions can be evaluative, like "really hot," emotive, like "angry," referential, like "sounding like a woodpecker," or metaphoric, like "muddy," "dirty," "cloud-like," "spaced-out," "flowing," and so forth. An example of such descriptions is provided by Dominic Milano:

> Playing chords in the bass register will produce your basic spooky noise. Playing seconds in the upper register gives that old Penderecki-meets-Friskies-cat-food-commercial effect. Playing the filter cutoff frequency manually produces B-grade space movie computer sounds. (Milano 1987, p. 16)

Sometimes the composer or producer will request a sound using familiar words in idiosyncratic ways. It can be difficult to make literal sense of such language, and sometimes there is no sense to be found behind the terms. But it is best to be as sympathetic as possible; part of the problem is that there really is no language that describes the world of sound well. This is particularly true of the world of synthetic sound, which is so young and poorly charted. If words could well describe the effects of music, we'd have less need for musicians.

The best guideline is to be logical and rigorous whenever necessary but not to impose such a working method on a sound search where the request is vague or enigmatic. Use your intuition and imagination, and think laterally. If the sound doesn't start to move in the right timbral direction fairly quickly, start over again, from either the same or a different sonic vantage point.

COMPUTER SOFTWARE

The final major resource for the synthesizer performer is the wide range of computer music software currently available. Many such programs can directly affect synthesizer performance. Others that do not have an impact on the synthesist's working conditions and options, so that an understanding of the range of resources provided by computer software is extremely handy. The main functions of existing commercial software can be summarized as follows.

Sequencing

In general, a sequencer is a device that can record a timed sequence of (musical) data and play it back. The contemporary MIDI-based sequencer is a powerful and high-resolution software environment enabling multitrack recording, advanced and comprehensive editing, some compositional transformations, and multitrack playback of recorded MIDI messages. Storage of system exclusive data and external synchronization to SMPTE via MTC are becoming standard features (see chapter 3). Video and film production assistance software exists separately and is also incorporated to a considerable degree in some sequencers. A much more detailed description of the features and use of sequencers in live performance is given in chapter 7.

Algorithmic Composition, Compositional Environments, and Intelligent Instruments

The term *compositional environment* is used here to mean a set of software features allowing such things as computer composition, computer transformation of input MIDI data, and *interactive composition* between computer instrument and the performer, either directly via the computer's input devices or through a MIDI performance device such as a synthesizer or master controller. Often the computer is acting as a compositional assistant; when the computer composes music independently, it is operating under the guidance of its programmer's *algorithms,* and so computer-composed music may be called *algorithmic composition.* An algorithm is a precise step-by-step set of instructions that allow the computer to carry out a task. When a played electronic music system shows independent decision-making capacity in interpreting the performer's actions, it may be called an *intelligent instrument.* Some intelligent music software produces both sound and visual effects. See chapter 7 for the use of these environments in synthesizer performance and chapter 11 for a look at future directions in this area.

Score Production

A number of software programs now produce musical notation of varying degrees of sophistication and stylistic compass. This notation may be input in a number of ways, but the basic option is between *non-real-time input* (*step-time input*), where the user enters the symbols to be used from a QWERTY keyboard, mouse, MIDI keyboard, or special input device, and *real-time input,* where the music is played into the program from a keyboard or other performing device and the program automatically notates it. Such autotranscription routines are steadily improving in quality but always require subsequent editing. Some programs feature automatic part production from an input master score. Discussion of the use of synthesizers with such routines is given in chapter 7.

Score production may also be integrated with MIDI playback facilities, or with a sequencer and compositional routines, or with both. These different functions may be combined in one program or readily set in communication through a multitasking environment, producing an integrated sequencing/printing/composing production facility.

Editor/Librarian Software

An editor provides vastly improved graphic representation of the synthesis parameters in a specific machine. It also may provide algorithms to do useful tasks that the original machine doesn't achieve well or at all. For example, routines for special kinds of tunings, and automatic patch generators, are widely found. Editing software is linked to specific synthesizers and therefore may have a shorter half-life than other software.

Machine-specific librarian software is either found bundled with an editor or on its own. It simply allows the display and rearrangement of programs and the storage of this information. Generic librarians exist that can store patches from many different manufacturers in one software environment; these often have generic templates for editing.

Music Programming Environments

These are programming environments that include considerable musical intelligence, which the programmer can use to create such things as new instruments, composing routines, MIDI transformation procedures, and other musical innovations.

MIDI Programming Languages

These are separately devised high-level languages that allow the user to program using MIDI.

Direct Digital Synthesis

The programs referred to here are Music N-type direct synthesis languages that have been adapted for microcomputer use.

Sound Synthesis, Analysis, Resynthesis, and Sound File Manipulation

One type of program allows sound to be synthesized by software, usually using icons representing familiar synthesis sources and processes such as oscillators and modulation, which are patched together on the screen. The sounds are produced by the computer's own DSP (digital signal processing) chip or by using special cards or external devices to achieve higher (usually 16-bit) resolution. Another type of program is concerned with actual display of acoustical signals, in time or frequency plots, which may be two- or three-dimensional. Audio can be entered from data transfer (for example, via MIDI from a sampler), or directly by ADC, and then manipulated before being reconverted to sound. Cut-and-paste editing, splicing, looping, filtering, and resynthesis are typical features. Playback of sounds can be via a sampler, or directly, by DAC.

MIDI Analysis

These programs display MIDI data in lists and graphs to facilitate analysis or system troubleshooting.

MIDI Mapping

These programs convert incoming MIDI data to a different set of outgoing data in systematic ways, using a variety of built-in operations. Equivalent hardware modules are available; these modules are usually called MIDI mappers or MIDI transformation boxes.

Musicianship and Ear Training

The skills of traditional musicianship are taught by a number of available programs. These include basic theory (e.g., scales, key signatures, chord and interval spelling) and aural perception (pitch, chord and interval identification). Most such programs provide different levels of difficulty and a self-assessment system to allow the user to monitor progress.

Data Storage

These programs allow bulk storage of MIDI data, but come without significant editing features.

Music programs are written for all existing computers. Best known for their music applications are Macintosh and Atari (with built-in MIDI connection); also widespread are IBM, Amiga, and, in Japan, NEC. NeXT computers have made a strong impact among music researchers, and machines by Silicon Graphics seem set to do the same.

Commercial software is often copy protected, either by software or hardware. The trend away from copy protection is clear in most other fields but less so in music. Whether this is a comment on the greater unscrupulousness of musicians over other computer users or the small size of the market available to programmers is left for the reader to decide.

REFERENCES

Balzano, J. "The Group-Theoretic Description of 12-Fold and Microtonal Pitch Systems." *Computer Music Journal* 4,4 (Winter 1980): 66–84.

Barnes, John. "Bach's Keyboard Temperament." *Early Music* 7,2 (April 1979): 236–49.

Blackwood, Easley. *The Structure of Recognizable Diatonic Tunings*. Princeton: Princeton University Press, 1985.

Bregman, A., and S. McAdams. "Hearing Musical Streams." *Computer Music Journal* 3,4 (Dec. 1979): 26–43, 60, 63.

Carlos, Wendy. "Tuning: At the Crossroads." *Computer Music Journal* 11,1 (Spring 1987): 29–43.

Chowning, J. "The Synthesis of Complex Audio Spectra by Means of Frequency Modulation." *Journal of the Audio Engineering Society* 21,7 (Sept. 1973): 526–34.

Reprinted in *Foundations of Computer Music,* ed. Curtis Roads and John Strawn. Cambridge, Mass.: MIT Press, 1985.

Chowning, John, and David Bristow. *FM Theory and Applications.* Milwaukee: Yamaha Foundation and Hal Leonard, 1986.

Deutsch, Diana. *The Psychology of Music.* New York: Academic Press, 1982.

Dodge, Charles, and Thomas Jerse. *Computer Music.* New York: Schirmer, 1985.

Emmerson, Simon, ed. *The Language of Electroacoustic Music.* London: Macmillan and Co., 1986.

Erickson, R. *Sound Structure in Music.* Berkeley: University of California Press, 1975.

Fokker, Adrian. *Just Intonation and the Combination of Harmonic Diatonic Melodic Groups.* The Hague: Nijhoff, 1949.

Grey, John. "An Exploration of Musical Timbre." Ph.D. diss., Stanford University, 1975.

Hall, Gary. "The Dimensions of Delay." *Electronic Musician* 6,9 (Sept. 1990): 48–75.

Le Brun, Marc. "Digital Waveshaping Synthesis." *Journal of the Audio Engineering Society* 27,4 (April 1979): 250–266.

Lloyd, Llewelyn, and Hugh Boyle. *Intervals, Scales, and Temperaments.* New York: St. Martin's Press, 1978.

McAdams, S. "The Auditory Image." In *Cognitive Processes in the Perception of Art,* ed. W. R. Crozier and A. J. Chapman. Amsterdam: North-Holland, 1984.

Manning, Peter. *Electronic and Computer Music.* Oxford: Clarendon Press, 1985.

Milano, Dominic, ed. *Synthesizer Programming.* Milwaukee: Hal Leonard, 1987.

Moog, R. "Granular Synthesis Explained." *Keyboard* 14,12 (Dec. 1988): 117–18+.

Moore, F. Richard. *Elements of Computer Music.* Englewood Cliffs: Prentice-Hall, N.J. 1990.

Partch, Harry. *Genesis of a Music.* New York: Da Capo Press, 1974.

Pierce, J. *The Science of Musical Sound.* New York: Scientific American Books, 1985.

Risset, Jean-Claude. "Digital Techniques and Sound Structure in Music." In *Composers and the Computer,,* ed. C. Roads. Vol. 2, The Computer Music and Digital Audio Series. Madison, Wisc.: A-R Editions, Inc., 1985. (Originally published by William Kaufmann, Inc.)

Roads, C. "A Tutorial on Nonlinear Distortion or Waveshaping Analysis." In *Foundations of Computer Music,* ed. C. Roads and J. Strawn. Cambridge, Mass.: MIT Press, 1985.

———. "Introduction to Granular Synthesis." *Computer Music Journal* 12,2 (Summer 1988): 11–13. See other articles in this issue for more information on granular synthesis.

Schaeffer, P. *À la recherche d'une musique concrète.* Paris: Éditions du Seuil, 1952.

———. *Traité des objets musicaux.* Paris: Éditions du Seuil, 1966.

Slawson, W. *Sound Color.* Berkeley: University of California Press, 1985.

Smalley, D. "Spectro-morphology and Structuring Processes."In *The Language of Electroacoustic Music.* ed. S. Emmerson. London: Macmillan and Co., 1986.

Smith, Julius O. "Musical Applications of Digital Waveguides." Stanford University Department of Music Report, STAN-M-39, 1987.

Wessel, David. "Timbre Space as a Musical Control Structure." In *The Foundations of Computer Music,* ed. C. Roads and J. Strawn. Cambridge, Mass.: MIT Press, 1985.

Wilkinson, Scott. *Tuning In: Microtonality in Electronic Music.* Milwaukee: Hal Leonard, 1988.

Yasser, Joseph A. *A Theory of Evolving Tonality.* New York: Da Capo Press, 1975. (Originally published New York: American Library of Musicology, 1932.)

MIDI

I too was encompassed by the popular assumption that the *present,* in relation to the *past,* means progress. It involved no small inner struggle to emerge from that spell, to discover that present "progress" clothed a skeleton of bondage to a specific and limited past.

- Harry Partch, *Genesis of a Music* (1974)

MIDI stands for Musical Instrument Digital Interface. It is the widely used standard used for communicating information about sound and musical performance between different musical devices, be they synthesizers, computers, sequencers, or other electronic devices. Conceived and refined in 1981 and 1982, its functional date is January 1983, when it was first used to connect instruments made by different manufacturers at a National Association of Music Merchants convention in the United States.

The technical details of MIDI are by now well established, although the basics continue to be supplemented by other possibilities as new needs emerge. The current MIDI specifications are contained in a document entitled *MIDI 1.0 Specification,* available from the International MIDI Association (IMA; for address see the General Bibliography). New additions and alterations are made periodically, resulting in successive document versions (e.g., document version 4.1). A recent explication of MIDI is found in Rothstein (1992). Changes and supplementations to the MIDI master document are made on an ongoing basis by the MMA (the U.S.-based MIDI Manufacturer's Association) and the JMSC (Japanese MIDI Standards Committee).

The focus in this chapter will not be on a full explanation of all the facets of MIDI. Nevertheless, the MIDI messages commonly of direct relevance to the performer will be described, both functionally and in terms of precise coding. While understanding of the functions of the various MIDI messages is important for all performers, a detailed understanding of the MIDI code is not essential for most playing situations. Knowledge of MIDI code can, however, be extremely useful when diagnosing and fixing MIDI system faults, using MIDI mappers, designing the performance interface for more advanced effects like velocity switching and controller cross-fade, and avoiding technical problems in live performance. Those readers who do not require this level of detail are advised to gloss over the details of the provided code and use this book as a reference text for the specific situations requiring MIDI programming.

MIDI consists of a number of different kinds of messages, or commands, most of them designed to correspond to the actions of a synthesizer performer. Other types of messages refer to such things as the actions of a sequencer, modes of sound production, synthesizer programming data, or the transfer of stored MIDI files.

Each MIDI message consists of one or more *words.* The term is used here, just as in normal language, to stand for a unit of meaning. Each word consists of ten *bits* of information. A bit is the smallest unit of digital information, usually represented by a digit that can be either 1 or 0. The symbols 1 and 0 are arbitrary, and we could just as readily use up or down, on or off, yes or no, + or −, or any other two symbols. The essential idea is that of binary logic, based on two possibilities.

The first and last bits of all MIDI words are called, respectively, the start and stop bits, and they serve to delineate the message carried in the word; they do not themselves contain information. (The start bit is always 0 and the stop bit is always 1.) The eight bits in the middle are the real information carriers, and they form a *byte*. From this point on we will talk primarily about bytes rather than words. A byte can be considered to be made of two parts, each containing four bits and called a *nibble*. This terminology is shown in figure 3.1. Note that the prefix "kilo" normally means 1,000, but in the digital world of bytes, a kilobyte is $2^{10} = 1,024$ bytes, and a megabyte is $2^{20} = 1024 \times 1024$ bytes, or 1,048,576 bytes.

MIDI information is sent in *serial* digital format (one bit after another) at a *baud rate* (transmission speed) of 31,250 bits per second, or 31.25 kilobits per second, or 31.25 kbaud. (Note that here kilo is used to mean 1,000.) Hence, each MIDI word of ten bits takes about 320 microseconds to be transmitted down a MIDI cable. A *parallel* transmission protocol, in contrast, sends all its message bits out simultaneously on different wires. Although faster, parallel transmission is more expensive.

NUMBER SYSTEMS

To understand the way MIDI code is read, we will have to make a short digression to understand the nature of number systems. A *number system* is a set of symbols that provides a way to count and do arithmetic. Every number system has a *base*, which is the number of distinct symbols used to express values in it. Our familiar decimal system uses ten symbols: 0,1,2,3,4,5,6,7,8,9. The binary system uses the two symbols, 0 and 1. The octal system, base 8, commonly uses the symbols 0,1,2,3,4,5,6,7. But note that most manufacturers who use octal numbers for storing patches, such as Roland and Korg, begin counting with 1, so their symbol set is 1,2,3,4,5,6,7,8.

In general, a system uses the familiar Arabic numerals from 0 to 9, and if it requires more than ten symbols, letters are used. In the hexadecimal (base 16) system, the symbols are thus 0,1,2,3,4,5,6,7,8,9,A,B,C,D,E,F. Hexadecimal arithmetic is often distinguished by putting either a $ before the number or an H after it. For example, $7F and 27H are both hex numbers. In this book the H notation will be preferred.

To learn how to use the binary system, the one actually used to transmit MIDI information, it is best to begin by analyzing our familiar decimal system. Consider what we mean by a decimal number such as 6,235. This has the value $(5 \times 1) + (3 \times 10) + (2 \times 100) + (6 \times 1000)$. The rule we are following is to add the digits together from right to left, but only after

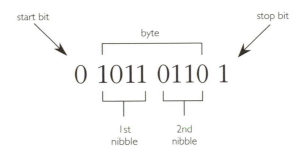

start bit

stop bit

byte

0 1011 0110 1

1st
nibble

2nd
nibble

FIGURE 3.1 The MIDI word.

multiplying them by the value associated with their position (or "place" or "column"). Each position (or place) is worth ten times the value of the position to its right. Here 5 is in the ones column, 3 is in the tens column, 2 is in the hundreds column, and 6 is in the thousands column.

In general, the value associated with each position in any number system is just the base b raised to the appropriate power. The appropriate power is just the position number, when we number the positions from right to left, starting with position zero (0). In other words, the digit in the rightmost position (position 0) is multiplied by the base to the zero power, b^0, which is always 1, so any number in this column represents itself. The next digit to the left (position 1) is multiplied by b^1, the next digit to the left (position 2) by b^2, the next digit (position 3) by b^3, and so on. In the base 10 system, as shown above, the associated values are $10^0 = 1$, $10^1 = 10$, $10^2 = 100$, $10^3 = 1000$.

We evaluate binary numbers using this same rule, where the successive positions from right to left are powers of 2: 1,2,4,8,16,32,64,128, and so on. For example, 10011 would be, in decimal notation, $(1 \times 2^0) + (1 \times 2^1) + (0 \times 2^2) + (0 \times 2^3) + (1 \times 2^4) = 19$. The 8-bit byte 10010001 would have a value of $(1 \times 1) + (1 \times 16) + (1 \times 128) = 145$.

The hexadecimal system will also be useful in describing MIDI. Its successive right-to-left positions are based on powers of 16: 1, 16, 256, 4096, and so on. But with regard to MIDI, we will rarely need to go beyond two digits. For example, the number 27H is equivalent to $(7 \times 16^0) + (2 \times 16^1)$, or 39 in decimal notation. Remembering that A is used for decimal 10, B for 11, C for 12, and so on, 4CH corresponds to 12 + (4×16), or 76.

It is important to note that each nibble in the binary system corresponds to a single hexadecimal digit. Hence, a byte of eight binary digits (as in a MIDI message) may be expressed as two hexadecimal digits. Since hex numbers are much easier to remember than binary for most people, and since hex is usually used in MIDI displays in software and hardware, we will express each MIDI byte as two hexadecimal numbers, setting off bytes from each other with a period (".").

The correspondence between decimal, binary, and hexadecimal notations for the first twenty-one numbers is given in table 3.1. Included for comparison is the two-digit octal representation as well, with 1 (not 0) as the first digit, as commonly used by synthesizer manufacturers, and decimal notation starting with 1 rather than with 0, as is used in synthesizers to list such things as MIDI channel numbers and program numbers. A conversion table between these number systems up to decimal value 128 is given in Appendix B.

MIDI MESSAGES

We are now in a position to make sense of MIDI messages. Each such message is made up of one or more bytes. These bytes are of one of two types: status or data. A *data byte* typically gives the numerical value of a performance variable—for example, it may indicate the note number depressed by the keyboardist or the physical position of a controller on the keyboard. A *status byte* defines the meaning of data bytes that follow it, or indicates system states or events that have no associated data bytes. For example, a status byte may turn on a sequencer, or indicate that the data bytes following it refer to pitch bend. In binary, all data bytes start with 0 and all status bytes start with 1. In hexadecimal this means that all data bytes start with 7 or less and all status bytes start with 8 or more.

MIDI messages contain a single status byte, followed immediately by zero, one, two, or, in some cases, possibly more, data bytes. These messages fall into two types: channel and system. A *channel message* is addressed to only one channel in the receiving device. In practical terms, a channel number is simply an identifying numerical label that can have one of sixteen values. The receiving device looks for the channel number and acts on the information in the message only if the device has been configured to respond to that channel.

Channel messages divide further into two types: channel voice messages and channel mode messages. *Channel voice messages* give values corresponding to physical gestures by the performer. *Channel mode messages* send information about the synthesizer's mode of operation on the specified channel. The channel messages, in hexadecimal, are summarized in table 3.2.

DECIMAL	BINARY	HEXADECIMAL	DECIMAL (STARTING AT 1)	OCTAL
0	0000	00H	1	11
1	0001	01H	2	12
2	0010	02H	3	13
3	0011	03H	4	14
4	0100	04H	5	15
5	0101	05H	6	16
6	0110	06H	7	17
7	0111	07H	8	18
8	1000	08H	9	21
9	1001	09H	10	22
10	1010	0AH	11	23
11	1011	0BH	12	24
12	1100	0CH	13	25
13	1101	0DH	14	26
14	1110	0EH	15	27
15	1111	0FH	16	28
16	10000	10H	17	31
17	10001	11H	18	32
18	10010	12H	19	33
19	10011	13H	20	34
20	10100	14H	21	35

TABLE 3.1   Decimal, binary, hexadecimal, and octal number systems. The octal system here begins with 1 (not 0), as is the practice with most manufacturers.

System messages, in contrast, are addressed to the entire synthesis system, without restriction by channel. They fall into three categories—system exclusive, system common, and system real time—and are summarized in table 3.3.

Channel Voice Messages

The status bytes of channel messages divide into two nibbles. The first nibble identifies the kind of message it is, and the second gives the MIDI channel number. The next one or two bytes are data bytes, which vary from 0 to 127 (0H to 7FH) in all cases. (Bytes in the range 80H to FFH are status bytes.)

Since a nibble is four bits long, the channel number can have only 2^4 or sixteen possible values: Customarily these are numbered 1 to 16 in synthesizer parlance. But in the MIDI message format itself, the range 0 to

CHANNEL VOICE MESSAGES

Message	Status	Channel	Data byte 1	Data byte 2
8n.kk.vv	Note Off	*n*	*kk* = key number	*vv* = off velocity
9n.kk.vv	Note On	*n*	*kk* = key number	*vv* = on velocity (00 = note off)
An.kk.pp	Polyphonic Pressure	*n*	*kk* = key number	*pp* = pressure value
Bn.cc.vv	Control Change	*n*	*cc* = control number	*vv* = control value
			00–1F continuous*	MSB
			20–3F continuous	LSB
			40–5F switch†	0–126/127 = off/on
			60–78 undefined	—
			79–7F channel mode	—
Cn.pp	Program Change	*n*	*pp* = program number	—
Dn.pp	Channel Pressure	*n*	*pp* = pressure value	—
En.bb.BB	Pitch Bend	*n*	*bb* = LSB bend value	*BB* = MSB bend value

MSB = most significant byte
LSB = least significant byte
channel number *n* ranges 0–F hex, 1–16 decimal
*when programmed as a switch, off = 0–63, on = 64–127
†may be assigned as continuous

CHANNEL MODE MESSAGES

Message	Status	Channel	Data byte 1	Data byte 2
Bn.7x.yy	Mode Message if *x* = 9 = F	*n*	79 = Reset All Controllers	*yy* = 00
			7A = Local Control	*yy* = 00/7F = off/on
			7B = All Notes Off	*yy* = 00
			7C = Omni Off	*yy* = 00
			7D = Omni On	*yy* = 00
			7E = Mono On	*yy* = number of sequential channels†
			7F = Poly On	*yy* = 00

†equals number of independent voices at synthesizer

TABLE 3.2   MIDI channel messages.

SYSTEM EXCLUSIVE MESSAGES

Message	Status	Data bytes
F0.*ii.aa.bb....nn*.F7	F0 = Begin System Exclusive	*ii* = Manufacturer identification number*
		aa = first data byte
		bb = 2nd data byte
		nn = last data byte
	F7 = End System Exclusive	

*ID 7EH reserved for generic non-real-time data, 7FH for real-time data

SYSTEM COMMON MESSAGES

Message	Status	Data bytes
F1.*tt*	Quarter Frame	*tt* = MIDI Time Code data
F2.*pp*.*PP*	Song Position Pointer	*pp* = LSB location in beats
		PP = MSB location in beats
F3.*ss*	Song Select	*ss* = number of song
(F4, F5)	(Undefined)	
F6	Tune Request	
F7	End System Exclusive	

SYSTEM REAL-TIME MESSAGES

Message	Meaning
F8	Timing Clock
(F9)	(Undefined)
FA	Start
FB	Continue
FC	Stop
(FD)	(Undefined)
FE	Active Sensing
FF	System Reset

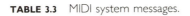

TABLE 3.3 MIDI system messages.

15 (0 to F in hex) is used, since computer number systems normally start with 0. Hence we must remember to add 1 to the channel number in message format to convert to common synthesizer format. For example, the status byte 90H corresponds to a Note On command (depress key) on channel 1. (In binary this command would be 10010000.)

Table 3.2 summarizes the channel messages, but a little discussion is necessary to understand it. To begin with, the defined Note Off (release key) message 8nH is rarely used; instead, 9nH with velocity 0 is. Some machines will respond to both options, but the 9nH message with velocity 0 is the message normally sent when a synthesizer key is released; only a few keyboards actually send release velocity. Following are a few examples:

81.40.40H	Note Off, channel 2, key number 40H (64 decimal), off velocity 40H (64) = half maximum value
9A.3F.7FH	Note On, channel 11, key number 3FH (63 decimal), on velocity 7FH (127 decimal) = maximum possible velocity
9A.3F.00H	Note Off, channel 11, key number 3FH. This message would turn off the previous note

The two pressure-based status bytes AnH and DnH in table 3.2 are based on the existence of force sensors (or some equivalent design) beneath the keys of the synthesizer. The synthesizer periodically scans these sensors and sends a message when there has been any change in the force applied after the keys have come to rest on the keybed. This *scanning rate* (*scan rate*) will vary from manufacturer to manufacturer but typically needs to be in the range of at least 100 to 200 times per second to produce audible smoothness in certain controlled parameters (Moog 1986). Some interfaces are much faster than this. For example, the Synthophone, a saxophone-based controller, scans its keys at rates of up to 4,000 times per second (admittedly while looking for more than just pressure data). Channel Pressure (DnH), also called Monophonic Pressure or Aftertouch, typically measures the total force exerted by the performer on all depressed keys and has one associated data byte. Polyphonic Pressure (AnH), also called Polyphonic Aftertouch, measures the force exerted on each individual key, and has two associated data bytes. Two examples follow:

A2.40.7FH	Polyphonic Pressure on channel 3, note number 40H (64 decimal), with full force 7FH (127 decimal)
D0.2BH	Channel Pressure on channel 1, applied pressure 2BH (43 decimal)

The Program Change message CnH allows a new program to be selected. The data byte can vary from 0 to 127, and the corresponding synthesizer patch numbers may either be identical or range from 1 to 128, or they may be in octal or other equivalents (see table 3.1 for a comparison of these different numbering conventions). This message is normally sent out when a program button is pushed on the front of the synthesizer, unless this option has been disabled in programming. For example:

C3.05H   Program Change 5 on channel 4. Interpreted as program 5 on a 0-starting decimal system, as program 6 on a 1-starting decimal system, and as program 16 on an octal system that starts with 11

The Pitch Bend message EnH has two data bytes to allow 14-bit resolution. Hence, one byte (the second of the two, labeled *MSB*, for most significant byte) provides the coarse resolution, and the other (the first, labeled *LSB*, for least significant byte) provides the fine control. In fact, many manufacturers use only one meaningful data byte here, the MSB, and this means that under certain relatively uncommon conditions the coarse steps of the "continuous" pitch bend can be heard. A few manufacturers use an LSB of limited resolution (e.g., 2-bit). In any case, this message is sent, at a rate determined by the manufacturer's scan rate for the physical device, whenever there is a change in the physical device (usually wheel or joystick) controlling pitch bend. The pitch bend controller can bend up or down and takes as its zero effect position the midpoint value 00.40H. For example:

E0.00.00H   Pitch Bend, maximum negative displacement, on channel 1

The Control Change status byte BnH is a general catchall message that is used to describe the state of change of all other possible ancillary controllers (performance devices) in the system besides the pitch bend device and the pressure sensors. The message has two associated data bytes. The first is a label telling which controller is being referred to and which can vary from 0 to 121 (0H to 79H). The second gives the current value of the controller. Messages are sent only when there is a change and only at a rate corresponding to the instrument's scan rate for the controllers in question. The resolution of most controller messages is 1 byte (7 bits, excluding the initial 0 of data bytes), or one part in 128. If additional resolution is required, Control Change messages can be combined to achieve 14-bit resolution, or one part in 16,384. This is done by using controllers 0 to 63 (decimal) in the following way. Controller numbers 0 to 31 send the most significant byte of the controller message, and controller numbers 32 to 63 send the corresponding least significant byte of the same controllers. For example, controller 33 will code the LSB of the Control Change for controller 1. Whether this fine control is necessary is a decision made by each manufacturer; so far, 14-bit controller resolution is very rare because of the expense of more accurate detection, lack of internal accuracy, perceptual limits of a changing value, and MIDI clogging (see "The Limitations of MIDI" below).

Controller numbers can be set to have any synthesis function built in by the manufacturer at the receiving module. Furthermore, some synthesizers can change the controller numbers assigned to each physical controller at the sending or receiving end of the MIDI path. This means that, in principle, any controller number or device can be set to do anything. However, to avoid causing needless confusion between manufacturers, there is a standard set of assignments that show what controller number corresponds to what control function. These are listed in table 3.4. The most widely implemented numbers are 1 for modulation, 4 for foot controller, 7 for volume, and 64 for sustain pedal (all numbers are in decimal, as is usually done in all documents except the MIDI specification itself).

Not all manufacturers have followed this table, although nearly all do now. Sometimes the names are changed, even though the function is the same: For example, controller 64 is called damper pedal on some Akai machines, hold 1 on some Roland machines, and sustain on some Korg devices. Note that in some cases this control function is not spelled out in very much detail; for example, the type of modulation effect produced from controller 1 data will depend on settings at the receiving sound engine.

Controller 7 (volume) is widely implemented and requires special comment because it is far from the only factor affecting overall synthesizer volume. The other factors include velocity and other MIDI volume programming, preamp volume on the sound module, other controllers, and external amplifier gain. Controller 7 and other MIDI messages affecting volume act only within the range of volume available from the preamp (controlled by the volume control on the front panel of the synthesizer or synthesis module) and the external amplifier (controlled by its gain settings and separate channel faders, as available). This is in fact not all: Nearly all synthesizers have a volume parameter that operates internally on the sound programs. Sometimes this turns out to be the same as controller 7 volume (and hence will be changed by this message), and sometimes it is independent (and will not be affected by this command). Some multitimbral synthesizers even have two volume parameters per part, one changed by controller 7 and one set independently.

Controllers can be continuous (like a modulation wheel or slider) or discrete (like a foot switch or button). A *continuous controller* actually

CONTROLLER NUMBER (2nd byte value)		CONTROL FUNCTION
Decimal	Hex	
0	00	Bank select MSB
1	01	Modulation wheel/lever
2	02	Breath controller
3	03	Undefined
4	04	Foot controller
5	05	Portamento time
6	06	Data entry MSB
7	07	Main volume
8	08	Balance
9	09	Undefined
10	0A	Pan
11	0B	Expression controller
12	0C	Effect control 1
13	0D	Effect control 2
14–15	0E–0F	Undefined
16–19	10–13	General-purpose controllers 1–4
20–31	14–1F	Undefined
32–63	20–3F	LSB for values 0–31
64	40	Damper pedal (sustain)
65	41	Portamento on/off
66	42	Sostenuto pedal
67	43	Soft pedal
68	44	Legato foot switch
69	45	Hold 2
70	46	Sound variation
71	47	Harmonic content
72	48	Release time
73	49	Attack time
74	4A	Brightness
75–79	4B–4F	Undefined
80–83	50–53	General-purpose controllers 5–8
84–90	54–5A	Undefined
91	5B	External effects depth (effects 1)
92	5C	Tremolo depth (effects 2)
93	5D	Chorus depth (effects 3)
94	5E	Celeste (detune) depth (effects 4)
95	5F	Phaser depth (effects 5)
96	60	Data increment
97	61	Data decrement
98	62	Nonregistered parameter number LSB
99	63	Nonregistered parameter number MSB
100	64	Registered parameter number LSB
101	65	Registered parameter number MSB
102–119	66–77	Undefined
120	78	All sound off
121–127	79–7F	Reserved for channel mode messages

TABLE 3.4 Common controller assignments.

sends a range of quantized, discrete values from 0 to 127 (or 0 to 16,383 in principle, as discussed above). A *discrete controller* sends only two values, an on value and an off value. Some performance interfaces allow discrete controllers (switches) to be set as either toggle or momentary. A *toggle switch* toggles between two values. That is, it sends its on value when pressed and nothing when released. It then sends its off value when next pressed and again nothing when released. At the next press it sends its on value, and so forth. In contrast, the *momentary switch* sends its on value when pressed and its off value when released. In terms of performance, the two types of switches require different techniques. The momentary switch is always primed to produce the same result. The toggle switch's current state must be remembered if it is to be played effectively. Following are some examples:

B2.01.40H	Controller 1 on channel 3 changes to the value 40H (64 decimal). Interpretation: The modulation wheel is moved to its half-way position.
B0.07.7FH	Controller 7 on channel 1 changes to value 7FH (127 decimal). Interpretation: Turn channel volume to maximum possible (within the range set by the amplifier).
B1.40.7FH/ B1.40.00H	Controller 64 (40H) on channel 2 changes to maximum and then minimum. Interpretation: sustain pedal on, then off.

Note that foot switches exist either as normally closed mechanisms (Roland, Yamaha) or as normally open (most other manufacturers), and so these are not readily interchangeable. Some machines (e.g., several by Kurzweil and Ensoniq) allow the user to program the system to work with a foot switch of either type.

Controller messages 98 to 101 correspond to nonregistered and registered parameter numbers. These messages allow the receiving synthesis device to be configured for control of specific synthesis parameters. Registered parameter numbers have been agreed to by the MMA and JMSC and currently consist of:

LSB	MSB	FUNCTION
00H	00H	Pitch bend sensitivity
01H	00H	Fine tuning
02H	00H	Coarse tuning
03H	00H	Change tuning program
04H	00H	Change tuning bank

These should work for all manufacturers. Nonregistered parameter numbers are assigned separate synthesis functions by each manufacturer. In either case this procedure usually works by sending the appropriate Control Change messages to select a given parameter and then using Data Entry, Data Decrement, or Data Increment messages to change the parameter's value.

Channel Mode Messages

Channel mode messages are in general simpler (see table 3.2). They use the same status byte as the Control Change message, BnH, but with first data byte values ranging from 122 to 127 (7AH to 7FH). These messages allow local control and omni to be turned off or on, mono or poly mode to be chosen, and All Notes Off and Reset All Controllers commands to be sent.

The Local Control command (7AH) refers to the connection between the synthesizer keyboard and its internal sound engine. If Local is on, the synthesizer plays normally from the keyboard; if Local is off, the keyboard is disconnected from its own sound engine and the sound engine can only be driven externally via MIDI.

The message 7BH is an All Notes Off command. It is designed to cure stuck-note syndrome. However, not all modules respond to it. Therefore, some devices such as master controllers do not use this command but instead have a panic button that individually turns off all notes and resets all controllers to their normal (zero effect) positions. Its sibling command is Reset All Controllers (79H), which orders the receiving module to return the values for pressure, pitch bend, and all controllers to their rest values. It is unfortunately rarely implemented.

Omni is a variable that can override the channel choice. If the receiving module is set to Omni On (7DH), messages will be responded to regardless of channel. If the receiving module is set to Omni Off (7CH), only the channel(s) chosen at the receiving end will produce any effect.

Mono (7EH) and Poly (7FH) correspond to first approximation to monophonic and polyphonic. The polyphonic case in particular corresponds to the traditional use of this term; the receiving module will play as many voices as it is physically capable of playing. Mono mode, however, means more than simply monophonic. On older synthesizers, monophonic had its traditional musical meaning of a single musical line or voice. If you played more than one note, then only one would sound—perhaps the lowest or highest or most recently struck. Some MIDI-based digital synthesizers still have this feature internally. In the MIDI specification, however, *mono mode* is a multitimbrally oriented mode of synthesizer operation corresponding to the message Bn.7EyyH, where nH is the basic MIDI channel (numbered 0 to F in hex) and yyH is the number of acceptable MIDI channels (in effect the maximum number of independent timbres). In this mode, a transmitter sends its voice (note) messages on channels $n + 1$ to $n + yy$ (numbering now in decimal 1–16), one per channel. For example, a four-voice instrument in mono mode with basic channel 2 (message B1.7E.04H) would transmit note messages on channels 2, 3, 4, and 5. A receiver in this mode receives monophonically on each of its acceptable MIDI channels. The value $yy = 0$ is a special case directing the receiver to assign its voices, one per channel, from the basic channel $n + 1$ to 16, until all available voices are used. Mono mode allows usefully variable multitimbral effects from a single performance interface.

These classifications allow the definition of the four standard MIDI modes: 1—Omni On/Poly; 2—Omni On/Mono; 3—Omni Off/Poly; 4—Omni Off/Mono. Mode 3 is most commonly used and is known as "poly" mode. Mode 4 allows the mono mode trick just mentioned. Mode 2 is rarely used. This classification of modes is really incomplete now, since most synthesizers are multitimbral and can therefore play a number of separately allocated MIDI channel messages at once, with more than one voice per channel—acting, in essence, like more than one synthesizer in a box. The multitimbral situation, though strictly speaking not a defined MIDI mode, is often called "multi" or "combination" mode.

System Exclusive Messages

The system exclusive (or sysex) message has a variable length and is used to send manufacturer- and model-specific synthesis data, certain kinds of standardized MIDI files, and certain control protocols. The system exclusive message itself (see table 3.3) begins with F0H, is followed by a manufacturer identification number, and then contains any number of data bytes operating under the manufacturer's specification. It ends with F7H.

When the sysex message used is manufacturer-specific, it acts primarily to allow bulk transfer of programs and sets of programs (bulk dump request) and real-time alteration of synthesis parameters (parameter change). In this case, its internal format is completely unspecified in the MIDI specification document, and manufacturers all use different systems, which are mutually unintelligible.

Many manufacturers use a one-directional data transmission protocol in system exclusive information, and others use a handshaking protocol. *Handshaking* means that the sending and receiving devices require two-way communication (MIDI IN/OUT from both devices). Typically, the sending device will not initiate transmission until it receives an appropriate message from the receiver. It then sends all or part of the requested information, and this is typically checked for self-consistency by the receiver, either at the end of the first packet of data or the end of the entire dump. If part of the dump had an error, the sending machine can ask the transmitter to send it again. The advantage of handshaking is that it helps to minimize errors in data transmission.

Such sysex data can be recorded on many sequencers, though not all can handle the handshaking type, and some may have a buffer that is too small to record the entire data dump and hence will not record data from certain machines that produce big sysex files. This problem doesn't occur if large sysex data messages are broken up into smaller chunks, called packets, with pauses in between. This system is used, for example, by both Roland and Yamaha.

It is worth noting that small packets of parameter-specific sysex data are sent out by some synthesizers (e.g., most professional Yamaha products, Roland JD-800) when parameters are being changed in edit mode. These can be recorded on many sequencers in lieu of using channel controller messages, or they can be used to affect an external synthesizer of identiical type. Other machines may transmit nothing upon editing or send information on controller 6 (and possibly also controller 38), as with some Kurzweil machines.

Many manufacturers have special numbers that act as a sort of channel within the system exclusive message. This is often the third byte in the sysex message. Yamaha has an internal device number used to tell one Yamaha machine from another; on most multitimbral Roland machines, the basic MIDI channel in effect when the bulk dump is sent is used as an internal device identification number inside the system exclusive bulk dump commands. If the basic channel of the machine is not set to the same value later when data are to be transferred back, the bulk dump message will be ignored. The solution for the synthesis worker is always to use the same basic channel or note the basic channel used at the time of storing.

Some generic formats have been developed within the system exclusive message by reserving the "manufacturer" ID numbers 7EH (for non-real-time data) and 7FH (for real-time data). The MIDI Sample Dump Standard and MIDI Time Code are two prominent examples. MIDI Sample Dump Standard allows samples of sounds to be transferred along MIDI and between different types of machines. The Sample Dump Standard contains a device ID byte, which must be matched between sending and receiving machines. As it turns out, the MIDI transmission rate is too slow to make this a very attractive option for samples that are not quite small. (A faster parallel data transmission protocol like SCSI—the Small Computer

Systems Interface—is preferable.) MIDI Time Code (MTC) uses a combination of system common and system exclusive information to transmit SMPTE time code over the MIDI cable (see "Synchronization and MIDI").

System Common Messages

System common messages have variable functions. F1H is a Quarter Frame message, used as part of MIDI Time Code. F2H, Song Position Pointer, allows the specification of location in a song stored on a sequencer or drum machine to a particular sixteenth note. F3H, Song Select, allows the selection of a numbered song in such a device. F6H, Tune Request, asks the synthesizer to tune itself. Only older analog machines will generally respond to this. F7H is used to end the system exclusive message described above.

System Real-Time Messages

System real-time messages are generally concerned with timing and have in mind commands sent to a sequencer or drum machine. F8H, Timing Clock, is a timing clock pulse sent twenty-four times per quarter note. FAH, Start, tells a sequencer to start a song (at the beginning). FBH, Continue, tells a sequencer to start from the point where it last stopped. FCH tells a sequencer to stop. FEH is the Active Sensing message, which assures the receiving module that the sender is still on-line. This is sent about three times per second. If a device receives this command, it will expect to continue doing so and will turn off any sounding notes if it does not. However, this feature tends to be optional. If the signal is never received, most receivers aren't bothered. FFH is a System Reset command, which will have variable effects depending on the receiving module. Most current modules do not respond to this command.

Running Status

Performers should be aware that all MIDI modules are required to respond to a convention known as *running status*. This means that a message received without an associated status byte is presumed to be operating under the status byte of the last status byte received. This was designed to save needless duplication in data transmission. For example, the series of numbers D0.00, 03, 07, 09, 0B, ... 7C, 7FH would correspond to moving from zero to full force with aftertouch on channel 1. Some intervening numbers are not present because of the limitations of the device's scan rate. The status byte D0H is presumed to apply to all subsequent data bytes.

STANDARD MIDI FILES

MIDI also defines a standard format for files containing MIDI information. Increasingly, all sequencers are moving to store sequence information in this format, allowing ready interconversion. The files can contain any type of MIDI data, including sysex data, and various kinds of *meta-events* such as tempo, time signature, key signature, markers, SMPTE offset, names of tracks and instruments and sequences, lyrics, copyright notices, and other types of information. There are three types of such MIDI files. Type 0 is a single multichannel track of data; type 1 contains multiple tracks in parallel; type 2 refers to a set of independent sequences or patterns.

MIDI IMPLEMENTATION CHARTS

Each piece of MIDI equipment should have in the back of its manual a *MIDI implementation chart*—a chart specifying the equipment's characteristics with respect to receipt and transmission of MIDI messages. The chart has a standard form prescribed by the MMA and the JMSC. When in doubt about the basic features of a synthesizer or other MIDI device, consult this chart. The IMA can provide them, and general compilations are available (De Furia 1986). A sample chart, for the Korg Wavestation, is included as figure 3.2. The chart indicates the implementation of a certain feature by a symbol in the legend at the bottom, usually "O." "X" is used to indicate that the feature is absent. Although much of the chart is self-explanatory, some comments are needed.

Under Mode, "default" refers to the settings that apply when the device is first powered up, "messages" lists the transmitted and recognized MIDI modes, and "altered" refers to the MIDI mode used by the machine when it does not implement a certain MIDI mode and must substitute one for another (here this is not relevant, as the Wavestation ignores all sent MIDI mode messages). "True voice"—under Note Number—gives the range of received note numbers that lie within the range of true notes produced by the instrument. Under "velocity" we can read that the Wavestation does not respond to the $8n$ type Note Off commands but uses the $9n$ velocity = 0 command. Note that the vector synthesis joystick on this machine is shown to send out information with controllers 16 and 17, though different numbers can be assigned. "True #," under Program Change, gives the range of program change numbers that correspond to the actual number of patches selected (here the 0 to 127 range is used unambiguously). The Remarks

Function ***		Transmitted	Recognized	Remarks
Basic	Default	1 - 16	1 - 16	Memorized
Channel	Changed			
Mode	Default	3	1, 3, 4	
	Messages	✕	✕	Mode Messages
	Altered	**********	✕	Ignored
Note		0 - 127	0 - 127	
Number :	True voice	**********	0 - 127	
Velocity	Note ON	O (9N, v=1~127)	O (9N, v=1~127)	
	Note OFF	✕ (9N, v=0)	✕	
After	Key's	✕	O	
Touch	Ch's	O	O	
Pitch Bend		O	O	
	0 Bank (msb)	O	✕	
	01 Mod Wheel	O	O	
	04 Foot Cntrl	O	O	
	06 Data	O	O	
Control	16 Joy-X	O	O	
	17 Joy-Y	O	O	
Change	32 Bank (lsb)	O	O	
	38 Data (lsb)	O	O	
	64 Damper	O	O	
	100 RPN (lsb)	O	O	
	101 RPN (msb)	O	O	
	1-95 Controls	. ✕	O	Assignable
Prog		0 - 127	0 - 127	
Change : True #		**********		
System Exclusive		O	O	
	: Song Pos	✕	✕	
Common :	Song Sel	✕	✕	
	: Tune	✕	✕	
System :	Clock	✕	O	
Real Time :	Commands	✕	✕	
Aux :	Local ON/OFF	✕	✕	
	: All Notes OFF	✕	O	Note 1, 2
Mes- :	Active Sense	O	O	
sages :	Reset	✕	✕	
Notes			1. Ignored in OMNI mode.	
			2. Also Reset All Controllers message.	

Mode 1 : OMNI ON, POLY   Mode 2 : OMNI ON, MONO   O : Yes
Mode 3 : OMNI OFF, POLY   Mode 4 : OMNI OFF, MONO   ✕ : No

FIGURE 3.2 A MIDI implementation chart.

column tells us All Notes Off is recognized, but not in Omni mode, and that the device does respond to Reset All Controllers (but presumably doesn't send it). Note that the chart refers only to what is sent out or received over MIDI. For example, this machine neither sends nor responds to a Local command. However, it might still have an internal Local Control-type function that disconnects the keyboard from the sound engine—and this synthesizer does, in fact.

MIDI CONNECTIONS AND CONFIGURATIONS

MIDI data travel through MIDI cables, which have five-pronged *din* plugs at each end (din stands for Deutsche Industrie Norm, or German Industrial Standard). The recommended maximum cable length is 50 feet; greater lengths may produce sufficient signal degradation to cause data loss or misreading. (In practice, this will vary with the devices used, and usually somewhat longer lengths will work without problem.)

Three types of ports are found on MIDI devices: IN, OUT, and THRU. An IN port receives MIDI messages. An OUT port sends out MIDI messages that are produced or processed in the device. A MIDI THRU port puts out what comes in the MIDI IN.

Some devices, primarily master keyboards, sequencers, and computers running music programs, provide a soft THRU or ECHO BACK option that puts out from MIDI OUT what comes in MIDI IN. This is a useful feature when the performer wishes to have two devices such as a keyboard and a computer both play an entire synthesis system while the keyboard is also feeding the computer. Without this feature the keyboard and computer cannot both control the system at the same time. The reason for this is that two MIDI message streams cannot be simultaneously combined by doing anything as simple as routing them into a Y-cord. Special processing is required to synchronize the incoming message streams and avoid possible message ambiguities due to such things as running status.

To combine MIDI message streams in general a special process called *MIDI merge* is available. A merge combines two MIDI signals, allowing both to control whatever follows in the signal path. The above soft THRU option is one kind of merge. Merge boxes can be purchased separately, and many MIDI patch bays now have this feature built in. Since the merge process requires some computer processing, it can cause small delays in MIDI propagation.

It should be kept in mind that MIDI merge and soft THRU functions can enable MIDI feedback loops to occur if connections are set improperly, resulting in clogged data transfer and MIDI buffer full messages from the system components. (See "The Limitations of MIDI.")

When one MIDI device controls another MIDI device by sending messages, the first device is called the *master* and the second the *slave*. (This terminology actually predates MIDI and is used wherever one device controls the operation of another, as in the cases of a master oscillator to which others are synced or a master clock that determines the timing of other devices.) In terms of MIDI connections, the relationship in its basic form is master OUT to slave IN. But there can be more than one slave. If this is the case, all the slaves can be driven from the master by repeated IN/THRU connections between the MIDI slaves, producing a so-called *chain configuration* or *chain network*. In this case, all MIDI signals are going through one signal path, or *bus*. Another option is to split the master OUT into a number of parallel MIDI OUTs by using a MIDI THRU box or patch bay. This cabling arrangement is usually called a *star configuration* or *star network*. Still another option, sometimes essential for very complex music, is the use of separate MIDI buses (each containing distinct information) coming from the master device, since this minimizes the risks of delays and data clogging and also allows the use of more than sixteen MIDI channels (since each bus has sixteen separate channels). A thorough discussion of possible performance configurations involving MIDI will be deferred until chapter 7.

NAMING MIDI NOTES

All keyboards have a standard configuration for the location of MIDI note numbers. Note number 60, for example, is in middle C position on an 88-note keyboard; the lowest A is 21, and the highest C is 108. On a 61-note keyboard the lowest note is MIDI note number 36 and the highest 96. But note that this standard assignment can be changed on master keyboards and some synthesizers.

Even in standard configuration, the frequencies produced by depressing these keys depend entirely on the programming of the synthesizer engine connected to the keyboard. Often we will want to refer to these note numbers or their corresponding keys by their customary pitch labels. Here there is an unfortunate problem. The literature of music has a well-observed standard that says that the sounding pitch middle C, and often by implication its corresponding keyboard position, are labeled C4. The note above it is C♯4, the one below it B3, and so on. However, Yamaha, an early leader in MIDI synthesis, chose to define the middle C keyboard position (note number 60) as C3, and this convention has been widely followed in the synthesis field. (But not by a few manufacturers, notably Kurzweil and Roland, who call this position C4.) This action was presumably done either in ignorance of musical standards or in a conscious attempt to change standard practice so that the nomenclature for a 61-note keyboard could begin in a "natural" way with C1. An interesting coincidence is that MIDI note number 60 translates to 3C in hex.

Accordingly, in this book we have to make a choice for one system or the other while remaining aware of the problem. We will use C3 for middle C position (note number 60), in line with the most common usage in the synthesizer industry. A 61-note keyboard then extends from C1 (36) to C6 (96), a 76-note keyboard from E0 (28) to G6 (103), and an 88-note keyboard from A−1 (21) to C7 (108). The full range of MIDI notes is C−2 (00) to G8 (127).

MIDI DIAGNOSIS

Performers will not usually need to use detailed MIDI codes. However, at certain times this knowledge is essential. In MIDI programming, or in using MIDI transformation hardware and software, hexadecimal coding often appears. Another situation is when there is a need for a system diagnostic tool. Performers of even mildly complex synthesis setups will be well aware that things sometimes do go wrong. Some bits of the system appear, inexplicably, not to be talking or listening to other bits, and the source of the problem is difficult to locate. In this case the recommended procedure is to use a program that displays sent MIDI information, like the Kurzweil Corporation's public domain program MIDIScope for the Macintosh, to find out what the sender is in fact sending and the receiver is in fact receiving. Normally, this readily solves all such system connection difficulties. Other pieces of software and increasing numbers of hardware devices include this sort of MIDI message display. Often the status bytes may be translated into mnemonics like NON for Note On, which simplifies the diagnosis procedure considerably.

SYNCHRONIZATION AND MIDI

Synchronization means the time coordination of two or more devices. There are many systems that exist quite apart from MIDI, with drum sync, FSK (frequency shift keying) and SMPTE being the best-known among them. MIDI offers two options: the use of MIDI clocks and

MIDI Time Code. The MIDI options can be converted to and from the other codings (with suitable devices) and also used to drive a sequencer to produce regular audio sounds (usually clicks) that set down a specific tempo, forming a *click track*. Some tape recorders can respond directly to MIDI, but as of this writing this is uncommon. MIDI itself cannot be recorded accurately onto tape, as its bandwidth is too high (31.25 kHz is considerably higher than the audio bandwidth of ca. 20 kHz).

All such synchronization codes fall into two types: relative time and absolute time. *Relative sync codes* (also called click sync codes) give regular pulses but do not show precise time location — they produce a relative time base; *absolute sync codes* show exact temporal locations, giving an absolute time base. FSK, drum sync, and MIDI clocks are relative-time type syncs, and SMPTE and MIDI Time Code (MTC) are absolute time types. The absolute types have undeniable advantages.

Drum sync is a series of short electronic pulses, used to synchronize drum machines. *FSK* is a regularly occurring signal that consists of the alternation of two audio tones, normally an octave or more apart. Early forms of FSK could not synchronize unless the sequenced track was played from the beginning each time, since they indicate only pulse and not absolute location. Later versions, so-called *smart FSK*, do contain information about song location. FSK is an inexpensive and reliable technique, but it tends to be different from device to device, with different clock rates and audio frequencies all being common. This means it is not readily transferrable when devices become obsolete or are used in different environments.

SMPTE is a synchronization format adopted by the U.S. Society of Motion Picture and Television Engineers (and the European Broadcasting Union — EBU). It allows the synchronous playback of tape machines, computers, videos, cameras, and other units. It has become the preferred method of synchronization where audio and MIDI devices must be synced together.

SMPTE consists of a stream of 80-bit words, each giving a precise time label to its physical location. Time is recorded in hours, minutes, seconds, and frames. Resolution is determined by frame rate, which can be 24, 25, 29.97, or 30 frames per second (fps). It tends to be half the local alternating current (AC) frequency throughout the world: 25 is used for video in Europe and Australia, whereas 30 or 29.97 is found in the United States (30 is used in recording studios and for black-and-white video; 29.97 is the NTSC — National Television Standards Comittee — color video rate). The 24 fps rate is standard for film. In audio production, SMPTE is used in the following way. A SMPTE track is recorded onto one track of a multitrack tape or video; this is called "striping" the tape. This track is then used to drive sequencers and other devices when the tape recorder or video is played back. Its advantages are that it can coordinate overdubbing and that it is fully compatible with video.

The MIDI clock option uses the MIDI Timing Clock command F8H, which is sent twenty-four times per quarter note. This message is used to synchronize the tempi (not events per se) of two sequencers or a sequencer and a drum machine (playing its internal patterns). Its resolution is normally quite adequate for its chosen purpose of tempo locking and interpolation. It naturally coordinates with the MIDI Song Position Pointer message F2H, which gives the location of the sequencer starting point to within an absolute sixteenth note from the start of a song (piece of music). These two messages are sometimes collectively called *MIDI sync.*

MIDI Time Code is typically used in conjunction with SMPTE devices and has two advantages in this context. It is an absolute system of time location (not dependent on sequencer tempo), and it allows a much greater resolution of entry point than that enabled by the Song Position Pointer message.

When either FSK or SMPTE is to be used to coordinate MIDI systems, there must be conversion between the different sync formats. These are handled by special devices called SMPTE-to-MIDI or FSK-to-MIDI converters—generically, *time code converters.* They allow MIDI systems to be synced to tape. Performance sync boxes also exist that allow the performer's playing of recurring sounds to produce MIDI or other types of time code. These are described further in chapter 7.

Two other developments deserve mention here. MIDI Show Control (MSC) is designed to coordinate lighting (and other) cues or sequences in theatrical productions. MIDI Machine Control (MMC) enables the design of MIDI devices that can remotely control the transports of tape decks.

GENERAL MIDI

MIDI provides a highly useful standard of communication between electronic devices, but in some situations it may offer too much flexibility. Data designed for use with one MIDI setup will not function properly with a different setup without substantial reprogramming—sounds must be matched with program numbers and with MIDI channels, pitch bend range sensitivities set, controller numbers assigned, note ranges matched, transpositions reset, velocity responses matched, and so forth. Such conversions must be commonly done when new synthesizers are substituted for old in a setup, and when commercial MIDI files of repertoire are purchased, whether on disk, CD-ROM, CD + MIDI, or any other format. To facilitate interconversion between

MIDI systems, the idea of *General MIDI* has been introduced. The General MIDI protocol establishes a set of conventions for the parameters that commonly vary between different MIDI setups. Synthesizers adhering to the standard are generally identified as General MIDI mode synths and should be able to play GM standard MIDI files with minimal (perhaps no) fine tuning of parameters and sounds, regardless of the synthesis procedures they employ. Synthesizers that allow options beyond General MIDI mode can have this mode turned on or off, either internally or by special Universal Non-Real Time Sysex messages.

Specifically, General MIDI provides a standard set of timbre types in a bank of 128 programs. These timbres are largely imitative in character, and divide into sixteen families as shown in the General MIDI Instrument Map found in table 3.5. General MIDI is a multitimbral specification, and (un-tuned) percussion must be located on MIDI channel 10. Table 3.6 shows the GM Percussion Key Map that identifies standardized locations of such percussion sounds. While hardly comprehensive, the timbral pallete of these two tables will service many common uses of MIDI systems. Such standardization may be of particular use to less experienced MIDI users (e.g., those using "consumer" type modules). At the same time it should not restrict the potential of professionals.

In addition, General MIDI specifies the minimum performance of a participating sound module as given in table 3.7. The reasonableness of these choices would seem to ensure that General MIDI finds a useful niche in certain kinds of electronic music production.

MIDI DEVICES

In chapter 1 the use of MIDI was described for synthesizers, master controllers, sound engines, samplers, and computers. But its rapid growth since inception has meant that a remarkable array of additional devices and gadgets is now controllable by MIDI. Many of these are traditional devices adapted for MIDI control. Others are new in conception. A list of such hardware devices might run as follows:

MIDI sequencer

MIDI display device

MIDI switcher and THRU box

MIDI patch bay

MIDI merger

MIDI processor

Prog#	Instrument	Prog#	Instrument
1–8	PIANO	33–40	BASS
1	Acoustic Grand Piano	33	Acoustic Bass
2	Bright Acoustic Piano	34	Electric Bass (finger)
3	Electric Grand Piano	35	Electric Bass (pick)
4	Honky-tonk Piano	36	Fretless Bass
5	Electric Piano 1	37	Slap Bass 1
6	Electric Piano 2	38	Slap Bass 2
7	Harpsichord	39	Synth Bass 1
8	Clav	40	Synth Bass 2
9–16	CHROM PERCUSSION	41–48	STRINGS
9	Celesta	41	Violin
10	Glockenspiel	42	Viola
11	Music Box	43	Cello
12	Vibraphone	44	Contrabass
13	Marimba	45	Tremolo Strings
14	Xylophone	46	Pizzicato Strings
15	Tubular Bells	47	Orchestral Strings
16	Dulcimer	48	Timpani
17–24	ORGAN	49–56	ENSEMBLE
17	Drawbar Organ	49	String Ensemble 1
18	Percussive Organ	50	String Ensemble 2
19	Rock Organ	51	SynthStrings 1
20	Church Organ	52	SynthStrings 2
21	Reed Organ	53	Choir Aahs
22	Accordian	54	Voice Oohs
23	Harmonica	55	Synth Voice
24	Tango Accordian	56	Orchestra Hit
25–32	GUITAR	57–64	BRASS
25	Acoustic Guitar (nylon)	57	Trumpet
26	Acoustic Guitar (steel)	58	Trombone
27	Electric Guitar (jazz)	59	Tuba
28	Electric Guitar (clean)	60	Muted Trumpet
29	Electric Guitar (muted)	61	French Horn
30	Overdriven Guitar	62	Brass Section
31	Distortion Guitar	63	SynthBrass 1
32	Guitar Harmonics	64	SynthBrass 2

TABLE 3.5 General MIDI instrument map, showing sixteen instrumental families.

Prog#	Instrument	Prog#	Instrument
65–72	REED	97–104	SYNTH EFFECTS
65	Soprano Sax	97	FX 1 (rain)
66	Alto Sax	98	FX 2 (soundtrack)
67	Tenor Sax	99	FX 3 (crystal)
68	Baritone Sax	100	FX 4 (atmosphere)
69	Oboe	101	FX 5 (brightness)
70	English Horn	102	FX 6 (goblins)
71	Bassoon	103	FX 7 (echoes)
72	Clarinet	104	FX 8 (sci-fi)
73–80	PIPE	105–112	ETHNIC
73	Piccolo	105	Sitar
74	Flute	106	Banjo
75	Recorder	107	Shamisen
76	Pan Flute	108	Koto
77	Blown Bottle	109	Kalimba
78	Shakuhachi	110	Bagpipe
79	Whistle	111	Fiddle
80	Ocarina	112	Shanai
81–88	SYNTH LEAD	113–120	PERCUSSIVE
81	Lead 1 (square)	113	Tinkle Bell
82	Lead 2 (sawtooth)	114	Agogo
83	Lead 3 (calliope)	115	Steel Drums
84	Lead 4 (chiff)	116	Woodblock
85	Lead 5 (charang)	117	Taiko Drum
86	Lead 6 (voice)	118	Melodic Tom
87	Lead 7 (fifths)	119	Synth Drum
38	Lead 8 (bass + lead)	120	Reverse Cymbal
89–96	SYNTH PAD	121–128	SOUND EFFECTS
89	Pad 1 (new age)	121	Guitar Fret Noise
90	Pad 1 (warm)	122	Breath Noise
91	Pad 3 (polysynth)	123	Seashore
92	Pad 4 (choir)	124	Bird Tweet
93	Pad 5 (bowed)	125	Telephone Ring
94	Pad 6 (metallic)	126	Helicopter
95	Pad 7 (halo)	127	Applause
96	Pad 8 (sweep)	128	Gunshot

TABLE 3.5   Continued.

MIDI delay unit

MIDI panning device or spatial sound processor

MIDI filter

MIDI mapper (transformation box)

MIDI accelerator

MIDI arpeggiator

MIDI storage device

SPMTE-to-MIDI converter

Pitch-to-MIDI converter

MIDI-controlled signal processor and effects unit

MIDI-controlled mixer or audio patch bay

MIDI-controlled audio (e.g., tape) recorder

Wireless MIDI transmitter/receiver

The function of a number of these does not require special definition, and many of them will be discussed in musical context in later chapters. Those whose function seems to require elaboration are described below.

The MIDI switcher or THRU box or junction box takes a few MIDI IN signals and puts them THRU to a number of exit ports. The MIDI patch bay is a more extensive and programmable device and can route six to eight or more inputs to eight or more outputs, with each configuration of patching recallable via the device's own stored programs. Such devices normally have a merge function and often other data manipulation features as well. The MIDI merger merges two INs to one OUT. The MIDI filter blocks certain kinds of MIDI information. The MIDI mapper allows drastic transformation and processing of incoming MIDI data. The MIDI accelerator is a device used to process and selectively filter MIDI data, arranging it more efficiently to try to avoid MIDI clogging at high data transmission rates.

The MIDI arpeggiator produces arpeggiation-type patterns from held notes. In its basic form an arpeggiator steps one at a time, in programmable order, through a group of notes programmed or played into it, most commonly producing a steady stream of notes of uniform duration.

The pitch-to-MIDI converter analyzes acoustic signals and computes a fundamental pitch and possibly other spectral characteristics in real time. It then converts this information into equivalent MIDI information, primarily using Note On, Note Off, and Pitch Bend commands. See chapter 9 for a more detailed account of pitch-to-MIDI converters. MIDI control of signal processing and effects functions and mixing is now increasingly commonplace; it means that control of all these functions can be recorded on a sequencer for playback or performed live via MIDI. The MIDI audio

Midi Key	Drum Sound	Midi Key	Drum Sound	Midi Key	Drum Sound
35	Acoustic Bass Drum	50	High Tom	66	Low Timbale
36	Bass Drum 1	51	Ride Cymbal 1	67	High Agogo
37	Side Stick	52	Chinese Cymbal	68	Low Agogo
38	Acoustic Snare	53	Ride Bell	69	Cabasa
39	Hand Clap	54	Tambourine	70	Maracas
40	Electric Snare	55	Splash Cymbal	71	Short Whistle
41	Low Floor Tom	56	Cowbell	72	Long Whistle
42	Closed Hi Hat	57	Crash Cymbal 2	73	Short Guiro
43	High Floor Tom	58	Vibraslap	74	Long Guiro
44	Pedal Hi Hat	59	Ride Cymbal 2	75	Claves
45	Low Tom	60	Hi Bongo	76	Hi Wood Block
46	Open Hi Hat	61	Low Bongo	77	Low Wood Block
47	Low-Mid Tom	62	Mute Hi Conga	78	Mute Cuica
48	Hi-Mid Tom	63	Open Hi Conga	79	Open Cuica
49	Crash Cymbal 1	64	Low Conga	80	Mute Triangle
		65	High Timbale	81	Open Triangle

TABLE 3.6   General MIDI percussion key map (MIDI channel 10).

patch bay is a MIDI-controllable audio patch bay that can receive program changes.

THE MIDI STUDIO

Synthesizer performers often have occasion to work in traditional audio recording studios. Increasingly, such facilities have substantial MIDI facilities. But a separate design, the MIDI studio, has become common where MIDI-based sound engines make up the dominant part of the users' desired sound world. Potentially less expensive because of the reduced need for sound isolation and a variety of expensive microphones and extensive multitrack recording machines, this can range from the small personal studio to a large professional suite. In the low end of the range this facility will have:

a sequencer (dedicated hardware unit, workstation component, or computer plus MIDI interface plus software)

multitimbral sound modules (synthesizers, samplers, drum machine, etc.)

MIDI switcher or THRU box

Voices:			Controllers:	Description
			Controller #	

A minimum of either 24 fully dynamically allocated voices available simultaneously for both melodic and percussive sounds or 16 dynamically allocated voices for melody plus eight for percussion.

Controller #	Description
1	Modulation
7	Main Volume
10	Pan
11	Expression
64	Sustain
121	Reset All Controllers
123	All Notes Off

Channels:

General MIDI mode supports all sixteen MIDI channels. Each channel can play a variable number of voices (polyphony). Each channel can play a different instrument (timbre). Key-based Percussion is always on channel 10.

Registered Parameter #	Description
0	Pitch Bend Sensitivity
1	Fine Tuning
2	Coarse Tuning

Instruments:

A minimum of sixteen different timbres playing various instrument sounds. A minimum of 128 presets for Instruments (MIDI program numbers).

Additional Channel Messages:

Channel Pressure (Aftertouch)
Pitch Bend

Note On/Note Off:

Octave Registration: Middle C = MIDI Key 60. All Voices including percussion respond to velocity.

Power-Up Defaults:

Pitch Bend Amount = 0
Pitch Bend Sensitivity = ±2 semitones
Volume = 90
All Other Controllers = reset

TABLE 3.7 Minimal features required of a sound module under General MIDI.

a performance interface (usually a keyboard controller)

a multichannel mixer with effects bus and equalization

a stereo amplifier and speakers

a stereo or 4-track audio recorder (cassette, reel-to-reel, DAT, or digital)

an audio effects unit

A more professional setup will also include:

a MIDI patch bay/processor (instead of MIDI switcher)

a computer and MIDI interface

compositional assistance, sound analysis, editor/librarian and score production software

a printer (dot matrix or laser)

a SMPTE-to-MIDI conversion box (if not present in MIDI interface)

a pitch-to-MIDI conversion device

video unit and associated SMPTE interface

a multitrack audio recorder

DAT machine

assorted additional audio effects and processing units

The connections between MIDI and audio devices can become fairly complex in a large professional system. An example of a MIDI studio of moderate complexity is given in chapter 7, under "Standard Performance Configurations."

THE LIMITATIONS OF MIDI

Performance on a synthesizer is in no way intrinsically linked to MIDI. When a self-contained synthesizer is played, MIDI is not used. Other control protocols are also available, like control voltages. Yet since MIDI has become so dominant in synthesizer performance, it is necessary to understand some of its performance limitations and how they can be overcome to varying degrees.

The main problems or limitations associated with the musical use of MIDI are as follows:

timing delays

clogging, overflow, and data loss

limited bandwidth

feedback

conceptual orientation to the keyboard

scanning resolution

Delays occur for a number of reasons in synthesizers. Some of these are due to the design of MIDI itself, and some are due to speed limitations in the processing units of MIDI devices. For example, it takes a certain amount of time for the information from the performer's hands to be processed by the synthesizer to produce sound or to be formatted as MIDI messages. It then takes more time for the MIDI messages to actually be sent since MIDI has a fixed transmission speed and corresponding maximum bandwidth. There are also delays due to the processing of messages at the receiving end, where MIDI is used to control sound. If merge functions are used, there will be additional delay. The total delay from all these sources often approaches 10 milliseconds and can rise to or exceed 20 to 30 milliseconds in dense MIDI streams.

The amount of delay depends strongly on the total amount of data traveling through the data bus. Hence, the risk of audible delays is increased if a number of different synthesizers are used in a chain or parallel output star configuration, since in both cases each synthesizer must process all sent MIDI data to find the data to which it must respond. Only separate buses, as described earlier, will reduce this risk. A frequent point of confusion in this area is the idea that the MIDI IN/MIDI THRU connection itself produces audible delays. This is false. This data path runs only through an opto-isolator, and any delays produced are of the order of microseconds, which are inaudible. It is for this reason that there is normally no perceptible difference between the chain and star configurations with regard to MIDI transmission speed, despite folklore to the contrary. (The only way a star configuration can in principle reduce MIDI data transmission problems in comparison to the chain configuration is by the insertion of fast MIDI data filters in each cabling link of the star configuration, that only pass data needed for each synthesis unit, but this is very rarely done.) However, multiple THRUs do increase the possibility of signal degradation, possibly causing more "MIDI data error" messages or stuck notes, which might favor the star configuration when many modules are involved.

The dominant source of delay is therefore usually not MIDI but relates to the speed of the sending and receiving devices' processors. Since these delays will show up most at high data densities, it is unusual for this to occur with a solo performer, but it can happen if the performer is merging with a very busy sequencer into the same sound module or if the performer is sending lots of control change and pitch bend information at the same time. It is usually not noticeable in solo performance unless at least pitch bend and two controllers' worth of information are being sent (e.g., channel pressure and foot controller), although polyphonic pressure can cause problems on its own.

Research in music perception has shown that listeners can, under optimal conditions, hear asynchrony on the order of 1 to 2 msec in sounds (Small and Campbell 1962). Optimal conditions, however, mean that the sound sources are clicks and that the clicks are presented in isolation from other sounds. In something like a more normal musical situation, "spreads" of notes on the order of 20 to 30 msec are dependably heard as synchronous (Rasch 1979; Pressing 1987), and larger spreads may be as well, depending on musical context. Hence, the musical impact of delays will depend partly on the attack envelopes of the sounds in question. If rise times are not very quick, the effect will probably never surface at all. On the other hand, if attack times are rapid (such as for percussive sounds), delays on the order of 10 msec or less (which as we have seen can readily occur) may well be noticeable and are quite likely to affect the rhythmic feel of the music, often unfavorably. If such delays are consistent, they may be compensated for by the performer or by track shifting on a sequencer. If the delays are variable, there is no apparent compensation procedure.

In general there are at least two ways a synthesizer can fail to keep up with the data being sent it. Either its processing speed can be too slow or the buffer it uses to store information for processing can be too small. If the limitation is that the processing speed is too slow, the response to information will be delayed: Notes and controller information will be noticeably delayed and incorrectly synchronized. However, the information will eventually appear. If the limitation is in buffer size, MIDI logjams and clogging will occur, and some of the information will be lost: Notes will not sound, pitch bends will not bend to the right point, and so forth. A few synthesizers have the intelligence to send out data on MIDI that they cannot process themselves.

How can such effects be minimized? If the problem is too many notes going into the same module from different sources, the obvious solution is to try to split the signal by using different synthesizers and different data buses. If no extra modules are available, the preferred method is *data thinning* to eliminate redundant information. While this is often not musically sensible with note messages, it is the general method of choice for the controller-based clogging problem.

There are two approaches to thinning. First of all, controller information that is needed can be thinned out by a computer or MIDI processing box. If, for example, the modulation wheel information is controlling the depth of vibrato, it probably doesn't need the full resolution over its range of 0 to 127. Every other, or two out of three, Control Change Messages could be filtered out. This will reduce the density of the data stream without affecting the aural results, provided one is careful to choose controllers for thinning that correspond to synthesis effects with suitably limited audible resolution. This is not recommended for 7-bit Pitch Bend messages, for example. MIDI accelerators perform this thinning trick, along with more efficiently arranging the order of messages.

The second approach is to block out information that is not being used at all. This most commonly applies to channel or polyphonic pressure, since normal keyboard playing will trigger it even if it will have no effect at the receiving end. Either play lightly, without aftertouch, filter it out before it reaches the sound module, or, if your keyboard permits it, turn it off at the performance interface itself. If you need lots of real-time information, there may be no completely satisfactory solution.

The musical significance of delays, clogging, and data loss will vary. Moore (1987), in an important article, has convincingly discussed these problems, pointing out that what he calls a "degradation in control intimacy" will inevitably occur under certain conditions. Eventually a super-MIDI, running, say, ten or more times as fast, may evolve, though the likelihood of this seems small as of this writing. An alternative is some sort of universal digital communication protocol that can encompass MIDI, SMPTE, digital audio, SCSI, and other formats at higher transmission speeds. One example of this, a LAN (local area network) protocol called Media-Link, has already appeared.

Feedback is a special problem that occurs with MIDI Merge or SOFT THRU data streams that are routed back to themselves. A typical synthesizer feedback loop is created as follows: OUT and THRU are merged and routed back to MIDI IN. Consider what happens when a given note on a synthesizer is played: The Note On message passes out via MIDI OUT, merging with the THRU from the same unit, to enter the IN port. This triggers the note again, and the Note On message is passed out from the THRU port again, after a slight delay, which then triggers the same note again, is passed out the MIDI THRU port, and so on. This can be avoided by carefully checking connections to avoid loops. The symptom of this problem is usually the rapid clogging up and overflowing of data buffers. Sometimes synthesizers with MIDI feedback will freeze up and refuse to respond to normal commands, and resetting them may be necessary.

MIDI has a keyboard orientation, and this provides some limitations in its capacities as a control language. However, most of these limitations can be avoided by knowledgeable synthesis programming, as discussed later in this book. Some, however, can be circumvented only partially, including certain issues with note-by-note retuning, aspects of the expressive control of sustaining sounds, and certain properties of the interaction of notes (such as resonances between notes sounding simultaneously). These issues will be discussed further in chapter 9.

The final limitation is based on the technology used to scan keyboards and controllers to determine the information to be used for MIDI messages. The resolution of this process depends completely on the performing instrument's design; MIDI provides no limit here except its already mentioned data transmission rate.

How do controllers send their information? The process is simple. A certain number of times per second, a microprocessor device scans (updates) the state of the performance interface and compares it to the previous state. If a change has occurred, the new value is sent out. On commercial synthesizers and master controllers, this may happen 100 to 300 times per second or considerably faster. These sorts of minimum rates are required to avoid audible graininess in certain musical variables. How accurately is the state value measured? That depends on the design of the performance device, but normally it is geared to the resolution that can be sent over MIDI, which corresponds to either one or two 7-bit bytes. Controllers of 7-bit resolution field an accuracy of one part in 2^7, or one in 128. Controllers of 14-bit resolution and pitch bend provide a potential accuracy to one part in 2^{14}, or one in 16,384.

These two figures—the scan rate and the resolution of the sent data—determine whether the interface reports faithfully what we are playing. The limitations are those of any digital representation of analog data and are exactly analogous to the discussion of digital sampling of audio waveforms given in chapter 2. Some degree of approximation is always involved, and whether the approximation is satisfactory depends to a considerable extent on what musical function the information is controlling and on the sensitivity of the ear to those changes.

The ear is decidedly variable in its ability to perceive control resolution. Perceptual resolution on the order of 14 bits is enough for all synthesis variables. However, most machines send and respond to only 7 bits, for reasons of cost and economy of data transmission (avoiding clogging up the MIDI link), even with pitch bend, where the ear is extremely sensitive. Roughly speaking, we may classify the needed resolution as low, medium, or high. Some concrete examples are given in table 3.8.

With medium- to high-resolution musical functions, some situations may occur where an unwanted graininess of control appears in the sound with 7-bit resolution. The only solutions for the performer are to play the controller more rapidly or decrease the sensitivity of the receiving sound engine to the controlled variable.

MUSICAL FUNCTION	NECESSARY CONTROL RESOLUTION
Pitch bending	high
Frequency ratios	high
Volume change	medium to high
Modulation amount	medium
Panning	low
Filter cutoff frequency	medium to high
Pulse width	medium

TABLE 3.8 Control resolution necessary for common music synthesis variables.

REFERENCES

De Furia, Steve. *The MIDI Implementation Book.* New York: Third Earth Publishing, 1986.

International MIDI Association. *MIDI 1.0 Specification.* Los Angeles: International MIDI Association, 1983.

Loy, D. G. "Musicians Make a Standard: The MIDI Phenomenon." *Computer Music Journal* 9,4 (Winter 1985): 8–26.

Moog, R. "MIDI: Musical Instrument Digital Interface." *Journal of the Audio Engineering Society* 34,5 (May 1986): 394–404.

Moore, R. "The Dysfunctions of MIDI." *Proceedings of the 1987 International Computer Music Conference.* San Francisco: Computer Music Association, 1987.

Pressing, J. "The Micro- and Macrostructure of Improvised Music." *Music Perception* 5,2 (Winter 1987): 133–72.

Rasch, R. A. "Synchronization in Performed Ensemble Music." *Acustica* 43 (1979): 121–31.

Rothstein, J. *MIDI: A Comprehensive Introduction.* Vol. 7, The Computer Music and Digital Audio Series. Madison, Wis.: A-R Editions Inc., 1992.

Small, A. M., and R. A. Campbell. "Temporal Differential Sensitivity for Auditory Stimuli." *American Journal of Psychology* 75,3 (1962): 401–10.

CHAPTER FOUR

SYNTHESIZER TECHNIQUE

. . . .

Traditional music has always depended on its performers to stress those of its aspects they judge necessary to clarify its forward unfolding. This resource is assumed unthinkingly by most electronic composers to exist in the electronic medium, but since it does not, the forward unfolding of even the simplest forms is seriously impeded.

- Charles Wuorinen, in Elliott Schwartz, *Electronic Music: A Listener's Guide* (1973)

Skilled performance on the synthesizer, as on any instrument, demands an appropriate technique—a set of physical skills used by the performer to produce the desired sounds. Technique is the crucial link in the chain from musical conception to musical production and expression; through it, internally heard sounds become external. Obviously, technique must be both comprehensive and well founded if it is to allow the full detail and precision of the performer's musical conception to be expressed.

This conception often takes the form of an *aural image* (McAdams 1984), the performer's mental representation of the intended music. This representation acts as a guide or referent in execution, allowing the performer to minimize errors, make ongoing adjustments, and prepare for musical events to follow. The more precisely this image is conceived, the more reliable the outcome. This is, however, not to deny the potential benefits associated with improvisation; risks successfully negotiated can make exciting music.

In the case of the synthesizer, technique includes skills on both the note selector and the various ancillary controllers. The details of this technique can, of course, be affected by the synthesizer's programming, in some cases drastically. But, fortunately, there is enough of a fund of common experience to define a core of standard skills that are essential for all synthesizer performers. This chapter addresses these standard skills for keyboard synthesizers. More innovative and specialist keyboard performance practices will be treated in chapter 6. Performance issues on nonkeyboard controllers will be treated in chapter 9.

KEYBOARD TECHNIQUE: CONCEPTS

A keyboard is a board with keys (levers) on it. The standard musical keyboard is a set of levers arranged in a row and played by the hands or, in the case of the organ pedalboard, the feet. The optimal technique to use with any such set of levers will naturally depend on the details of its construction but also on hand size of the performer, body position, the character of the sounds being produced, musical style, and other factors. Synthesizer keyboards today are nearly all of the standard piano/organ form, with the seven white and five black keys per octave arrangement that no Western musician could fail to recognize. Many other keyboard designs exist, some of them still in active use, but they do not yet seem significant for the synthesizer performer, and we will ignore them in this book.

Much of the synthesizer's standard keyboard technique can be distilled from that of its major instrumental antecedents: the organ, the harpsichord, the clavichord, and the piano. (For a discussion of other traditional nonelectric keyboards such as the accordian and celeste see chapter 8.) Although these four instruments do have much in common, their differences are considerable, both in sound and technique. The main variables differentiating their traditions of technique from each other are action, key size, number of keys, number of keyboards, velocity sensitivity, and pressure sensitivity.

Action, strictly speaking, refers to the mechanism that causes sound production on a keyboard. From the standpoint of the performer, action also has the connotation of the responsiveness of keys to striking, the "feel" of the playing interface. It is affected by a number of physical variables. These primarily include the heaviness of touch, the depth of travel of the key, the lever-arm distance (the distance from the key's internal pivot point to its playing end), and the key mechanism's quickness of response. Some of these are illustrated in figure 4.1.

An optimal action is formed when these physical variables fall into appropriate ranges. Heaviness of touch depends on the amount of inertia in the key action mechanism and, to some degree, on the internal friction between moving mechanical parts. If touch is too heavy, playing may require too much force for rapid passages; if it is too light, there may not be enough resistance for comfortable or customary fingering practices. It is almost always easier to adapt a technique used for heavy-touch keyboards to light-touch keyboards than vice versa. If the depth of travel is too great, it may interfere with proper articulation; if it is too shallow, it may feel unnatural, although this is rarely a problem. If the lever-arm distance is too small, black keys may require much more force to play than white keys, which can be awkward. There is rarely a problem of lever-arm distance being too long. If the response time is too long the keyboard will feel sluggish, and repeated notes will be difficult to execute rapidly; it is hard to imagine any problem caused by the response time being very short (although some performers are unnerved by a keyboard that triggers a sound well before the key has traveled its full depth). Although actions differ widely, any specific instrument must have a certain internal consistency of mechanism and sound across the keyboard if it is to be comfortable to play.

KEYBOARD TECHNIQUE: HISTORICAL SOURCES

With this information, it is now possible to begin a quick survey of the historical sources of technique available to the synthesizer

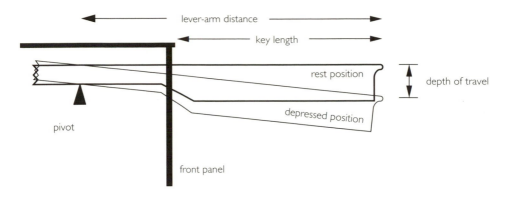

FIGURE 4.1   Schematic of key action (side view).

performer. The oldest keyboard instrument is the organ, and its roots go back at least 4,000 years, when it was hydraulically driven and had much larger keys. Keys were about the size of the hand, and the performer used one hand (or even the fist or elbow) per key rather than one finger. That technique is noticeably less common today!

The organs of contemporary practice come in tremendous variety, from the pop combo organ to ancient portative organ to the small positive to the electric theater organ to the massive pipe organ. From the standpoint of technique, the organ represents a light-touch keyboard tradition, often without velocity or pressure sensitivity (excluding recent electric organs that have synthesizer-like implementations). However, traditional pipe or-gans, though the keys are unweighted, do sometimes provide reasonably stiff resistance, especially where there is direct mechanical control of the pipes ("tracker action"), as is now widely preferred. Such control is pre-ferred in contemporary classical organ performance over pneumatic and especially electromechanical action because it allows the performer to gradually open the sounding pipe, enabling the player to control to some degree the attack time of each note, and also the release characteristic of the note. The degree of control depends on both the pipe and the specific design of the action, with the French suspended mechanical action being often considered most sensitive. There can also be a slight dynamic effect with changes in velocity. Mechanical action thus allows the traditional organ to be articulated as a wind instrument. However, many synthesizer players will primarily know the electric organ as played in jazz, blues, and popular music, an instrument which typically does not have such possi-bilities.

All but the smaller single keyboard organs have essentially the same key size as found on the piano. Larger organs, such as those installed in churches or concert halls, or those used by professional theater organists, have several (two to five) tiered *manuals* (hand-played keyboards), typically with sixty-one keys (C to C), although this can vary. Many inexpensive electronic organs have only one manual. Most organs also have a pedal-board played by the feet, and such pedalboards have a range varying from one octave on small organs to a fairly standard two octaves plus a fourth or fifth on larger ones. Pedalboards of one octave (found on smaller electric organs) usually lie flat on the ground, while larger ones (on church or concert organs) are often concave. Technique on the pedal-board uses the heel and ball of the foot and emphasizes the alternation of legs whenever possible. Although organs do not have very developed dynamic control from the keys, dynamic gradation is possible by pulling out drawbars, engaging or disengaging stops (extra voices), or, on many organs, the use of a swell pedal (foot volume control).

The organ tradition has some other aspects of significance for the synthesist. It is the most polyphonic of all traditional instruments due to the presence of the pedalboard. The experienced organist is likely to be better at playing a number of independent parts on different manuals than the pianist for this reason. The organ has also, among all nonjazz keyboard traditions, best kept alive the traditions of solo improvisation, most notably in France. Traditional church organists also are able to play undisturbed by the long delays in sound production that occur due to the large size of some traditional churches and the distance of the organ console from its pipes. Finally, the idea of the patch change in synthesis probably came from the idea of change of registration in organ performance, the idea of the keyboard stack from the multimanual organ.

The harpsichord dates back at least to the fourteenth century. Its keys are smaller than the piano's, and their depth of travel is less. Except for special models rarely seen today, it has no pedalboard. Like the organ it has no sustain pedal, no pressure sensitivity, and no dynamic control other than by the limited device of engaging extra stops (sets of strings) by using the hand (or foot on some models). It does have quite a distinctive feel in performance because, even though its touch is light, the method of sound production (the keystroke actually plucks the string or strings with a plec-trum) causes a noticeable tug part of the way down in each key depression. Too heavy a touch must be avoided, since it produces an undesirable "clunk" as the key strikes the keybed. Overall, its dynamic level is low, which was part of the reason it faded from popularity when the fortepiano was developed. Its contemporary range is often about five octaves, most commonly F to F, but other spans are common. It exists in single and double manual forms. Experienced harpsichord performers are used to improvising from a figured bass, which is a hallmark of the baroque period that can be of use to the synthesist in some playing situations.

The clavichord, like the harpsichord, can be traced back to the four-teenth century. It is a single manual device, with light touch and keys that are often smaller than standard piano size. It commonly has a five-octave span, from F to F, although smaller sizes are frequently found, and is normally pedalless. In many ways, its keyboard technique is more relevant to that of the synthesizer than the technique of any of the other three main keyboard antecedents. This is not a new opinion. In the words of Ludwig van Beethoven, "among all instruments the clavichord is that on which one can best control tone and expressive interpretation" (Lloyd and Boyle 1978, p. 286). This is because of its physical action, which causes a brass wedge called a *tangent* to directly strike and stop the string. This method permits both dynamic gradation and polyphonic pressure effects. Increas-ing pressure will raise the pitch of the depressed key so that both directly controllable vibrato and limited portamento or pitch bend effects are achievable by the skilled performer. There are also audible effects based on control of release velocity.

Unfortunately, the overall volume of the instrument is very low since the transfer of energy from the tangent to the string occurs near its end and is very inefficient. This means that the clavichord usually cannot be heard adequately in an ensemble of other instruments. The design of the instrument also makes acoustic miking and amplification challenging, so that the clavichord, the most expressive of all traditional keyboard instru-ments, remains a specialist rarity for most keyboardists. That this is due to no stylistic limitations of the instrument is amply demonstrated by recent studio recordings by people like Oscar Peterson and Keith Jarrett and of course many recordings of the solo instrument playing its traditional Re-naissance and baroque repertoire.

The piano, formerly the fortepiano (so named because of its ability to play both loud and soft), is distinguished by its relatively heavy action and its developed velocity sensitivity. It was invented by Bartolomeo Cristofori, who began work on it as early as 1698 and produced the first model by 1700. The early pianos actually had quite a light touch, like the organs and harpsichords that preceded them. Hence, they initally used the same tech-nique, which focused on exclusive use of the fingers, as illustrated by the idea that a coin placed on the back of the hand should not fall off. Initially, the thumb and little finger were largely neglected as being unsuitably short or weak. The use of all five fingers for scales and passage work was one of the radical innovations of J. S. Bach. Nevertheless, contemporary observers noted how he avoided as much as possible any other body motions besides those of the fingers. But as the piano action became more developed and powerful, the instrument came to have the heavier touch we know today, and a weight-control or application-of-weight method came into being, propelled to prominence by such masters as Rudolf

Breithaupt and Franz Liszt. This emphasized using the entire physical apparatus of hand, wrist, arm, shoulder, torso, and ultimately the solar plexus to apply weight to, rather than strike, the keyboard.

The standard contemporary piano has eighty-eight keys, from A to C. (A few have more: ninety-two, running from F to C, or ninety-seven—notably the Bösendorfer Imperial Grand—running from C to C.) It has, of course, no pressure sensitivity. The piano always has at least two pedals: a soft pedal and a sustain pedal. The soft pedal decreases the volume of the instrument and also alters its timbre by decreasing the number of strings sounded per key to one (so-called *una corda* playing, which diminishes attack and string resonance). Less expensive pianos imitate this effect by just moving the hammers closer to the strings, which scales down the volume without causing much change in resonance. The sustain pedal removes the dampers from all strings so that all keys sounding or struck after the pedal is depressed ring on until they die out naturally. The amount of sustain can be controlled by careful use of partial pedaling. Where a third pedal is present, as in most grands, it is a sostenuto pedal, which removes the dampers from the strings of all keys being held down. This allows the performer to sustain selected notes only. When all three pedals are present, the soft pedal is on the left, the sostenuto pedal is in the middle, and the sustain pedal is on the right. The left foot takes the soft pedal, the right foot the sustain pedal, and either foot the sostenuto pedal.

The piano's key size has now become standard for the vast majority of professional synthesizers, but there are some significant exceptions to this. Strap-on keyboard controllers often have smaller keys to keep the weight of the instrument to a minimum. Many cheaper synthesizers also use smaller key sizes, more like the standard harpsichord and clavichord keys or even smaller. Such smaller keys can be viewed as a limitation, particularly for performers with large hands or a fixed sense of key geography. But they also allow voicings and leaps that would be impossible on a full-sized keyboard—certain typical open voicings commonly used, for example, in traditional string writing are impossible for one player on a standard keyboard, but they become feasible on one of reduced size.

A summary of the typical control features of keyboard instruments and synthesizers is given in table 4.1. Some of the possible categories are unimplemented and seem likely to remain so.

CONTEMPORARY SYNTHESIZER KEYBOARD TECHNIQUE

While it is true that the techniques of all four main keyboard antecedents have influenced the development of synthesizer

Touch	Velocity sensitivity	Pressure sensitivity	Key size	Number of Keys	Examples
heavy	yes	yes	standard	88+	master keyboards
heavy	yes	no	standard	88+	piano, some synthesizers, some master keyboards
heavy	no	yes	—	—	—
heavy	no	no	—	—	—
light	yes	yes	variable	37–76	master keyboards, strap-ons, synthesizers, clavichord
light	yes	no	variable	variable	some synthesizers
light	no	yes	—	—	—
light	no	no	variable	37–61	organ, harpsichord, accordian, some synthesizers

TABLE 4.1   Typical control features of keyboards.

performance, piano technique is the main source for contemporary synthesizer keyboard technique, for the following reasons: (1) Virtually all synthesists have some exposure to it; (2) piano technique is normally considered essential for organists; and (3) piano performance has a substantial and influential technical literature. Therefore, it is worth examining sources for piano technique of special use to the synthesist. There is a large number of books on this topic, expressing a great diversity of viewpoints, and to examine them all thoroughly would take us too far afield. Likewise, to treat the full details of keyboard technique with musical examples would duplicate existing texts for the synthesizer's antecedents and needlessly swell the size of this book. Instead, I will mention some important texts and then simply survey basic aspects of technique that should be developed by all synthesizer keyboardists. Only in the case of the ancillary control devices unique to the synthesizer, notably pitch bend, will specific exercises prove necessary to build technique.

I have found Alfred Cortot's *Rational Principles of Pianoforte Technique* to be the best overall text on keyboard technique by virtue of its comprehensiveness and clearheaded discussion of the goals of its exercises. It is serious yet largely avoids the unrewarding rote prescriptions found in many texts. It also presents a quite contemporary view of musical materials (its year of publication—1928— notwithstanding). Other valuable works include Johannes Brahms's *51 Exercises,* the various studies by Czerny (e.g., *School of Velocity, 100 Progressive Studies,* and *31 Easy Exercises*), C. L. Hanon's *The Virtuoso Pianist,* Rafael Joseffy's *School of Advanced Piano Playing,* J. Pischna's *Technical Studies,* I. Phillip's *Exercises de moyenne force, Op 50,* Ernest Dohnanyi's *Essential Finger Exercises,*

J. B. Cramer's *Piano Studies,* and Muzio Clementi's *Gradus ad Parnassum.* Study of any of these distinguished texts is likely to improve technique, but they do suffer from focusing on mechanism to the exclusion of concept and are couched in an older (or at least different) harmonic language than that used by many synthesizer players.

For a series of short but more contemporary technical exercises I can point the reader to my own monthly column "Technique" in *Keyboard* magazine, which ran from January 1987 until mid-1991 and addresses technical issues at the keyboard, with special attention given to the synthesizer. The column is broadly based but focuses on the materials of contemporary music.

Although the details of successful technique may differ from player to player, the goals of a well-developed technique do not. They include finger and hand independence, strength, dexterity, mobility, suppleness, speed, appropriate relaxation, endurance, accurate timing, reliability, and evenness of touch. Coupled with knowledge of style and interpretation, good theoretical foundations, and a developed ability to hear internally, the result will be effective music.

The full development of technique cannot be learned from a book. However, there are a few universal concepts that describe how motion is to be directed to the relevant body parts. The most important of these are transfer of weight and playing from the center. *Transfer of weight* means the following: rather than depressing a key by using only the muscles of a finger, shift the weight of your torso from arm, shoulder, and solar plexus to the finger to cause key depression. This is the technique of choice in most situations on the piano and for many synthesists will be the first choice when the keyboard controller is weighted. With a light-touch controller much more direct finger technique can be used, in line with the historical variations in keyboard technique mentioned above. This lighter technique can be useful in keeping a strictly nonlegato articulation, which is essential for some types of monophonic playing. The two methods can also be combined in various ways.

Playing from the center refers to an attitude towards motion. If the player conceives of every action as coming from the center of the body and passing through the various muscle systems to reach the fingers, a better type of playing will normally result. This seems to happen because the various muscle groups reinforce each other and because it involves the body more completely in the required actions, meaning that inadvertent mistakes are made less often and rhythmic precision enhanced.

Good technique comes from enough practice of the right kind. I recommend that practice should consist of the following five components:

warm-up exercises

exercises and studies to improve technique in specific areas

practice on specific pieces

sight-reading practice

improvisation (chord-based, free, and in as many other styles as possible)

KEYBOARD WARM-UP EXERCISES

For warm-up exercises I can recommend those given by Alfred Cortot on pages 4–7 of his *Rational Principles of Pianoforte Technique*. Since this book is sometimes hard to find and is designed for the piano, I present here an independent and modified version of these for the synthesist.

The fundamental point of view of these warm-up exercises is simple: All muscle systems used by a keyboardist need regular exercise. These exercises are designed to systematically activate all the relevant major muscle systems used in keyboard performance: finger motion along three axes of motion and music-driven movements of the muscles of the hand, wrist, forearm, and shoulders. They are to be played using a nonsustaining timbre on the synthesizer. I will consider finger actions first and then move up the arm.

In some exercises, the thumb has to be handled slightly differently than the other fingers. The reason for this is that the thumb really has only two joints while the other fingers have three. But common sense will guide you in the adjustment. Similarly, the fourth finger has less independence than the other four since it shares a common extensor muscle with the third finger and will therefore require special attention in some circumstances.

The exercises begin as follows. Sit at the keyboard. All finger motions can be analyzed into movement along three basic dimensions—up and down, side to side, and in and out. Begin by placing your fingers as indicated in figure 4.2, with the right thumb on E, the left thumb below it on C, and the other fingers covering a whole-tone scale up or down. Silently depress the keys. Then, with both hands, perform the following exercises to a slow 4 count, using first the thumbs and then the other fingers in the order 1,2,3,4,5,5,4,3,2,1:

FIGURE 4.2   Hand position for warm-up exercises.

Exercise 1 (fingers)

    beat 1: strike key and hold it down

    beat 2: press into keyboard on that finger, transferring weight from the arm and shoulder

    beat 3: release pressure (key remains down)

    beat 4: raise finger as high as comfortably possible

Keep all other fingers down except the two concerned. Do the four-beat pattern two to four times using each pair of fingers before going on to the next pair. The overall exercise—going through the cycle of fingers—should be done a total of one to four times, depending on practice time available. These last instructions apply also to the next two exercises.

    Side-to-side finger warm-up is handled by the following:

Exercise 2 (fingers)

    beat 1: strike key

    beat 2: lift the finger and move it towards the other hand (inwards) as far as is comfortably possible

    beat 3: move the finger away from the other hand (outwards) as far as is comfortably possible

    beat 4: move finger up above key to prepare for the next stroke

    Finally, the third dimension of motion is catered to by:

Exercise 3 (fingers)

    beat 1: strike key

    beat 2: lift finger and extend it forward

    beat 3: curl finger back under hand

    beat 4: lift finger up to prepare for next stroke

When the fingers involved in this exercise are the thumbs, they should point down at the floor in beat 3.

Next we consider the hand and wrist. The main kinds of motions used in keyboard technique are up-and-down motions and the rotary actions used to play tremolo or repeated notes.

Exercise 4 (wrists)

beat 1: curl hands and wrists below arm level as far as is comfortably possible

beat 2: lift hands up and back as far as is comfortable.

This motion is like a slow and exaggerated waving goodbye and should be done with level forearms. Do it ten to twenty times at a slow to moderate tempo. It should be done, as all the others so far, seated facing the keyboard. Next, try the following exercise, which emphasizes circular motion.

Exercise 5 (wrists)

Clump the ends of the fingers of each hand together into a dull wad, fingers fairly straight. Put each wad on one spot on the keyboard (several white keys), and rotate the wrists and forearms as much as possible, first clockwise eight to ten times, then counterclockwise eight to ten times. Keep your wrists very flexible and each clump of fingers over the same spot on the keyboard.

Exercise 6 (wrists and forearms)

This exercise is best done standing up. Throw your arms down from shoulder level to their full length. When your arms are fully extended, rapidly rotate your wrists about the axis of the individual arms clockwise and counterclockwise in alternation, four or five times per throw of the arms. The motion should be like rapidly unscrewing jars. Do the entire operation about eight to fifteen times.

Further wrist exercises are not required for this basic warm-up set, but you may exercise them more by clenching and unclenching your hands to develop strength in both wrist and fingers. This is best done with a wad of newspaper or plastic foam in the palm to provide resistance.

Next we look at the arms. The forearms move most characteristically to and fro. Hence we have:

Exercise 7 (arms)

Seated somewhat back from the keyboard, with elbows bent and pointing straight down and hands in front of the shoulders, throw your forearms fully forward and let them quickly rebound to their initial position. Do this ten to twenty times.

Finally, the full arm and torso are also involved in the following:

Exercise 8 (arms, shoulders, trunk)

Take one arm and throw it rapidly from the highest note on your keyboard to the lowest, then back, taking care to strike only the desired key at each end with a single finger. Keep the hand low to the keys. This is best done on an eighty-eight-key instrument. If the length of your keyboard is significantly less than this, it may be better to touch the left- and right-hand edges of the instrument rather than the keyboard. Do this eight to fifteen times with each arm.

Regular use of these exercises can actually improve your technique, without any additional practice, for short periods. If used consistently, they will nearly always prevent your technique from backsliding, even without any other practice. However, the exercises must be done with awareness. Don't rush through them because the physical stress caused by hurrying might make them counterproductive. Treat these important body parts with the special care they deserve. Rather than grudgingly hurrying through them every day, do them every other day instead.

For those who are interested in further muscle development, there are a number of texts on muscle systems of the hand, although they are usually not written with the keyboard in mind. There is, however, one small pamphlet on hand exercises that is worth a look, as it contains 154 separate exercises for music-oriented muscular development: this is *The Musician's Handbook,* by Louise Curcio, listed in the end of chapter references.

Since the synthesizer keyboard can rely on either the organ, clavichord, or piano touch protocols, and since the synthesist must often switch frequently between them, there is a certain degree of stress on the hand that is not characteristic for any other instrument. The synthesist can be particularly prone to tenosynovitis problems. This can commonly occur with the extensive use of pressure, which can cause hand soreness if care is not used. The best cure for such troubles is rest from the offending techniques; the best prevention, regular warm-up as given in this chapter.

THE COMPONENTS OF TECHNIQUE

Even though we will not provide exercises in standard keyboard technique, it can be useful for keyboardists to assess areas of strength and weakness in their technical skills. The maximally versatile keyboardist should develop technique in all the following areas:

smooth two-handed playing of chromatic and diatonic scales, at the octave and at other intervals

smooth playing of arpeggios and broken chords in thirds, fourths, fifths, and larger intervals

tremolo

trill

thumb passing under

fingers other than thumb passing over and under

displacements and leaps

accents

grace notes and figurations

hand extension for larger intervals

hand independence

finger independence (striking and pressure)

dynamic control via attack velocity

pedaling techniques: sustain, soft, sostenuto

repeated notes

octaves

double stop technique in all intervals

single line interval studies: thirds to tenths

hand crossing

part balance in polyphonic passages (e.g., inner voice technique)

strength and independence of fingers 3, 4, 5

alternating hand technique

block chords

glissando

staccato articulation

nonlegato articulation

legato articulation: pedaled, fingered polyphonic, fingered mono-phonic

split keyboard techniques

multimanual techniques

pressure techniques: channel and polyphonic

portamento

release velocity techniques

velocity switching techniques

pitch bend

continuous controller techniques: wheel, joystick, slider, ribbon, foot controller, breath controller

Most of these skills apply to nearly all keyboards and are well known enough to require no special discussion here. However, the last ten are to varying degrees fairly specific to the synthesizer, and they will now be reviewed. Some of these techniques are best discussed in musical context since the demands they make are more conceptually novel than physically demanding. This applies to split keyboards, which will be discussed in chapter 6, multimanual techniques, which will be discussed in chapter 7, and portamento effects, which will be deferred until chapters 5 and 6. Some techniques—notably repeated notes—are usually easier on a light-touch keyboard than on a piano action model keyboard, and different fingerings are often preferable because of it. For a detailed look at the differences in this case and at accompanying exercises see Pressing 1988.

The remaining discussion begins with the staccato–legato distinction, an intriguing one for the synthesist since there are several ways these effects can be achieved, each based on different conceptual models of instrumental performance. To explore the issue it becomes necessary to consider that, because synthesizers are programmable, sound and hand articulation are no longer inextricably linked: For example, sound may ring on considerably after release due to slow release envelope or high reverberation setting, so a staccato touch may produce a legato sound. Staccato musical effects, if achievable at all, might then be reached only by playing staccatissimo. Analogously, a sound with a very slow attack envelope requires notes to be played much more legato than normal if they are to sound without use of the sustain pedal. Since partial pedal sustain effects are not possible on most synthesizers, legatoness, particularly with sustaining sounds, must often be controlled to a much greater degree by the fingers than with the pedal. By *legatoness* is meant the degree of legato used in performance.

In general, needed articulation may be affected by many aspects of the synthesis programming, particularly voice assignment. Voice assignment effects are described in the section immediately below, while exotic techniques requiring substantial reconceptualization by the performer are discussed in chapter 6 in "Extended and Reconfigured Instruments."

Even without exotic programming, the synthesist must be aware of a primary distinction in the nature of legato playing based on the two most common kinds of sound envelopes found on traditional instruments: One style of legato playing holds for monophonic instruments, another for polyphonic. Legatoness with traditional polyphonic instruments is commonly created by note overlap, as on traditional keyboards; legatoness with traditional monophonic instruments is not achieved by note overlap but rather by tenuto (hold full value) playing that avoids additional onset noise (corresponding to bowing or tonguing noise) at the start of phrases and slurs. The keyboardist must be fluent in both legato and strict tenuto touch if imitations of traditional articulations are to achieve maximum realism. In situations where such imitation is not relevant, this simple dichotomy will be modified by the synthesizer's programming and the demands of musical context.

Another example of the effect of sound on technique is found when playing drum kit or percussion ensemble setups from the keyboard. The small finger motions characteristic of piano technique do not seem to naturally provide the right type of gestural link to the power and required rhythmic precision of percussion. Consequently, either a large amount of special practice is necessary or a two-arm technique that uses the fingers like the mallets in classical multimallet percussion technique. (See chapter 8 for a detailed look at this situation.)

The use of channel pressure is straightforward for most performers: simply assign it some function, such as vibrato, volume, or brightness, and press down in proportion to the desired intensity of the effect. Commonly, it is the sum of all the force being applied that produces the effect, as the sensors are usually placed under the entire keyboard frame; therefore, big chords may need only a little pressure per key. However, with keyboards that have both channel and polyphonic pressure, channel pressure is often determined from the maximum individual key pressure, and this requires a quite different attitude to technique. It is also important to make sure that velocity effects do not carelessly spill over into pressure—notes strongly attacked may need to have their force quickly reduced after striking if the aftertouch function is not to be automatically engaged. Practice soon makes this a natural integrated action. In general the shoulders must not allow too much of the weight of the arms to rest on the struck notes if superfluous aftertouch is to be avoided. This may require a change of habit for some pianists and organists used to resting the arms' weight on held notes.

This carefulness in the areas of velocity independence and shoulder support is also essential when using polyphonic pressure. In addition, since polyphonic pressure allows each depressed note to separately articulate pressure values, some special practice on the part of the performer is usually required to achieve proper finger independence. In a complex texture, poly pressure provides an excellent way to bring out a given voice, most commonly by selectively adding vibrato or increasing dynamics. Polyphonic pressure is still transmitted by only a limited number of synthesizers and master controllers, although a larger number of sound modules respond to it.

With either type of pressure, many keyboards have the problem that the physical force required to get a full range of values tends to tire the hand rapidly, sometimes causing strain or pain. If you use pressure effects extensively, it can be best to program a rather sensitive response to pressure. In any case, if any pain develops, stop using pressure in favor of some other controller, or make the resultant sonic effect stronger for the same amount of pressure.

The use of pressure can be practiced by modifying exercise 1 above, as follows: instead of a decaying sound, use a sustaining timbre, and route pressure to control volume, setting it so that at zero pressure there is no (or very low) volume and at preferred maximum pressure there is maximum volume. In the course of the exercise you should then be able to calibrate your pressure sense. Pressure's main disadvantage as a means of control is that it can rise from zero only after key depression and must fall to zero before release. A closer look at specialist pressure effects will be given in chapter 6.

Release velocity, the speed at which a depressed key is allowed to rise, is a feature available only on a few synthesizer keyboards or master controllers, and only a limited number of sound modules respond to it. The relevant MIDI message is 8*n.xx.yy*H, where *yy* is release velocity. Where present, it is usually in sophisticated devices that allow it to be routed to a number of different synthesis functions; most commonly, it controls release time or other aspects of the decay process, but there is no reason it need be confined to this. Release velocity is a variable that does occur in older standard keyboards, notably on the clavichord and mechanical action pipe organ, but since few synthesists are experienced on these instruments, it remains an area with much undeveloped potential. This is despite the fact that timbre can be influenced strongly by release envelope. Certainly the synthesist who comes to the instrument from the piano or electric organ will need special practice to master its use.

Velocity switching requires that the performer give special attention to the control of velocity production if the desired timbre is to be chosen consistently. The difficulty of the technique depends on the number of different velocity zones and the degree of difference between the selected timbres. The best way to practice the technique is to play familiar scales and arpeggios, achieving sufficient regularity such that only one timbre sounds throughout. With a two-way switch, this is easy; with a three-way switch, more difficult; and with four or more switching zones it is really quite challenging, and special practice is required.

This completes our outline of keyboard technique, except for one little fact: Synthesizers are not always played horizontally in a sitting position, as older keyboards are. Standing and crouching positions are also used.

There is little resulting difference in keyboard technique if the keyboard is horizontally suspended on a stand or table, but the use of pedals is affected, as the feet, rather than a stool or chair, now support the body. The simultaneous use of two pedals while standing may decrease the player's balance and affect surety of execution, although it's not impossible for those with good spatial sense and agile ankles.

If the performer is using a strap-on synthesizer or remote controller, changes in technique are more pronounced. Not only do these typically have restricted ranges of three or four octaves and smaller than full-size keys, but they are normally played in a guitar-like position. They often have a short neck with ancillary controllers, which are played by the left hand by reaching around the back of the instrument, as in a stringed instrument like the guitar. The keyboard is played by the right hand alone, or both hands when required. Strap-on controllers are more likely to have more developed pitch bend facilities (such as ribbons) since they play a lead-line function more frequently than most synthesizers. Program change buttons, continuous controllers, and other switches are located in a variety of places on the bodies of different strap-on controllers.

With the right hand (and left, when it plays the keyboard), the angle of attack, body stance and quality of physical support are different than with keyboards in a horizontal position; however, most players can readily adapt to this change, especially if they have played some guitar. A light touch is usually necessary, particularly when both hands play the keyboard, since then the left arm no longer functions as a support and only the body strap holds the instrument in position. Strap length should be adjusted to make sure the arms are not unnaturally cramped—holding an awkward position is tiring and undermines precision. Many experienced strap-on synthesizer players develop a system of one-to-one gestural mapping between musical effect and body motion, linking the small appropriate finger motions to larger expressive body gestures. It not only makes for a more engaging performance visually but is objectively effective in increasing the rhythmic precision and integrated musicality of performance.

VOICE ASSIGNMENT: MONOPHONIC AND POLYPHONIC MODES

Many synthesizers can operate in monophonic mode or polyphonic mode. In *polyphonic mode* the synthesizer plays all notes, up to its voice limit (or the number of voices programmed for a particular layer or split). In *monophonic mode* (occasionally called *stack mode* or *unison mode*), only one note at a time is sounded. Different technique is required in the two cases. To understand exactly what the differences are, we must first address the issue of voice assignment.

Voice assignment refers to how the sound generators inside the synthesizer are assigned to the depressed keys. Each independent monophonic sound generator is called a voice, as defined in chapter 1, and every synthesizer has a maximum number of voices it can cause to sound at once. Whether the synthesizer is operating monophonically or poyphonically, it must have a *voice assignment algorithm* that allows the machine to decide which notes to play (assign a voice to) when the number of keys depressed exceeds the voice limit of the machine or assigned part(s).

In the monophonic case, the voice assignment algorithm will come into play when more than one note is depressed simultaneously. This will happen when notes are sounded together intentionally but also if they are played sufficiently legato to overlap even a tiny amount. In terms of voice assignment, the common algorithms are low-note priority, high-note priority, and last-note priority. In *low-note* and *high-note priority* respectively, the lowest and highest depressed key at any given time is sounded; *last-note priority* sounds the last key depressed. These possibilities are important for the performer because a different technique is required to play the same figure with different priorities. Figure 4.3 shows how two short examples would actually sound under the three priorities. It is also possible to set these same note priorities by the use of certain external MIDI mapping devices.

To further complicate the monophonic case, some synthesizers allow a choice between single and multiple triggering. This option is still available on a number of devices but was more common on older analog synthesizers than it is today. With *multiple triggering* each new note will retrigger the envelope(s) of the sound, robbing the sound from any previous note. This means that the remaining portions of the previous note's envelopes will be chopped off. With *single triggering* new envelopes are triggered only when there is no overlap between notes — in other words, when nonlegato articulation has been used. If two notes are played legato, the second note will begin its pitch where the envelope(s) of the first note left off, chopping off the front of the new envelope(s). This can make a useful legato-like effect, or at least increase the variability of the shape of note attacks. (Some of the classic single line solos of the 1960s and 1970s made use of single trigger mode.) Some synthesizers supply only single trigger monophonic mode.

The implications for the performer are as follows. If a nonlegato touch is used consistently, voice assignment priorities and triggering modes will be irrelevant since notes will never overlap. This is such a useful possibility that the ability to play consistently nonlegato must be considered a

FIGURE 4.3 The effect of different monophonic voice assignment priorities on two simple motives.

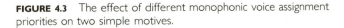

basic part of the synthesist's technique. If legato touch is used with single trigger mode, the starts of note envelopes will be truncated, producing a kind of sonic legato, while if multiple trigger mode is used the ends of note envelopes will be truncated, producing more like a tenuto nonlegato effect. In either case, pitch selection will be determined by the chosen voice assignment algorithm.

In the polyphonic case, the details of voice assignment depend both on the number of available voices, and the presence and degree of multitimbrality. Consider the monotimbral case first. If the number of notes played exceeds the voice capacity of the machine, then some previous note must be dropped (the word *stolen* is often used) if the most recent note is not to be ignored. Just how this is done depends on the intelligence and stylistic suppositions programmed into the synthesizer by its designer. The simplest common voice assignment algorithm is *first-in-first-out*, meaning that the note held longest will be cut off when voice capacity is exceeded. Some machines have a feature or variable, called *forced damp* (Yamaha) or *steal release rate* (Kurzweil), that drops this oldest note unobtrusively to zero to avoid a possible glitch in the sound caused by the envelope cutoff.

First-in-first-out can work very well, but it fails notably in some common cases, as for example when the attempt is made to hold a bass tone with the sustain pedal through immediately following treble figurations (as is common in piano style passages). In such cases, the bass will drop out as soon as the voice total is exceeded. Some machines, such as the Kurzweil synthesizers, have the intelligence built in to avoid this kind of limitation — in this case, by not stealing the highest and lowest sounding notes. Some machines allow the assignment of voice-stealing priorities for voices in different zones. Others have the option of choosing from a menu of voice-stealing algorithms, such as stealing the voice that is at the softest dynamic, stealing from repeated notes that are being sustained by the pedal, and so forth. Some recent musical modules, such as those by Ensoniq, Kurzweil, Oberheim, and Sequential, have the option of sending out through MIDI the notes that cannot be handled in the machine itself, allowing the number of voices to be increased by a factor of two, three, or more by chaining duplicates of the original module together via MIDI. This option is usually called *overflow mode*.

Most of the time, these voice assignment algorithms will not directly affect the performer. Remember, however, that in imitating a monophonic sustaining instrument in polyphonic mode, note overlap must be avoided if the notes are to sound as intended. The performer must play strictly nonlegato, ranging only from staccato to tenuto (hold to full value).

In the multitimbral situation, several different parts (different sounds on different MIDI channels) in the synthesizer can receive notes at the same time, and voice allocation can be either *fixed*, specifying a fixed maximum number of voices per part, or *dynamic*, changing according to the needs of the musical situation. With well-designed dynamic voice allocation, a single multitimbral synthesizer can give the impression of having considerably more voices than its rated capacity, especially if the parts being played are designed with this limitation in mind. Some machines allow the assignment of voice-stealing priorities (low, medium, high priorities) between the parts. Extra notes will then be dropped according to their voice assignment priorities.

Even with fixed voice allocation, some quite interesting effects can occur. Some synthesizers with fixed voice allocation (for example, the Oberheim Xpander) permit the input notes to circulate among the selected sounds in various preset orders. *Rotate* mode circulates through the different parts (programs) with each new note: If six voices (parts) are possible, then note 1 might be assigned to part 1, note 2 to part 2, ... note 6 to part 6, note 7 to part 1, note 8 to part 2, and so on. An equivalent effect occurs with controllers that can send out in so-called *cycle* mode (a Kurzweil term), where, beginning with a basic channel, each successive note is assigned to the next higher MIDI channel until a maximum number is reached, after which it starts the cycle of channels over again. Some MIDI mapping boxes allow this effect and variations on it. If this controls a number of synthesizers set to receive on the channels selected, a timbral rotation will occur. If the different timbres have very different transpositions, a simple line can generate complex leaps and changes of register.

Another possibility is *reset* mode (an Xpander term), where nonlegato playing resets the system to a starting timbre (let us say part 3), and each additional simultaneous voice engages the next part (4, 5, 6, 1, etc.) so that a nonlegato line will keep the same timbre if all other voices hold. These options can be an effective way for a single keyboardist to create complex multitimbral textures. It is also sometimes possible to set these voice-allocation options separately in different keyboard zones. Figure 4.4 shows the timbral results of playing the same passage with three different voice-allocation configurations: rotate, reset, and rotate (treble zone = C3 and above)/reset (bass zone = below C3). An effect similar to reset or rotate can occur with MIDI mono mode (see chapter 2).

VELOCITY AND PRESSURE MAPS

Most synthesizers allow a flexibility of performance inflection not found on the older keyboard instruments. This is primarily *not* due to their ability to change the physical aspects of touch (key weight,

FIGURE 4.4 Polyphonic (multitimbral) voice allocations under three different priorities: rotate mode (a); reset mode (b); rotate/ reset mode (c). The part (voice) number assigned to each note is written next to each note head, and the final arpeggiation is upwards.

speed of key mechanism response, etc.) of the keyboard, although at least one master controller (the KTI GZ1000) does offer adjustable hammer action. Rather, they are able (in varying degrees) to alter the production of actual performance data (in MIDI or control voltage format) resulting from keyboard actions (notably velocity and pressure). This programmability can occur in three ways. At the transmission end, the MIDI (or other) output produced from the interface for a particular physical gesture can be modified. At the receiving end, both the nature and sensitivity of the response of the sound engine to pressure or velocity data can be set. Lastly, an intervening device may alter the message sent. Changes at any point in the chain of control will affect the way the performer must play that particular sound.

The degree of programming sophistication and versatility available varies considerably from device to device. At the receiving end, attack velocity can most commonly be routed to control such target variables as overall volume, the volume(s) of selected sound components, attack time(s), and filtering. In some machines, a much greater range is available. Where release velocity is available, a similar range of functions is commonly found as for attack velocity. Pressure can be most commonly routed to control overall volume, the volume(s) of selected sound components, pitch shift, and depth of LFO modulation (pitch or amplitude). Again, some synthesizers, notably some by Kurzweil, Oberheim, Ensoniq, and E-mu, make available many more target parameters. Audio processing devices and synthesizer "workstations" with built-in audio processing increasingly offer a host of audio target variables such as reverberation time, reverberation depth, decay time, and so forth.

The sensitivity of the target variable will normally also be programmable, allowing the depth of the effect to be set. However, the nature of the shape of the response curve is not normally programmable, and where it is it involves a very limited choice of options.

At the transmission end, the situation may offer more flexibility. Some master keyboards and synthesizers allow a number of aspects of the relationship between applied velocity or pressure and MIDI output to be programmed. Similar versatility can be programmed by using special MIDI mapping boxes like the Oberheim Navigator between the note source and its target module to reshape the velocity and pressure data.

This programmed correlation between physical action and output signal is an example of a map. A *map* is simply a function relating two variables, input and output. A velocity map thus determines how played velocity will be transformed to MIDI velocity data in Note On or Note Off messages. (This is sometimes called "velocity scaling.") A pressure map determines how applied force ("pressure" applied to the key sitting on the keybed) will be transformed to MIDI pressure data in Channel or Polyphonic Pressure messages. Velocity and pressure maps determine, along with the keyboard's physical design, the "feel" and responsiveness of the keyboard controller.

Maps can have any possible shape in principle. Linear, exponential, logarithmic, and polynomial shapes are most common. Some synthesizers and master controllers allow the selection of such maps from a menu of presets; a few allow curve editing. Examples of common velocity or pressure map shapes are shown in figure 4.5. The precise mathematical form of such curves is not as important as an understanding of how their shape affects the performer's feel at the keyboard.

Figure 4.5a shows linear maps. In map 1, perhaps most common, a linear and full range relationship exists between the played and sent data. Map 2 has a threshold; it produces no output below a certain value (like, for example, the velocity variable on an acoustic piano). Map 3 produces a reduced range such as occurs on some synthesizers, notably Yamaha's X series, where velocities are put out only in the approximate range 11 to 110. Map 4 is "hot"—it saturates to its maximum output value of 127 in the middle of its input range (for example, the Kurzweil MIDIboard tends to do this). Map 5 is an inversion, allowing cross-fade effects.

In figure 4.5b, nonlinear maps are shown. Map 1 is "hot"; it does not saturate but just gives out generally high values. Map 2 is "cool"; high velocity or pressure values are sent only when the player strikes or pushes the keys very hard. Map 3 is a flattening curve that compresses the player's range of actions to emphasize mid-range MIDI data. Map 4 features an inverted dull response—the performer must strike the keys very lightly to get high velocity or pressure values.

The usefulness of such maps is that the performance interface can be customized for each performer. However, it is not confined to this. The potential for cross-fading exists, as shown in map 5 in figure 4.5a and map 4 in figure 4.5b, when such maps are combined with other sounds driven by "normal" (positive slope) maps. More generally, it can occur that when several synthesizers are used together the response of the different sound sources is uneven—a correct mix at one value of velocity may not be correct at another, or one machine is programmed for a different range of velocities or aftertouch than another, creating either distortion and unwanted brightness or dull and insipid sounds. The use of different maps on different channels allows such problems, which can range from minor irritations to major headaches, to be ironed out. If velocity and pressure maps are not available on the controller used and are needed, they must be approximated either by reprogramming at the sound modules—a tedious business—or using a MIDI mapping device to rescale the MIDI data that come out of the controller before they reach the sound modules.

One well-known example of this is the Yamaha X synthesizer series (DX7, DX21, etc.—but not the KX88 and KX76 controllers), which puts out a restricted range of velocities, as mentioned above. The programs were consequently designed to function for this range of velocity input. If an X synthesizer is controlled by a normal velocity range machine, the sounds come out too loud and shrill. If an X synthesizer acts as a controller for other synthesizers that are programmed to respond to normal touch, then brightness, presence, and dynamic range are lost.

The solution in the first case is to remap the velocity range piecewise to fit the X machine, but only on the channels controlling it. Some controllers even have a DX7 velocity map as an option (Kurzweil MIDIboard). The

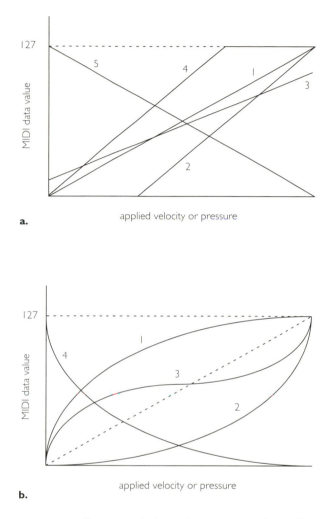

FIGURE 4.5 Common velocity and pressure map shapes: linear maps (a); nonlinear maps (b).

alternative of reprogramming all the sounds in the X synthesizer to respond to the normal range of velocities and playing the instrument only with Local Control off via MIDI cable OUT to IN is possible in principle but is not often done since some internal performance features can be lost in such a setup. If, as in the second case above, it is desired to use the X synthesizer as an external controller for devices with full velocity range, the options are increasing the velocity sensitivity of the receiver or rescaling the X machine's velocity output using a MIDI mapper.

ANCILLARY CONTROLLERS

Ancillary controllers are controllers that work as adjuncts to the main note selection interface. These include devices on the synthesizer or master controller that send out Control Change messages (the MIDI controllers), other sensors that send different MIDI messages (including pitch bend devices, channel and polyphonic pressure, and program change buttons), and controls that may operate only internally (for example, data entry sliders and master volume knobs on synthesizers). Although already discussed above, the pressure variables are mentioned here because they are typically programmed with the same range of functions as the other controllers.

In general, satisfactory performance on these devices is readily achieved by nearly all players without extensive or special practice. There are two exceptions to this rule. First, the coordination of controllers of all kinds with the playing of notes at the keyboard can require special attention, particularly when dramatic effects like volume or pitch bend are involved. This will be discussed separately below, and exercises will be given for the development of this skill. Second, because the ear is acutely sensitive to pitch gradations, pitch bend devices require careful control and special practice; these will therefore also be discussed separately, with accompanying technical exercises, at the end of this chapter.

The general process of playing an ancillary controller is shown in figure 4.6a, which indicates control routings and functions. The physical device played by the performer is assigned to transmit specific MIDI message types. The sound module must be set to receive that MIDI message type, including correct controller number if it is a Control Change message. The corresponding data stream must then be assigned some control *function* so that the data will cause a specific sonic effect (e.g., modulation, MIDI volume, panning, sustain on/off). Some synthesis modules have very little flexibility in assigning function, while others have a great deal. Similarly, some transmitters have a great deal of flexibility in assigning message types to ancillary controllers (especially master controllers), while others are far more restricted. For example, the possibility of setting the transmitted and received controller numbers is becoming more widespread, while pitch bend devices are, with very few exceptions, hard-wired to send out Pitch Bend messages and hence control pitch bend function.

Another option is the use of a MIDI mapping device, as shown in figure 4.6b, which typically allows both the conversion of MIDI message types and data byte transformations. Such devices can produce dramatic keyboard reconfigurations, and these will be discussed in chapter 6. Less fanciful uses of direct relevance to standard synthesizer technique are the

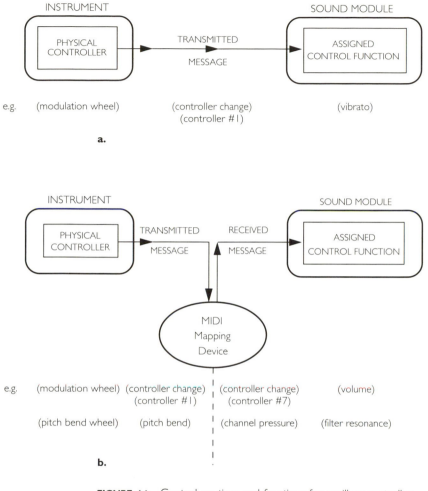

FIGURE 4.6 Control routings and functions for ancillary controller (a) and for ancillary controller with intervening MIDI mapping device (b).

fine tuning of inconsistencies in data ranges (such as discussed above with velocity and which happens quite often with pitch bend range) and the conversion of controller numbers. For example, if the performer is playing a breath controller sending out controller 2 and wishes to affect a sound module that cannot be programmed to respond to this controller number, a MIDI transformation device could change the data to controller 1 (modulation), which could then be assigned a control function in the receiving synthesis module. Some synthesizers allow this sort of conversion internally.

Note that certain naming conventions with regard to controllers can be confusing here. For example, the physical "modulation wheel" is often assignable to things other than modulation, such as volume. Some synthesizers assign the incoming controller message an internal label, like "pedal 1" or "lever," and these labels must then be assigned to a control function. These can become confusing when there may well be no pedal or lever involved in the playing process. It also needs to be remembered that sent information need not follow the recommended controller conventions given in chapter 3, although nearly all manufacturers do. All the communicating machines care about is whether controller numbers match. If a slider is set to controller 1, then it will function as a "modulation wheel." If data from the physical modulation wheel are sent out on controller 64, then it will act as a sustain pedal—not that this is a particularly useful controller assignment.

Most ancillary controllers have become fairly standardized in physical form, perhaps partly since they are almost all based on either position or force. In contrasting the pros and cons of various controllers, the main issue is what sort of real-time control they offer the performer. One natural division is between continuous and discrete devices, as described in chapter 3: Continuous controllers give out a full range of values, normally ranging over at least 128 values, so they can approximate continuous output; discrete controllers give out only two or occasionally several values. The resolution of continuous controllers allows enough control to achieve certain quasi-continuous nuances of musical expression like crescendo, pitch bend, and so forth.

Commonly encountered real-time control mechanisms (and, in parentheses, their typical functions) are: wheel or two-dimensional joystick (pitch bend); wheel, joystick, breath controller, foot controller, channel pressure, polyphonic pressure, control sliders, dial, knob, lever, drawbar, ribbon (all assignable according to the synthesizer's design); foot switches (sustain/soft/sostenuto pedals plus limited assignability); buttons and switches (toggle or momentary, variably assignable); and switch bank (program change). These controllers are typically built into or plug directly into the main instrument, but some are available as separate devices, such as Jeff Tripp's Tripp Strip (a one-dimensional ribbon controller with fixed or movable zero point whose data output is arbitrarily assignable), the Dorns Research Group's MIDI Performance Bar, special three-dimensional joysticks, etc. When used with synthesizers, they must be merged with the note selection interface by a separate merge device. Such merge functions are normally built in to master keyboards or other remote pitch controllers.

The above controllers are all used in play mode; on many machines, the data entry devices can also be used in edit mode to affect any programmable parameter in real time. This may offer real-time control within a sounding note or only with each change of note. Other more exotic control devices (pitch-to-MIDI converters, two-dimensional touch pads and surfaces, proximity detectors and accelerometers, etc.) will be discussed later.

PERFORMANCE WITH STANDARD CONTINUOUS CONTROLLERS

To understand the strengths and limitations of the various continuous controllers in performance, it is necessary to look at the type of real-time control they offer. The choice of correct controller is an important decision: The controller should have enough message resolution to do the job, it should provide a natural feel for its musical function, and it should be ergonomically designed, especially where two or more controllers must be played simultaneously. If the controller that is best ergonomically cannot be assigned by the sound module to control the desired synthesis variable, then it may in some circumstances be best, if possible, to convert the sent messages to a controller number or status byte type that can offer such control.

Table 4.2 summarizes the control features (cybernetics) of the main continuous MIDI controllers. The first column lists the controllers, with the note selection interface included for comparison. Column 2 lists the number of dimensions of control (degrees of freedom) each controller offers. Column 3, polarity, refers to whether the range of control is unipolar (allowing movement in only one direction from zero effect position or other nominal value) or bipolar (allowing movement in both directions from zero effect position or a nominal value). For example, the modulation wheel is nearly always monopolar, while the pitch bend wheel is bipolar. Bipolar controllers typically have a small *dead band* (*dead zone*), or null effect zone, around their center null effect position for playing convenience.

Return or hold (column 4) refers to whether the controller snaps back to a nominal value or keeps its position on release. In playing terms, the first situation requires the performer to hold the controller accurately to its selected value for the duration of the resultant effect; the second means it can be left once the effect is satisfactory but must be turned off manually when no longer needed. For example, breath controllers are necessarily

Controller	Dimensions of control	Polarity	Return/ hold?	Skips possible?	Sensory reinforcement	Fully independent?
mod wheel	1	uni	hold	no	good	yes
pitch bend wheel	1	bi	return	no	good	yes
joystick	2	bi	both	no	good	yes
slider	1	uni/bi	hold	no	very good	yes
ribbon/strip	1	uni/bi	both	yes	very good	yes
breath controller	1	uni	return	no	good†	yes
foot controller	1	uni	hold	no	fair†	yes
channel pressure	1	uni	return	no	good†	no
poly pressure	multi	uni	return	no	good†	no
note selector*	1 or multi	—	—	yes	variable	yes

*keyboard, etc.
†tactile feedback only; visual reinforcement is nil

TABLE 4.2   Cybernetic features of the common controllers.

return-to-zero-effect devices, while modulation wheels are hold-on-release devices. Spring return, typically necessary on pitch bend controls, allows a good deal of playful manipulation—flips, snaps back to zero, and so forth.

Most controllers cannot skip to arbitrary points in their ranges but must send out intervening values; those that can skip have a yes in column 5. This is one advantage of ribbon controllers. Column 6 refers to the sensory reinforcement of the controllers. Most controllers offer good sensory re-inforcement, but there are two components beyond the ever-present sonic link: First, there is the direct tactile feedback of the body part in contact with the controller; second, there is visual sensory redundancy, which reinforces accuracy of performance by allowing the performer to see as well as feel and hear the control. Four controllers have limitations in this area and are marked with "†". Finally, some controllers can be used only in tandem with other controls and are therefore not fully independent (column 7)—this refers to the pressure variables, since they are inaccessible without a previous key depression.

The details of the feel of playing continuous controllers will depend, as in the cases of velocity and pressure, on the relation between gesture and MIDI output at the playing end and MIDI input and sonic response at the receiving end. Controllers do not in general have a range of possible programmable maps to choose from, as some machines offer with velocity and pressure, and they are probably unlikely to develop such options. Often, their playing technique can be adjusted only by setting the sensitivity (amount of effect) at the synthesis receiving end, although there is increasing refinement at the transmission end (e.g., some foot controllers offer a range control knob, and the Yamaha breath controller has a set screw offering similar control). It is wise to remember that controller sensitivity will also depend on the sensitivity of the ear to the musical effect the controller is controlling.

We turn now to a survey of playing techniques on the most common controllers, examining hand controllers first. We begin with the wheel. Which finger(s) should be used, and how? That depends on both the wheel design and personal preference. Any finger is possible, but 1, 2, and 3 (of the left hand) are most common. Where no other controllers are being simultaneously used by the same hand, the thumb is normally preferred for bipolar controllers, since the hand can pivot up and down most easily with that fingering choice. The weight of the arm then rests on either the other fingers or the ball of the hand. If finger 2 or 3 is used instead, the arm weight rests on the thumb and remaining fingers. With monopolar wheels, fingers 1, 2, and 3 are used similarly. The details of hand position and action are a matter for personal preference. A few wheels have a raised projection at the center, making solo thumb action less secure and requiring the performer to use two fingers (1 and 2 or 1 and 3) to grip the projection loosely: Either the thumb is used to push up and the other finger to pull down, or both grip the end together and produce all movement as a unit.

If two wheels are present they are typically adjacent and can be played simultaneously with the left hand. This necessitates some changes in technique. It will not be possible to play both controllers accurately at the same time with the left hand unless the thumb is on the right (normally, modulation) wheel, and finger 2, 3, or 4 is on the left (normally, pitch bend) wheel. Even with this fingering, it can be awkward for most hands to turn the modulation wheel to high levels when the pitch bend wheel is pulled strongly towards the body. The arm must also support the hand without a resting point in this case. Try it and you'll see that certain effect combinations are not particularly comfortable, but with practice the technique will become usably consistent. There is a good solution for your individual hand—experiment and find it.

The synthesizer joystick is a two-dimensional controller and is played by grasping the end of the lever with fingers 1 and 2 or 1 and 3 (1 and 4 or 5 is of course also possible but rarely used), with arm weight typically resting on the ball of the hand. Here the performer must think in a two-dimensional field to keep track of the separate effects being produced. Special practice along separate x and y directions may be required to keep the two dimensions conceptually separate, especially when one is a highly sensitive variable like pitch bend. Control is easier to learn when it causes panning or cross-fading (as in vector synthesis machines).

The slider is typically played with the index or middle finger. When only one is used at once, there seem to be no special playing problems. When two, three, or four sliders are used simultaneously by the left hand, as occasionally occurs on master controllers, one finger is allocated to each slider, and arm weight rests on the performing fingers. With two sliders, fingers 1 and 3 or 2 and 4 seem most common.

The ribbon controller is in many ways the best of the lot in terms of its control potential since it has unrivaled visual feedback, a larger physical range of movement that allows better resolution (in principle), the possibilities of a floating zero point and no center dead zone. But as of this writing it is only rarely found as a standard feature, notably on strap-on controllers. Older machines used it more frequently than newer machines. Because of this, for the purposes of this discussion, we will assume that the ribbon is controlling pitch, its most common assignment.

The techniques used in playing a ribbon controller depend on whether it is set for hold or return mode. In return mode, it is played very much like an unfretted string instrument with only one string—in other words, gently rocking the controller around the held position produces a vibrato effect, and sliding motion between positions produces a portamento. With the use of more than one finger, skips can be made. In hold mode, vibrato is produced the same way, but the hand can leave the ribbon at any time, allowing skips to be produced by the same finger and more flexible hand positioning.

Ribbon technique also depends on the position of the ribbon in relation to the performer's body. If it is laid out from left to right on top of the instrument panel, the hand is palm down, and fingers 1, 2, and 3 are used predominantly; required technique becomes similar to that of the left hand of the pedal steel guitar or some styles of dobro. If the ribbon is part of the neck in a strap-on controller, use of the thumb may be impractical, and fingers 2, 3, 4, or 5 may be optimal, as in slide guitar performance.

The remaining continuous controllers (breath, the two pressures, and foot controllers) do not require a hand to leave the keyboard, a fact that gives them strong advantages in any part requiring real-time control and two hands' worth of notes. They have obvious mechanical differences in playing technique. The breath controller, which senses air pressure, probably has the fastest physical response. This makes smooth coordination of the breath with the attack of notes on the note selection interface particularly critical. Currently made only by Yamaha, the breath controller should be played with the air passage unobstructed for best results (e.g., do not put tape over the air exit hole, as is occasionally done), with its range calibrated by inset screw. Onsets of various shapes of whatever effect the breath control is controlling can be produced by using different consonant sounds to start or interrupt the airstream, with "d," "t," and "k" being traditional on wind instruments. Other consonant sounds can also be used for subtle effects, and the use of "doodle-tonguing" (saying "doodle" to make a more liquid transition between quick successive notes than is possible with the classical "tuh kuh") in jazz brass playing should not go unmentioned. Those who can execute a tongue trill will be able to produce fairly rapid amplitude modulation with the breath controller. Experimentation is in order.

The foot controller is probably not quite as accurately controllable as other real-time devices, but its response is quick, and there can be some crude visual feedback. The use of pressure was discussed earlier, as part of the traditions of the keyboard itself.

In playing and programming continuous controllers, it is important to consider the *timing onset* of the control function. In other words, some programmed functions, like envelope attack time, will necessarily have little or no effect on notes currently sounding; changes will first be heard with the next played note. Also, some control functions on some synthesizers do not upgrade the sound until the next note, even if the effect would have been audible, due to design limitations. Other control functions in the same machine may produce immediate effects, while in other synthesis modules all parameters may upgrade in real time. This distinction has an effect on the optimal playing of continuous controllers, particularly with sustaining sounds.

Occasionally, continuous controllers may be mapped to discrete control functions such as the choice of synthesis algorithm or discrete levels of volume. When this is the case, movement of the controllers must be slow and carefully timed if sonic glitches are not desired.

Finally, the resolution of the ear for the synthesis variable being manipulated may affect needed technique. Most variables are well covered by the common 7-bit resolution of a single MIDI message. However, with medium to high ear-resolution musical functions, some situations may occur where an unwanted graininess of control appears in the sound. This is most commonly apparent with volume changes (controller 7). Pitch bend graininess can also become readily noticeable if the range is set to a large value (six to twelve or more semitones) and the bends are slow. The only solutions for the performer are to play the controller in a way that disguises the synthesis limitation (making changes more slowly in the case of volume, more rapidly in the case of pitch bend) or to decrease the sensitivity of the receiving sound engine to the controlled variable. Other variables that may exhibit aural graininess at 7-bit resolution include frequency ratios between oscillators, filter cutoff frequency, and envelope times (Moog 1986).

DISCRETE CONTROLLERS

Discrete controllers are switches, normally with two states. They do not require any specialized performance techniques; they must simply be pressed at the right time. Most switches, like piano-style foot pedals and program change buttons, are momentary switches, that send the same message or set of messages whenever they are depressed and released. The remainder are toggle switches, which, when successively depressed, alternatively send one of two messages and then the other.

Foot pedals require further comment, partly because they are most commonly used in piano pedal-type function. But their use with synthesizers differs greatly from their use with pianos. Notably, an authentic piano sustain pedal is a continuous controller capable of considerable nuance; not so the sustain pedal switch as implemented on most synthesizers, since it just turns the effect on and off. A few synthesizers have begun to introduce the half-pedal effect, which is helpful, but there is no reason a foot pedal should not be built as a continuous controller to make a full range of nuance possible; as of this writing this is very rare. Likewise, the soft pedal on the piano does have some gradation of effect, although it is not very great on most instruments, so it is most commonly used as a simple switch. On those synthesizers that can respond to this message, playing technique is not much different from that for the piano. Sostenuto pedal technique is a simple switch on the piano, and for those machines that respond to it, an identical technique can be used. Kurzweil has introduced the idea of a "freeze" pedal, which sustains (without change— regardless of normal decay settings) all notes sounding at the time the pedal is depressed.

Foot pedals have other uses, of course. They are frequently available for program change or for turning off and on specific effects like audio processing, portamento, or single-trigger legato.

Program changes require further discussion because what really happens when a program button is pushed can vary from machine to machine. On some devices (notably some master keyboards) a program change will not be implemented until all notes are off and all controllers are at their null state. This means the performer must time note and controller release carefully and not worry about precise timing of the patch change push. More commonly, a patch change overrides whatever is going on at the keyboard, forcing a change of program immediately so that timing of the patch change button push can be very important. On some machines a patch change has the effect of cutting off the existing sound. On others it is possible to hear the previous sound dying away (via the decay portion of its envelope) as the new program is implemented; in some cases, the decay envelope of the final note(s) played before the program change can be lengthened to cover the gap by assigning decay time to a controller. On still other synthesizers (and this is increasingly common), notes held down through the patch changes will continue to produce the old sound until released. These last options avoid possibly unwanted gaps in the sound at each program change. Patch change issues in complex performance systems are discussed in chapter 7.

Some synthesizers, mainly the older analog keyboard types and the woodwind or brass controller types, have dedicated octave switches or transposition buttons, and the use of these in the middle of musical passages does require some careful timing. For the wind instrument player, these will be a familiar part of technique; for the keyboardist, a small amount of practice may be necessary. The use of such octave transpositions can be very helpful in certain musical passages that feature large leaps.

SPECIAL CONTROLLER PERFORMANCE EXERCISES

Coordination with Note Selection

Figure 4.7 contains two exercises for the coordination of controller effects and notes at the keyboard (or nonkeyboard controller). Try these exercises for each kind of continuous controller available in your setup: wheel, joystick, slider, ribbon, breath controller, foot controller, channel pressure, and polyphonic pressure. The controllers should be programmed to produce very large audible effects; master volume or pitch bend at high sensitivity are in particular recommended. The notation indicates depth of controller effect between two lines representing zero and maximum effect. The main point here is to make rapid controller transitions between notes without audible glitches, holding each note as much as possible to full value. In figure 4.7a, the controller must be dropped quickly from full effect to zero just before the start of each note. In figure 4.7b, the controller must change from zero effect to full effect with similar quickness.

Pitch Bend

Pitch bend is probably the single most challenging real-time technique specific to synthesizer performance. Skillful pitch bend performance is based on the ability to produce accurate, musically appropriate, and well-timed intonation. This skill has three components: a correct

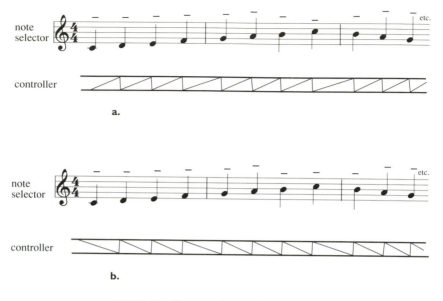

FIGURE 4.7   Exercises for synchronizing note selection with controllers. The controller drops from full effect to zero just before the start of each note (a), and rises from zero to full effect just before the start of each note (b).

conception of the necessary tuning for the piece in question, the ability to hear fine pitch gradations, and manual dexterity in operating the controller. In performance this skill is made more tractable by appropriate programming.

The first skill component is piece-specific and is discussed in chapters 2 and 6. The second and third components are of a technical nature and will be treated here. We turn first to pitch perception, which can be improved by many traditional exercises, including the following.

aural dictation: Identify intervals and notes played or sung by another musician, either live or on recordings. Transcribe musical examples that interest you.

sight-singing: Sing notated but unfamiliar melodies. After singing a piece without accompaniment, sing the piece again and check intonation frequently at the keyboard immediately after or as you sing. Use a sustaining timbre if possible, and strive to eliminate beating effects between your voice and the held tone. Note that there are often different tuning systems in use between single-line instruments and fixed tempered instruments. Hence, use a keyboard tuning system that is relevant for the musical context. (For more on tuning systems, see chapter 6.)

improvisation: Improvise a slowly moving melody, singing the notes as you play them. Again, use an appropriate tuning system. Keyboard, percussion, guitar, and string instruments (or controllers) are most useful here, although woodwind and brass performers can sing through their instruments while playing.

unison singing and playing: Sing or play along with a composed line featuring pitch bend. The line may be recorded on tape, disc, or sequencer. The best sources are often blues-based. The unison vocal and guitar techniques of such performers as Jimi Hendrix and George Benson are also worthy of study.

singing against a drone: Sing all the intervals within the octave in long sustained tones against a sustained drone, beginning with the minor second and progressing to the octave. Sing first without vibrato, and then, if you have such control, with vibrato. Fine tune each note to find where its pitch best sits. The tuning system here will be some form of just intonation since you will be trying to eliminate beating.

listening: Listen to music emphasizing fine pitch control. Two of the best sources are the Indian raga, particularly vocal *alap* (opening) sections, and certain jazz singers such as Sarah Vaughn.

Next we turn to controller dexterity, which requires appropriate physical gestures with the controller and proper coordination with the note-playing hand. The details of finger action in pitch bend are, of course, highly dependent on the physical form of the controller. Most common are wheels, joysticks, and ribbons, with the first two currently dominant. Yet other types of continuous controllers can be routed to pitch bend function in many synthesizers, notably channel and polyphonic pressure, foot controllers, control sliders, and breath controllers. These modulation routings may have different names and be achieved by different software and hardware inside the synthesizer, though these details are not particularly relevant to the performer. I will call such routings *pitch control* or *pitch deflection* when it is necessary to distinguish them from pitch bend. With the use of MIDI mapping devices, virtually any type of control can be routed to pitch bend, including discrete controllers, which do not cause bends but sudden leaps. Pitch bend control produced from these continuous controllers has the limitation of being monopolar, so that bends can only proceed in one direction. However, they can be useful for performing trills, "shakes," or parallel harmonizations over a preprogrammed range.

There are generally two philosophies of pitch bend control. The first and most versatile is to bend to and from definite pitch goals. This philosophy is used when the synthesizer is operating within a grid-like pitch framework in which there are things called notes and scales that represent discrete categories of pitch. Here the pitch bend range is most commonly set to ±2, ±3, or ±4 semitones so that the performer must divide each side of the pitch bend range into at most two, three, or four parts to bend to intervening notes (unless microtones are being used). Given below is a set of exercises providing a comprehensive workout for pitch bend skills for these common ranges. A range of ±2 semitones is the easiest, but it cannot achieve many kinds of effects. (The default range on many synthesizers without programmable pitch bend range is ±2 semitones.) Plus or minus three is quite frequently encountered, as it allows most common bend effects. For those with the full range of effects in mind (notably electric guitar imitation), ±4 semitones, though noticeably more difficult, is the most versatile.

The range of ±1 semitone will not be treated here, as it is rarely encountered, and its use in bending to notes of the chromatic 12-note scale presents no performance problems. In microtonal systems it may be handy, however, and in such cases may reduce to the same physical gestures given here for the other pitch bend ranges. If a range of ±1 semitone is used with quartertone tuning, for example, the bends to quartertones will use the same motion as bends to semitones when pitch bend range equals ±2 semitones. A few synthesizers allow pitch bend range to be set in quartertones (notably some Kurzweil products).

Larger ranges can also be used in this way, but the additional effort required to accurately subdivide a pitch bend controller range of ±5 semitones or greater is rarely worth the trouble. Of course, larger ranges are easy to use if the only pitch goals chosen are the end points of the controller's range; these require no special technical exercises. Likewise, larger ranges are easier if the intervening steps are quantized to semitones; however, this produces a glissando rather than a portamento effect and is hardly the point of pitch bend.

The second pitch bend philosophy operates where there is little concern with note goals—it is more the overall shape of the pitch bend gesture that is important. This will be the case when pitch bend shapes or special "effects," rather than note-oriented melodic motion, are the intended musical result. With this approach, there is no need to limit pitch bend range to small values; larger values (±7 semitones to $\pm$ several octaves) are often more effective, as they may make the shape of the gesture easier to hear. Generally, such effects do not require the refinement of performance skill to anything like the degree required by the first pitch bend philosophy; they are also harder to notate and more dependent on musical context for their correctness. Therefore, I do not consider special technical exercises to be necessary, and this second control philosophy will be looked at in musical passages in chapters 5 and 6.

In general there is more than one possible method of execution for most bend figures. This may be understood by looking at isolated up or down bends. Each of these can always be executed in at least two ways. We will use the terminology of the wheel, with an up-and-down axis of motion, when mention of specific pitch bend device is necessary. If the bend goes from the starting pitch to the goal pitch, then

to bend up:	strike the starting pitch key with wheel in center, then move wheel up to sound goal pitch;
or	strike the goal pitch key with wheel down (sounding starting pitch), then move wheel up to center
to bend down:	strike the starting pitch key with wheel in center, then move wheel down to sound goal pitch;
or	strike the goal pitch key with wheel up (sounding starting pitch), then move wheel down to center.

Consider the whole-tone bends indicated in figure 4.8a, which correspond respectively to these four options. The required played actions are indicated in the upper staff of each system, showing two options in each case. Pitch bend range must be set to at least ± 2 semitones. Deviations to be produced with the pitch bend device are indicated by the numbers of semitones $+$ or $-$ above the notes. In fact, this does not exhaust the possibilities. If pitch bend range is $\pm n$ and the bend has a span of m semitones, then there are $2(n-m)$ additional ways to play any specific bend, for a total of $2(n-m+1)$ possibilities. Figure 4.8b shows additional possibilities introduced when the range expands to at least ± 3 semitones, and figure 4.8c shows the additional options beyond this when pitch bend range increases to at least ± 4 semitones. It should be apparent that these additional fingerings are typically not first choice and are even counter-intuitive since they do not use the zero effect position very often, and effectively require the performer to think in a foreign key. Despite this, they are not without some uses.

Notice that we do not list bending through the center dead zone (dead band), without pausing to sound the middle note, as an option. The reason for this is that the rate of change of pitch cannot be very well controlled here (except when special effects are the intention, typically with larger pitch bend ranges), and this region usually produces an unsatisfactory plateau. A few older synthesizers, like the Minimoog, had no dead band, but this is not typical today.

A warm-up exercise that focuses on the preferred more natural pitch bend fingerings is given in figure 4.9. Here the sound consists of a repeating quarter note, F3, which the performer plays by countering changes in the pitch bend device by striking different keys. The first version is for

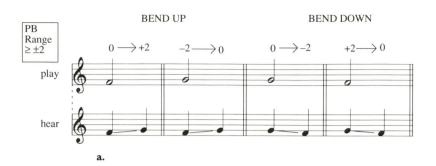

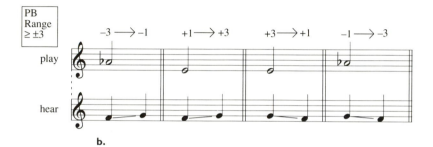

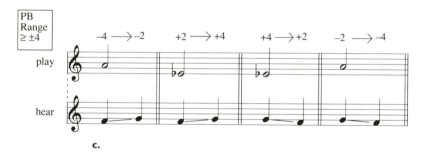

FIGURE 4.8 Twelve ways to perform two pitch bends: with pitch bend range ≥ ± 2 semitones (a); further possibilities with pitch bend range ≥ ±3 semitones (b); still further possibilities with pitch bend range ≥ ±4 semitones (c).

pitch bend range ≥±1 semitone; the successive versions increase the pitch bend range to ≥±2, ±3, and ±4 semitones.

The following exercises are organized to give variety in pitch bend range, direction of movement, polarity (moving above or below null position), and initial position (null or bent). Since they consist of sequences of two to five notes, only the first few motives will be written out in full; the reader should be able to continue the remainder from the indicated

FIGURE 4.9 Pitch bend exercises for a repeated note.

starting motives. The exercises are all based on common scale formations: major, minor, pentatonic, diminished, whole-tone, and augmented. Figure 4.10 gives these as part of a complete list of the tonal scales in common current usage; from these "parent" forms all the familiar and many not-so-familiar modal variants can be derived by starting on a different scale degree but keeping the same pitches (Pressing 1978). The first set of exercises (figure 4.11) is playable by all range settings of ±2 semitones or more, the second (figure 4.12) by all settings of ±3 semitones or more, and the last (figure 4.13) by all settings of ±4 semitones or more. Several different notation systems are used, but they should be transparent to the reader since all intervals are to be bent; notation for pitch bend is discussed more systematically in chapters 5 and 6.

Each of the given exercises can be practiced in a number of ways. First, it may be executed with different settings of pitch bend range since any range greater than or equal to the largest bend can be used. (Sometimes smaller ones can be used as well, if larger bends are capable of being

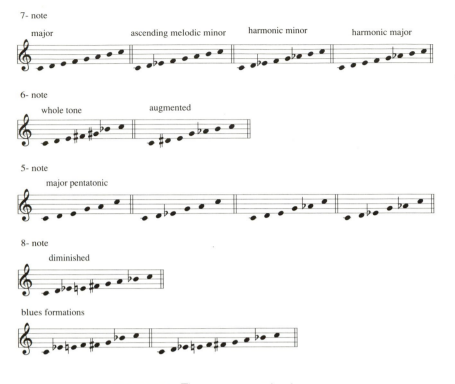

FIGURE 4.10   The common tonal scales.

"faked," or if largest bends can straddle the center position. See chapter 5.) Different ranges will require different physical gestures for the same musical figure. Second, it may be executed on various controllers in so far as more than one type is available (wheel, joystick, and ribbon). If monopolar controllers are used, bipolar bends will require a greater range to execute than monopolar bends and will typically be more difficent to play. Pressure-controlled bending has the further limitation that bends must start and end with zero pitch deflection, unless the sound is rapidly decaying or several keyboard zones are set up interactively (see chapter 6). Third, each exercise may be executed with two or more distinct fingerings (as described above), due to the nature of pitch bend. This requires the performer to think, in principle, in more than one key for each sounding chord. Fourth, different scales may be used, selecting from figure 4.10, with different transpositions and modal forms. Fifth, instead of being executed exactly as written, each exercise may be executed (when practicing) in piecewise alternation with the same figures played without pitch bend.

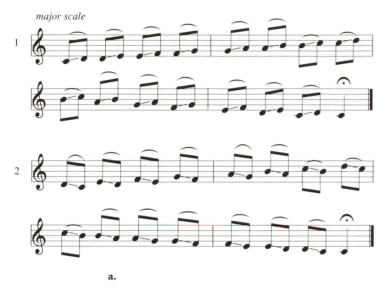

a.

FIGURE 4.11 Pitch bend exercise patterns for pitch bend range ≥ ±2 semitones: two-note patterns (a); three-note patterns (b); four-note patterns (c); five-note patterns (d).

"Piecewise alternation" means that correct pitching is reinforced by playing each motive (small piece) of the passage first by fingering the actual notes at the keyboard, without pitch bend; then the pitch bend version of the same motive is played, and so on. This technique is useful in practicing full musical passages as well: Simply divide a passage into small, musically sensible pieces of perhaps two to five (or more) notes in duration. Try this by performing selected pitch bend exercises (or a melody you know well) in pieces of one or two quarter notes' duration.

The exercises can be varied in yet other ways. One way is by varying the tempo. Another is by changing the rhythm by assigning different durations to the notes. This is important in making the exercises of optimal relevance to real playing conditions and can be achieved as follows. All the exercises consist of two- or three-note units or can be built up from two such units. For each two- or three-note unit, substitute another unit as given in figure 4.14. The same principles will of course work with basic note values other than the eighth note.

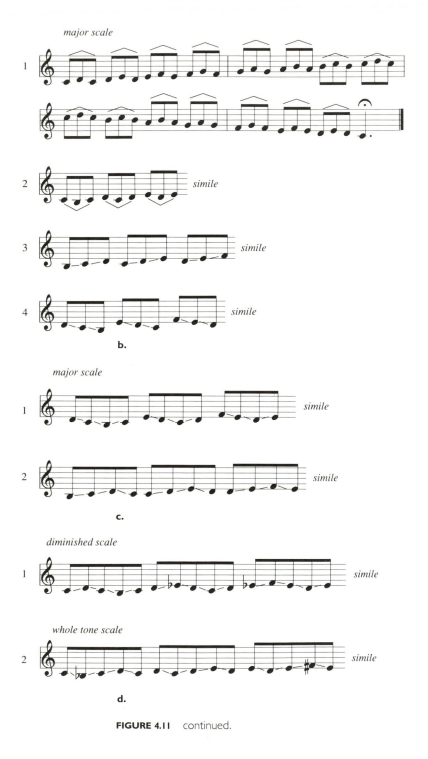

FIGURE 4.11 continued.

a.

b.

FIGURE 4.12 Pitch bend exercise patterns for pitch bend range ≥ ± 3 semitones: two-note patterns (a); three-note patterns (b); four-note patterns (c); five-note patterns (d).

The recommended practice procedure is to choose one pitch bend range and go through a variety of relevant exercises. Stick with this pitch bend range until you have explored it fully, then try another.

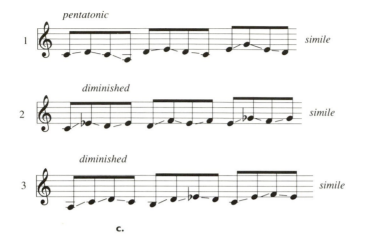

c.

d.

FIGURE 4.12   continued.

a.

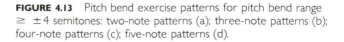

FIGURE 4.13   Pitch bend exercise patterns for pitch bend range
≥ ±4 semitones: two-note patterns (a); three-note patterns (b);
four-note patterns (c); five-note patterns (d).

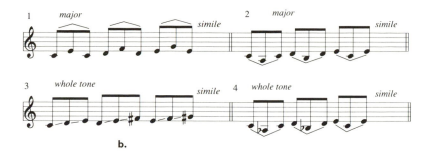

FIGURE 4.13 continued.

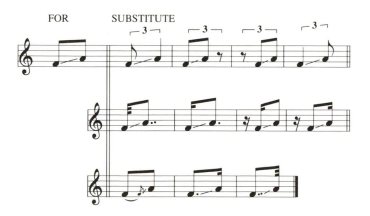

FIGURE 4.14 Substitute rhythmic units for pitch bend exercises.

FOR   SUBSTITUTE

FIGURE 4.14   continued.

REFERENCES

Aikin, J., Anderton, C., Coster, T., Darter, T., De Furia, S., Duke, G., Fryer, T., Gleeson, P., Moog, R., Powell, R., Tomlyn, B. *Synthesizer Technique*. Milwaukee: Hal Leonard, 1987.

Cortot, Alfred. *Rational Principles of Pianoforte Technique*. Trans. R. Le Roy-Métaxas. Paris: Editions Salabert, 1928.

Curcio, Louise. *The Musician's Handbook*. New York: Joseph Patelson Music House, 1968.

Haynes, S. "The Musician–Machine Interface in Digital Sound Synthesis." Ph. D. diss., Southampton University, England, 1979.

Lloyd, Llewelyn, and Hugh Boyle. *Intervals, Scales and Temperaments*. New York: St. Martin's Press, 1978.

McAdams, S. "The Auditory Image." In *Cognitive Processes in the Perception of Art*, ed. W. R. Crozier and A. J. Chapman. Amsterdam: North-Holland, 1984.

Moog, R. "MIDI: Musical Instrument Digital Interface." *Journal of the Audio Engineering Society*. 34,5 (May 1986): 394–404.

Pressing, J. "Towards an Understanding of Scales in Jazz." *Jazzforschung/Jazz Research* 9 (1978): 25–35.

———. "Technique." Monthly column appearing in *Keyboard* magazine, 1987–1991 (ca. 40 articles).

———. "Synthesizer Technique II: The Repeated Note." *Keyboard* 14,1 (January 1988): 107.

PLAYING A SINGLE LINE

. . . .

While the ear can recognize several thousand distinct pitches, less than one hundred can be written on a musical score, and the development of significant musical ideas takes place in a considerably smaller range than this. Although our musical notation is not capable of providing the performer with more than a bare indication of the composer's desire to depart from the set of preferred pitches, players of expressive instruments do regularly make these departures and they constitute an important point of departure from the polyphonic instrument of the organ type [having fixed pitches], and certain types of pitch flexibility are impossible on such a polyphonic instrument, the basic feature of which is the separation of each musical part into discrete tones which are supplied from separate generators. The monophonic instrument is thus the most important musical instrument, and the starting point of all musical thinking; and the polyphonic or organ-like instrument is simply an expedient necessary in view of the difficulty of assembling the required number of monophonic instruments and performers.

- Hugh Le Caine (1956)

Playing a single melodic line is a central skill in synthesis performance, whether it occurs live or as input to a sequencer or audio recorder, for from it parts of any complexity may be assembled, either by overdubbing or ensemble performance. The correct technique for such playing, as we have seen in the last chapter, will depend strongly on the sound and control functions programmed into the synthesizer. The final aural result will also depend on the degree of development of the performer's general musicianship and of the performer's musical conception of the specific piece. In this chapter we focus on the musical issues in synthesizer performance, assuming that technique and programming skills have been developed.

In so doing, I will use a variety of musical styles to emphasize the synthesizer's versatility. This variety will be far from comprehensive, since the synthesizer is so malleable that almost any single-line style—from plainchant to raga to blues to Lieder to hot rock lead—can be imitated, and completely new ones can be conceived. Leads may also have various aesthetic orientations: hot, laid-back, lyrical, sparse, angular, busy, static, and so forth, as may any musical part. In general, the synthesized lead line may follow the expressive traditions of older instruments, follow them only in part, or disregard them entirely.

To keep the discussion as broadly conceived as possible, I will break the musical line down into its fundamental parameters. The plan shall be to discuss these fundamental parameters of musical expression from the standpoint of synthesis and present a number of musical examples that show how the synthesizer performer can control them, basing this on some general and powerful models of instrumental sound production.

What are these fundamental parameters? They include pitch, timing, timbre, dynamics, articulation, and phrasing. In understanding them it is useful to consider each parameter to have macro and micro aspects. By *macro aspects* we mean the level of detail normally found in composed scores and notated improvisations; *micro aspects* are those left unspecified by such sources and therefore handled by the performer's *interpretation.* (Obviously the level of detail can differ from score to score, but it is the norms of contemporary practice we have in mind here.) These micro aspects are often what bring the music to life and are based on controlled (often small) deviations from the notated or literal choices of the parameters, especially with regard to pitch, timing, timbre, and dynamics. Such small deviations can be called *microstructure* or *expressive microstructure* and are critical in many styles of music. In contrast, we may refer to the composed score (or transcribed improvisation) as specifying *macrostructure.* Many micro and macro effects are achievable both by performer actions (real-time synthesis) and preprogramming (fixed synthesis).

There are also aspects of musical expression that do not fall neatly into micro and macro distinctions. These are the underlying musical assumptions of the culture, which typically remain unstated and of which many listeners are not consciously aware. Primary among these are: the timbral choices made available by instrument designers; cultural preferences for sound palette, ensemble types, and methods of musical development; the contexts in which music is presented; and tuning systems. The synthesizer, with its tremendous sonic diversity, forces us to confront these assumptions to a much greater degree than when making music with traditional Western instruments.

REAL-TIME CONTROL OF PITCH

Our survey of the parameters of music in performance begins with pitch. The pitch macrostructure of a given piece of music is formed primarily by the choice of performed notes, and the performing synthesist chooses these from the keyboard or other performance interface. The synthesizer typically tracks the keyboard, selecting the pitch for the triggered note on the basis of the note number. It is also possible on most synthesizers to operate in *fixed-pitch* mode, where the same sound is triggered regardless of MIDI note number selected.

Other pitch effects that are often large enough in scale to feature in scores are glissando and portamento, which are often confused or used interchangeably to refer to pitch movement between notes. Strictly speaking, the *glissando* distinctly (if briefly) sounds all semitones or all of a selection of diatonic tones in the range connecting the two end notes. The true *portamento*, in contrast, is a continuous frequency glide, and the term *glide* is sometimes used as a synonym. Both these effects are achievable either by controller manipulation (e.g., pitch bend) or by fixed programming. The first method is often preferred since it offers better real-time control of rate, but the second is sometimes indispensable, as when the music requires a greater range of pitch sweep than the maximum pitch bend range of ± 12 semitones found on some contemporary synthesizers. With fixed programming, the portamento or glissando function is usually programmed by rate rather than by time, so that the time taken to move from one pitch to the next will depend on both the programmed rate and the intervallic separation of the two notes. Glissando is also achievable directly, by hand action at the keyboard, as well as by MIDI transformation techniques (see chapter 6).

Sustain pedal and finger articulation technique often govern the occurrence of synthesized portamento and glissando. For example, programming may be set so that notes sustained only with the sustain pedal are not affected by portamento, while those held by the fingers are (this is called

sus-key p retain by Yamaha). Another option that occurs, often in monophonic mode, is for the portamento effect to occur only between two
notes that actually connect by overlap-style legato. If staccato, normal, or
even portato touch is used, no portamento effect will occur. This option
goes under such names as *auto-glide* or *fingered portamento*.

Finer pitch control usually falls into the categories of *microtonal inflection* and *vibrato* and may or may not be notated. The first term refers
to slight changes in the pitch of a given note. Microtonal inflection (or
pitch microvariation or *expressive intonation*) may consist of a short tuning correction near the start of the note, a change of pitch on the note
release, fine differences in the steady state pitch of a note each time it is
repeated, or overall qualities of pitch variability for a held tone (e.g.,
so-called *pitch jitter*). In performance, microtonal inflection may be handled by a pitch bend device or other controller, depending on programming.
Or, if microtonal inflection is to be achieved by fixed programming, designs such as frequency modulation by sources of randomness (e.g. noise,
sample-and-hold) or pitch envelope generators are required.

On traditional instruments capable of fine tuning, like the bowed strings
or trombone, intonation is an expressive device of considerable importance. In a wide range of musics, from the Indian raga to the early origins
of Christian plainsong, to blues lines, to gospel singers "worrying" a note,
such detail is of high importance. In the words of cellist Pablo Casals:
"Intellectual awareness, intuitive perception and critical listening all play a
role in the determination of the precise degree to which the instrumen-
talist adjusts his pitch. . . . Expressive intonation, when observed continuously
throughout a composition, becomes a foremost factor in the commmuni-
cation of emotional content" (Blum 1977, pp. 107–108). The synthesizer is
fully capable of projecting this degree of nuance in the single line, but this
potential has been developed by only a small number of performers so far.
Also, pitch bend is primarily a global function on today's synthesizer, and
the synthesis capacity to fine tune each of the notes of, say, a four-note
chord is still rare. Nevertheless, this is more of a practical than a conceptual limitation.

VIBRATO AND PITCH MODULATION

The second kind of fine pitch control, vibrato, is such a
stylized facet of musical expression that it requires special discussion.
Synthesizer vibrato very commonly imitates the musical vibrati found on
different traditional instruments (for a discussion of these nuances see
chapter 8); but of course it is not confined to this. Vibrato of whatever kind

is primarily the result of low frequency modulation of the basic sound. Often there is also some effect due to amplitude modulation, though in general this must be kept limited if an unsuitable tremolo is to be avoided. The balance of these two effects is a programming decision.

Vibrato can be programmed to have a fixed onset and contour with each note, as is sometimes found in commercial samples of breath and string instruments, but more musical versatility will result when real-time control is programmed. Most commonly this is achieved by one of three procedures: controller (normally wheel, joystick, pressure, foot controller, or breath controller) routed to LFO depth, controller routed to pitch deflection, or by the use of a dedicated pitch bend device. No matter which procedure is used, the main factors characterizing vibrato include depth, speed (rate), waveform, regularity, polarity, and onset point, where polarity refers to whether the pitch deviation is to one side of nominal note pitch (monopolar), as on the classical guitar, or on both sides (bipolar), as is common with the human voice. In playing "traditional" vibrato correctly, the performer should bring in the vibrato effect a variable amount of time after the note begins to sound: rather slowly on long notes, more rapidly on medium duration notes, and not at all on passages of quick notes. If, as is preferable, vibrato rate is controllable in real time, a slightly slower than normal rate can be used to good effect at the point of onset, notably for notes of long duration; the rate then speeds up to normal for the style in question. Realism is enhanced if the performer makes continual slight changes in rate and depth.

We examine the LFO method first. In a typical synthesizer configuration, a monopolar modulation controller affects the depth and onset point of LFO-driven vibrato in real time, using either a sine or triangular waveform. The onset phase of the LFO may also have a significant effect, especially where depth is large and rate slow. The LFO's rate is most often fixed, typically in the range of 3 to 8 Hz, with 3.5 to 6 Hz the range most common in synthesis, traditional instruments and the voice. The exact rate depends on style and personal preference. If the frequency drops to about 2.5 Hz or less, the integrated sensation of vibrato tends to be supplanted by noticeable pitch movement of a vibratoless sound. If the applied frequency moves to the range of 12 to 15 Hz or higher (enters the critical band), the sidebands of the modulation process begin to become audible, and the sound changes spectral characteristics, becoming noticeably "buzzy." Vibrato depth commonly varies from the threshold of audibility to 6 percent (approximately a semitone) of the basic frequency. For example, some studies have found a 3 percent depth for violin vibrato and a 6 percent depth for the operatic singing voice (Campbell and Greated 1987). The jazz or commercial singer uses less depth than this, sometimes virtually none. Greater depth than 6 percent tends increasingly towards the effect of rapidly recurring portamento.

Many synthesizers allow modulation rate to be controlled simultaneously in real time by a separate controller, often a slider or foot controller. This is a useful effect, particularly in slow-moving and expressive passages or where the irregularities of realism are to be mimicked. This variability may be approximated via fixed programming by slightly modulating the vibrato-producing LFO's rate with another LFO, noise, or a sample-and-hold source. In many commercial styles, such subtlety may be less essential.

The second method of vibrato production routes a controller to pitch deflection, a possibility increasingly available on contemporary synthesizers. As described in chapter 4, this is a synthesis function independent of pitch bend and often having a greater range, although its effect can be very much like pitch bend, or portamento when pronounced. Like pitch bend, this technique has the advantage that, as on an acoustic instrument, the degree of micropitch variation is directly controllable by physical contact rather than indirectly through the use of a low frequency oscillator. This improved directness of control gives improved realism of expression. In terms of vibrato production in performance, it differs from the pitch bend method (discussed in the next paragraph) primarily in the fact that it has no dead zone, and the controller usually provides only monopolar action. The lack of dead zone is a plus, but monopolar action means that this method can be successful only with a vibrato that is not too deep. Otherwise the perceived center pitch will become noticeably sharp or flat, depending on programmed direction of pitch deflection—unless, of course, the bend effect is treated like pitch bend and a key above or below the goal note is struck, with appropriate controller deflection, a rather uncommon procedure so far. One reason this may be uncommon is that the controller usually available for this technique is pressure, so that any bend must start from zero deflection. However, this can be overcome if the key is struck and pushed down hard so that the quick bend to starting pitch becomes virtually inaudible. Pressure is otherwise a very comfortable controller for vibrato, as it allows the performer to use a kind of gentle rocking or bouncing with the hand common with stringed instruments.

The third option, chosen by a minority of synthesists, uses pitch bend itself for vibrato production. This procedure has somewhat limited applicability with the most common dedicated pitch bend devices, the wheel or joystick, because they normally contain a dead zone in the middle, designed to give the performer some leeway in returning the wheel to its zero effect position. If the performer tries to achieve bipolar vibrato around the null pitch bend position by rocking the wheel or lever back and forth, the flat portion of the pitch change corresponding to the dead zone normally destroys the suitability of the effect. On the other hand, if monopolar vibrato is musically desirable, this approach can be very effective.

However, pitch bend vibrato with wheels and joysticks can be quite generally successful when preceded by a pitch bend that takes the device away from its null position. Since the pitch bend device has left the dead zone range, a slight wobble around the new "correct" position will produce a successful bi- or monopolar vibrato, although the performer must give special attention to avoid drifting away from the correct center pitch during the course of the wobble. When correctly played, this is the most expressive type of synthesizer vibrato.

Some pitch bend devices are particularly well suited to this technique. A few synthesizers, for example, have bipolar sliders or wheels without dead zones, routable to pitch bend. The appropriate performance gesture is then the wiggle, shake, or gentle rock. Yet the best controller for pitch bend function vibrato in many ways is the ribbon controller. The physical gestures required here are those of a bowed or plucked string instrument, and these gestures can be readily mastered. Unfortunately, the trend in modern synthesizers is away from ribbons; older analog machines by Moog and Buchla used to have them as a standard feature. Some strap-on keyboards, and specialized ancillary performance devices like the Tripp Strip, have kept this tradition alive.

OTHER PITCH AND AMPLITUDE MODULATION EFFECTS

Vibrato is only one kind of pitch modulation, achieved when the parameters of a periodic modulation source fall in certain ranges. The results of other types of modulation sources and parameter ranges are very usable yet often have no simple description in traditional musical terms. If, for example, the modulation source is a noise generator and the modulation target a sample of a fork falling on a table, the sound may be something like a grainy irregular collision of metal and wood. It is clear that traditional notation and theory will have little to say about how such a sound can be used musically. On the other hand, some sets of sources, targets, and parameter ranges produce musical effects for which names other than vibrato apply. These relate primarily to LFOs modulating oscillators. For example, square wave subaudio or low audio frequency modulation produces a trill or tremolo, depending on the modulation depth. The depth of the effect must be carefully set if the two pitches are to be in tune with the prevailing musical background. Sample-and-hold modulation produces a string of random pitches (not in tune with traditional tempered tuning) at regular time intervals. LFO modulation above about 50 Hz yields a characteristic rough sound a little like the growl on wind instruments achieved by singing through the instrument as it is played. These effects are commonly used in the same way as the traditional musical function they imitate most closely. But they can also be played in novel ways to create vibrantly active electronic textures or outrageously virtuosic single lines, most easily when waveform, speed, and depth can be chosen in real time. See "Examples of Single Line Performance Techniques" for a notated example of such effects.

Amplitude modulation by LFOs produces an analogous range of effects, but amplitude rather than frequency is affected. The main parameters affecting the resultant sound are depth, rate, waveform, regularity, and onset point. LFO modulation by waveforms that do not have sharp rises, such as sine, triangle, and sawtooth down, will produce various kinds of tremolo when the frequency is below about 12 Hz; as rates increase beyond this point, a buzziness or graininess becomes increasingly significant, regardless of waveform. Below about 12 Hz, for waveforms with sharp rises, such as square, pulse, sample-and-hold, and sawtooth up, amplitude modulation of sufficient depth will effectively produce repeated notes at the LFO frequency. Real-time control of rate, depth, onset point, and regularity can produce a wide range of effects. Sample-and-hold modulation is a particularly interesting case from this standpoint.

TIMING

Musical timing is controlled primarily by the note selection interface, though controller effects must also be correctly timed. The primary concepts include pulse, meter, rhythm, synchronization, subdivision, polyrhythm, syncopation, rubato, and swing, among others. These phenomena differ little, in performance, from their customary usages in nonsynthesized music, and therefore most require no detailed comment beyond emphasizing the cardinal importance of accurate timing. Sequencers and computer-controlled systems, of course, can achieve an accuracy and complexity of rhythmic execution that far exceed what human performers can do; but this is not our main focus here.

Two of these concepts do require examination, however, because they are used in conflicting ways by differently trained traditional musicians, and the synthesist, because of the instrument's versatility, may be called on to straddle conflicting traditions. First, rubato. *Rubato* is the systematic speeding up or slowing down from notated durations or steady pulse in one or more parts of a piece of music. In song-form-based jazz and commercial music, rubato that actually changes the tempo is comparatively rare, occurring primarily in song introductions and endings. Rubato effects on a foreground vocal or instrumental line do occur, but only over a steady rhythm section tempo. In classical music, in contrast, rubato is employed extensively to support cadences, emphasize the expressiveness of a lead line, and mark phrase structure. This typically occurs as a decelerando at the ends of phrases, with a return to original tempo at the start of the next phrase. Another way to put this is that timing is pulse-driven in jazz and rock music but phrase-driven in classical or "art" music.

These different traditions are responsible, more than anything else, for the difficulties that classical and jazz musicians have in playing with each other. As an ensemble member, the maximally versatile synthesist must be able to play off a well-grounded rhythm section tempo as well as follow the rubato tempo map of a conductor or specified lead line player. As featured soloist, the synthesist must be able to lead others on the basis of these contrasting protocols.

Second, we look at *swing*, a complex phenomenon, common in tune-based jazz, that entails "activating" a melodic line by increasing the duration of notes on the beat in relation to those between beats, while accenting these offbeats dynamically. Certain characteristic articulation patterns form part of the vocabulary, and offbeat phrasing is used. Sometimes the timing of the line shows consistent slowing down or speeding up in relation to the underlying pulse (followed by realignment). There is little in print that really elucidates this term well, though Giuffre (1969) makes perhaps the most precise attempt for the performer; this skill must be gained by aural tradition. The term *swing* can also refer to precisely consistent rhythmic coordination between members of a group. In the first case the melodic line is said to swing, whereas in the second it is the band that swings.

TIMBRE

Timbre may be controlled by fixed programming or real-time programming and performance. The possibilities are so vast that no generalizations about it are worth much, beyond the discussion given in chapter 2 and the observation that the most common parameters of real-time timbral change available on synthesizers are those associated with brightness/filtering, modulation, envelope characteristics, and the amplitude of components. The most expressive traditional instruments, like the violin and electric guitar, can produce tremendous variability in all these parameters. In traditional music scores, timbre is at best very crudely indicated, rarely going further than the use of mutes and a few special markings. In much contemporary art music, the level of detail has increased considerably. The synthesist, lacking clear traditions of instrumental performance, must program in both macro and micro changes in timbre, letting the ear be the guide, if the synthetic sound is to approach the variety of color that acoustic instruments possess.

DYNAMICS, ACCENT, AND STRESS

Control of dynamics is perhaps the area most neglected by the novice synthesizer performer. The meaning of this term is best clarified by distinguishing here dynamics from amplitude (volume). *Amplitude (volume)* change alters the loudness of all components of the sound equally. It refers to the overall sonic level or the amount of gain applied to a signal. The term *dynamics,* on the other hand, refers to the changes that occur when a traditional instrument is played with increased intensity (or force). The sound becomes louder, but its timbre also changes in tandem, usually by becoming spectrally brighter and being governed by more quickly rising attack portions of its overall or component envelopes. Brass instruments provide a clear example. They become brighter with increasing volume (Dodge and Jerse 1985).

Real-time control of dynamics requires programming of key velocity or some continuous controller to affect the variables just mentioned. Which type of control is preferable depends on whether the sound is sustaining or decaying: Key velocity is most appropriate for decaying sounds, a continuous controller for sustaining sounds (although key velocity is often used here as well). Key velocity does not allow crescendo or decrescendo within a note but only within a series of notes. With controller-programmed dynamics, control can be effected at any point. Dynamic control can also be allocated to more than one source: two controllers or key velocity plus controller.

When a note is played at a greater dynamic level (or volume) than its surroundings, we have *stress.* This is different from *accent,* which simply means emphasis. The reason they are different is that accent can come from sources of emphasis other than stress: lengthened duration (*agogic accent*), small delays or anticipations in the placement of a note, a preceding interval of silence, pitch ornamentation, timbral changes, and others.

ARTICULATION AND PHRASING

Articulation refers to the manner in which successive notes are joined to one another by a performer (Fallows, Lindley, and Wright 1984). Such joining necessarily involves the beginnings (attacks) and ends (decays) of notes, and is expressed by musical terms such as legato, staccato, and tenuto. These three words are somewhat arbitrary signposts on a large proving ground of possibilities, as can be clearly heard in expressive performance in any style. But, simply, *legato* means that adjacent notes are connected. What exactly is meant traditionally by connection varies from instrument family to instrument family and is discussed further below. *Staccato* means that the notes are short and unconnected. *Staccatissimo* means even shorter than this. *Tenuto* means that a note should be held to its full value but not connected to the next note. (It is also sometimes considered to mean a slight accent, and has further subtleties of interpretation that are specific to individual instruments, but we will not treat these subtleties here.) The term *portato,* used notably on string instruments, means "something intermediate between legato and staccato," and is achieved by playing short notes but not changing bow direction. No marking at all means that the note is neither short nor connected, and in practice this might mean that it lasts anything from 60 to 95 percent of its notated value. The main point is that keyboard articulation can be strongly affected by the envelopes used in sythesized sound. For example, an exaggerated legato technique is often required for sounds with long attack times. An exaggerated staccato may be needed for notes with built-in reverberation (medium to long release times).

Phrasing, a term based on the analogy of music to language, refers to the connection between larger groups of notes. It is accomplished by the conceptual joining together of notes into larger units via shared patterns of articulation, dynamics, and timbre.

NOTATION FOR SYNTHESIZER

Notation for the synthesizer is by no means standardized. This is particularly true of performance on the ancillary controllers and is hardly surprising considering the continual rush of new products to the marketplace. However, nearly all parts written for it can be scored using the three major written sources of Western culture: classical notation, jazz (and commercial) notation, and contemporary notational innovations by twentieth-century composers. We will survey the most commonly used systems here and make some suggestions.

The few sources that treat the problem of synthesizer notation are in contemporary keyboard and guitar magazines, such as *Keyboard, Guitar Player,* and *Modern Keyboard,* and some transcriptions of albums by notable artists in this field, such as Aikin et al. (1987), Corea (1986), and Marshall (1988), the last two presenting detailed legends for pitch bend and modulation usage. Jimi Hendrix's solo sections to *Purple Haze* are transcribed for synthesizer in Doyle (1989).

Other transcription sources that are useful are those of ethnomusicologists describing the many unfamiliar tuning, timing, timbral, and articulatory nuances of the musics of many different cultures. This is a vast literature, which may be initially contacted through the journal *Ethnomusicology* or the classic texts by Hood (1982), which has a useful survey of notations, and Nettl (1983).

For a look at the tremendous variety of contemporary music notation innovations, the reader should consult Karkoschka (1972), Read (1974), Cole (1974), Rissatti (1975), Schäffer (1976), Gaburo (1977), Stone (1980), and Burton (1982). A few sample scores of electronic music notation are given in Karkoschka's book, and a discussion of the analysis of electronic music via notation is given by Fennelly (1976). For a listing of notated scores for the synthesizer the reader is referred to chapter 7. The usefulness of many of these scores is sometimes compromised by their having been written specifically for equipment that is now obsolete.

In synthesizer notation, one staff usually suffices for a single line, with two staves required for more complex parts, and possibly three or even more for multikeyboard setups. Figure 5.1 presents the most common notational practices for note articulation and controller performance. It will be readily seen that many of these follow standard jazz notational conventions.

For vibrato, where it is indicated at all, the most common system is to draw its shape schematically above (or occasionally below) the notehead, similar to a trill without the opening *tr*. This allows depth, onset point, and speed to be schematically shown as necessary. For other continuous controller effects, one system is a band of variable thickness, above or below the notes, that indicates the depth of the effect. An alternative notation is to put an auxiliary staff made up of two (for monopolar controllers) or three (for bipolar controllers) dotted lines above the notated music, as shown in the figure. For discrete controllers, on and off points need to be indicated for momentary switches, depression points alone for toggle switches. To show the fine-time behavior of any of these effects, held notes may need to be written as tied groups notes of shorter duration.

The notation for pitch bend requires more detailed discussion since alternative notations abound. The following methods seem most common: (1) portamento markings between noteheads; (2) horizontal lines or arrows above or below the notes; (3) vertical arrows above or below the notes; (4) use of a separate (possibly smaller) additional staff to show fingerings and controller actions.

Examples of these notations used with the same musical excerpt are shown in figure 5.2. Of these, the most common methods seem to be numbers 1 and 2. Method 1 has the advantage of precision and correspondence with traditional notation, but portamento markings can be troublesome to read when they habitually cover small intervals, as is normal in pitch bend. Method 2 seems to be used increasingly in commercial publications and has the advantage of clarity and simplicity. It has limita-

FIGURE 5.1   A lexicon of single line synthesizer notation.

tions, however, in not being able to show enough detail about the bending of individual notes in some situations, as for example when one note bends in a chord but the others do not. Of the two options presented, method 2a seems simpler and has the advantage that it will not be confused with a notation used by some ethnomusicologists and jazz transcribers for slight note displacements, that is, a horizontal arrow over the notehead, showing delay if pointing to the right, anticipation if pointing to the left.

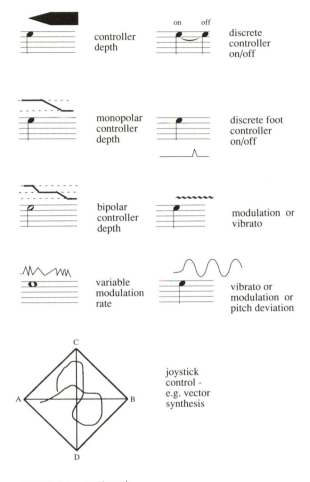

FIGURE 5.1 continued.

Method 3 occurs only infrequently and is not generally recommended for synthesizer notation; it is, however, the method used in indicating micro-tonal inflection in some jazz and ethnomusicological transcription, and it may be usefully co-opted when the synthesist performs that sort of action. In such cases, the arrow is always put on top, and the length of it may show the extent of the microtonal bend. A separate example using this notation is given in figure 5.3. Method 4 is somewhat cumbersome since it requires two staves per melodic line, but it is the only method that shows how the bend is actually to be executed, both in terms of fingering and the explicit time shape used on the controller. Although this system is rare in synthe-sizer writing, a closely related use occurs in certain texts on interpretation

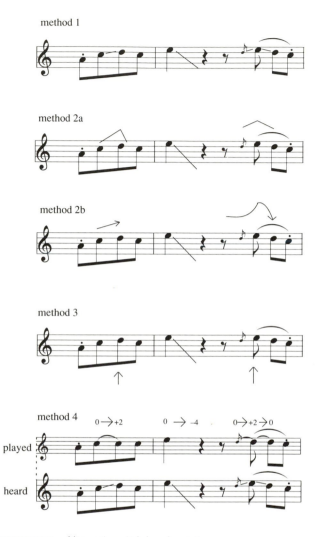

FIGURE 5.2   Alternative pitch bend notations.

FIGURE 5.3   Notation for microtonal inflection.

(e.g., Giuffre 1969) and in composers' use of *ossia* (alternative versions of certain passages). We will use a mixture of systems, as appropriate; methods 1 and 2 will be preferred, with method 4 used when the actual actions of the performer's hand need to be shown.

MUSICAL EXPRESSION

All the parameters above affect musical expression, a term defined in chapter 1. Behind this term lie many effects that music can create but that words cannot easily convey. Part of music's indescribability lies in the integrated quality of the musical statement, the "rightness" of it, its "authenticity," the difference between a mechanical and an inspired performance. These are the nuances that bring the music to life. Such success comes not only from the performer's musical sensitivity but from concern for detail, sympathy with the musical goals that are implied by the material in question, and appropriate hard work. Much of this lies in the correct use of microstructure in performance. When this expressive detail applies to a single line, we may use the term *line expressivity*. The word *interpretation* is closely related when referring to notated music.

It must be acknowledged that some music, notably a substantial body of music for synthesizers, makes only limited use of some of these expressive microvariables in performance. In a part that imitates a repeating percussion figure or an underlying vamp, there may be little need for dynamic variation or rubato, for example. Some synthesizer voices also evolved to commercial familiarity in an age before key velocity sensitivity was common and work best without it. However, this is true of a minority of sounds; other programs fail to develop their full potential because they lack correctly expressive programming or performance. In general, such sound design is a critical part of successful synthesizer performance.

THE SYNTHETIC IMPLEMENTATION OF EXPRESSIVITY

How then is the synthesizer performer to reproduce these shades and nuances of expression? There is no one answer to this question; rather, the best strategy in each case will depend on the musical demands of the particular piece.

There are, however, a number of useful guidelines, many based on the study of expressivity on traditional instruments. We start by characterizing all sounds as either decaying or sustaining. *Decaying sounds* eventually decay to zero; *sustaining sounds* have a nonzero steady state. On all acoustic decaying instruments, the time taken to decay to the background noise level depends on the register of the pitch: Low notes last longer than high notes. Most synthesizers allow this effect to be mimicked. Second, all traditional instruments are either monophonic, partially polyphonic, or fully polyphonic, where *partially polyphonic* instruments can sound only a severely limited number of notes simultaneously and *fully polyphonic* instruments have no limit as far as normal musical textures are concerned. Thus, the piano is a decaying fully polyphonic instrument, the saxophone is a sustaining monophonic instrument (excluding multiphonic techniques), the guitar is a partially polyphonic decaying instrument, and the synthesizer is a partially polyphonic or monophonic instrument that may be either decaying or sustaining.

The usefulness of these classifications is that many of the central parameters of expressivity and interpretation—dynamics, articulation, and timbre—in fact, everything except the fine details of timing and tuning, depend critically on them. Consider decaying instruments: such things as pianos, dulcimers, guitars, marimbas, gongs, and percussion instruments of all kinds. The amplitude of a note played on such an instrument is based on the force with which it is struck or otherwise set in vibration, and its timbre is based on the nature of that same attack (type of material, type of stroke, etc.). Unless a special technique such as rubbing, which allows continuous excitation, is used, no further control is possible after the instrument is set in motion, except through another attack. A more technically precise term for such sound production might be *one-shot excitation*. Hence in terms of synthesis, information at the start of the note—notably key velocity—can convincingly select both dynamics and timbre of the sound without substantial degradation of the performance information. In contrast, a sustaining sound such as a note played on the trumpet or arco violin entails the *continuous excitation* of the resonating object(s). Therefore, dynamics and timbre can be changed at any instant, not only at the note onset. In synthesis, key velocity, a one-shot burst of information, cannot possibly supply the right kind of current information to achieve continuous expressivity; one or more continuous controllers must be used.

The effect of the monophonic–polyphonic distinction is related much more to articulation and in particular the way legato is achieved. On a fully polyphonic instrument, legatoness can always be achieved by temporal overlap of adjacent notes. We call this *overlap legato*. Figure 5.4b shows how overlap legato is achieved with the decaying sound of figure 5.4a. On a monophonic instrument, and in many musical situations on a limited polyphonic instrument, this will not be possible. Instead, the notes are played tenuto, but without a special onset attack noise (often called *chiff*).

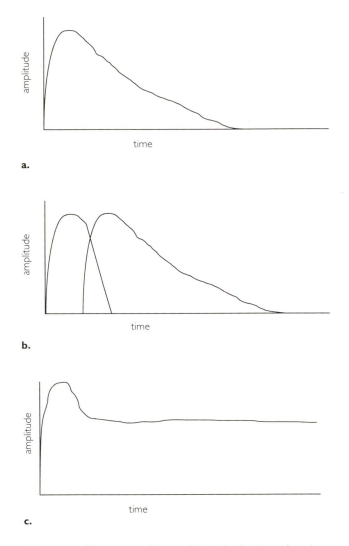

FIGURE 5.4 Two types of legato. In overlap legato, a decaying envelope sound (a) achieves legato by note overlap (b). In nonchiff legato, a nonlegato sustaining envelope sound (c) is modified by the performer to reduce its attack transients (d), producing the effect of legato with an adjacent note (e).

This performance technique may therefore be called *nonchiff legato*, or *attack attenuation legato*. In woodwinds and brass this attack noise comes from retonguing the note, usually with a "t," "k," or "d" phoneme, depending on the passage and interpretive tradition. In string instruments, chiff

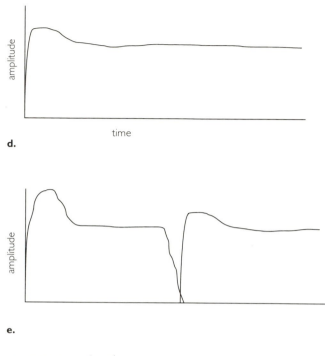

d.

e.

FIGURE 5.4   continued.

comes from a change in bow direction or, much less commonly, from a strong reattack in the same bow direction. On the guitar, it is the noise of the pluck. Figure 5.4c shows a sustaining envelope sound and how it is modified to produce legato (figure 5.4d). Figure 5.4e shows how this type of nonlegato note connects to a following legato note.

PRIMARY PERFORMANCE MODELS

If these two classifications are combined, we get four sonic possibilities and four resulting performance models: decaying mono-phonic, decaying polyphonic, sustaining monophonic, and sustaining polyphonic. These classifications are far from being equally common. Mono-phonic melody instruments, in particular, are nearly always sustaining, while polyphonic melody instruments, with some notable exceptions like the accordian and organ, are mostly decaying. This leads to our being able to define two primary performance models based on traditional instrument characteristics. These performance models will be widely applicable. The first is the decaying polyphonic model; the second, the sustaining monophonic model. The *decaying polyphonic model* uses key velocity for all note-by-note dynamic effects including crescendo, decrescendo, and stress; it uses overlap legato (by fingering and use of the pedal) for note connection. The *sustaining monophonic model* uses continuous controllers for dynamic (and timbral) effects and nonchiff legato for note connection. We define the less common *sustaining polyphonic model* as a secondary model, requiring dynamics to be shaped by controller, legatoness by note overlap.

There is a bias in the programming implementation of these models. The decaying polyphonic model is the most natural for the keyboardist since the piano is such a well-known example of it. That model is frequently found in commercial synthesizer programming even for sustaining sounds, partly through ignorance and partly because it can be successful in a number of situations such as short punchy figures, staccato passages, or where electronic nonimitative timbres are used. But its limitation becomes quite apparent when it is realized that it is impossible to crescendo a held note (without assigning additional controller functions).

The sustaining monophonic model requires more conceptual adaptation for the keyboard performer. Here dynamics must be routed to a continuous controller of some type, such as a standard MIDI controller or a data entry slider, if things like crescendi and decrescendi within a note are to be accomplished. It can be best to use no key velocity sensitivity at all in programming the dynamics of such voices, unless the part consists largely of notes of short duration, since the instrument's ability to control timbre and legatoness after onset will be diminished by whatever such control is allocated to key velocity. An alternative is to choose to distribute aspects of dynamic control across both velocity and a continuous controller.

Although in principle any continuous controller can work, the most versatile choices are those that will allow both slow and rapid dynamic change, enabling not only crescendo and decrescendo but accents and the execution of figures like *fp*. The best controller for this purpose, in many ways, is the breath controller. Unfortunately, this is available only on Yamaha synthesizers (and the Synclavier) and is seldom used in any case to its full potential, partly because synthesizer players have predominantly been keyboardists and are not used to breath control. The other controllers can also be quite effective, with wheels, joysticks, foot controllers, sliders, pressure, and ribbons all usable. The foot controller is probably the least reliable due to its relatively poor sensory feedback; if not used with great care, it can cause balance problems in live performance. Pressure is sometimes not a plausible choice because it must start and end with zero effect: To avoid extraneous crescendi at the start of notes and decrescendi at their ends, the performer must play with quite a sudden, hard touch. Of course, if the volume effects desired occur only after note onset, then pressure could be ideal.

Articulation in this model is based on both finger action (the pedal can be used only with great caution, to avoid note overlap) and control of chiff. Staccato is primarily a finger effect. To achieve legato, chiff may be turned off by continuous controller or, since it is largely an on–off phenomenon, by discrete controller (button or foot switch) or key velocity. Although all three are usable, the quick response and link to note depression makes key velocity the control variable of choice. This performance design does, however, require a different attitude to keyboard technique. It can seem quite unnatural at first to select articulation by striking the key harder while controlling dynamics with, shall we say, the modulation wheel. In many ways this is the best system, however, and it can be essential on some synthesizers that have a very limited number of assignable paths from the control sources to the dynamics of the sound components. The only minor disadvantage with this setup is that it can sometimes be difficult to play rapid passages completely detached (achieved by using consistently high key velocities). Just how troublesome this can be depends to some degree on the built-in velocity response curves of the synthesizer in question.

The two primary performance models are compared schematically in figure 5.5; sample implementations are given in the right-hand columns. Shading indicates viable control sources. To summarize, sounds corresponding to the decaying envelope model can be played like a modified piano, while the sustaining case requires one continuous controller for dynamics (with breath controller, modulation wheel, joystick, slider, data entry control, and foot controller all possible, roughly in decreasing order of suitability), the use of nonlegato keyboard touch, and key velocity or a second independent controller (continuous or discrete) for articulation changes.

There are actually two other useful ways to achieve legatoness in many circumstances. The first is to use very quick pitch bends in imitation of portamento-based legato as found on an instrument like the trombone. If the first of two legato-connected notes is played, followed by a very quick (hence virtually inaudible) pitch bend to the second, then there will be no extra attack on the second note, effectively producing legato of the non-chiff type. Impressive realism can be achieved with very simple sound sources with this technique. Figure 5.6 illustrates the concept. Its main limitation is that it is not available between arbitrary notes and ranges but must carefully negotiate the limits of pitch bend use. But with careful planning, this can be widely useful. We will refer to this technique as *pitch bend legato*.

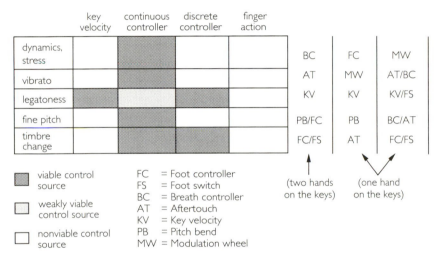

DECAYING POLYPHONIC MODEL

	key velocity	continuous controller	discrete controller	finger action
dynamics, stress	▓			
vibrato		▓		
legatoness			▓	▓
fine pitch		▓		
timbre change	▓	▓	▓	

EXAMPLES

key velocity

aftertouch/mod wheel

fingering/sustain pedal

pitch bend device

slider or switch

SUSTAINING MONOPHONIC MODEL

	key velocity	continuous controller	discrete controller	finger action			
dynamics, stress		▓			BC	FC	MW
vibrato		▓			AT	MW	AT/BC
legatoness	▓	░	▓		KV	KV	KV/FS
fine pitch		▓			PB/FC	PB	BC/AT
timbre change		▓	▓		FC/FS	AT	FC/FS

(two hands on the keys)   (one hand on the keys)

▓ viable control source

░ weakly viable control source

☐ nonviable control source

FC = Foot controller
FS = Foot switch
BC = Breath controller
AT = Aftertouch
KV = Key velocity
PB = Pitch bend
MW = Modulation wheel

FIGURE 5.5 The two primary performance models, with an indication of viable control sources.

The second option was first mentioned in the last chapter. This is the use of single trigger mode on monophonic synthesizers (*single trigger mode legato*), which produces a quasi-legato effect by omitting early portions of the envelope (and hence chiff) when overlap legato is played at the keyboard. Note that although the physical key depressions overlap, the sound never does, as it is strictly monophonic. It is now possible on some synthesizers to quickly switch such legatoness on and off via legato foot switch, controller number 68.

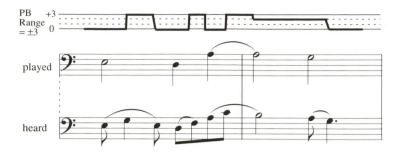

FIGURE 5.6   Pitch bend legato.

The remaining secondary sound model found significantly on traditional instruments is that of sustaining polyphonic instruments. The organ, melodica, harmonium, and accordian are best known in Western culture. Here legatoness is determined by fingered note overlap and sustain pedal, and dynamics by continuous controller. Sounds that have organ-like timbre are often played this way. Since these parts are polyphonic, a nonhand controller must usually be used for dynamics, with foot controller, breath controller and pressure being most common. Sustain and sostenuto pedals can be used profitably here, even though they are not available on the traditional instruments whose design is being mimicked.

EXAMPLES OF SINGLE LINE PERFORMANCE TECHNIQUES

To play the examples given in this section, first implement the two primary performance models (decaying polyphonic, sustaining monophonic) and the secondary model (sustaining polyphonic) on whatever synthesizers or samplers you have available. In the decaying polyphonic model, route key velocity to control dynamics: Volume and brightness (e.g., filter cutoff on a low pass filter, feedback, upper harmonics) should increase with key velocity, while attack time should decrease (if such control is available) on at least some sound components. If some of these aspects of sound, for example the attack time, are not directly controllable, their impact can be simulated to some degree by using key velocity to increase the volume of a component that has a short attack time.

In the sustaining monophonic model, find a combination of key velocity and continuous controllers, or several controllers, that is effective for you. The recommended starting point is key velocity for articulation control and continuous controller (breath or wheel or joystick) for dynamics. Use these to imitate expressive lines played by strings or brass. The controller for dynamics should (as above) optimally control volume, brightness, and attack time, either directly or by affecting the amplitude of components with those qualities. For articulation, use key velocity or a discrete or continuous controller to make legato and nonlegato audible by controlling the amplitude of a short and appropriately noisy transient.

Then implement the secondary model, as described earlier in this chapter. Of course, you will have many sounds not reducible to these basic models, and you should try these as well to see how well they are able to achieve the effects required in the examples.

The first six examples all contain significant pitch bend. Figure 5.7 is a rock-style bass line with pitch bend (indicated by portamento) and vibrato (indicated by a modulation symbol above some notes). It should sound one or two octaves below the written pitch. Use a pitch bend range of ± 3 (or possibly ± 4) semitones and LFO modulation cued to modulation wheel or pressure. Figure 5.8 presents a simple diatonic melody emphasizing articulation and dynamics effects, for which the sustaining monophonic model is appropriate. Quite a different sort of example suited to the same model is found in figure 5.9. This is in a contemporary art music style, with large leaps, as might be played on a violin. It poses several problems. First of all, the large leaps mean that two hands should be used. This means that dynamics must be handled by something like a foot controller. Second, the articulations are quite variable and will require careful attention to detail. Third, the tremolo figure at the end can be executed in various ways: by fingering the notes, playing an octave tremolo for simplicity, switching to a sampled repeated note sound, or trilling between the Bb3 key and some other key, like Db4, that does not occur elsewhere in the passage, tuned to the pitch Bb3. A square-wave-based amplitude modulation effect is even possible, though not if this is to sound like a traditional instrument.

A blues and guitar-based passage is shown next in figure 5.10. This will require a pitch bend range of at least ± 2 semitones. The motive in bar 4 is a well-known figure borrowed from guitar playing. Figure 5.11 shows a more extended lead pattern composed in jazz-rock ballad style. Pitch bend range of ± 2 semitones will suffice here.

When learning to play and improvise in the style of such lines, it is well to explore alternate bend fingerings, as discussed in chapter 4, and also to play the progression in keys that are one to several semitones sharp and flat of the actual passage. This second skill is useful in situations where, after a bend away from center position, the passage continues with notes without any pause to return the wheel to null position. The pitch bend controller is therefore held in its displaced position, and the performer

FIGURE 5.7   Rock electric bass line featuring pitch bend and LFO modulation.

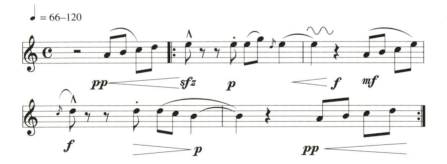

FIGURE 5.8   Diatonic melody emphasizing articulation and dynamic variation.

must transpose the part by the interval of the pitch bend device, but in the opposite direction. For example, if the range is ±2 semitones and the pitch bend device is at full positive deflection with a C chord sounding, the performer must play in the key of B♭. If half negative deflection is being held, the player must play in the key of D♭.

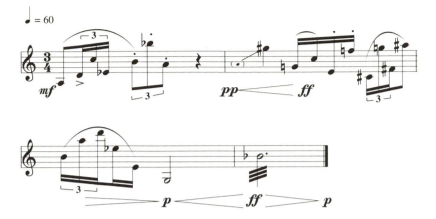

FIGURE 5.9 Contemporary violin-like passage emphasizing leaps, dynamic variation, and tremolo.

The pitch bend ranges chosen for such lead examples are a personal matter, as discussed in chapter 4. Where pitch bending to specific goal tones is the norm, the ranges ±2, ±3, and ±4 semitones are by far the most widely used. On a number of machines, or with any machine and the aid of a MIDI mapping device, different pitch bend ranges can be set for bends above zero and below zero.

It should always be remembered, of course, that pitch bend of intervals greater than the range can be "faked," often very convincingly. Figure 5.12 shows how. The performer simply bends as much of the distance as the pitch bend allows and just at that instant releases the initial key and strikes a key corresponding to the final pitch goal (with pitch bend at full deflection). In this example the goal is B♭, five semitones from the starting key F. Just as the upward bend runs out of steam, the A♭ is struck, approximating the impression of pitch bend to B♭.

Pitch bend can also be used to create *harmonic thickening*. In this case, the single line controls two or more sound modules that are set to have different pitch bend ranges. For example, if two modules are controlled, one with pitch bend range of 0 and the other with range of ±7, then when the bender is full up the line will be harmonized in fifths above, and when it is full down the line will be a harmonized in fifths below. If three sound sources are used, with ranges ±2, ±6, and ±12, then a half-bend up of the note C will yield the voicing D♭E♭G♭, which could function as part of an A♭ suspended chord or an E♭mi7 chord; a full bend will yield DF♯C, a dominant seventh voicing for D. The same bends down yield the intervallic inversions of those voicings, respectively F♯BA and CG♭B♭. If intervening quantization to the nearest semitone is invoked, an entire series of

FIGURE 5.10   Blues-influenced lead excerpt.

chromatically shifting trichords can be produced over the range of the pitch bend device. Because such effects produce exact rather than diatonic transposition, they readily go outside the prevailing modes used in tonal contexts.

The remaining examples in this section emphasize the use of controller effects. Figure 5.13 shows notated use of vibrato and both portamento rate and on/off effects. Figure 5.14 shows possible notation for the cross-fade and real-time control of attack time and reverb time parameters. The velocity switch is also shown. Similar notations can be used for any other control parameter. The notations here are only suggestions, as there are no standard forms as of this writing. In figure 5.15, some effects obtainable with square wave and sample-and-hold frequency modulation are indicated. Again, there is no standard notation.

Finally, there are some interesting effects that can be obtained from a single line that is routed to a fixed-pitch sound source (a module operating in what is called *fixed-pitch mode*), one where the same pitch sounds regardless of the key struck. Most commonly this setup applies to playing percussion-like parts. One main point is that repeated note figures, which are common in percussion playing, and one of the more difficult keyboard techniques to execute with precision with one hand, can be played as trills or tremolos, which are easier. The basic idea is shown in figure 5.16. The heard line (on the lower staff) can be executed on a "normal" variable pitch setup either with one hand or by alternate use of the two hands, as indicated. Connected to a sound module operating in fixed-pitch mode, the performer can play as indicated on the upper staff to achieve the same sound.

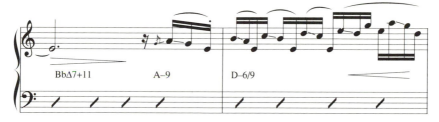

FIGURE 5.11 Jazz-rock ballad melody featuring a variety of pitch bend figures.

A highly useful variant of this procedure is available on samplers and synthesizers that allow substantial retuning of each note. In this case, without using fixed-pitch mode, notes in the neighborhood of a given note can be tuned to be only "slightly" different in pitch—microtonally different if the sounds have a clear fundamental, and perhaps as much as several semitones different if the sound is noisy and without clear fundamental.

FIGURE 5.11 continued.

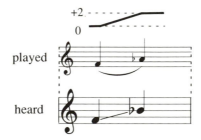

FIGURE 5.12 The "faked" pitch bend.

Then the trill-like figures of figure 5.16 achieve something like small timbral variations with each different note, timbral variations that typically
enhance realism by avoiding exact repetition. This is normally the preferred programming design for imitating realistic percussion parts and is
discussed further in chapter 8.

A more sophisticated example based on the same idea is shown in
figure 5.17. Here a single line is routed to two independent sound sources
(which could, of course, be the same sound if so desired), at least one of
them operating in fixed-pitch mode. The result is the production of two
lines from the single played line, with one line containing the notes of the
other. This kind of rhythmic structure is very common in Latin music, and

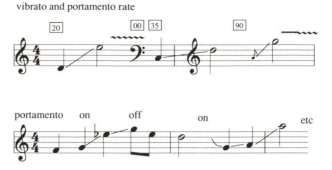

FIGURE 5.13   Vibrato and portamento effects.

the example given corresponds to the clavé and stick parts for the *guaguanco*, a kind of rhumba. The fundamental stick pattern is first given, in figure 5.17a, and its adaptation to produce the stick and clavé patterns simultaneously is given in 5.17b.

How can this be done? One way is on a master controller or synthesizer capable of sending out notes on more than one channel simultaneously. Zone A (MIDI channel 1) is set to cover the entire keyboard and is routed to a fixed-pitch module. As a result the upper (composite) rhythm of the bottom staff (figure 5.17b) is produced. Zone B (MIDI channel 2) is set to send notes only from the upper part of the keyboard, with a lowest note in the range G♯3 to D4, and is routed to either a fixed-pitch mode sound module producing G3 or a normal mode sound module transposed down a perfect fifth, and with a sustaining timbre. As a result the lower rhythm in the bottom staff is produced. (If the full durations of this part are required, which is not customary for this percussion piece, a sustaining voice in monophonic mode can be used.) An even simpler way to achieve the two-lines-from-one effect on multitimbral synthesizers with split points is to split the keyboard between G3 and D4, routing the pattern's top note to produce both D4 (timbre 1) and the fifth below (timbre 2), and the G3 to sound a fifth higher (timbre 1). Such tricks are also possible via external keyboard splitting devices that turn a standard synthesizer effectively into a master keyboard.

OTHER PERFORMANCE MODELS

Many of the above examples can be used with any type of sound; others are obviously most effective or meaningful when coupled

FIGURE 5.14 Examples featuring various types of real-time parametric control.

with one of the main models described above. But while it is clear that these two models are widely useful, they primarily specify the nature of dynamics and articulation, and even there they hardly encompass the full range of options, which are limited only by the imagination.

For example, it is possible to use a number of discrete controllers to provide variation in sound. On some machines, such as some of those made by Kurzweil and Ensoniq, a set of buttons can allow the substitution of selected components of a sound, achieving timbral variety without the

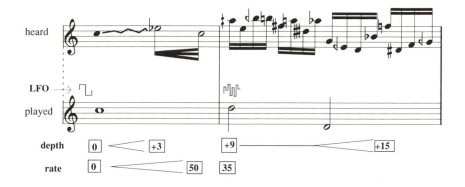

FIGURE 5.15 Performed effects of square wave and S/H pitch modulation. The depth is given in semitones, rate in arbitrary units. ♮ = approximately 1/4 tone sharp; ♯ = approximately 3/4 tone sharp; ♩ = approximately 1/4 tone flat.

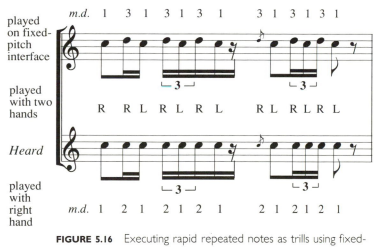

FIGURE 5.16 Executing rapid repeated notes as trills using fixed-pitch mode.

danger of glitches associated with a full program change. If enough articulatory variety can be achieved, this approach can be developed into a full performance model in lieu of the alternatives given earlier.

It is also possible to effect such changes in sound and articulation on nearly all synthesizers using program changes (but without the risk of glitches) by adopting the following strategy. Consider, for example, the

b. Method: Zone A, all pitches, Ch 1, to fixed pitch source. Zone B, notes above G3, Ch 2, sounding a fifth lower.

FIGURE 5.17   Producing two percussion lines from one with fixed-pitch mode: Latin rhythm pattern (guaguanco) with traditional handing (a); the same pattern recast to produce an included rhythm (b).

melodic line for cello or cello-like sound given in the top staff of figure 5.18. This can be dissected into four types of articulations:

1. a nonlegato attack produced by change of bow direction (e.g., first note)
2. a legato type attack produced without change of bow direction (e.g., second note)
3. pizzicato (last three notes of measure 1)
4. a slow gentle bowed attack (e.g. the G♯ of measure 2).

To realize this, set up two identical (or compatible) synthesis modules or two parts within one synthesis module to have four patches—P1, P2, P3, P4—that correspond to these four articulation sounds. Set one part/

FIGURE 5.18 Splitting a line into two different MIDI channels to allow varying articulations to be executed via program change.

module to MIDI channel 1 and the other to channel 2. The strategy works by splitting the line between the two channels to allow enough time for the insertion of program changes, as shown in the realization in the second system of the figure. The arrows attached to the P labels indicate patch change points. This strategy—which might be called *line splitting*, although there is no standard term for it—is a kind of hocketing and can be readily extended to more programs and more channels. It is most viable as a compositional technique within a sequencer. It can be realized in live performance only by some intensive programming and virtuosic button pushing, with access to two MIDI channels achieved by two separate keyboards or two keyboard zones on the same controller or perhaps even velocity-based channel assignment, using a MIDI mapping device. In my experience this usually introduces an unwelcome degree of complexity when used in live performance as well as reducing the number of available MIDI channels.

A more general and dramatic novelty occurs when by suitable programming the synthesist alters the customary relationship between "physical" articulation and "sound" articulation. One dramatic case of this is when envelope parameters are set to make decay-to-zero time (with key held down) short, and release time (decay after key release) medium to long. Since most envelopes have the property that releasing the key immediately instigates the release portion of the envelope, this has the effect of reversing legato and staccato: Playing legato creates staccato articulation, and playing staccato causes legato.

Another rupture with familiar keyboard physicality occurs when reversed or nonmonotonic tuning systems are used at the keyboard. These effects are more drastic than those of fixed-pitch mode, and will be treated in chapter 6.

A quite different kind of single line performance orientation bases itself on gestures rather than discrete note events. In fact, one criticism that has been leveled at the "MIDIfication" of electronic music is the resultant preoccupation with note-type events at the expense of the general sound sculpturing and processing functions available in direct digital synthesis. A gestural orientation can help to avoid this limitation. The basic method is quite general but easiest to demonstrate in the language of pitch bend. Consider figure 5.19. Here the pitch shape is a path with only occasionally marked goals. It would normally be executed using one or more of the following: pitch bend (with pitch bend range as large as possible), pitch deflection, and portamento, using a foot switch for on/off control and a continuous controller or data entry slider to allow variable portamento rate. Coordinating these effects to create a specific gestural shape does require some practice. Note that effective maximum pitch bend range here can often be not the usual twelve semitones, but rather twenty-four, since bends through the center that are rapid and on this scale will usually not reveal the objectionable irregularities associated with the dead zone that are so audible with more traditional musical gestures. Similar gestural shapes can be used with any musical parameter, such as volume, filter cut-off, reverberation depth or LFO speed. Such an orientation is even more natural with such parameters, where no universal traditions of notation other than those of general graphic layout exist. The conception of such music should be shape- and texture-oriented rather than precisely timed. Often such shapes can proceed from a painterly or architectural orientation, as in Edgard Varèse's pioneering work in such pieces as *Poème électronique.*

Several other alternatives revolve around the issue of the *sonic identity* of a line. This has to do with: how similar sounds must be to be interpreted as coming from one source; how different they can be and still be accepted as coming from one source; and how different they must be to be heard as separate sources. If, for example, a given program, while ostensibly monotimbral, varies widely in timbre from note to note due to real-time

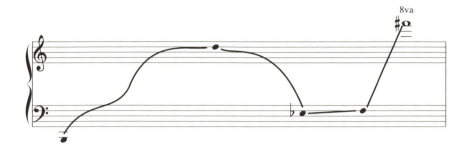

FIGURE 5.19 Gestural pitch bend.

programming and control, the effect may well be one of several independent tone colors. The same effect occurs if a single program is composed of sampled sounds of great diversity spread across different registers or activated differentially by velocity switching, or if velocity switching changes between different programs. If a line is multitimbral, and operating in rotate or reset mode, a similar effect is again obtained. The performance issues of such setups have to be handled on a case-by-case basis, depending on required musical effect.

If, as a second example, a monophonic line leaps rapidly between several different registers, even without timbral change, the line may break up perceptually into several different parts, each more slowly moving. This concept is called *compound melody* and has been used to great effect by J. S. Bach in his solo music for violin and cello. It is found in music of many styles. A third and final example occurs with the layering of sounds that occurs so naturally when sound modules are MIDIed together. How similar do the sounds have to be, in terms of such things as tuning, envelope, and spectrum, to fuse perceptually and function as a single melodic line? Such issues of identity can affect harmonic considerations like dissonance and rhythmic effects like syncopation. This will be explored more deeply in chapter 7, when we look at performance configurations.

Still another relaxation of the concept of the single melodic line is the use of sound effects. Here sounds are designed more for their individual impact than for their concerted formation of a line. In other words, the sound or line does not act as a melodic carrier. Such effects may have a substantial performed component to their success, but it is difficult to generalize, and these must be fine-tuned on a case-by-case basis, as part of a hunting expedition in timbral space.

REFERENCES

Aikin, J., Anderton, C., Coster, T., Darter, T., De Furia, S., Duke, G., Fryer, T., Gleeson, P., Moog, R., Powell, R., Tomlyn, B. *Synthesizer Technique.* Milwaukee: Hal Leonard, 1987.

Blum, David. *Casals and the Art of Interpretation.* New York: Holmes and Meier, 1977.

Burton, S. *Orchestration.* Englewood Cliffs, N.J.: Prentice-Hall, 1982.

Campbell, Murray, and Clive Greated. *The Musician's Guide to Acoustics.* London: J. M. Dent and Sons, 1987.

Cole, Hugo. *Sounds and Signs.* London: Oxford University Press, 1974.

Corea, C. *The Chick Corea Elektric Band.* N. p.: Third Earth/Hal Leonard, 1986.

Dodge, Charles, and Thomas Jerse. *Computer Music.* New York: Schirmer, 1985.

Doyle, Frank. "Purple Haze on the DX7-II." *Modern Keyboard* 1(4): 62–64, 1989.

Fallows, D., H. M. Lindley, and M. Wright. "Articulation." In *The New Grove Dictionary of Musical Instruments,* ed. Stanley Sadie. London: Macmillan and Co., 1984.

Fennelly, Brian. "A Descriptive Language for the Analysis of Electronic Music." In *Perspectives on Notation and Performance* eds. Benjamin Boretz and Edward Cone. New York: Norton, 1976.

Gaburo, Virginia. *Notation.* La Jolla, Calif.: Lingua Press, 1977.

Giuffre, Jimmy. *Jazz Phrasing and Intepretation.* New York: Associated Music Publishers, 1969.

Hood, Mantle. *The Ethnomusicologist.* Kent, Ohio: Kent State University Press, 1982.

Karkoschka, Erhard. *Notation in New Music.* Ruth Koenig, trans. Universal Press, 1972.

Marshall, Wolf. *Van Halen OU812.* Guitar/vocal edition. Port Chester, New York: Cherry Lane Music, 1988.

Milano, Dominic, ed. *Synthesizer Programming.* Milwaukee: Hal Leonard, 1987.

Nettl, Bruno. *The Study of Ethnomusicology.* Urbana: University of Illinois Press, 1983.

Read, Gardner. *Music Notation.* London: Victor Gollancz, 1974.

Rissatti, Howard. *New Music Vocabulary.* Urbana: University of Illinois Press, 1975.

Schäffer, Boguslaw. *Introduction to Composition.* Krakow: PWM, 1976.

Stone, Kurt. *Music Notation in the Twentieth Century.* New York: W. W. Norton, 1980.

CHAPTER SIX

POLYPHONIC PERFORMANCE AND EXTENDED TECHNIQUES

The introduction of a new kind of music must be shunned as imperiling the whole state, for styles of music are never disturbed without affecting the most important political institutions. . . . The new style, gradually gaining a lodgment, quietly insinuates itself into manners and customs, and from these it . . . goes on to attack laws and constitutions, displaying the utmost impudence, until it ends by overturning everything.

▪ Plato, as quoted by Will Durant, *The Life of Greece.*

In this chapter we look at more advanced musical performance problems—more advanced in terms of required technique, compositional design, or real-time programming. We start by discussing some additional parameters of music, complementing those given in chapter 5, needed to describe polyphonic music. Primary among these are harmony, texture, and density.

Harmony refers to the vertical arrangements of notes, best known in terms of the formation of chords, but it is not confined to this. It can vary stylistically over the great wealth of Western musical styles—early music, baroque, classical, romantic, jazz, blues, rock, neoclassical, twentieth-century intervallic and pitch class set orientations, and so forth, or the harmonic devices in many world cultures (notably those of Africa, Southeast Asia, and the Pacific). The synthesizer's versatility means that all such traditions are potentially accessible.

Texture refers to the configuration of musical parts. It can be described in many ways, including metaphors such as busy, thick, fluid, simple, tight, and sparse, or in the more precise terms of traditional music: unison, monophonic, homophonic (melody plus accompaniment or block chordal), heterophonic (slightly different versions of the same material operating at the same time), call-and-response (or the related antecedent-consequent), and polyphonic. Traditionally, polyphony refers to the presence of two or more independent voices; there is no limit to the number of parts in general, though the usual practical solo keyboard maximum is five. It should be noted that the term *polyphonic* is being used differently in the title of this chapter, to mean more notes than monophonic; this is a common usage in synthesis.

Density usually means the number of events per unit time. It can be high, medium, low, fluctuating, and static, to name a few possibilities. Density also sometimes refers to vertical density, which is better known as spacing, chordal spacing, or harmonic density.

The central keyboard problems of polyphonic performance, beyond those already discussed with monophonic music, are rhythmic coordination among parts, balance, and correct musical reading. In other words, the parts must be played with proper timing, with proper relative dynamics (in classical music, the term *voicing* is used for this), and appropriate musical conception. These notions apply to all polyphonic instruments, including the synthesizer. Indeed, there are many similarities in these areas between the synthesizer and other polyphonic instruments, especially when the music being performed operates under the models of notes, chords, melodic lines, and stable timbre and uses a standard keyboard configuration. These similarities will not be given detailed discussion. Rather, we shall emphasize techniques specific to the synthesizer.

What differences there are in such standard contexts are due primarily to the effects of controllers (notably polyphonic pressure, which allows vibrato, continuously variable dynamics, or other effects to be achieved simultaneously on individual notes, increasing the distinguishability of different lines or notes in a texture) and multitimbrality (which increases both voice distinguishability and variety of voice function). Other differences are based upon the need to imitate a great range of nonkeyboard performance gestures and styles by suitable programming and real-time control.

PART DISPOSITION

By *part disposition* we mean the way a musical part is placed on the keyboard(s) (or range of the general performance interface) for performance. The most basic decisions are the octave placement of the part and whether any (nonoctave) transposition will be applied to it.

There are several considerations here. If the part comes from another instrument and is written as a transposed part rather than a concert part, it is a simple matter to avoid mental work by programming the transposition into the chosen sound. For example, if the part is for alto saxophone, the part can be transposed to sound a major sixth below the written (played) notes so that the player can read directly from the saxophone part. See chapter 8 for a survey of such standard transpositions.

In some cases, it will also be necessary to change the octave in which the part is played, either to bring the hand into an appropriate part of the keyboard or simply to make sure that the part will fit on the available keys. This is true of parts played by certain transposing instruments like the bass clarinet and certain nominally nontransposing instruments that sound in a different octave than written, like the bass, guitar, celeste, glockenspiel, tubular bells, crotales, and xylophone. If the part is very high or very low in pitch, adding appropriate octave transpositions will bring the line more into the center of the keyboard, making it more naturally playable in the standard sitting position. With bass register one-hand parts, for example, where left hand controllers are used, it can be advantageous to transpose the notation up and the sound down by an octave to make right-hand playing more comfortable. With high treble parts, just the reverse can be useful.

EXTENDED AND RECONFIGURED INSTRUMENTS

When the synthesizer's design and programming require more radical changes of attitude or technique from the performer, one may speak of it as an extended or reconfigured instrument. An *extended instrument* is one that adds new physical controls to an existing (traditional) control interface; a *reconfigured instrument* is one that has an unchanged control interface but has been reprogrammed or rebuilt so that traditional performance gives distinctly different results, requiring changes in technique. If the control mechanisms and resultant effects are changed radically enough, we have essentially a new instrument rather than an extended or reconfigured one. These definitions can apply to many innovations in the history of acoustic instruments. Historically, the French term *luthier nouvelle* has been used for such developments.

I will first consider the extended keyboard idea. The term raises the question: extended relative to what? All synthesizers are extended relative to the piano, due to their ancillary controllers (even as they are more limited in certain ways such as pedaling). But if we use as our reference instrument the generic MIDI keyboard synthesizer described in chapter 1, then the extended synthesizers or controllers are those that include very uncommon or novel features. Keyboards of greater than normal control capacity include the Kurzweil Midiboard, which offers four dimensions of control per voice: key number, key-on velocity, release velocity, and polyphonic pressure. There is nothing conceptually novel here, simply a high degree of completeness of design. A step beyond this, however, is Key Concepts' Notebender keyboard, where keys can move in and out as well as up and down, giving five dimensions of control for each note, two of them of the continuously monitoring type. Big Briar's multiple-touch sensitive keyboard goes even further, sensing key number, key-on velocity, release velocity, polyphonic pressure, and two further dimensions of control derived from two-dimensional finger position on the chosen key (Moog 1987). This yields six dimensions of control per note, and the full potentials of such systems have barely begun to be explored. Devices such as these last two are expensive, highly specialized, and only rarely seen, and they will not be featured in this book.

The reconfigured keyboard is much more accessible since it relies on clever programming rather than expensive special sensors. Synthesizer programming that produces effects drastic enough to deserve this label include:

splits and zones, which allow different timbres and control functions to be allocated to different ranges of notes;

keyboard retuning, which allows notes to sound quite unconventional pitches from traditional finger configurations;

mathematical or logical functional combination of several performance control sources (as found on the Kurzweil 2000, for example);

MIDI transformations, which can completely change the nature of control that standard keyboard actions produce.

These reconfiguration effects can either be programmed into the controlling keyboard or the receiving sound module or created by interposing a MIDI transformation device between keyboard and sound engine. I will comment on the relative viability of these options in the following discussions.

NOTATION

There are very few novel notations required for the polyphonic situation that are not readily generalized from the monophonic. Thus, if a whole chord is modulated, the modulation notation can be put at the top of the chord, and it will be assumed to apply to all voices. The primary novelty required is when notes in a chord are controlled separately—usually by a special pitch bend mode, the use of zones, or polyphonic pressure. The solution is to put the effect notation immediately following and at the same level as each notehead, as shown in the pitch bend case in figure 6.13. If this is too messy, the part may be divided onto two staves for clarity.

We now turn to the specialist techniques of polyphonic synthesizer performance.

ALTERNATING HAND TECHNIQUE

One two-handed technique that can assume more importance on the synthesizer than with traditional keyboards is *alternating hand technique*. This simply means that the hands alternate as they play notes or chords. The feel of such motion is familiar enough to experienced keyboardists, but because the synthesizer's sonic identity is so variable, the technique forms a particularly useful alternative to the typical dispositions of hands and fingers found in such keyboard textures as polyphony, melody and accompaniment, or rhythmic unison—especially when certain kinds of musical statements are required. One of its most useful attributes is its ability to imitate strumming effects. It is often the technique of choice for repeated notes, repeated chords, and tremolos involving three or more notes. Trills can also be played this way to good effect.

A passage using alternating hand technique is shown in figure 6.1. This passage is just an arpeggiation of three-note voicings in each hand with a sustaining middle part. Chordal alternation works in exactly the same way but really gains something over traditional technique only with unison tuning, as discussed below. An extension of basic alternation technique is where at least one hand plays more than one note or chord in sequence. For example, the left hand may play one note, followed by two notes in sequence by the right, consistently. Or each hand may play two sequential notes before control shifts to the other. Such fingerings produce different types of performance gestures and typically allow more forceful and rhythmic playing. An example of this is shown in figure 6.2.

DOVETAIL VOICINGS

When chords are voiced in overlapping fashion, they are said to *dovetail*. Voicings that dovetail are a standard feature in arranging and composition. They are used, for example, to promote homogeneity of sound across woodwind sections, and the term is adapted from that source. When played on the keyboard, with the right hand above the left, this means that at least the thumbs of both hands (and possibly other fingers) overlap. This is found in keyboard music long before our own time, as for example Sergei Rachmaninoff's Prelude in C♯ Minor. If the hands are crossed as well as dovetailed, then the fifth fingers (and possibly others) overlap. It is also possible for the span of one hand to completely contain the other, producing what might be called an *included* voicing. After a little practice, such hand positions become second nature, although their difficulty does vary considerably, depending on the number of notes overlapped and the black/white geography of the voicings.

Figure 6.3 shows a voicing recast into several different dovetail arangements. In the last case, some notes appear in octave transposition. Obviously, not all voicings can be so transformed without transposition. But it is clear that all dovetail voicings can be recast to have no overlap. Whether such modifications are musically appropriate or not depends of course on context.

Dovetail voicings can be played as block chords, either in unison or alternation. One use of such dovetailing is to allow a specific inner voice to be brought out by virtue of its being assigned a special finger—normally the top of the lower chord (left hand thumb). This effect becomes particularly noticeable when the two hands are playing different sounds, using different keyboards or differently timbred zones on the same keyboard. The allocation of voices to different hands will then determine the timbres of some of the overlapped inner voices.

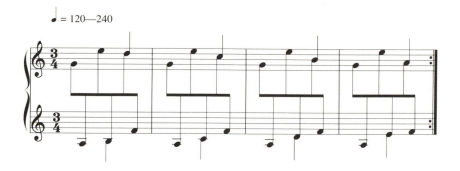

FIGURE 6.1   A vamp using basic hand alternation technique.

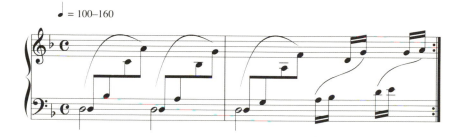

FIGURE 6.2   Alternating hand technique with two notes per hand.

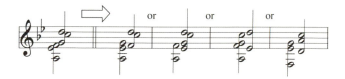

FIGURE 6.3   Recasting voicings to produce dovetailing.

But perhaps the main point of dovetailing comes to the fore when such voicings are executed as arpeggios. Here the overlap between the voicings means that the contour of the sound will be different from the contour of gesture that performers are used to from "normal" low-to-high voicing arrangement of the hands. Well-worn arpeggio patterns suddenly take on a fresh sound. The hands also act more as a unit, and the resultant feel is a useful addition to the synthesist's technique. Figure 6.4 shows dovetail

con pedale

FIGURE 6.4   Dovetail arpeggiation, with hand crossing.

arpeggiation, with various degrees of overlap, including the crossing of hands.

The number of ways in which a given dovetail voicing can be arpeggiated varies, depending on the total number of notes used. If the number of notes is n, then there are $n! = n(n-1)(n-2)...1$ possibilities. If three notes are used, there are $3 \times 2 \times 1$ or six different patterns; if four notes, twenty-four; if five notes, 120; if six notes, 720; and so on. If some notes are repeated, the number of possibilities is even larger. In terms of the feel of various types of arpeggio, we can think of each movement between notes as being based on the choices of (1) using the same hand or the opposite hand and (2) motion up or down in pitch.

These simple choices aggregate to produce a specific gestural shape. Figure 6.5 shows some possible dovetail arpeggiation patterns for chords of five, six, seven and eight notes. Figure 6.5a uses five-note patterns; figure 6.5b uses six notes in hand alternation style; figure 6.5c alternates three-note patterns against four-note patterns; and figure 6.5d uses eight notes in contrary motion. The patterns that are easiest to play are those in which each hand plays all its notes in only one direction before repeating any of them, and those in which hand alternation uses a very simple pattern, such as left, right, left, right. Indeed, the point of this technique is to use the easier strumming patterns to generate those that are less "natural" for the keyboardist. Hand alternation is one consistently attractive option.

Clearly, if the two hands' cycles are not the same length, then the composite pattern will not repeat until both hands produce an integer number of cycles at the same time. If the number of notes in the left-hand cycle is n_L and the number in the right hand is n_R, then the number of notes required in each hand before the overall pattern repeats will be

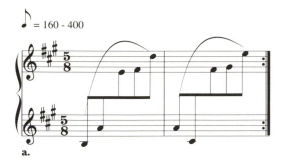

a.

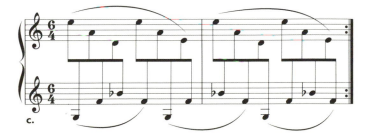

b. *Ped.*

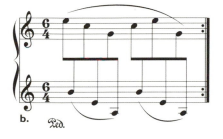

c.

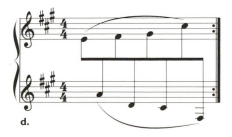

d.

FIGURE 6.5 Various dovetail arpeggiations, using alternating hand technique.

$n_L n_R$, divided by any common factors in n_L and n_R. The total pattern duration will therefore be twice this (since there are two hands). For example, a 3 by 4 pattern will take 24 notes to finish, a 4 by 5 pattern 40 notes, and a 4 by 6 pattern 24 notes.

MULTITIMBRAL TECHNIQUES

The multitimbral effects described in chapter 5 are also applicable in polyphonic context. The rotate and reset modes, in particular, can have additional interesting effects. For example, if the same chord is repeated at a steady rhythm in rotate mode, slight changes in the relative attack times of the notes will continually revoice the chord. The effect of variability is increased if the number of synthesis voices available is different from the number of notes in the chord, so that a different set of voices (timbres) is used at each chordal attack, and if the different voices have markedly different transpositions. The first part of the effect also occurs in reset mode; the reader will recall that this can also occur by using MIDI mono mode, where available.

More generally, multitimbral effects are used with split keyboards and zones, to which we now turn.

SPLITS, ZONES, AND LAYERS

A keyboard is split if it has one or more *split points* that separate the keyboard into nonoverlapping *zones* that may be assigned distinct sounds, MIDI channels, or other properties. If there are n split points, there are $n + 1$ zones. The separate zones can be routed to different programs, either via separately assigned MIDI channels or through the internal signal paths of a synthesizer. Split points are programmable but are normally fixed within each chosen program. A few systems can vary the split intelligently during performance, using cues from the consistency of the player's style to shift the split point(s) up and down in real time. Such split points are said to be *floating*.

If the keyboard in use does not allow splitting, the equivalent effect can be achieved if the receiving sound module(s) allow range limiting—in other words, they can be set to respond only over certain ranges (zones). For example, if the keyboard is connected to sound module A (or part A on a multitimbral synthesizer), which is set to respond only from C−2 to B2, and also connected to sound module B (or part B on a multitimbral synthesizer), which is set to respond only from C3 to G8, then a keyboard split has been achieved. In this case both modules can operate on the same MIDI channel or in Omni mode.

The same effects can be achieved if an intervening MIDI mapping device is used to change the character and range of the MIDI messages coming from the keyboard before they reach the sound module(s). Zones can also be effectively defined on samplers by assigning samples to certain ranges. If splits and zones can be engineered both at the sending and receiving ends, and in between, quite complex interface designs can be achieved.

The most general situation is where zones can actually overlap or include each other, and this has some special uses. In such cases there are no split points but simply zone end points. This can be configured on any master keyboard controller worth its salt, some synthesizers, and by any keyboard using the receiving range-limiting method mentioned above. The basic types of zone relationships are illustrated in figure 6.6. The entire range of MIDI notes from C−2 to G8 is indicated, although it is not very often available on one keyboard simultaneously. Arrows at the bottom of each figure show the placement of typical sixty-one- and eighty-eight-note keyboards in this range, although this can of course be changed by programming. The number of splits can be as large as the number of keys minus 1, and the number of zones is in principle unlimited. When zones coincide or share common notes, they function as *layers,* or components of a composite sound. Ranges of the keyboard where two or more zones overlap are said to be *layered.*

What are the playing implications of splits and zones? Let us begin an answer to this question by looking at the single split keyboard case. In its most common, practical, and perhaps least imaginative incarnation, this allows two timbrally distinct parts to be played with their customary function by one performer at one keyboard. For example, a bass could be played by the left hand and a lead line or brass section by the right, each hand basically staying in its own zone, except to help execute a flourish or fill out a chord in the other zone when its own voice drops out momentarily or sustains previously played notes. An example of this is seen in figure 6.7. To play this pattern with optimal smoothness, the left hand must shift to the upper zone for at least the last chord of bar 1 and probably for all chords except the first two of that bar.

In any such split, each zone will have to be played and programmed in an idiomatic style. In figure 6.7 the bass zone would probably be best set up without sustain pedal, but sustain (and other) pedals should function over the treble zone. If the two zones had saxophone and tamboura (an Indian plucked drone instrument) function, sustain pedal and key-velocity-driven dynamics would be needed on the tamboura side, and continuous

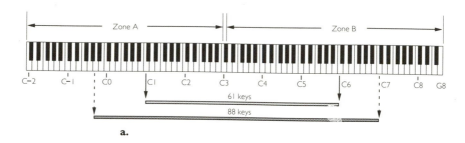

a.

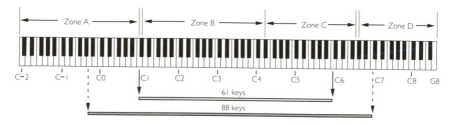

b.

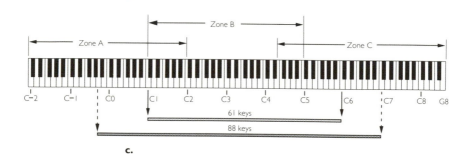

c.

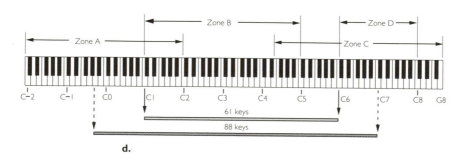

d.

FIGURE 6.6 Zone configurations: two zones created by a single split point, C3 (a); four zones, created by three split points, C1, E♭4, and G6 (b); three overlapping zones, C−2 through C2, C1 through C5, and E4 through G8 (c); and zones with overlap and inclusion, C−2 through C2, C1 through C5, E4 through G8, and C6 through C8 (d).

FIGURE 6.7 A split keyboard vamp.

controller control of dynamics (via foot, pressure, or breath) without sustain pedal over the saxophone zone. With only two zones, there are usually enough hands, feet, and other body parts to go around for any necessary allocation of control along the lines of the major performance models discussed in chapter 5. But if the sounds on both zones use extensive real-time shaping, such controls may have to be operated in alternation.

Such configurations can be varied by transposition. It may be useful to shift one or both zones up or down by some interval to allow certain normally impossible voicings or to gain access to certain ranges. Passages that require the complex interleaving of fingers on a normal keyboard can also be "pulled apart" and made more tractable in this way. If desired, the hands can even reverse their usual function by assigning the treble part to the left-hand zone (transposed up) and the bass part to the right-hand zone (transposed down). This is a useful practice technique that can free up musical conceptualization and promote hand independence.

The splits described so far achieve their effects by allocating a distinct part function to each zone. The resulting performance demands are the sum of the musical demands of each of the component zones plus the technical difficulties of coordinating the parts simultaneously.

A quite different conception occurs when the zones of the split interact with each other to form a composite result. A very simple example of this is to assign the same basic sound to different zones but slightly vary such properties as vibrato speed and brightness between zones to improve timbral richness. (This is even more effective with three or more zones.) A more dramatic example is *hocketing* (dividing a single part between two or more instruments—here, zones). Another common usage occurs when the two zones are assigned the same sound and are transposed so that their ranges overlap significantly. One well-known example of this is *unison tuning*, where two different zones are tuned to cover the same range. This can be achieved a number of ways: by internal programming on many synthesizers, by routing separate zones on a master controller to two identical sound modules, by playing two separate identically programmed keyboards in the same range, by properly tuning the ranges of samples on a sampler, and so forth. Since nearly all pitches can be found in two places on the keyboard, patterns that might be difficult to play in normal configuration can be much easier in split configuration. For example, cramped dovetail voicings can be split apart and executed much more easily. New kinds of melodic designs suddenly fall "naturally" under the hands. Hand alternation technique on different keys can also be used to achieve comfortable repeated notes and chords, as shown in figure 6.8.

To execute this last example, use some sort of tuned percussive sound like vibraphone or electric piano, with the split point at G3, the treble zone transposed down one octave, and the bass zone transposed up one octave relative to standard pitch. To achieve the sounding pattern, play the right hand part 8va above and the left hand part 8va below what is written. A light degree of random pitch function is recommmended if your synthesizer has this feature, as this will produce occasional mild beating between slightly mistuned versions of the same notes (akin to chorusing in a real ensemble).

Some further possibilities with the same zone setup are shown in figure 6.9. Three distinct ostinato figures are given there—first as played and then as they will sound. These patterns are taken from a recently comissioned piece of mine called *Rotating Gesture,* in which a computer simultaneously performs real-time sound editing as the performer improvises on patterns like those given, emphasizing hand alternation technique.

Another use of unison tuning technique is in executing bass patterns. See chapter 8 for an example.

Unison tuning is not the only way in which different keyboard zones can profitably interact. For example, controller information from one zone can be routed to another zone. This occurs automatically in some synthesizers with splits and can otherwise be generally arranged by the use of MIDI mapping devices. One instance of this that I've found useful is to have pressure from one zone control pitch deflection on another zone. Consider figure 6.10, with the following programmed configuration: electric blues guitar patch on both sides of a keyboard split at E3; E1 tuned to the lowest note of the guitar, with pitch deflection up resulting from aftertouch (in either zone) active only on the top zone (full pressure corresponding to two semitones); sustain pedal operating only on the bass zone; treble zone transposed down an octave relative to standard pitch; bass zone at standard pitch.

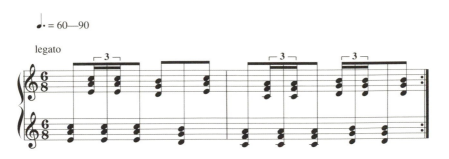

FIGURE 6.8 A chordal vamp using unison tuning and alternating hand technique.

The sustain pedal is set to function in the lower zone to allow the left hand to be used in the top zone for big leaps and special effects without the bass dropping out. It does not affect the treble zone, so the right hand has complete freedom to play quick passages without blurring. The split point is set high enough so that the right hand can readily play across it to produce melodies with leaps from conjunct keyboard technique. In this example, the channel pressure contributed by each hand is indicated as a small plot between two dotted lines above its respective staff.

One point of this setup is that it allows pitch deflection in the treble zone to be controlled from any key in either hand. Pitch deflection up can be handled in the normal way, by attacking the note and then adding pressure in either zone. Pitch deflection down can be handled by first pressing down with the left hand on accompaniment notes already being sustained (which will not themselves bend, since they are in the lower zone), and then striking the treble key(s) one or two semitones above the desired pitch, as appropriate, and easing up on the left-hand pressure. If you maintain full pressure with the left hand on sustained chords, you will actually need to play in the key of D to sound in E. A variant on this effect is to use different sensitivities and/or polarities of controller response in the two zones. In this way a variety of contrary and oblique motion pitch bends can be obtained (see "Polyphonic Pitch Bend"). This effect of "cross controller action" can, of course, be used with any control function.

With three or more zones, we can distinguish the same options but also some additional possibilities. One function provided by multiple zones is to allow certain figures to be played that would be very difficult, or impossible, on a normal keyboard. The timbre of all the zones might well be the same in this case. Figure 6.11 shows such an example. Here there are two split points and three zones. The indicated setup allows a normal tremolo figure to map into a pattern that would require an impossibly large hand and is distinctly unpianistic. Figure 6.12 shows another usage of

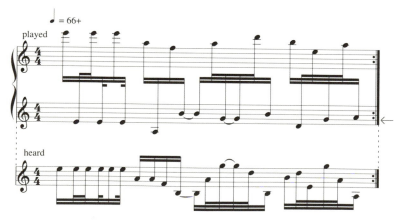

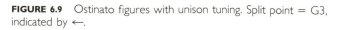

FIGURE 6.9 Ostinato figures with unison tuning. Split point = G3, indicated by ←.

FIGURE 6.10 Using pressure in one zone to achieve pitch bend in another. Split point = E3. Left hand channel pressure is indicated above the bass clef, right hand channel pressure above the treble.

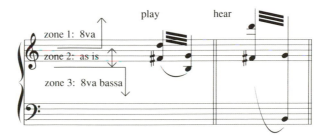

FIGURE 6.11 Using three zones to perform an otherwise impossible tremolo.

multiple zones: *selective harmonic thickening.* Zone 1 plays the notes untransposed, zone 2 transposes them up a major third, and zone 3 transposes them down a fifth. Simple lines can blossom into chords.

The traditional multizone approach is where each zone has a distinct musical function and normally a separate timbre. Here zones most commonly do not overlap. Common approaches are to straddle the middle zone between the two hands or keep one hand in one zone (most commonly the bass) while the other hand jumps between the other two zones as required. This second approach can be duplicated in a single split point setup if one zone can be programmed to have a velocity switch function. In this alternative, you just play with more force when you want the third

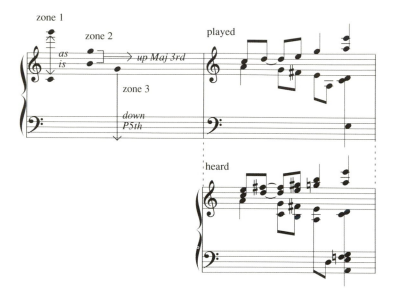

FIGURE 6.12   Using zones to achieve selective harmonic thickening.

timbre. With four or more zones, at least one hand is typically changing registers frequently so that timbral variety can compensate for the loss of available range for each sound.

THE USE OF POLYPHONIC PRESSURE

Where available, polyphonic pressure provides additional control that can be achieved in no other way. Its most common functions are pitch shift and modulation, but some instruments (notably those made by Kurzweil and Ensoniq) allow many more. It is really the only performance technique that can continuously and independently affect the separate notes in a chord. Its main limitations are that it is still quite uncommon, is monopolar (primarily a limitation with pitch bend function), has minimal visual (but good tactile) feedback, and must always start and end with zero effect. Its use is best discussed in terms of a particular assigned function, and the reader will find its properties integrated into the sections on polyphonic pitch bend, cross-fade, and MIDI mapping.

POLYPHONIC PITCH BEND

Figure 6.13 shows a number of examples of the use of polyphonic pitch bend. The cases with two voices are most common and may be described in terms of traditional principles of voice motion: parallel, similar, oblique, and contrary (figures 6.13a–d). The programming and realization of these figures vary in difficulty. Parallel motion (figure 6.13a) requires no special design since all controllers routed to produce pitch bend except polyphonic pressure will normally move all notes in parallel. For other types of bending, polyphonic pressure routed to pitch deflection is the most versatile configuration for producing arbitrary types of relative pitch motion in different voices. If you have access to a poly pressure keyboard, use it to try all parts of figure 6.13. Two types of techniques will need to be used: explicit pressure by individual fingers and, where feasible, shifting of the weight of the arm onto selected fingers. However, the comparative rarity of poyphonic pressure means that we will focus predominantly on other pitch bend techniques.

Oblique pitch bend motion with two voices can often be handled by increasingly common special modes: *low mode,* which bends only the lowest sounding note, and *high mode,* which bends only the highest sounding note (figures 6.13e and 6.13f respectively). If not directly available the effect can be mimicked if each note falls on a different zone on the keyboard by setting pitch bend on for one zone and off for the other. When three or more notes are present, the same selective zone system will work if the notes to be bent can be segregated into a zone or zones separate from those notes not bending. This, of course, is not always possible. Alternatively, special modes and zones can be combined. For example, if an inner voice alone is to be bent selectively, proceed as follows: Split the keyboard just above the note to be bent, and set the upper zone to have no pitch bend response (e.g., range = 0) and the lower one to have high mode response. The result is that the inner voice will be bent selectively. Likewise, the note in question could have been put as the bottom voice of a higher zone operating in low mode.

The special oblique cases of *bend to unison* (figure 6.13g) and *bend from unison* (figure 6.13h) recall a very common guitar technique. There are several ways such figures can be obtained. Bend to unison can use low mode if the bend is up, high mode if the bend is down. Key on mode and zone techniques can also apply, as above. Bend from unison can be achieved in the same way if the notes are returning from a bend to unison; if this figure does not immediately precede the desired bend from unison but a slight pause exists, then the bend to unison can be executed first, with channel volume turned to zero and the volume then rapidly raised to

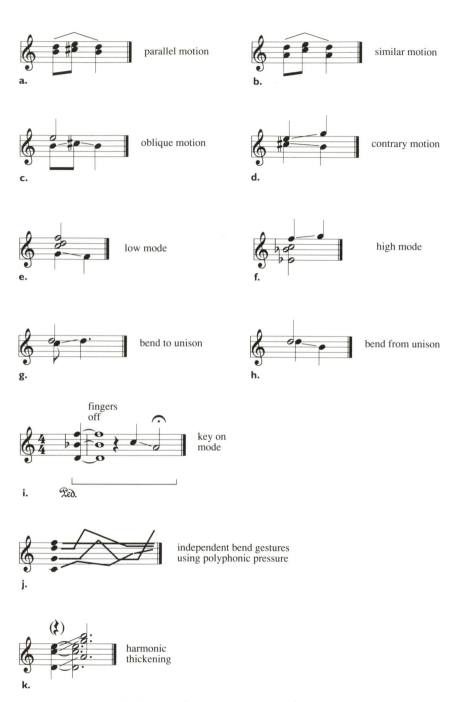

FIGURE 6.13   Polyphonic pitch bend figures.

execute the bend from unison. Otherwise, either the initial note must quickly be struck twice, and then high/low mode or key on mode techniques used, or two zones used with unison tuning. These two effects are often most expressive if the bend is not to exact unison but to a slightly detuned pair of notes.

Oblique pitch bend on chords of three or more notes can also be obtained by so-called *key on* mode (a term used by Yamaha), which applies pitch bend only to the notes actually fingered; notes held by the sustain pedal are not bent, as shown in figure 6.13i. (Notes held by the sostenuto pedal typically are.) When these different modes are combined with use of the sustain and sostenuto pedals, some complex pitch bend effects can be achieved.

Pitch bend in similar motion (figure 6.13b) is often easiest to achieve by causing a parallel bend motion with the pitch bend device and "faking" the pitch bends that don't move exactly in parallel (as described in chapter 5). The faked bends may be more easily faked if they are inner voices. Hence, where there is a variety of bend intervals, usually the top voice (or that of the majority of voices) should be unfaked. If the notes to be independently bent happen to fall into separate keyboard zones, then different range settings on different zones can create the desired effect. This will, of course, be possible only in certain circumstances.

If the musical needs of the situation require either similar motion where zones and faking will not work, or actual contrary motion (figure 6.13d), a fairly sophisticated programming environment is required. Such effects are not possible on every synthesizer because each note must have independent bend range and possibly direction. Even on sophisticated machines that allow each note in a MIDI channel to have its own pitch bend range, as the Oberheim Xpander, the notes will not be fully independent under bending but will simply move in proportion to their range settings. Real independence (figure 6.13j) requires either the differential use of polyphonic pressure or separate zones and separate pitch bend control devices. As an example, a breath controller might control pitch deflection on one side of the split, while channel pressure might control it on the other. Polyphonic pressure remains more versatile, but it is harder to control.

Polyphonic pitch bend can be used to create harmonic thickening, as in the single line case, when two or more sound sources are MIDIed together with different pitch bend ranges. Here it readily produces new chord voicings. For example, if two modules are set with pitch bend ranges 0 and ± 7, then a full bend up of a C triad produces a C major ninth chord, a full bend down of a C minor triad an F minor ninth chord. Figure 6.13k includes a comparable example. If a diminished seventh chord is fully bent and MIDIed to three separate modules with ranges 0, ± 1, and ± 2

semitones, a complete chromatic scale (set) will be produced. This technique obviously becomes more versatile where individual notes can have different pitch bend ranges. It can also be extended, as described in chapter 5, by using a MIDI mapping device to scale the up and down ranges and polarities of a single pitch bend device, so that, for example, a full bend up moves all tones by a second, while a full bend down moves all notes down (or, alternatively, up) by an octave (as in the imitation of electric guitar finger bend and whammy bar effects). Some synthesizers allow this kind of design internally. Furthermore, if the pitch bend function can be quantized, all the intervening positions of transposition are readily available, producing, if different ranges have been set, entire strings of successive chords whose rhythms would be determined by the quantization protocols.

KEYBOARD RETUNING

Changing the tuning system of a synthesizer has many uses, and several kinds of standard retuning procedures exist in commercial synthesizers. Explicitly programmable systems, as of this writing, primarily use *note-by-note retuning,* where every note can be assigned its own frequency, or *basic octave retuning* (or *pitch class retuning*), where the basic octave is tunable and is copied by octave transposition to cover the full range of the instrument. Many synthesizers and samplers, commonly those with the basic octave system, allow only a limited range of frequency tuning of each note, say ± a quartertone or semitone. Others, more pleasantly versatile, allow any note to have any frequency to the accuracy of a fraction of a Hertz. Synthesizers and samplers without such options that have a software basis for their operating system can potentially be upgraded to allow retuning on a global basis, and some third parties have developed such software and made it commercially available. See Wilkinson (1988) for a list of such possibilities.

Some machines have sufficiently flexible modulation architecture to allow a third approach to retuning. This is achieved when the depth of frequency modulation of the oscillators (or other sound sources) that comes from the keyboard note number (in other words, keyboard tracking or key following) can be altered. If the amount of modulation (tracking) is reduced from the standard level, the number of pitches available per octave will increase; if modulation is increased, the number will decrease. Negative tracking will produce keyboard reversal. The effect of this is limited to producing different equal-tempered systems; arbitrary retuning is not possible. The results may need to be fine-tuned by ear since the modulation process may introduce some nonlinearities, and there is no automatic octave duplication of pitch. This third approach is made much easier on synthesizers that allow direct programming of intonation "slope" in frequency ratios, as for example some Korg devices.

A fourth method is available on all samplers. Since each sample can be individually tuned, note-by-note retuning is effectively available to the limit of the number of distinct samples and keygroups (allocations of samples to ranges) that can be contained in a single program. Other tuning controls may be available as well.

On machines that have dedicated retuning software (methods 1 and 2 above), tunings will have their own separately allocated patch memory. These will be accessible from the front panel but normally not directly by MIDI Program Change message. A few synthesizers allow the tonic of a nontransposable (irregular) tuning to be changed at any time during performance by selecting a note from a special keyboard octave (e.g., some Kurzweil machines) or even a small supplementary keyboard (Wendy Carlos's instruments). Where more makeshift tuning procedures are used (such as methods 3 and 4), different tunings can normally be stored in memory only as part of an overall synthesis or sampling program, although some synthesizers allow such tunings to be output via sysex dump for external storage. Hence, with any of the indicated methods, external change of tuning system normally can be effected only by calling up a main synthesis program that has the tuning attached to it. The only other external option is to use system exclusive commands specific to the synthesizer to make the changes.

There is yet another way to bring about retuning: by the use of computer programs (or, with less versatility, MIDI mapping devices) that interface between the note selection interface and the sound module. The device can be programmed to take an incoming MIDI message at a given key number, change its key number, and add an appropriate amount of pitch bend to it to achieve a consistently different tuning. If this is done for a number of layers, entire chords can become associated with each played MIDI note. Since pitch bend is a channel message, only one such voice can operate per channel; hence, if n parts are required, they will need to be routed to n independent sound sources on n distinct channels, perhaps via MIDI mono mode. However, if the performance system has polyphonic aftertouch that can be routed to pitch deflection, then the computer program can similarly retune each note separately by adding a Polyphonic Pressure message of appropriate size to each incoming note message. This setup allows the completely arbitrary retuning of a single sound module, with any number of voices.

All of the retuning procedures except this last one are nearly always based on a fixed tuning system conception, where each MIDI note has a fixed associated central pitch. If each note in the tuning system can be altered independently in real time, the tuning system can be called *floating*, or real-time retunable. This is currently quite rare and usually achieved only with computer programming assistance.

PRACTICAL EXAMPLES OF ALTERNATIVE TUNING SYSTEMS

There is an infinity of tuning systems available to the synthesist with the methods described above. Historical temperaments, non-Western tunings, and freely invented systems can all play a significant role. The fundamental creative position was enunciated over 100 years ago: "The construction of scales and harmonic tissues is a product of artistic invention, and by no means furnished by the natural formation or natural function of the ear, as has been hitherto most generally asserted" (Helmholtz 1885, p. 365).

For the purposes of examination, we can divide our approaches into the following categories, which will be treated in turn and without any illusion that this list is comprehensive:

monotonic twelve-note-per-octave systems

microtonality

"macrotonality" and redundancy

microtonal inflection

keyboard reversal

self-accompaniment

octave remapping

"incompatible" tuning systems

Monotonic Twelve-Note-per-Octave Systems

The most straightforward systems are those where the-monotonic left-to-right design of the keyboard's tuning is undisturbed. In other words, the frequency of notes at the keyboard increases steadily from left to right, as in all the traditional tuning systems mentioned in chapter 2. The many possible tuning systems of this type can create a remarkable variety of compositional effects and moods, but if they are based on twelve categories per octave, even if microtones (intervals smaller than a semitone) are present, there are few changes of technique required of the performer. Performers must of course attempt to hear a piece internally in its correct tuning to produce an integrated performance, and sometimes acclimatization to different tuning systems can take a very long time since we have all had so much exposure to the cultural norm of tempered twelve.

Yet if the piece is completely notated, the player can initially approach the score as a sequence of required actions and, through practice, successfully build an aural image, and from this an interpretation, no matter how unfamiliar the tuning system initially. If, however, improvisation is required, then the performer must construct a far more detailed set of cognitive relations that represent the tuning system and its musical potentials, since actual composing in the system in real time is required. If the tuning system is based on twelve notes per octave with small deviations from tempered or just systems, it is relatively simple to think and play functionally in the new tuning system—even if the acoustic novelty of the tuning relations is jarring at first, since the relationship between sound and hand spacing will be preserved to a fair approximation. The fine details of just how each system works must be worked out on a case-by-case basis. The reader may wish to experiment with the historical and international tunings discussed in chapter 2 at this point. Many other scale systems may be tried, such as those that are basically standard diatonic but contain one or more "outside" tones. For example, scales with one or a few notes roughly a quartertone flat or sharp from their twelve-note tempered equivalents are found widely in the Middle East. Try the following scales (♮ = three quartertones flat, ♯ = three quartertones sharp): C,D ♮,E,F, G,A ♮,B,C, and C,D ♮,E,F♯ ,G,A,B,C.

Microtonality

More substantial changes to performance concept and practice occur when the tuning system is based on a number of notes other than twelve to the octave, since many or all of the traditional links between visual spacing and sound may be changed. By *microtonality* we refer to the presence of microtones—intervals significantly smaller than a semitone. Hence, tuning systems of n notes per octave ($n \leq 12$) may or may not be microtonal, depending on their arrangement of pitches, but all $n > 12$ systems are certainly microtonal. In this section we will be concerned primarily with $n > 12$ cases, since they most drastically alter the nature of the performance interface. There is a tremendous variety of possibilities here, certainly more than can be included in a general book on synthesizer performance.

In setting up such systems for performance, there are two basic designs: Either put all notes on one keyboard, with a commensurate reduction in available range; or distribute the notes across two or possibly more keyboards so that full range or something approaching it can be kept intact. The second method can often require the performer to use alternating hand technique since only some of the notes are available on each keyboard. The two common approaches to the multikeyboard method are either to divide the range between the keyboards, so that keyboard A has all the notes below, say, C3, and keyboard B has all notes from C3 on up, or to interleave the notes, so that each pitch falls in an octave more commensurate with its traditional location. The best known example of this second approach is when quartertone tuning is achieved by stacking two twelve-tone keyboards that are tuned a quartertone apart. This allows seen and heard intervals to have their familiar spatial correspondence within each keyboard.

Equal-tempered systems are one common kind of microtonal strategy. They have certain limitations in return for their transposability. But they have the advantages that they are more widely available than nonequal systems (as described above) and that they are very easy to set up using some synthesizer editing software. The most accessible $n > 12$ microtonal systems for the synthesist are probably the nineteen and twenty-four equal-tempered systems. We will examine approaches to microtonality by looking at just these two systems, leaving readers with deeper interest to consult the literature listed in the General Bibliography.

Our look at the nineteen-tone equal-tempered system will be brief. Like every other tuning system, it has its subjective qualities or "mood." Available as a standard tuning option on at least one synthesizer, its primary rationale is that it gives what many consider a better approximation to just intonation than equal-tempered twelve can offer yet still offers modulation to twelve (or more) keys. As a comparison, the errors in the two systems, relative to the just intervals of the overtone series, are as indicated in table 6.1.

This system's thirds are much purer, and the fifth is still acceptable. Because it involves adding seven notes to a twelve-note conception, traditional notation can be readily extended to accommodate it by dis-

DEVIATIONS FROM JUST INTERVALS (CENTS)

Notes per octave	Fifth	Major 3rd	Minor 3rd
12	−2.0	+13.7	−15.6
19	−7.2	−7.4	+0.1

TABLE 6.1 Deviations from common just intervals produced by equal-tempered twelve- and nineteen-tone systems.

tinguishing sharped notes from their (twelve-note) enharmonically equivalent flat forms. The chromatic scale can then be notated C, C♯, D♭, D, D♯, E♭, E, F♭ (= E♯), F, F♯, G♭, G, G♯, A♭, A, A♯, B♭, B, C♭ (= B♯). It can be seen that each whole tone is divided into three parts. Hence, if an interleaved two-keyboard setup is used, notes can be arranged as in figure 6.14. The black keys are tuned the same on both keyboards. (This same setup can be used with a just-tuned, or any other, nineteen-tone system.)

If a single keyboard is used, the aural octave becomes a played perfect twelfth; the standard five-octave synthesizer keyboard will have a range of only three octaves and a major second. Figure 6.15 shows major and minor triads and major-scale structures as they would be played on such a keyboard. A useful introduction to the practicalities of this tuning has been given by Aikin (1988). Deeper treatments of this temperament are the classic works by Yasser (1975) and Mandelbaum (1961). The same idea of adding extra keys in groups of five or seven in line with the predilections of the familiar keyboard system can be used in the seventeen (twelve plus five) and thirty-one (nineteen plus twelve) systems.

Our second example, the twenty-four equal-tempered (quartertone) system, will be treated in a bit more depth. This tuning system has a not inconsiderable repertoire, and is probably the most widely commercially available non-twelve system. The use of quartertones can be traced back at least as far as ancient Greek music. To many Western ears the results at first are startling, even disturbing; but after only a short time, the user begins to find a way to put a fresh sheen on familiar musical ideas as well as to produce completely unprecedented effects.

The main hurdle for most newcomers to quartertones is getting a point of reference. We will therefore use the single keyboard system for realizing these examples, initially focusing on learning the new keyboard patterns required to produce familiar musical patterns, and only then branching out to new possibilities. The new keyboard patterns turn out to be conceptually simpler than patterns based on semitones, although bigger keyboard stretches are required.

In the following discussion, it will be useful to employ the familiar musical terms *triad, octave,* and *whole tone scale* in two ways: to refer to both sound and a corresponding visual pattern on the traditional tempered-twelve keyboard. This usage is too handy to forgo, but it must be used with caution to avoid confusion.

In quartertone tuning, all musical intervals from the tempered-twelve system now span twice the number of steps (keys) at the keyboard, so that all semitone-based patterns use the keys from one tempered-twelve whole tone scale and cover twice the physical distance. Consequently, in each set of twelve consecutive keys (which define an octave in the tempered-twelve system) there are at most only six keys involved in semitonal sonic

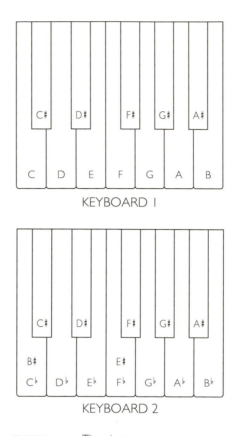

FIGURE 6.14 The nineteen-tone-per-octave tuning system arranged across two keyboards in a way that preserves interval distances.

patterns and at most half the usual number of different fingerings to be learned in transposing any musical figure.

Consider a concrete example: Figure 6.16a shows a C major scale starting on the key C3, notated for a twenty-four tone equal-tempered system. The scale is played as an arpeggio that draws on two triads from a two-octave tempered-twelve whole tone scale: a C augmented triad followed by a Bb augmented triad (with its octave). Transposing this to any other key is easy—just double the distance from C3 to the starting point of the new scale, and then use the same keyboard pattern. The sounding D major scale will be played as tempered-twelve E+ and D+ triads, F major will be played as tempered-twelve Bb+ and Ab+ triads, and so forth.

Other keyboard patterns besides that for the major scale are easy to remember and transpose. Figure 6.16b shows a major triad arpeggio. The diminished scale (fig. 6.16c) can be seen to consist of only four note names

major chord   minor chord   major scale

FIGURE 6.15 Traditional tonal structures on the single keyboard nineteen-tone-per-octave system.

a.

b.

c.

d.

FIGURE 6.16 Quartertone keyboard patterns for familiar tonal structures, on a single keyboard: for a major scale (a); for a major triad arpeggio (b); for a diminished scale (c); for a blues scale (d).

(C, E, F♯, B♭) from the tempered-twelve system, and every (semitonal) transposition of this scale can use the same fingering. The seven-note blues scale (fig. 6.16d) shows a less symmetrical pattern.

Figure 6.17 shows how quartertones can be used to embellish such a scale to create "in-the-cracks" blue note effects that keyboards usually can't manage. The excerpt is in the form of the first eight bars of a blues; the process can be carried on by making similar quartertone substitutions for the other tones of the blues (and chromatic) scale. The use of sequences and embellishment figures is a good way to carry this further.

FIGURE 6.17 Using quartertone tuning to create "in-the-cracks" blues embellishment.

Quartertone repertoire can be played to gain experience in using this tuning system. Recommended are Charles Ives's *Three Pieces for Quartertone Pianos* (1924), Ivan Wyshnegradsky's (also spelled Vishnegradsky) *Dithyramb* (1926), *Prelude and Fugue* (1929), and *24 Preludes for Two Quartertone Pianos* (1934/75), Hans Barth's *Concerto for Quartertone Piano and Strings* (1930), Béla Bartók's *Concerto for Violin and Orchestra* (1938) and the third movement of his *Sonata for Solo Violin* (1944— original unpublished version), John Eaton's *Concert Piece for Synket and Symphony Orchestra*, Teo Macero's *One-Three Quarters* for chamber ensemble, Toru Takemitsu's *Voice* for quartertone flute, and numerous works by composers Julián Carillo and Alois Hába. Quartertone piano music is commonly written for two pianos tuned a quartertone apart. Works featuring quartertones and other microtones have also been written by George Rimsky-Korsakov, Györgi Ligeti, Mordecai Sandberg, Heinz Holliger, Julián Carrillo, Alois Hába, and Jean-Etienne Marie.

"Macrotonality" and Redundancy

One kind of process that is inverse to microtonality might be called *macrotonality*, meaning that fewer than twelve notes per octave exist. This term is not very satisfactory and is used only because there seems to be no other. Other writers would call such temperaments microtonal, using microtonality to mean all systems that do not use the familiar twelve-tone temperament.

It is apparent that $n < 12$ systems need not require as much novelty in keyboard technique as $n > 12$ systems. If fewer notes per octave are needed, some keys can simply be omitted or tuned in unison with others so that the visual and heard octaves continue to coincide. Diatonic systems are particularly tractable since they can be easily mapped onto familiar scale formations. For example, the white keys could be tuned to an equal-tempered seven-notes-per-octave scale (as approximated in traditional Thai music), with the black keys left silent. Asymmetrical scales, like the five-note Indonesian slendro (readily mapped onto the black keys) and the seven-note Indonesian pelog (white keys) could be treated similarly.

Alternatively, the notes of such tuning systems can be mapped onto consecutive keys, so that the aural octave becomes less than the tempered-twelve octave (twelve keys). For example, a seven-note scale would cover a visual fifth. Such a setup would correspondingly increase the range of the keyboard but require a completely reconceptualized technique.

The idea of tuning some keys in unison with others nearby can be called *note redundancy,* and it has some special uses. For example, consider the following tuning set-up, in each octave:

KEY		PITCH		KEY		PITCH
C	→	C		F♯	→	G
C♯	→	C		G	→	G
D	→	D		G♯	→	A
D♯	→	D		A	→	A
E	→	E		A♯	→	B
F	→	F		B	→	B

Here the black keys are copies of the white. If the correct scale is C major, this makes it pretty hard to play a wrong note. This tuning also allows repeated notes to be executed as trills (except for E and F), and the interval of the unison becomes available without use of the sustain pedal. For example, if black- and white-key glissandi are played simultaneously, a composite glissando containing repeated notes (as on the harp) becomes feasible. In a purely diatonic piece or passage, such a tuning will provide other conveniences. This effect of turning the chromatic universe of possibilities into a diatonic one has been called "tonal quantization" (Roos 1989). In machines that allow it, notably samplers, an interesting effect is to give the black keys slightly different timbre parameters from their identically pitched neighbors for variety in performance.

If the performer can call up a series of distinct diatonic mappings of this kind, it is possible to play through a series of chord changes by giving very little attention to note choice (since all played notes will be mapped to the correct scale) and to focus on gesture and textural aspects of performance alone—for example, by playing trills, tremolos, and large leaps around the keyboard. Each different scale mapping can be called up by program change, or, with a few sequencers, these changes can be called up by stored MIDI mapping tables that operate for a preset number of bars at a time.

Microtonal Inflection

An interesting variant of the redundancy concept is where the "redundant" notes are not tuned to exact unison with the notes they are doubling but instead differ by a microtonal interval—a sixth or an eighth of a tone or less, say. The effect here is one of microtonal inflection. If two such microtonally inflected notes are played in alternation, they will have an effect that varies from microtonal step movement to repeated note, depending on the size of the microtonal inflection. One useful version of the technique makes the interval small enough to emphasize the latter effect without completely abandoning the former. In this case, when trills of two microtonally inflected notes are sustained, a beating effect occurs that adds apparent warmth and resonance to the sound. The following tuning table shows such a setup, where the intended tonic is B♭, and ↓ means microtonally flat:

KEY		PITCH		KEY		PITCH
C	→	C		F♯	→	F♯
C♯	→	D ↓		G	→	G
D	→	D		G♯	→	G♯ ↓
D♯	→	E♭		A	→	A
E	→	F ↓		A♯	→	B♭
F	→	F		B	→	B♭ ↓

Hence trills of C♯ and D, or E and F, and alternations between A, B♭, and B will produce such resonance. The microtonal alternatives can also be used as grace notes or as alternative notes in building chords, promoting realism by their variable pitch. If very slight amounts of microtonal inflection are used, the realism of synthesized string instrument glissandi will be enhanced (as on the harp or zither).

Keyboard Reversal

The last keyboard tuning given is nonmonotonic: It goes down in pitch as you move up from A♯ to B. When this idea is developed further, many possibilities unfold. One of the best known is keyboard reversal, where the keyboard is configured high to low moving from left to right. This requires a note-by-note retuning capacity or a MIDI mapping device that has an invert note number function, as most do. Playing a reversed keyboard is a useful mental exercise and can have practical implications. If a normal and inverted tuning system are MIDIed together, they automatically produce mirror harmony.

Partial keyboard reversal can be readily achieved with MIDI mapping devices. For example, if the tuning of odd-numbered notes is reversed, and the tuning of even-numbered notes left intact, the keyboard divides into two interlocking whole tone sets (scales), one ascending in pitch and the other descending. If each keyboard whole tone set is mapped to a sounding chromatic scale (intervals are shrunk by a factor of two) the keyboard might sound, in part, as follows:

KEY		PITCH	KEY		PITCH
C3	→	C3	G3	→	A♯2
C♯3	→	C♯3	G♯3	→	E3
D3	→	C♯3	A3	→	A2
D♯3	→	C3	A♯3	→	F3
E3	→	D3	B3	→	G♯2
F3	→	B2	C4	→	F♯3
F♯3	→	D♯3			

Any figure played in one tempered-twelve whole tone set (which, with this retuning, will sound chromatically) will be inverted when played in the other. A conjunct tempered-twelve diatonic or chromatic single line played near the center of the keyboard will stay relatively conjunct; away from this region, it will be converted to a leaping and perhaps pointillistic texture that may create the effect of several independent parts.

Self-Accompaniment

The previous example can be considered a primitive use of retuning to enable self-accompaniment. One standard procedure here is to combine (either by MIDI or internal synthesizer programming) two or more sound sources that use different tuning systems, but different only to the extent that they arrange the notes of one temperament differently. When done properly, this allows a single line to generate its own accompaniment; more complex textures will also be thickened accordingly. The usefulness of this procedure depends on whether the retuning capacity of the instrument extends to every note or uses the basic octave system. In either case, straightforward effects like doubling a part a diatonic third below may be achieved:

KEY		PITCH 1	PITCH 2	KEY		PITCH 1	PITCH 2
C3	→	C3	A2	G3	→	G3	E3
C♯3	→	C♯3	A2	G♯3	→	G♯3	F3
D3	→	D3	B2	A3	→	A3	F3
D♯3	→	D♯3	C3	A♯3	→	A♯3	G3
E3	→	E3	C3	B3	→	B3	G3
F3	→	F3	D3	C4	→	C4	A3
F♯3	→	F♯3	D3				

If the note-by-note system of retuning is available, the produced accompaniment may provide a second part of more genuine independence—such as a bass line or countermelody designed to anticipate the probable melodic function of the note to be harmonized, as in the following setup:

KEY		PITCH 1	PITCH 2	KEY		PITCH 1	PITCH 2
G2	→	G2	C2	F3	→	F3	B♭2
G♯2	→	G♯2	F1	F♯3	→	F♯3	A2
A2	→	A2	F2	G3	→	G3	E3
A♯2	→	A♯2	E1	G♯3	→	G♯3	F2
B2	→	B2	G1	A3	→	A3	C3
C3	→	C3	E2	A♯3	→	B♭3	G2
C♯3	→	C♯3	A1	B3	→	B3	G2
D3	→	D3	B1	C4	→	C4	C2
D♯3	→	D♯3	G2	C♯4	→	C♯4	G3
E3	→	E3	C2	D4	→	D4	F♯3

Figure 6.18 uses this setup; playing the treble melody will automatically produce the notated bass line. This technique can be readily applied to more complex material, and to three or more sound modules with distinct tuning systems, to produce harmonically complex chords from very simple arrangements of played notes.

Octave Remapping

Another option that produces something like self-accompaniment is *octave remapping*. This shifts a number of notes up or

FIGURE 6.18 Using keyboard retuning to create self-accompaniment.

down by one to several octaves while staying within conventional temperaments. Hence, all pitch class relations are preserved, but conjunct motion is converted into irregular leaping motion. The familiar can become well hidden, yet tonal relations are left intact, or at least not altered beyond usability. Part of such a (diatonic) retuning is given below:

KEY		PITCH	KEY		PITCH	KEY		PITCH
C1	→	C0	C2	→	C4	C3	→	C0
D1	→	D5	D2	→	D1	D3	→	D5
E♭1	→	E♭2	E♭2	→	E♭5	E♭3	→	E♭1
F1	→	F1	F2	→	F6	F3	→	F4
G1	→	G3	G2	→	G4	G3	→	G6
A1	→	A1	A2	→	A3	A3	→	A5
B♭1	→	B♭2	B♭2	→	B♭6	B♭3	→	B♭1
						C4	→	C4
						D4	→	D4

Figure 6.19 shows the result of playing a diatonic passage in parallel tenths with this tuning system. The leaps produced change the character of the line markedly, creating something like a virtuosic and unconventional Latin vamp from a slightly syncopated conjunct scale pattern. If octave remapping shifts only some notes by one octave up or down, closed position chords can be revoiced to imitate, for example, string voicings in the orchestra, which are impossible to articulate with only two hands at the keyboard.

Of course, this only begins to tap the potential of the idea of note remapping. One can produce completely novel arrangements of pitches based, for example, on the intervallic properties of the twelve-note system, as follows:

KEY		PITCH	KEY		PITCH	KEY		PITCH
C1	→	C1	C2	→	C2	C3	→	C3
C♯1	→	F1	C♯2	→	D♯2	C♯3	→	E3
D1	→	B♭1	D2	→	F♯2	D3	→	G♯3
E♭1	→	E♭2	E♭2	→	A2	E♭3	→	B3
E1	→	A♭2	E2	→	B2	E3	→	D♯4
F1	→	D♭3	F2	→	D3	F3	→	G4
F♯1	→	G♭3	F♯2	→	F3	F♯3	→	F♯4
G1	→	B3	G2	→	A♭3	G3	→	B♭4
G♯1	→	E4	G♯2	→	G3	G♯3	→	D5
A1	→	A4	A2	→	B♭3	A3	→	C♯5
B♭1	→	D5	B♭2	→	D♭4	B♭3	→	F5
B1	→	G5	B2	→	E4	B3	→	A5

In this example the C1 octave is mapped onto a cycle of fourths, the C2 octave onto a set of cycles of minor thirds, and the C3 octave onto a set of cycles of major thirds. Such schemes can be programmed on some MIDI transformation boxes and software, also introducing different channelization to each note as well.

"Incompatible" Tuning Systems

The tuning systems combined to this point have been rearrangements of notes from one master temperament, but it is possible also to combine different tuning systems, even those that are seemingly incompatible. One ready possibility is layering together quartertone and semitone tunings, as in my own composition *Constellation,* enabling the improvising player to think in either tonal space. The semitones can be heard as unconventional "overtones" for the quartertone organization, or the quartertones can be heard as the overtones, depending on volume and envelope settings, which are changeable in real time by using control sliders or pedals. Fingerings for familiar musical materials must then be learned for both tuning systems.

The possibilities of combining tuning systems that have different versions of the same intervals or were created for very divergent musical purposes have been little explored. This field has considerable scope for development.

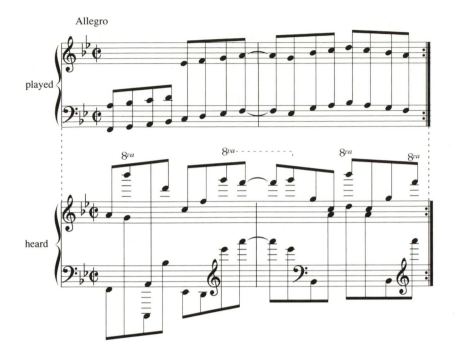

FIGURE 6.19 A vamp using octave remapping.

VELOCITY EFFECTS

Velocity in polyphonic context has basically the same musical functions as in the monophonic situation: to control onset dynamics, as in the decaying envelope model; to control onset articulation, as in the sustaining model; or to allow velocity-based switching, fading, and layering effects. To the first two cases there is little to add, but in the last category there are many potential refinements of the basic procedure, to which we now turn.

To review, the velocity switch chooses one from among two or more distinct sounds on the basis of key velocity. In cross-fading, the relative volumes of two or more components of a mix are determined by the applied velocity. In velocity-based layering, new sound layers enter as a function of velocity, without the fading out or switching out of sounds already present. As mentioned in chapter 5, such designs require the performer to adopt new modes of thinking about velocity. Where the different sounds or components do not function as different aspects of the same sound source, this design requires the synthesist to think of velocity no longer as a dynamic control but as a timbral selection control.

To investigate the nuances of these techniques, let us consider one or two practical examples. Assume we want to switch or layer four sounds. If the synthesizer or sampler has such features built in, fine. If not, or if we wish to switch or layer sounds on two different sound modules, the equivalent steps must be programmed into a MIDI mapping device. A possible way to do this is as follows: If the velocity range is 1–127, the incoming notes of Note On message $9n.xx.yy$H can be routed to channels $n, n + 1$, $n + 2$, and $n + 3$, based upon whether they fall in ranges such as 1–32, 33–64, 65–96, or 97–127 (decimal). In hex, these ranges are 1–20H, 21–40H, 41–60H, and 61–7FH. This creates a velocity switch effect, with only one sound sounding at a time. If, instead, the ranges are chosen to be 1–127, 33–127, 65–127, and 97–127, an increase in velocity progressively layers the different sounds one on top of the other. If the ranges chosen are 1–32, 1–64, 1–96, and 1–127, an increase in velocity will progressively silence the sound layers.

We are assuming for the purpose of demonstration that the keyboard's velocity range splits into four equal sections covering the range 1–127. This will, in real life, hardly ever be the case; trial and error, the ear, and player preference must guide the selection of actual boundaries that produce a good feel at the keyboard. For example, one common setup I have used has the ranges 1–54, 55–85, 86–108, and 109–127.

Furthermore, since we want to retain the dynamic characteristics and timbre of each of the selected sounds, it is best (if possible) to rescale the velocity after selecting a voice so that it covers the approximate full range. For the first mentioned case (velocity switching), the lowest range can be multiplied by 4, the second lowest range is multiplied by 4 after decimal 32 (20H) is subtracted from it, the next range is multiplied by 4 after subtracting 64 (40H), and the top range is multiplied by 4 after subtracting 96 (60H). In short, our message would be processed as shown in figure 6.20. The reader should be able to make a similar set of conversions for the velocity layering protocol. Note that in the diagram, $yy = 0$ (Note Off) messages must be treated separately to avoid leaving notes hanging (on). If possible, the message is routed to the correct channel; if such information is not stored, it must be routed to all channels. This may not be necessary if rapidly decaying timbres are used.

Velocity cross-fading, if not available internally on a machine or if needed between machines, can be comparably arranged with a MIDI transformation device. Figure 6.21 shows a simple two-way cross-fade, achieved in

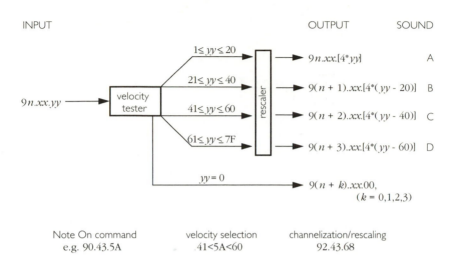

INPUT   OUTPUT   SOUND

$1 \leq yy \leq 20$ → $9n.xx.[4^*yy]$ A

$21 \leq yy \leq 40$ → $9(n + 1).xx.[4^*(yy - 20)]$ B

$9n.xx.yy$ → velocity tester $41 \leq yy \leq 60$ rescaler → $9(n + 2).xx.[4^*(yy - 40)]$ C

$61 \leq yy \leq 7F$ → $9(n + 3).xx.[4^*(yy - 60)]$ D

$yy = 0$ → $9(n + k).xx.00,$
$(k = 0,1,2,3)$

Note On command   velocity selection   channelization/rescaling
e.g. 90.43.5A   41<5A<60   92.43.68

FIGURE 6.20 Creating velocity switching and rescaling using MIDI mapping. All numbers are in hex.

two ways: If the patches are strongly velocity sensitive, the 9nH messages alone will suffice. If the sounds do not have significant dynamic relationships with velocity, then the Bn.07H (MIDI volume) messages must be used instead or as well. This will achieve cross-fading but of a rather idiosyncratic variety in polyphonic context: all sounding notes will be recross-faded on the basis of the velocity of each successive note.

Other velocity effects can occur by the use of MIDI mapping devices. For example, velocity switching can be used not to select between sounds but to cause transposition or octave doubling. This can greatly expand the dynamic power of a sound. Also, sporadic revoicing can be introduced by using a MIDI mapping device that takes only every velocity value divisible by a small integer, such as 3 or 4 (see the section on modulo filtering, p. 250) and transposes it up or down one octave. This type of numerical "filtering" can also be used to effectively increase the size of the keyboard if notes in top and bottom octaves are often transferred below and above the keyboard's nominal span. Some devices allow velocity to be set from a controller, and this effect is even found as a dedicated feature on a few master controllers (for example, the Cheetah 7P). Even more radically, if the first and second data bytes of the note message are swapped, then played velocity will determine note number, and the played note number will determine velocity. This requires a very different keyboard technique. For velocity related effects of status byte conversion, see "MIDI Mapping Devices and Status Byte Conversion," below.

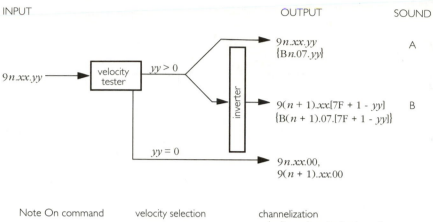

INPUT   OUTPUT   SOUND

$9n.xx.yy$ → velocity tester

$yy > 0$

$9n.xx.yy$
$\{Bn.07.yy\}$ A

inverter

$9(n + 1).xx.[7F + 1 - yy]$
$\{B(n + 1).07.[7F + 1 - yy]\}$ B

$yy = 0$

$9n.xx.00,$
$9(n + 1).xx.00$

Note On command   velocity selection   channelization
velocity and controller inversion

e.g. 90.43.5A   5A>0   90.43.5A, 91.43.26
$\{B0.07.5A, B1.07.26\}$

FIGURE 6.21 Creating velocity cross-fading using MIDI mapping. Both velocity and controller 7 effects are shown. All numbers are in hex.

ATTACHMENT

Attachment is a term used here to mean the attaching of a number of MIDI events to a single MIDI note. Chords can be attached (via layering or internally on those synthesizers that offer this sort of chord play) or motives can be (by so-called *riff attachment*). In the first case the attached notes may be transposed, delayed, and rechannelized (or any combination of these three) to produce a complex sound object. In the second case, one or more motives or riffs are attached to each key, either by sampling played motives, using wavetable loop options, using digital delay with pitch shift, or using MIDI mapping devices that have delay. Some synthesizers—such as the Kawai K1 and K4—allow the oscillators to be transposed and delayed, giving this effect inside one patch. The riffs added may be transpositions of each other or all different. If several riffs are attached to each key, velocity switching can be used to choose between them. They may all be cued to a common pulse, play back at speeds proportional to the note number or velocity value, or have no common rhythmic denominator. In all these cases the effect will be one of producing motivic mosaics, either coordinated or uncoordinated.

USING UNPREDICTABILITY

Unpredictability is a useful quality in a performance setup in certain circumstances. This idea, well known to those who habitually operate in the home-built low-fi end of the technological resource spectrum, means that the performer gets out at least partially unpredictable output for the same input. This requires a reconceptualization of performance actions and an attitude more like improvising in conjunction with another performer. Such effects are typically programmed on synthesizers by using random or sample-and-hold generators, unrememberable interface complexity, or "pathological" synthesis parameter values that produce partially erratic output due to quirks in the synthesizer's operating system.

MIDI ARPEGGIATORS AND DELAYS

Many performance effects available on older analog synthesizers can readily be duplicated in the digital MIDI environment without being at the mercy of external signal processing noise. Prominent among these are functions like arpeggiation and delay, often available in separate devices.

The arpeggiator is basically an accompaniment-producing device that arpeggiates the held notes through various octaves and possibly other transpositions. The performer either plays with the orientation of guiding the chord production or plays a lead melody or counterline against the arpeggiation pattern, which is played on another zone or keyboard. In the MIDI environment, this device seems to be developing considerable programmability: the Oberheim Cyclone arpeggiator, for example, allows arpeggiation modes with multichannel output and embedded transpositions, real-time control of the direction and rate of arpeggiation, multiple arpeggios in synced rhythms, and other such features.

Performing with an echo unit, whether analog or digital, MIDI or audio, stand-alone or on-board, is a technique easily abused. MIDI delay or echo may allow real-time control of delay time, rate of decay, and possibly other variables. Since a MIDI echo may be either a direct copy or one that is melodically transformed, the possibilities of self-accompaniment are considerable—especially if MIDI delay and depth are controllable in real time. Such units are similar in effect to those of audio processing units that may have delay and pitch shifting. One useful but rare effect as of this writing is for a MIDI delay to be set to have certain rhythmic values and to be synchronized to performance by the use of MIDI clocks.

MIDI MAPPING DEVICES AND STATUS BYTE CONVERSION

MIDI mapping devices (data processors, transformation boxes) allow input MIDI data to be changed before they affect the sound sources. Some of the most powerful keyboard reconfiguration effects can be obtained by these devices, the best known being the Yamaha MEP4, Digital Music Corporation's MX-8, the Forte Mentor MIDI Event Processor, and the Axxess Mapper. Equivalent software is becoming more wide-spread; even some sequencers (such as C-Lab's Notator) have these real-time mapping capacities. Although MIDI mapping devices enable many features, like cross-fading and switching, splits and zones, retuning, velocity and pressure scaling, MIDI delays, monophonic assignment modes (low, high, last, etc.), and renumbering of controllers, all of which are already found on some synthesizers and master controllers, many others are unique to them. Such devices allow MIDI data to be altered by multiplication or addition, modulo filtered, range limited, inverted, time delayed, or completely reinterpreted by changing MIDI status bytes, all in real time. (*Modulo filtering* means that all data values exactly divisible by a given number, called the *modulus,* are filtered out. For example, if the modulus is 3, then 3, 6, 9, 12, etc. are culled.) A few mapping devices also allow data lists to be triggered, with variable entry points, or a number of notes (possibly on different MIDI channels) to be slaved to each key of the performing keyboard. Others allow lists of system exclusive data to be loaded in and sent out at the push of a single foot switch or front panel button (a feature found on some master controllers). This can allow the construction of macros that perform real-time editing operations. On some machines, these sysex lists do not have to be separately constructed byte by byte but can be recorded from a connected synthesizer as the real-time editing changes are made. Unfortunately, many MIDI mappers do not deal with system real-time messages.

Particularly powerful data transformations are associated with MIDI *status byte conversion,* producing *functional conversion.* Here the status bytes of MIDI commands are altered so that commands sent out by the hands are functionally completely reinterpreted by the synthesis module. A few examples will show some of the potentials of this method, without any illusion that a comprehensive set of possibilities can be enunciated.

Example 1

If Note On commands from selected keys are converted to Program Change messages, program changes may be automatically cued from special notes without hands leaving the keyboard. These could be used to program numbers not otherwise easily accessible from the front panel.

Example 2

If Note On messages 9*n.xx.yy*H are converted to 9*n.yy.xx*H and then copied to also produce Pitch Bend commands E*n.yy.xx*H, velocity will select pitch bend amount and note number, and note number will select velocity. With each played note, the tuning basis of the entire keyboard will change. Notes played softly will be low in pitch, with little pitch bend, while notes struck hard will be high, with substantial pitch bend. To make this work practically, the incoming Note Off commands 9*n.xx.*00 should be filtered out since they will not be able to turn off the notes turned on and will just continually reset pitch bend to zero (if 7-bit information is used in pitch bend) or near zero (if 14-bit information is used in pitch bend). Hence decaying sounds must be used. When used in moderation with percussive-enveloped timbres, this is an especially expressive technique.

Example 3

If Polyphonic Pressure messages are converted to Note On commands, repeated notes are produced from each key at a rate proportional to the rate of change of pressure (but limited by the pressure sensor's scan rate), with a key velocity given by applied pressure. If the Polyphonic Pressure messages are converted to Note On commands with the data bytes swapped, pressing on a key after striking it produces hypervirtuosic glissandi. These can be changed to scales or arpeggios by selectively filtering out some Note On messages. Since the Note On commands produced are not automatically followed by corresponding Note Offs, this technique should be tried with sounds that have nonsustaining envelopes. Alternatively, appropriate Note Off commands can be paired with the Note Ons, delayed by a certain time. This last possibility can also avoid the rather small possibility of confusing or crashing some devices or programs that require Note Offs to follow Note Ons.

Example 4

If channel commands can be converted to system commands, the output from controllers or the keyboard can be used to turn sequencers on and off, decide on their start points, change their tempi of playback, and so forth, or to perform arbitrary real-time editing of data using system exclusive formats where the synthesizer allows such external control. Some of these functions are increasingly available as standard features on sequencers.

Some devices allow further possibilities. For example, a list of notes or other data can be stored, accessed at variable entry points in real time, and used to generate note sequences or determine a floating transposition point or mix with played data. Notes currently depressed by an input keyboard can be stored in a buffer and used as a basis for chordal attachment. Groups of messages can be combined to produce new messages. Such possibilities are most readily developed in a computer-assisted environment and will be explored further in chapter 11.

REFERENCES

Aikin, Jim. "19-Tone Temperament." *Keyboard* 14,3 (March 1988): 74–80.

De Furia, Steve. *Power Play DX*. Milwaukee: Hal Leonard, 1988.

Helmholtz, Hermann von. *On the Sensations of Tone*. Reprinted New York: Dover, 1954. (Originally published 1885.)

Mandelbaum, M. Joel. "Multiple Division of the Octave and the Tonal Resources of 19-Tone Temperament." Ph.D. diss., Indiana University, 1961.

Moog, R. A. "Position and Force Sensors and Their Application to Keyboards and Related Control Devices." *Proceedings of the AES 5th International Conference: Music and Digital Technology*. John Strawn, chair, Los Angeles. New York: Audio Engineering Society, 1987.

Roos, Randy. "Tonal Quantization: MIDI Guitar Meets PVG." *Keyboard* 15,10 (Oct. 1989): 102–104.

Wilkinson, Scott. *Tuning In: Microtonality in Electronic Music*. Milwaukee: Hal Leonard, 1988.

Yasser, Joseph. 1975. *A Theory of Evolving Tonality*. New York: Da Capo Press, 1975. (Originally published New York: American Library of Musicology, 1932.)

PERFORMANCE CONFIGURATIONS AND PRACTICALITIES

We must, then, distinguish two tendencies or purposes: the commercial—to which standardized production belongs, and the educational—to which the work of art properly speaking belongs. In the first case the success is immediate. In the second it is delayed. In the reality of our present organization the two tendencies coexist, despite the fact that they are contradictory. This is not rare, however, as contradiction is the way in which natural forces live and act.

- Carlos Chavez, *Toward a New Music: Music and Electricity* (1937)

In the previous two chapters we have focused on the performer and instrument in comparative isolation from the performance context. In this chapter we look at the practicalities of performance configurations: how things such as keyboards, sound modules, sequencers, computers, and audio and MIDI processors should be configured for optimal performance in a variety of situations, whether live or in the studio. Before doing this, there are some issues common to all performance configurations that will first require some attention.

LAYERING

Contemporary synthesizer performance practice routinely doubles musical parts by layering two, three, or more timbres to increase the level of complexity and sophistication of the sound objects. This can be done within one multitimbral synthesizer or by controlling two or more separate sound engines from one synthesizer or master keyboard via MIDI. In this section we systematically examine the issues involved in such layering.

The idea of layering is very similar to the central idea of additive synthesis, as discussed in chapter 2. The difference, albeit a minor one, is that we are combining already completed sounds rather than simple components of sounds. To discuss layering in general terms, we must attempt to classify sounds with regard to their general potentials for musical combination. This is no easy task. Although some sounds have very unusual characteristics that strongly suggest specific musical uses, many others are quite versatile. In any case, no one can definitively say what a sound might or might not be good for, even considering the goals of some particular musical style. Tomorrow someone may come along and show new possibilities that throw traditional wisdom out the door.

But there are a number of perspectives that will prove of value. Of primary importance is the *sonic goal* of the layering. Does it seek to imitate another sound, reinforce the basic sound, brighten the spectrum of sound, change its coloration, change its envelope characteristics, add special sound effects, add a canon by the use of delay, add reverberation, or create a chorus effect by detuned unisons? Or is its goal more compositional and metaphoric, as in the production of a "restful" sound, a sound of anguish, a sound befitting the weightlessness of outer space (where, of course, there is literally no sound), or an inner sound of meditation? When such goals can be clearly formulated, the criterion for successful layering is simply whether the addition of a new layer adds to or detracts from the desired goal. At other times, a more exploratory or trial-and-error approach is useful.

The idea of a sonic goal leads naturally to the question of whether or not a sound is *complete* for a given purpose. If a sound is not yet properly fine-tuned for its function, it may need reprogramming, simple layering, or both reprogramming and layering. Adding some attack noise to a plucked string sound that is otherwise too dull may make the result more realistic. Likewise, a sound consisting of just occasional bleeps and sonic smears may be too sparse and benefit from the addition of some complementary bleeps and smears in a different register.

Worth examining in some depth is the common goal of *reinforcement.* Some sounds are not rich or powerful enough for their intended use, or they may lack "warmth." Adding layers that are identical except for slight detuning will "fatten" the sound. Adding similar sounds that have somewhat different timbral details will give the sound increased richness and can imitate the effect of an instrumental choir. (This is a very useful technique for enhancing the realism or credibility of a wide variety of sounds, from "plucked string" instruments to "brass" or "voice.") The doubling of a sound at one or more octaves is another typical kind of reinforcement. If doubling uses intervals other than octaves and unisons, parallel harmony results. If doubling at such intervals occurs at reduced volume, the effect can be that of adding harmonics, or stops, as on the organ.

This raises the question of whether the sound layers are intended to perceptually fuse or retain their separate identities. In the first case we will hear one resultant sound, and in the second we will hear more than one. Such perceptions may be unequivocal or depend on musical context or personal predilection.

The practicalities of such perspectives can be discussed further by looking at the structural relationships between the layers. The following factors seem to be the most important in combining two or more sound layers:

pitch relations

onset times

relative volumes

envelopes and time behavior

timbral similarity

spatial positioning in the mix

responses to real-time control

The relationship between layers can be fixed or made dynamically variable by the performed effects of controllers, keyboard range, key velocity, and so forth.

The importance of the *pitch relations* between the various layers is unmistakable. Just how this works depends to some extent on the use to which the composite sound is to be put and to some extent on the frequency spectra of the different layers. It is useful to distinguish here the different spectral types, as discussed in chapter 2: pure sounds, harmonic sounds, pitched nonharmonic sounds, formant-like sounds, and noise. The first three types may be classed as being of definite pitch, and the last two as being of indefinite pitch.

We also distinguish two modes of keyboard control of the frequency of the sound engine: keyboard tracking or fixed pitch. With keyboard tracking, the frequency of the programmed sound changes with MIDI note number in accordance with the set tuning system; in fixed-pitch mode, the frequency of sounds does not change with MIDI note number. The first three spectral types can function as carriers of traditional melody and hence are usually used with keyboard tracking. If any such sound component is used with fixed-pitch setting, the effect is to add an ostinato or drone.

Formants and noise may be keyboard tracked or operate at fixed pitch, depending on musical function. If they are keyboard tracked, melodic gestures at the keyboard will produce audible contours, where relative judgments like high and low are valid even though specific intervals will not be distinguishable. One term for the resultant musical shapes is *registral melody.* If fixed-pitch mode is used, such sounds commonly function as vocal formants, percussion-like instruments, or noise components of melodic carrier sounds; of course, they can be used in many conceivable ways. Percussion instruments with spectra of this sort are often explicitly classed as indefinite pitch instruments.

When definite pitch sounds are combined, so that the composite sound will usually be acting as a carrier of melody, the primary pitch variable is of course the interval of transposition between them. Transposition intervals are most commonly the familiar intervals of consonance: unison, one or more octaves up or down, a fifth, one or more octaves plus a fifth, and similar combinations. The addition of a fourth produces similar effects in some styles, such as contemporary jazz, but yields a more dissonant effect requiring resolution in other styles—notably that of traditional tonal harmony. The intervals used to this point add only very limited chromaticism to modal or diatonic music.

Next most common are major and minor thirds and sixths, possibly combined with one or more octaves. These intervals will take a diatonic line more out of its modal context than the preceding intervals, and so they require more careful use in such musical situations; in harmonically freer contexts, they are quite generally useful. Often, decreasing the volume of layers standing in this relation will allow them to be heard as overtones rather than as parallel harmony. Such a predilection is enhanced by separation by one or more octaves. A number of organ stops use this principle (see chapter 8).

Transposition intervals based on seconds, sevenths, or tritones and one or more octaves tend to be associated with special effects or with passages of short duration where melodic doubling is intended. As above, the use of one or more octaves of separation with these intervals in a layer reduces the perceived dissonance, although perhaps to a lesser degree than with thirds and sixths. Such intervals may also be used to facilitate the production of clusters—for example, a diminished seventh chord with a second layer tuned a whole tone above will produce the eight-note diminished scale. Yet another use is to add nonharmonic components of short duration to a sound.

Some pitched sounds that have highly inharmonic spectral components will not follow these general guidelines since certain nominally "dissonant" intervals may actually prove to combine the inharmonic partials in a dissonance-reducing manner. Hence, experimentation in the combining of such sounds is essential.

Quite different types of pitch relationships can occur when two or more component layers carry definite pitch but each sound corresponds to a different tuning system. Such effects were discussed in chapter 6.

The above transposition ideas can change when we consider combining the other spectral categories. Indefinite pitch sounds may work well along the lines of the same hierarchy of intervals, but the contrary can also be the case, and sometimes it is register or absolute interval size more than specific interval type that is relevant. For example, with drum, gong, or colored noise sounds, combination at the interval of a seventh or a ninth can thicken a sound and keep pitch indefinite. Combination at the interval of a third or a fifth may produce more "resonance" but will also create a sense of fundamental pitch that may be musically inappropriate.

When definite and indefinite pitch sources are mixed, there are many possibilities. One standard idea that imitates the chiff function of woodwind instruments is the combination of a short noisy onset transient (often in fixed-pitch mode or with a shallow keyboard tracking, where pitch changes only very little across the keyboard) with a steady state sound in (full) keyboard tracking mode. The chiff component can be velocity dependent. Of course, this can often be done internally in a synthesis program, without the need for layering. If definite pitch layers are to be perceptually fused with indefinite layers, it is best to voice them into tight clusters or have either the duration of the noise components or the pitched components be very short.

The *onset times* of different components, relative to the depression of a key, can have important effects on layering. The perceptual fusion of sounds is possible only if their onset times are not too different. Just how asynchronous the sounds can be and still be heard as a single sound depends quite a bit on the sounds' envelopes, as discussed later in this section and in chapter 3. With slowly rising envelope shapes, relative onset times lose their primary importance. If attack envelopes are more rapid, different onset times may cause the listener to hear two or more separate notes. When the time difference is small, these attacks may merge into a timbral perception that simulates the complex pluck effects of claviers and double-strung string instruments (like the twelve-string guitar).

The optimal *relative volumes* of the layers in a composite sound will depend on whether they are to be heard as equal partners or with some components subordinate to others. Sound components at noticeably lower volume than the others will tend to be heard as timbral coloration (e.g., under- or overtones) in many cases. Perceptual fusion will be promoted where the most contextually novel components of the sound are lower in volume than the others.

Envelope relations and time behavior is a phrase used to cover a multitude of temporal possibilities in layering. First of all, envelopes can affect any number of variables: dynamics, volume, pitch, filter parameters, panning, reverberation, and so forth. Second, such envelopes can also assume a great number of different shapes and operate over time scales varying from milliseconds to minutes. Very complex time behavior can be built up when the different envelopes of different layers are superimposed. It seems therefore impossible to be comprehensive here about the possibilities of their combination; the ear of the musician must act as the guide. However, there are some clear-cut generalizations. For example, it is clear that layers guided by similarly shaped envelopes (over similar time scales) will tend to be heard as a single sound.

To partially systematize the idea of "similarly shaped" envelopes we can point to five basic *time shapes,* which include some notions of both shape and duration. There are 5 basic types, illustrated in figure 7.1: the transient envelope, the decaying envelope, the swelling envelope, the stabilizing envelope, and the evolving envelope.

The boundary between a transient and a decaying envelope falls roughly in the range 200 to 500 msec, although there is no hard psychoacoustic barrier here. Some musicians consider that a categorical difference exists between transients in the range 50 to 200+ msec and those in the range 0 to 50 msec, which might be called "short" transients or pulses. (These numbers are only suggestive and can vary as a function of timbre, pitch, and individual perceptual differences.)

The swelling envelope is just the reverse of the decaying envelope. The fourth type—stabilizing—is also called "sustaining" if it refers to volume or dynamics. It may stabilize to a constant level, as shown in the figure, or to a repeating shape. Some synthesizers, such as the Prophet VS and Kurzweil 1000 series, have looping envelopes that produce this latter effect. The evolving envelope is one that retains unpredictability indefi-

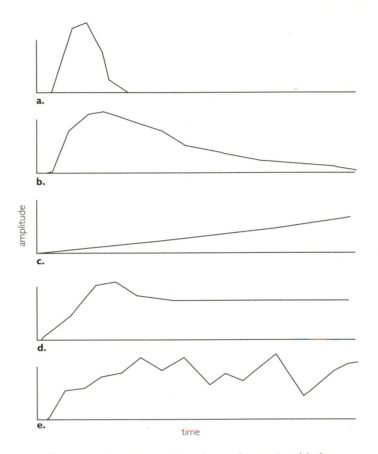

FIGURE 7.1 Five basic envelope shapes: the transient (a); the decaying (b); the swelling (c); the stabilizing (d); and the evolving (e).

nitely; in other words, it keeps coming up with substantial amounts of new information. The most common sources for this are noise and sample-and hold waveforms; highly complex modulation routings effectively imitate it.

These basic envelopes may be combined in many different ways. Three common possibilities are shown in figure 7.2. In figure 7.2a, *multiple attacks* are achieved by layering variously delayed transients. In practical terms, this could be approximated by using a sample-and-hold LFO to modulate an oscillator's amplitude or frequency in one or more layers. In figure 7.2b, the attack transient masks the more gradual onset of the sustaining time shape. Figure 7.2c shows the combination of decaying and swelling envelopes to produce a *temporal cross-fade*, where one sound gradually turns into another.

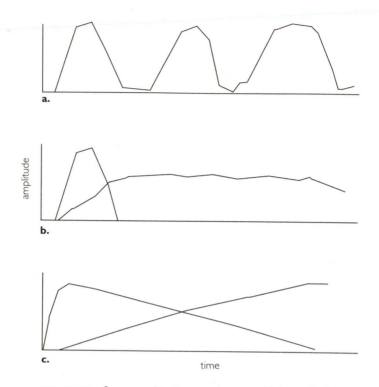

FIGURE 7.2   Some combination envelopes: multiple attacks (a); masking (b); temporal cross-fade (c).

These combinations are limited by one factor: The temporal resolution of the auditory system is greater than what MIDI transmission (or indeed the CPUs of most synthesizers) can achieve (information that was given in chapter 3). This means that the precise coordination of envelopes in different layers to anything like the limits of peceptibility (millisecond resolution) is not normally possible—unless perhaps by two synthesizers with identical response times (identical models) listening to the same channel. The best that can otherwise be achieved is coordination or dovetailing over the time scale of a few 10s of milliseconds.

Timbral similarity is a catch-all phrase referring to the qualities of the sounds that have not been specifically mentioned under previous categories. Similarity or difference in timbre, respectively promoting fusion or independence in perception, can be refined here along the lines of the aspects of sound color discussed in chapter 2.

Well-designed *spatial positioning in the mix* can promote clearer perception of the music's intentions. Its primary role in layering is to promote fusion or fission of sounds. Sounds that come from the same direction and apparent depth of field, whether fixed or in apparent motion, are more likely to fuse than those that do not. If the position of layers is changeable in real time by the use of controllers routed to panning and reverberation, then the effects of similarity or differentiation can be enhanced.

Responses to real-time control can quite generally promote fusion or differentiation of the components in layering. For example, two lines that otherwise fuse might be given different pitch bend ranges or modulation depths. Then, when the controller is applied, the single line splits into its components. Another example is to have the volume of one component of a sound determined by aftertouch so that it can be brought in whenever required for reinforcement or coloration.

STANDARD PERFORMANCE CONFIGURATIONS

The development of increasingly complex MIDI systems has led to a number of standard configurations suited to different playing conditions. The most basic setup is one performer playing one keyboard, which in turn drives one or more sound engines. This keyboard may be a separate master controller or it may be part of a synthesizer or sampler that includes its own sound engine.

Figure 7.3 shows some basic configurations. Configuration 1 corresponds either to a master controller driving a single sound engine or a self-contained keyboard synthesizer or sampler. Configurations 2 and 3 correspond to a single keyboard driving a number of separate sound engines. The difference between these two configurations is in the MIDI connections: Configuration 2 uses a star network, where the MIDI signal is split into separate paths by a junction box or MIDI patch bay before routing to the sound engines, while configuration 3 uses a chain network, based on a chain of MIDI IN/THRU connections. Such systems may include a MIDI mapping device, as indicated. Audio processing, not indicated in the diagram, may be built into the sound engine or available in outboard devices. Also not shown is the system mixer, where audio outputs from the sound engines are mixed and given final panning, equalization, and perhaps other treatments.

A more complex performance system—configuration 4—is shown in figure 7.4. Here the keyboardist plays multiple keyboards, which are assigned to various sound engines on the basis of the patch configurations set on the patch bay. The use of a patch bay is increasingly essential in this case since different sets of connections may be required for different pieces and the rather unpalatable alternative is the continual replugging of

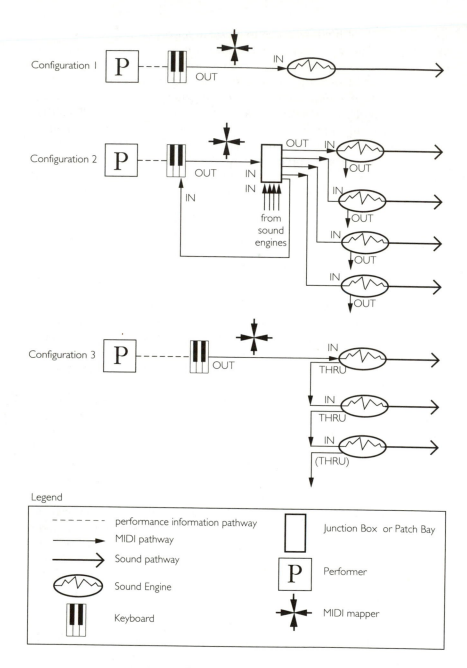

FIGURE 7.3   Three performance configurations.

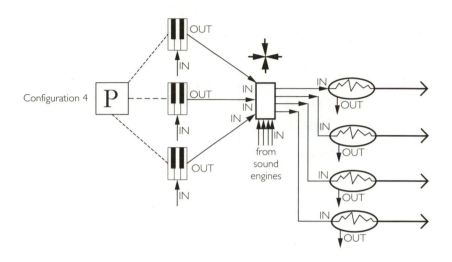

FIGURE 7.4   A multiple keyboard performance configuration.

MIDI cables. Typically, a separate MIDI channel is used for each musical part, and each such part may engage all or part of one or more sound engines. An alternative used by a few performers is to use Omni mode for all modules and bring up their volumes as required by the use of a number of separate foot controllers, one for each timbre. The effect of independent MIDI channels may also be achieved by the direct patching of each keyboard to the desired sound module.

These setups have live performance in mind, without the use of sequencing. When a sequencer (either hardware or software) is used, either for recording or playback, the system setup changes slightly. If the sequencer and keyboards play different modules then the sequencer merely takes the place of one of the keyboards in configuration 4. However, if both the keyboard and the sequencer/computer need to control the same sound-producing parts of the system, keyboard and sequencer/computer must be able to merge their output. Four ways this can be done are illustrated in figure 7.5. A computer icon is used, but in reality it can be a sequencer or a computer running sequencer- or other MIDI-based software.

Configuration A uses the so-called *soft THRU* option available on sequencers/computers. This option merges OUT and THRU. The main limitation of this method is that if the sequencer/computer is not on, or is running a program without soft THRU, the system will not be playable

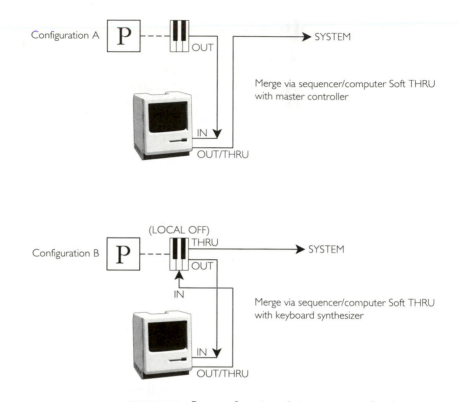

FIGURE 7.5   Four configurations that use a merge function to allow both a keyboard and sequencer to control a system of sound engines.

from the keyboard. This setup is generally suitable only for controller keyboards, since any sound engine built into the keyboard device itself cannot be controlled by the sequencer/computer. However, the same method can be readily modified for synthesizers and keyboard samplers that have a Local Off function using the design shown in configuration B.

Configuration C uses the built-in merge function, available on master controllers and a few synthesizers, where MIDI data sent to the IN port are echoed out the OUT port. Soft THRU on the sequencer/computer must be off if a MIDI feedback loop is to be avoided. Configuration D uses an external merge device, as in a dedicated merge box or patch bay. To avoid feedback loops, sequencer/computer soft THRU must be off, and any built-in merge functions of the keyboard itself must be turned off.

Figure 7.6 (configuration E) shows a more intricate system containing two keyboards, patch bay, computer, and multiple sound modules, as

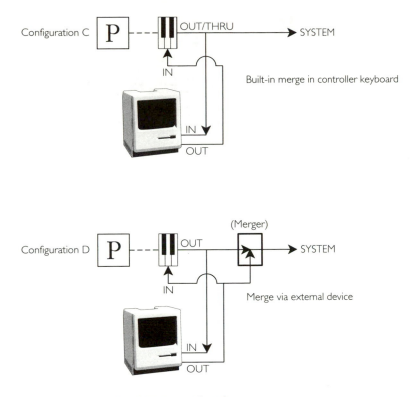

FIGURE 7.5   continued.

might be used in a studio or live performance. As above, outboard audio processing and mixing are not shown. Merging of controlling keyboards and sequencer/computer is assumed to be achieved by the MIDI patch bay. It should be remembered that sequencing is only one type of computer function, and other software packages, notably editor/librarian software, compositional environments, sound file display, software synthesis, music and MIDI analysis, and music notation programs, form a pool of other resources. In these cases the performer can also perform on, or at least operate, the computer via QWERTY keyboard and mouse.

In such a complex system the use of a patch bay is essential. Although INs and OUTs from every device are shown, it is not feasible to show every possible set of connections for all possible functions for which the system may be used. However, the most common kinds of connections may be readily described. For performance with and recording into a sequencer or compositional environment, the connections indicated in figure 7.6 or any of the options of figure 7.5 will serve. These will also be suitable for MIDI performance, autotranscription into music notation, and MIDI

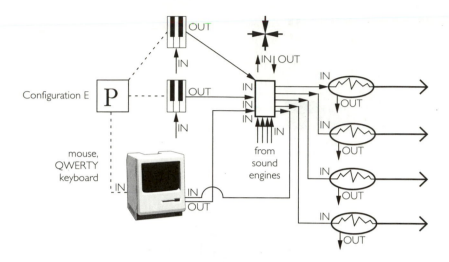

FIGURE 7.6   A configuration for stage performance or MIDI studio.

analysis. To use editor/librarian software for a specific device the MIDI connections must run as follows:

computer → device;

device → computer.

If a MIDI mapping device is used to alter the performer's output, the connection runs:

keyboard → MIDI transformation box → system + computer;

computer → system;

(*System* refers to the sound engines and controllable audio devices.)

In complex MIDI systems, it is useful to have two or more distinct MIDI ports from the sequencer/computer or MIDI interface. Each ouput port can then drive a separate data bus, which provides the twin advantages of reducing the chances of data clogging and making possible more than sixteen MIDI channels. Two separate outputs, for example, will allow thirty-two MIDI channels: A1–16 from port A, and B1–16 from port B. (Commercial systems currently allow up to fifteen independent MIDI ports, for a total of 240 channels.) An example of an actual MIDI studio with two separate MIDI buses is given in figure 7.7. This diagram shows MIDI and audio connections in one of the composition laboratories at La Trobe

I. AUDIO

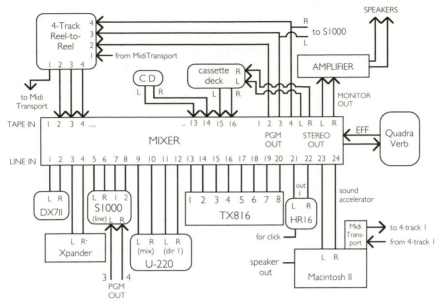

II. MIDI

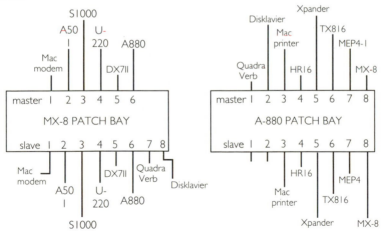

FIGURE 7.7 Signal routings in a moderately complex MIDI studio (at La Trobe University, Melbourne, Australia).

University in Melbourne Australia, as of March 1990. This setup used the following equipment:

DX7II-FD synthesizer

Akai S1000HD digital sampler with 8 Meg of RAM

Oberheim Xpander

TX816 FM tone generator rack

Roland U-220 sound module

Alesis HR-16 drum machine

Roland A-50 master keyboard controller

MX-8 MIDI patch bay/processor

Roland A-880 patch bay

Yamaha MEP4 MIDI event processor

Tascam M-224 mixer

Macintosh II computer: hard disk, 5 Meg RAM, Digidesign Sound Accelerator Card

Passport MIDI Transport MIDI interface

Alesis Quadraverb

Yamaha Disklavier

stereo Amplifier

Two speakers

cassette deck

compact disc player

reel-to-reel tape recorder (4-track)

Fairlight Voicetracker (pitch-to-MIDI converter)

The number of MIDI devices necessitated two patch bays.

SAVING AND LOADING SYSTEM EXCLUSIVE DATA

In using such systems, one major issue is the efficient bulk storage of patches. This can be handled in a number of ways. Each sound module, synthesizer, or sampler has its own specific range of storage devices—special cartridges, cassette tape, or floppy disk. Cartridges are quick but tend to be expensive and rapidly outdated; cassettes are slow, cumbersome, and sometimes unreliable; floppy disks are normally the best system (where a built-in disk drive is available), being inexpensive and readily available, though they may be less rugged than other storage media (although this is not a significant problem, especially with $3\frac{1}{2}''$ floppies).

Today, nearly all devices also provide sysex bulk data dump via MIDI. This allows the storage and retrieval of such information from many different devices to be done centrally, if a suitable generic system exclusive data storage device is available. Its practical use requires a patch bay since different patchings are required to save sysex data to the central device from each sender, although data saved in the central device can be downloaded into all peripheral devices in the basic playing configuration.

The special central storage device can be software or hardware. If central storage is to be in a synthesizer or master keyboard via its on-board floppy disk drive, configurations 2, 4, and E are viable. If storage is to be in a sequencer/computer, then configuration E should be used. With the computer, such generic bulk dump storage is available in special programs and as a normal part of sequencer environments. Dedicated hardware sequencers also include bulk data dump storage. Only a minority of such devices allow the sysex data to be examined byte by byte and edited. Small hardware devices dedicated to bulk data dump storage are widely available, and may be especially useful for the touring performer.

There is one caveat here. Some bulk dumps require handshaking, the reciprocal communication of devices, whereby the sending module must first be sent a signal (and possibly others subsequently) from the receiver before data transmission can begin. Many MIDI recorders will not record such bulk dumps properly. On devices that allow the display and editing of sysex data, such as the Roland MC-500 or C-Lab's Creator, handshake request codes, if known, can be specifically assembled and sent. A few bulk dump drives are intelligent enough to have some hardware protocols built into them. For detailed information on sysex coding the reader should refer to the MIDI specifications in the users' manuals or the IMA.

Samples can also be transferred via MIDI, but the MIDI baud rate is too slow to make this a preferred procedure in comparison to direct storage on floppy or hard disk.

PRACTICAL ISSUES IN LIVE PERFORMANCE

Program Changes

With any synthesis configuration, it is frequently necessary to change programs as the music progresses in a performance. With a single synthesizer or sound module this poses no particular problems;

one simply picks the program number of the next required sound. There is a major potential difference between improvised and composed music here, of course. If the sequence of programs is fixed beforehand, then the patch sequence may be memorized, presequenced in a variety of ways, or written down and taped to the front panel or put on a music stand and read. If the order of patches is variable, as in freer types of improvisation, then the performer must keep an aural image of each patch number clearly in mind, either by memorization or using a written legend.

The optimal arrangement of patches will in general depend on whether the order of programs is to be fixed or variable. If program order is fixed, it is often helpful to resave the programs needed for the music so that they run in numerical sequence in the order to be used. Or, many performing devices allow a foot pedal or other switch to advance one step in a pre-configured *chain* (sequence) of patches. In this case a chain of patches is programmed into the performing device before live performance: The first foot depression calls up patch 4, the second patch 32, the third patch 17, and so on. This has the advantage that the performer can focus purely on the music and not have to interact with numbers in any way—which can otherwise be distracting.

Patch chaining provides an effective way to reorder patches, which can frequently be necessary when the order of pieces (or actual repertoire) changes from one concert to the next. In this way, programs can be left in their same numerical positions for longer periods, facilitating memorization of their numbering scheme—useful when improvisation has a large role, or in emergencies. It may be advantageous in this regard to organize the programs into groups by similarity of sound or function.

In a more complex system, where there is more than one sound module in the system and possibly more than one keyboard controller interface, the problem of coordinating patch changes on different modules and MIDI channels can become tricky. From the performer's standpoint, things should be kept as simple as possible—it is always best if a single button or foot switch push reconfigures the entire system to the next desired state, calling up the right program number on each device in the system. But the best way to do this will depend on the way the system is set up and the features of its component parts.

Some master controllers (and synthesizers) can send out program changes on a number of different channels simultaneously, at the depression of a single front panel program button or foot switch. If the number of possible simultaneous patch change channels on the master controller is greater than or equal to the number of channels used in the setup, and only one sound engine (or independent timbre [part] on a multitimbral synthesizer) is used per MIDI channel, then all patch change programming can be achieved on the master controller.

If there are not enough channels to go around, or two devices share the same MIDI channel (as is often the case with layering or zone techniques) or are operating in Omni mode, then there are two alternatives. One way is to reshuffle the patches on the receiving sound modules so that they correspond to the sending patch change; however, this can be tedious and may require frequent updating. Alternatively, the sent patch change number(s) can be converted at the receiving end, or by an intervening MIDI transformation box, to the needed value(s). Increasingly, this first option is available on sound engines, usually in the form of one or more *program number conversion tables* (also called *patch conversion tables, program maps, patch maps* or *performance maps*) that can be called up, each of which will convert incoming patch changes to chosen internal patch numbers. Such a program table might read as does table 7.1.

The size of such tables will depend on the number of programs that can be held in the device at any one time, and is typically thirty-two, sixty-four, 100, 128, or 256. If two or more modules share the same MIDI channel and the same MIDI bus, this is the only method that will work. If for some reason these modules are not on the same MIDI bus, then a MIDI mapping device can allocate them different Program Change messages. If some receiving modules do not have internal patch number conversion but have different MIDI channels, then a MIDI mapping device can be generally used to convert input to required output, providing it has enough processors to put out revised patch change numbers to all receiving devices in the system (sound modules, MIDI mixers, MIDI-driven audio processors, etc.). There are two ways this can be done: Either the incoming messages are converted one by one to the needed Patch Change messages and passed on, or the incoming patch change is received by the MIDI mapping device, changing it to its own new program, which functions to send out the required patch changes.

Multitimbral sound engines typically have a *basic MIDI channel* that receives multitimbral program changes and often some other global commands (depending on the device). Each program number here will configure the entire machine for multitimbral sound and may change the MIDI channels that the machine responds to, since part of the multitimbral program data is typically the MIDI channel assignments used for the individual timbres. The individual parts making up the multitimbral configuration will also be independently able to receive patch changes on their respective channels, unless this feature is turned off. The basic MIDI channel and the other component channels may all have separate applicable patch conversion tables.

Let us look at an example to clarify this. Suppose that the basic MIDI channel (which must always be set by hand from the front panel, for there is no Change MIDI Channel command in the MIDI specification yet) is set

INCOMING PROGRAM NUMBER	INTERNAL PROGRAM SELECTED
001	024
002	112
003	015
....	....
....	....
127	101
128	079

TABLE 7.1   An example of a program map (program number conversion table), which converts incoming program numbers to internal program numbers.

to 1 and that three multitimbral programs will be used, with active component parts as follows:

Program 12:   Part 1 - MIDI channel 3; single patch 09

Part 2 - MIDI channel 4; single patch 02

Part 3 - MIDI channel 2; single patch 27

Program 13:   Part 1 - MIDI channel 1; single patch 44

Part 2 - MIDI channel 4; single patch 15

Part 3 - MIDI channel 2; single patch 27

Part 4 - MIDI channel 2; single patch 28

Program 24:   Part 1 - MIDI channel 3; single patch 05

Part 2 - MIDI channel 4; single patch 87

The single patches are the actual sound programs of the device. Assume that the following patch conversion table is applicable on the basic channel only and that patch changes are being responded to on all channels:

INCOMING PROGRAM NUMBER	INTERNAL PROGRAM SELECTED
001	024
002	012
003	013

Suppose we are currently in multitimbral program 24, so that the sound configuration is

PART	CHANNEL	SINGLE PATCH
	1	no sound
	2	no sound
1	3	05
2	4	87

Then if a Program Change message is sent from the controlling keyboard (or sequencer), what will happen? If program 1 is received on channel 1, very little, for the Program Change 1 simply calls up number 24, the existing multitimbral program. In most machines, this will produce at most a glitch, where sustaining notes are cut off.

If program 2 is received on channel 1, multitimbral program 12 will be called up, and the response of the machine will be:

PART	CHANNEL	SINGLE PATCH
	1	no sound
3	2	27
1	3	09
2	4	02

If program 3 is then received on channel 1, multitimbral program 13 will be called up, and if the individual parts are also sensitive to MIDI program changes, part 1 will change to program 3 as well, producing the following response:

PART	CHANNEL	SINGLE PATCH
1	1	03
3	2	27
4	2	28
	3	no sound
2	4	15

This type of response—where patch changes on the basic channel have the capacity also to produce separate program changes on individual parts with the same MIDI channel—can cause some confusion but is found in some synthesizers. In such cases separate program change tables for parts and the basic channel can usually be set to avoid confusion. Some synthesizers may exempt parts assigned to the basic MIDI channel from responding to Patch Change messages. A simpler alternative is not to set parts to the basic MIDI channel, assuming there are enough channels to go around. In the above example, if individual parts had been set to ignore program changes on their channels, the chart would be identical except that part 1 would be on patch 44.

If program change 5 is subsequently sent to channel 2 (not the basic channel), only channel 2 parts will respond, producing:

PART	CHANNEL	SINGLE PATCH
1	1	03
3	2	05
4	2	05
	3	no sound
2	4	15

Hence, although there is currently no Change Responding MIDI channel command in the MIDI specification, this can be effectively achieved by the use of such programming on multitimbral synthesizers. The other advantage in having parts inside multitimbral programs respond independently to program changes is that each component of a complex sound can be changed separately, and the glitch that may accompany this will in general be far less severe than when the multitimbral patch itself changes, potentially causing glitches on a number of channels simultaneously. (Some synthesizers, however, do retain sounding notes on program change.)

In setting up patch changes, it must be remembered that different synthesizers use different numbering conventions, and this can be a nuisance. Most synths begin numbering their programs at 1, but some begin at 0. Most synths number decimally in banks of 32, but some number decimally in banks of 64, 100, or 128, while others use octal, where the first number is 11. (The relations between these systems were described in chapter 3; for a complete table of conversions between them, see Appendix B.)

What happens when program numbers greater than the maximum internal storage location are received is variable. They may be interpreted as cartridge (or other external storage device) locations, reduced modulo the size of the internal patch bank, or ignored altogether. The user must find this out from the manual or by trial and error (this is the sort of detail that is all too often missing from manuals). Here are some examples:

Patch number 38 in a 1-starting decimal system will be usually converted to $38 - 32 = 6$ in a typical thirty-two-patch system; it will be 37 in program banks that start with 0; it will be 56 in an octal system that starts with 11 (since $(5 - 1) \times 8 + 6 = 38$).

Patch number 82 in a 0-starting bank of 100 will be cartridge 19 in a sixty-four-program 1-starting system that routes higher numbers to cartridge; it will be B33 in a 1-starting octal system that labels the first sixty-four programs "A" and the next sixty-four "B," as on some Roland machines.

Refer to Appendix B. There is also a Bank Select message, continuous controller 00, which allows the specification of larger numbers of patches.

Audio Processing and the Performance Space

In the optimal presentation of any live performance of music, the acoustics of the performing space must be carefully considered. The primary factors are the amount of natural reverberation, first reflection effects, and the frequency response of the room. Of course all performers must deal with these issues; the synthesist, by working with a PA system, has the luxury of adjusting the room's characteristics artificially, although there are clear limits—for example, the amount of reverberation in the room can be electronically increased but not commonly decreased beyond its natural values. In addition, audio processing quite different in character from the natural effects of halls can be created.

Reverberation

Artificial reverberation is commonly used to enhance the warmth of electronic sounds in a mix. It affects the perceived size of the room and the perceived distance from the source to the listener. It also affects frequency response, attenuating high frequencies more than low ones (Dodge and Jerse 1985). In any performing environment, some natural reverberation is also present, produced by the reflection of sounds from the ceiling, walls, and other surfaces. The synthesizer performer must often alter the amount of synthetic reverberation used to fit the acoustic environment. If the total reverberation level (natural and artificial) is too low (the room is "dry"), the performance environment lacks warmth and is uncomfortable to play in. If, on the other hand, the reverberation level is too high (the room is too "wet"), fast or complex passages will lose detail and the music's ability to project may be undermined.

If the overall reverberation level is unavoidably too high due to room acoustics, the player should try to adapt his or her style as much as is musically practicable. This is most possible when the music contains improvisation: One simply plays fewer notes. To counter the relatively greater attenuation of high frequencies, sounds can be made brighter, either by equalization or slight patch modifications. A lower dynamic level can also improve clarity, as can a slower tempo.

Sometimes reverberation problems are due to reflections from specific surfaces in the room, so-called first reflections or echoes. In a live room with hard vertical surfaces, care should be taken, if there is a choice, to set up the speakers in directions that will not cause coherent and unsatisfactory reflections.

Artificial reverberation is commonly added to sounds in various ways. First, a separate audio processing unit may be used at the mixing desk. Second, individual synthesizers now commonly have on-board audio processing capacity. These setups allow ready application of rich and varied types of artificial reverberation. The first setup puts the same type of reverberation on all system components, and this may not always be desired. The second setup allows separate audio processing for each device, and this may extend to allowing different processing for different parts or different stero output pairs within each synthesis device.

Reverberation may also be simulated by a third method. Here the synthesist alters the release envelope(s) of the sound at the synthesis source so that it decays slowly to zero after the key has been released. This built-in reverberation method has the advantage that its intensity can be separately programmed for each timbre or even timbral component. Its chief disadvantage is that the reverb and sound are not independently controllable. Any changes to volume, pitch bend, or other controllers will act on the reverberant part of the sound, whether or not this is desired. This makes it impractical to use the pitch bend wheel with full versatility, for example, for the reverb gets audibly bent after the nominal sound is finished. Although such an effect, like any, can be sometimes used to good purpose, it is more commonly a nuisance. Likewise, a program change will cut off the reverb abruptly on some synthesizers, and this is often not desired.

A fourth procedure exists which can be used to simulate reverberation. This is simply to add an additional sound layer that is considerably more sustaining and perhaps darker in timbre than the basic sound. Real-time control of the characteristics of this extra layer (e.g., via foot pedal or velocity switching) can create useful expressivity and coloration.

Balance and Mixing

Balance and mixing refer to the relative volumes of components of the overall music. These are set by the mixer and may be static or dynamic in character. The mixer is a multichannel device, with typical features on each channel including audio inputs and outputs, panning, gain, equalization, input attenuation, bus selection switches, and effects send (allowing external audio effects to be added).

In a traditional PA system, real-time changes are often overseen by a special operator—the soundman or soundperson—after approximate general levels are set. The mixing desk operator may thus act as a hidden performer. For larger ensembles involving synthesizers this remains a recommended option. For small group and even solo work, this is also widespread, but it is also common to run the mixing desk without an operator since the synthesis programming should include setting appropriate volumes for performance for each program within each synthesis device or rack of equipment, adjusted for equal or otherwise preset amplification of the channels of the PA system. The development of MIDI-driven mixers also means that where the material is substantially pre-composed, master mix volumes can be set at the sound check and then controlled within those amplification ranges by a sequencer, typically with greater reliability and scope than possible with a single human operator. Even where separate MIDI mixers are not used, sequencers can produce the same effects by the use of controller 7 messages for volume and real-time controller control of inbuilt or outboard audio processing devices.

Of course, volume control of separate parts of a system, as well as separate stations in a synthesis ensemble, can be controlled in real time by the performers themselves. The volume foot controller is the most widely used example of this, even though its visual feedback is limited. Some players find this highly useful; other performers, especially those working with highly prearranged music, prefer to avoid any real-time volume adjustment by foot controllers.

Equalization

This is a common function of the mixing desk. As described in chapter 2, there are various kinds of equalization that selectively boost or decrease certain portions of the audio spectrum. By selectively applying these to certain sounds the mix can be improved: by focusing the spectral distribution of the sounds to improve clarity, by the removal of any unwanted masking effects, and by compensating for limitations in the synthesis itself.

Sound Localization and Panning

These terms refer to the spatial placement of different components of a sound (or sounds) in the mix. With stereo, there are two speakers or sets of speakers placed at different locations in the room, normally stage left and stage right. In this familiar case there are two primary dimensions of spatial positioning: left-to-right, called *panning*, and *apparent distance*, sometimes called depth. If the amplification system has more than two independent channels of output (quadraphonic or even higher), then the speakers can be arranged to produce three-dimensional positioning or more refined two-dimensional positioning. Such sound placement can be either static or dynamic (the term *diffusion* is sometimes used for dynamic sound placement with multiple speakers). In this book, we will primarily refer to a stereo amplification system.

The effect of panning is achieved by routing different amounts of the same signal to the left and right sides of the stereo system. Perceived left-to-right placement of a sound is, however, based on two factors: the relative volume of the signal at the two ears and the relative onset times of (delays between) the signals reaching the two ears. The dominant factor of the two is actually the delay. If the listeners are using headphones, then these effects are clear and unambiguous. In public performance, of course, the audience is not wearing headphones, and the listener's position in the room will influence perceived localization substantially; this is something about which the performer can do little.

Direction effects are only really significant for frequencies above about 270 Hz (Dodge and Jerse 1985). Hence, dull kick drum or bass sounds will not be very localizable no matter where they are nominally put in the stereo mix.

When sounds are layered together, the component sounds' envelopes and relative volumes will determine perceived direction. If the sounds fuse into one, the resultant location may well be determined by the loudest component or the component with the quickest rise time. If the component layers are noticeably different in timbre, each component may have a separate perceived spatial location, and these can create a sense of motion in time. For example, try the following: MIDI together two sounds, one with a quick percussive attack and decay, and another with a gently bowed string-like envelope. Pan the first sound hard left and the second sound hard right, and play a passage in eighth notes at at least moderate tempo. If the sounds are of comparable volume, you will almost certainly hear the sound as originating from the left side—the pan position of the quicker attack component has dominated positioning. If a whole note is played, the sound will begin on the left and transfer to the right as the left side fades out. As a second example, if the left sound has an organ timbre, and the right a fade-up/fade-down envelope, a sustained note will sweep from left to right and return.

Distance cues are determined by reverberation levels, as described above. In a mix, the differential application of reverberation to specific parts can affect timbre as well, even creating a limited sense of spatial motion. In the first example above, reverberation could be set to affect one channel alone; if added to the left channel in large amounts it will cause the shift of attention from left to right side on long notes to proceed at a slower pace. The reverberation from the one channel can also be played back selectively to the opposite side to make a richer sound, and one showing more sense of motion in the mix.

Spatial Motion of Parts in a Mix

When sound locations are changed by the performer in real time, apparent motion of sources is created for the listener. This can be programmed in several ways. Some synthesizers allow the panning and reverberation to be driven by hard-wired functions, like envelopes or LFOs. Some also allow the placement of a sound in a mix by note number, velocity, or continuous controller. Alternatively, such effects may be available in outboard processing units such as MIDI mixers, MIDI-driven effects units, and spatial sound processing units. Volume pedals operating different sounds that are panned substantially to one side of the mix or the other will also create a sense of motion if increases in one pedal are linked to decreases in the other, even if the sounds are completely dissimilar.

The actual physical motion of sound sources creates the well-known Doppler effect, whereby the apparent frequency of sound sources moving towards the listener is increased, and that of sources moving away from the listener decreased. Although not commonly done with MIDI synthesizers, this effect can be imitated by combining pitch bend or possibly portamento with changes in panning and reverberation levels. For example, if a sound's reverberation level goes from high to low to high as it is panned left to right, while its pitch rises and then falls, an effect like the Doppler can be heard. Of course, this effect will be enhanced considerably if quadraphonic amplification is available so that the sound can appear to be routed through the listener, or if "left" and "right" speakers are located in front of and behind the listener instead of at their usual positions.

When speakers are arranged on the same plane stage left and right, there is (strictly speaking) no way in which sound can change its vertical position. However, it is possible to simulate this effect in the following way, though this has been expensive to do. The ears are normally in the same horizontal plane when listening. But the auditory system in such cases can judge changes in the vertical position of the source by corresponding changes in the timbre received at the eardrum; these changes occur due to the shape of the ears. If such changes are simulated in the synthesis process (a complex business that goes beyond the scope of this book), or obtained by sampling a binaural recording of such sound sources in motion, then the ear can be tricked into interpreting the sound as changing its vertical position. A number of commercial systems providing "spatially enhanced," or "3-D," sound from two speakers are now available.

More sophisticated types of sound motion usually rely on more than two speakers and a more imaginative distribution than stage left and stage right. Better movie theaters, for example, may use the Dolby matrix system, which has three speaker cabinets in front of the audience (left, right, and center), or the six-channel Omnimax system. Special wrap-around theaters for the production of light shows and so-called hypermedia typically have many more speakers than this. Examples are the San Francisco Audium and the Boston Science Museum Theatre. These systems require a number of separate amplifiers and some way to coordinate the motion of sound. MIDI-based sound processing units, notably Spatial Sound's Spatial Sound Processor, have been developed and facilitate the placement of sound at any point in a one-, two-, or three-dimensional space.

Spatialization can be controlled by live or sequenced MIDI messages or directly from front panel joysticks.

Stage Presentation

We have now discussed all the major technical aspects of live performance except the actual act of stage presentation. There is, of course, a wide range of styles of presentation of music in our culture, including pop concert, club music (for dancing or listening), concert hall recital, religious music, music as adjunct to other media (film, dance, or theater), multimedia, and performance art—to mention just a few categories most relevant to synthesis. The presenter must carefully consider the manner of presentation if the audience's engagement with the music is to be maximized. If stage actions are limited to those strictly necessary for musical performance, the result must stand or fall on the basis of the sound alone. If elaborate accompanying movements, visuals, and special effects are used, the presentation will be more stimulating but may lack depth, carrying the risk that the music will be received as only a backing soundtrack for the "main events" on stage (dance, rehearsed personality projection). Certainly the commercial video clip, where music is normally only mimed during filming, has frequently adopted this stance despite its vitality and stylistic innovations. Between these two extremes lies a range of possibilities open to the intentions of the music's creators.

One important general rule is that the visual presentation should allow the performer's actions, and their link to the sound, to be seen as much as possible. This helps the audience to engage. In synthesizer performance this can be a problem—particularly with multiple keyboards, which are sometimes stacked up so that the player can hardly be seen behind them. To avoid such difficulties, it is now common to stand or crouch over keyboard stacks, and not to stack them too high, but rather array them around the performer in separate columns. The use of the single master controller keyboard reduces this problem, and the strap-on remote controller allows the keyboard performer the luxury of choreography. Wireless MIDI boxes have become available, and these can eliminate the need for cables for some performers, although the would-be user should be warned that their reliability in stage performance may not be 100 percent.

PERFORMING INTO RECORDING DEVICES

Performing into a recording device is in many ways like live performance. Musicality and expertise in performance will be apparent in either context. But there are also many differences, both practical and conceptual. A recording situation often places the performer in a special studio facility, which usually requires the performer to monitor his or her playing with headphones, to listen to a balance that is not life-like or may later be changed, and sometimes to use a click track for synchronization. Visual contact with other performers may be reduced. Space may be limited. The recording room itself will typically be very dry. Adapting to such minor matters is basically a matter of experience. But in other ways, the studio requires a different set of mental attitudes because of the different resources it offers.

Audio Recorders

Let us first consider the audio recording environment. Here the precise resources offered will depend on the degree of sophistication of the studio and also on the format of storage of audio material. Thus there are differences depending on whether the storage is analog (magnetic tape, direct-to-disk) or digital (two-track, multitrack, PCM, videotape, optical, etc.). But there are a number of features common to all, and these result in certain distinct procedures that affect performance into any type of machine: *editing, overdubbing,* and *part-splitting.* Overall, their effect is to reduce the level of instrumental skill required of the synthesist. The main changes of conception arising from these for the performer are as follows.

Editing

The possibilities allowed by editing depend very much on the versatility of the editor, and this is in turn affected by the nature of the storage medium and format. All editing allows error correction: sloppy execution, improper balance, wrong notes, even poor tone can all be fixed to various degrees. In some cases, the corrections are so slight as not to be conceived as the correction of an error but as enhancing the part or refining its interpretation.

A different orientation uses editing as a compositional tool. Musical passages may be recorded without preconceived order or function; multiple versions of the same music may be recorded as resource material; or only the skeletons of musical passages may be entered. In all cases, complete compositional design and details are filled out by subsequent editing and overdubbing.

In analog tape recording, such effects are typically limited to choosing between alternate versions, punching in and out, splicing tape in and out, adjusting balance, modifying timing of isolated events, speeding up and slowing down the tape playback, and audio processing of the sonic product using the resources catalogued in chapter 2. The frequencies of the notes themselves are not commonly changed, for example, although this option exists with the pitch shifter. With digital multitrack machines, the sound can usually be treated in greater detail and without introducing noise in manipulation. Single notes can be excised more readily, drop-ins made more reliably, complex sequences of mix actions recorded for automatic performance at the final dub, and so on. The cost for this is that cut-and-splice editing and varispeed techniques are all but impossible. However, some analog machines at the top end of the market have these improved features as well.

The new generation of digital workstations that record directly to a computer's hard disk (*direct-to-disk recording*) allows further possibilities such as simultaneous multi-user access and more powerful sound editing and shaping procedures like note transposition, file editing, cutting and pasting, and the application of sophisticated digital processing techniques. The effect for the performer/composer can be to decrease the pressures of studio performance (as error correction procedures become more powerful) and to increase the viability of audio editing as a compositional tool. Alternatively, if studio time is extremely limited so that these techniques cannot be used, the player may be under greater pressure than usual to get it right the first time, since his or her output will be compared to studio sessions where the full range of editing options has been used.

Overdubbing

Overdubbing means that all parts need not be recorded simultaneously and that one person may play more than one part in the same piece. In practical terms, the performer must be able to play each chosen part with the proper feeling in relation only to a click track or an incomplete set of accompanying parts, as the complete piece is slowly built up by overlaying. The balance of the parts already recorded can be changed as needed, of course. Taken to the limit, this allows the "one-person band" approach.

Overdubbing of the same line on itself can also be useful, when the slight heterophonic irregularities of two performers playing in unison are required. This can impart a dynamism that may be missing in the too exact rhythmic precision of MIDI-based unisons or the consistency of the effects of added-on digital delay. Chorusing (chorale) effects can become quite pronounced on instruments that have some pitch microvariation in their note production or with singing.

Overdubbing also allows the recording of several versions of a passage so that either the best one can ultimately be selected or a new composite version pieced together in mosaic fashion by splicing and punching in and out. Different versions of the same passage may also be used simultaneously, as when an improvised musical conversation with oneself is called for. If there is plenty of recording time, these possibilities can allow the performer to adopt a more relaxed and experimental attitude in studio work than in live performance; if studio time is very limited, the opposite effect may occur.

Part-Splitting

Part-splitting refers to the division of a complex part into two or more simpler parts that are played in separately and then recombined. In this way performers can realize parts that they cannot play or realize parts they can play in far less rehearsal time. Part-splitting can either be done in a linear (sectional) fashion or a vertical (registral) fashion. The first approach divides the part into separate sections and subsequently pieces the sections together. This can work only if there are natural split points between sections (such as brief rests) so that glitch-free splicing can be achieved. Each section can then be separately rehearsed and played in. One common use of this sectional approach in popular music is to record the fixed material separately from any improvised solos or fills. Another is to record verse and chorus sections separately. On the other hand, some performers find such procedures lacking in spontaneity.

The other way part-splitting can occur is by dividing parts on the basis of register—for example, into treble and bass registers, with overdubbing. Naturally, the split point between the part components should float, making musically sensible allocations of different notes to the separate components. Each component can then be recorded separately while the performer listens to any previously recorded components and the click track as well (if one has been used) to ensure that the parts mesh properly. If balance of the components is fine-tuned, the result should be a perfect semblance of the required composite part.

Performing into Sequencers

Sequencers come in many sizes and shapes: as dedicated hardware boxes such as the Yamaha Q series and Roland's MC-500 series; as part of synthesizers and synthesizer "workstations"; as part of MIDI-driven instruments like MIDI player pianos (e.g., Yamaha's Disklavier series or Kimball's Imperial Grand Bösendorfer); or as computer software such as Mark of the Unicorn's Performer and Opcode's Vision for the Macintosh, C-Lab's Notator, Intelligent Music's and Dr. T's Realtime, and Steinberg's Cubase for the Atari, Magnetic Music's Texture and Voyetra's Sequencer Plus for the IBM, Microillusions' Music-X for the Amiga, and both Passport's Master Tracks Pro/Pro 5 and Dr. T's KCS for all four computers.

All sequencers store musical performance information in digital format. Information may be entered by performance (*real-time input*) or by non-real-time data entry (*step-time input*). The use of the standard MIDI sequence file format is becoming increasingly widespread and allows ready convertibility between different sequencers. Editing, overdubbing, and part-splitting are also of primary importance in the sequencing environment: Because of the nature of MIDI data, their scope of action is enormously enhanced over the case of audio recording. This is particularly true of editing.

In professional MIDI sequencer environments, the error-correction and part-refinement functions of editing know few limits: Incorrect note choices can easily be fixed, while timing can typically be adjusted to millisecond accuracy (depending on the tempo and the number of time divisions per beat—usually called *clocks*), tuning to better than 1 Hz in frequency, balance to less than 1 percent in volume, and timbre fine-tuned to the limitations of the synthesizer's or sampler's design and the musician's ear. All note and controller information can be arbitrarily cut, copied, pasted, merged, scaled, and otherwise subjected to global commands in most sequencers; on many sequencers status bytes can be changed as well. Data may be displayed graphically, in traditional music notation, or in precise lists.

Figure 7.8 shows three examples of the editing facilities of computer sequencing software. Figure 7.8a shows musical data in list format (Performer); mnemonic icons are used for MIDI message types (pitch bend, pressure, and notes), while locations are shown in bar number, beat number, and clock number. Figure 7.8b shows Note On data in graphical format (Master Tracks Pro). This type of display is now quite standard and may be called "scroll" or "player piano" format. Figure 7.8c shows the graphic display of pitch bend information (Master Tracks Pro). Someone with virtually no performance skills can make a virtuosic recording with such features—though they will have to spend a great deal of step input and editing time to get all the performance detail right.

Other editing features of the MIDI sequencer environment also reduce or alter the technical skills required of the performer. Best known is *quantizing* (occasionally termed *auto-correct*). Here a sloppily executed part is shifted to have improved metronomic precision. Attack points and durations (and sometimes end points) can usually be separately quantized. The basic system moves all played notes to the nearest appropriate beat subdivision specified by the user, most commonly the eighth, sixteenth, triplet-eighth or triplet-sixteenth note. This is the quantizing grid. Contemporary sequencers offer a number of options beyond this. Some of these are:

partial quantizing (x%), where the note is moved not into exact synchrony, but x% closer to the nearest appropriate beat subdivision. This feature is also called *strength* or degree of quantization.

range or sensitivity (x% or s clocks), meaning that only notes within x%, or s clocks, of the grid will be quantized. Opcode's

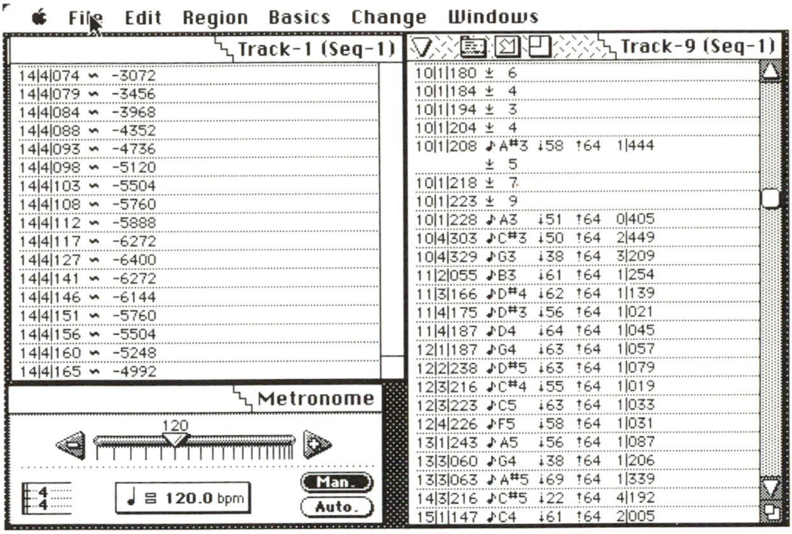

a.

FIGURE 7.8 Software editing of MIDI data: (a) data displayed in lists (Performer, Mark of the Unicorn); (b) notes displayed in scroll notation (Master Tracks Pro, Passport); (c) controller data (pitch bend) displayed in graphic format (Master Tracks Pro, Passport).

Vision allows negative sensitivity, meaning that notes outside the range window are affected and those inside left intact.

shift (*s* clocks), which can shift the quantizing grid relative to the beat so that slight consistent anticipations or delays can be accommodated.

swing (*x*%), where the beat subdivision at a certain duration level (e.g., eighth notes) is divided in a consistently unequal fashion (say 52%/48% or 60%/40%), and notes are subjected to this nonuniform rhythmic grid.

floating quantization, where the program can intelligently pick on a note-by-note or beat-by-beat basis which grid from among a user-specified range of quantization grids will be imposed on the notes. For example, all notes might be rounded to multiples of either triplet eighths or sixteenths.

An inversely related feature is *randomizing,* sometimes called *humanizing.* This simply takes the selected data and introduces a controlled amount of randomness to them. Small amounts of randomness can help reduce the stiffness of parts too rigidly quantized, but they can just as easily

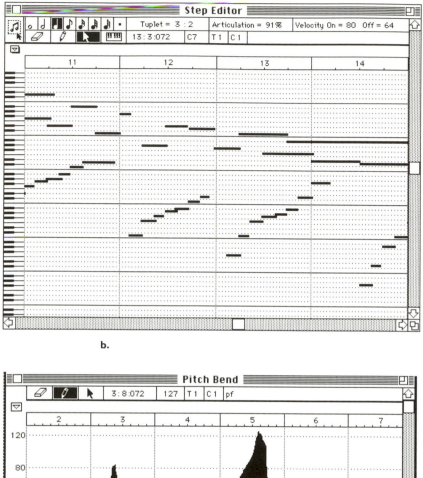

b.

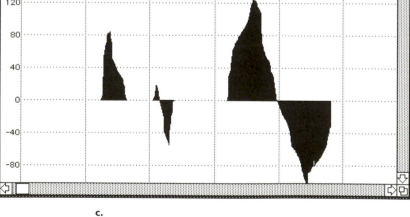

c.

FIGURE 7.8   continued.

vitiate the rhythmic vitality. Above all they will not provide the perfor-mance nuance of the experienced player—as the term *humanize* seems misleadingly to imply. The application of much larger amounts of random-ness to note onset times can rearrange note orders, effectively acting as a compositional tool. Some sequencers allow controlled randomness to be introduced to virtually all the stored parameters.

The general power of editing as a compositional tool is greatly ex-panded in a MIDI environment. Increasingly, more and more features characteristic of compositional environments are creeping into the various sequencers, whether hardware or software based. The details of the com-positional offerings vary from sequencer to sequencer, and any attempt at a comprehensive listing would be soon out of date. Features found widely include transposition (exact and sometimes diatonic), scaling and system-atic arithmetic alteration of all types of MIDI data, time reversal, arbitrary note remapping, inversion, algorithmic channel reassignment of notes, and time stretching (of selected parts).

One interesting idea becoming increasingly common is *conditional editing* (called also *logical editing, change filter,* or *transform*), which allows the selection of specific events based on a host of criteria such as note range, duration range, velocity range, bar number, adjacency to cer-tain time locations in the bar, event number (e.g., *modulus transform* in Voyetra's Sequencer Plus for the IBM, which selects every *n*th event), and so forth, before any of the actual change operations are performed. Any number of these criteria can typically be used in parallel as well. *Intelli-gent imaging* (called variously *echoing* and *ghost of*) is found in Finale, Vision, Creator/Notator, and Realtime: This means that one parent track or musical passage is linked to other tracks or passages (that may be derived from it), and all changes in the parent will be duplicated or echoed in the "progeny."

Some sequencers have on-screen faders that can graphically control performance variables and can themselves be controlled in real time by controllers on the synthesizer. For example, a foot controller could be set to vary the track tempo continuously. Although many of these ideas are compositional and do not directly affect the performer's fixed tasks, they affect the way newly produced material will be subsequently used and so ultimately require different attitudes from the improviser or composer/performer. It can become necessary to improvise or compose so that material will sound as intended after being subjected to such composi-tional transformations.

Another basic editing feature that has important implications for the performer is variation in tempo. Parts can be played in slowly, then brought up to full speed, reducing technical demands. The reverse procedure is occasionally useful as well. With slight tempo changes (on the order of 15 percent or less) the same playing attitudes used at normal tempo can be employed. For larger changes, the rhythmic and durational choices and conceptions used by the performer may require some modification. If rhythms are eventually to be substantially quantized, then little change to playing technique may be necessary. However, if notes are played with any noticeable lilt (as in the inequality of dotted-note figures of music of any style, the unnotated swing of jazz players, or the French *note inégale* tradition of the seventeenth and eighteenth centuries), technique modification will be necessary. This is because the long–short duration ratio of such figures varies with tempo, becoming more nearly equal with increasing tempo. If the performer records at reduced tempo (the most common case), the amount of swing or any other slight durational inequalities must be underplayed. Otherwise, notes played slowed down will sound quite ridiculous when sped up.

Overdubbing remains fundamentally the same in the MIDI sequencer environment as it is with audio recording. However, there are differences of detail. Monitoring can normally be done without headphones since synthesizers have direct line outputs. Also, the cut and paste functions of the MIDI environment are so much more developed that the piecewise splicing together of different versions of the same part becomes much quicker and more reliable.

Part-splitting becomes a considerably more wide-ranging technique than in the audio environment. Parts need not be separated on the basis of note register alone; for example, dynamics and modulation can be put in as separate controller parts, with notes on another track. Pitch bend can be added as a separate track to the note track, and so forth.

Some sequencers and notation packages have autotranscription routines that can be used to create musical notation from standard MIDI files or live performance. The best-known programs include Coda's Finale, Mark of the Unicorn's Professional Composer, and Passport's Encore for the Macintosh; C-Lab's Notator and Dr. T's Copyist for the Atari; Passport's SCORE and Coda's Finale for the IBM world; and Dr. T's Copyist for the Amiga. The performer plays relative to the sequencer's click track or, in some programs, can play the tempo directly by tapping an assigned MIDI controller such as a foot switch. All such programs currently have considerable limitations; the problem of discerning musical intention from a performer's physical actions is not a simple one. In using such a system to score music, it is sometimes best to use a rather mechanical approach to rhythm as much as possible to help the program do a better job of approximating the performer's intention. However, if carried too far, this can interfere with proper execution of both fixed and improvised music. Another alternative is to play normally but selectively quantize the subsequent recording in a passage-specific way before exporting it for translation to score. Some programs with floating quantization (notably Finale) do this automatically, and the quality of the output, while still quite imperfect, is steadily improving.

Figure 7.9 shows an autotranscription of the opening of the Courante from the J. S. Bach's Partita No. 2 in B♭, played by the author, with the score given below. The program is Encore and the result is a quite usable first approximation. The program has in most cases successfully distinguished between triplets and sixteenths as found in the original score. The similarity shows a certain degree of luck, however—when the precise note durations in the sequence are compared, it is shown that the performer was playing very close to triplets throughout (maximum deviation 6 percent in this passage), which is the standard interpretation of the written bass figures in this piece. Notational differences between the original music and the performance are found in the last treble figure of most bars and in the bass of the last measure. With music involving more complicated rhythmic figures (fives or sevens, for example), Encore is currently inadequate and a program like Finale sometimes more accurate. Besides these rhythmic problems, all such programs have inevitable limitations in assigning notes their proper clefs in keyboard music. With more complicated chordal input using the sustain pedal (still as of this writing not satisfactorily handled by virtually all such programs), the autotranscription can be really very different from the original, and it must be questioned whether direct step-time entry is not the more viable option.

Using Compositional Environments

The last category of program requiring special attitudes from the performer comprises the intelligent music programs such as Intelligent Music's and Dr. T's M (Mac, Atari, Amiga, IBM), or Jam Factory or Ovaltune on the Macintosh; Dr. T's Programmable Algorithmic Generator (part of the KCS sequencer) on the Atari; Cool Shoes' Sound Globs on the IBM; and Aesthetic Engineering's Music Mouse (Mac, Atari, Amiga). There are also music programming environments like Frog Peak Music's HMSL and Opcode's Max that can readily be configured for novel performance setups. Hardware with some such features also exists, as in Zyklus' MIDI Performance System. Here the performer can play material into the program, and it or some part of it (for example the note sequence, stripped of its timing) will form input material that can be transformed according to the nature of the program's features. This can typically all happen in real time, making of the composing environment also a performing environment.

These programs typically allow randomness and permutations of entered note material, often breaking the material into separate cycles of

FIGURE 7.9   Autotranscription of a played passage and the original score (Encore, Passport).

notes and durations. Rhythms can be overlaid at various speeds or stretched in certain ways. Algorithms generating harmony, note density, controller values, duration, and so forth and variations of various kinds may be present. Multiple sequences may be separately controllable with respect to start/stop/continue, transposition, and tempo, from QWERTY or musical keyboard. M allows its many algorithmic variables to be conducted using the mouse. Snapshots of configurations can be stored and recordings of produced pieces ported to sequencers for fine tuning. The interface for performance with M is shown in figure 7.10.

The performer interacts with the program, learning it as a novel interactive instrument. Such programs often allow the MIDI keyboard to be

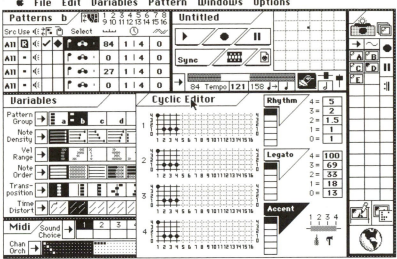

FIGURE 7.10   The performance interface for M (Intelligent Music and Dr. T's).

configured for selecting the various compositional options. Alternatively, the MIDI keyboard may be used as a music performing device, while compositional options are selected with the QWERTY keyboard, mouse, or both. Often, notes and rhythms may be selected from the QWERTY keyboard and mouse as well. In such cases, it is usually best to put the QWERTY keyboard and mouse pad at the front panel of the keyboard. A quite different set of performance skills must be developed for each program.

The performance skills developed in such programs are not limited to music. Intelligent Music's and Dr. T's Ovaltune program allows the production of computer graphic "videotapes" by performance with QWERTY keyboard and mouse and simultaneous music production from an attached MIDI keyboard. Figure 7.11 shows a black and white still from Ovaltune. Integrated multimedia are also catered for in Opcode's Max, which can currently be programmed to allow real-time control (via MIDI instrument or graphic object) of such things as synthesizers, complex MIDI software processes, digital signal processing boards, videodisc players, and the location and size of synthetic and scanned color images on the screen.

Max is based on an expandable set of simple graphic objects that the user connects via "patch cords." This has become one standard approach

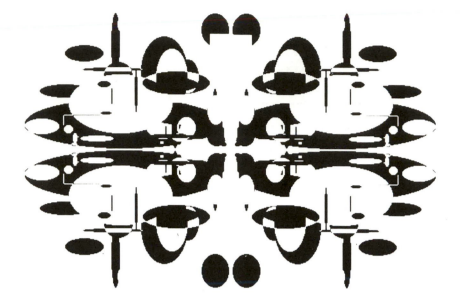

FIGURE 7.11 A graphic design linked to musical shapes (Ovaltune, Intelligent Music/Dr. T's).

to music programming environments. Figure 7.12 shows a simple Max program that transforms the nature of the familiar synthesizer interface. Pitch selection happens as normal, but controller 4 routes the interface to one of eight MIDI channels, and individual note duration is determined by controller 5. Both of these controllers are to be linked to foot pedals. An on-screen dial scales overall note durations. The program also produces color graphic figures that can be projected onto a screen for performance. The range and mean speed of movement of these figures are controlled by note number and note velocity respectively, as well as by two on-screen horizontal sliders. The programming details of the graphic part of the program are hidden within the object *graphcontrol*. For further examples, see Rowe (1992).

LIVE PERFORMANCE WITH PRERECORDED MUSIC

Often the synthesizer performer is called on to play live with previously recorded music. The recorded parts are most commonly in audio format (e.g., audio tape) or performance format (e.g., MIDI).

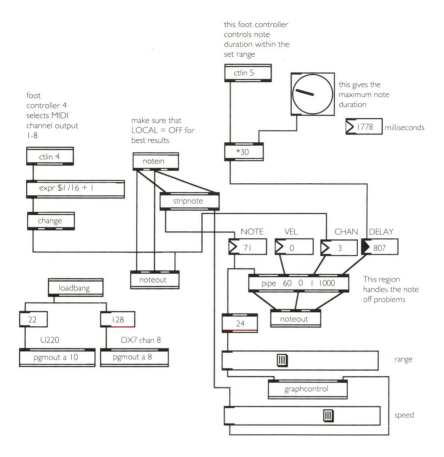

FIGURE 7.12   A Max program that reconfigures the performance
interface and produces color graphics.

Other possibilities, such as the invoking of musical processes that are
stored in computer composition environments and only realized at performance time, are also widely used. Regardless of storage format, the
main problems are similar enough to deserve parallel discussion.

Performing with Sequencers and Drum Machines

In this case, the prerecorded parts are stored in the form
of performance instructions and used to produce sound, via MIDI, only at
the moment of execution. The sequencer can also make changes in the
instrument(s) controlled by the performer. For example, one common
procedure is for the sequencer to handle all program changes. It can, of
course, do far more, changing dynamics and producing real-time synthesis

changes using controllers in both the performer's instruments and those solely sequencer controlled.

Playing with a sequencer or drum machine is in many ways like playing with a skillful but unintelligent and highly insensitive human performer. Current commercial sequencers do not respond to your actions in any but the most limited ways; you must respond to theirs. Exceptions to this are pulse followers (so-called "human clocks") now on the market; these follow a variable pulse played by the performer, continually interpolating a tempo that drives the sequencer. If deviations are too extreme, the devices may fail to follow properly. Some of these devices can follow fairly complex audio signals, as long as they contain the target pulse or simple pattern somewhere; some can directly accept MIDI Note On data as a clock source. Some of these machines can put out sync information in many different formats (MTC, FSK, SMPTE, etc.). There is a considerable amount of computer music research in progress that succeeds in allowing the player to drive the other parts in a piece simply by playing one part into a microphone (e.g., Vercoe and Puckette 1985) or at a MIDI controller, and this is beginning to have some commercial impact.

With these exceptions, the performer must still follow the sequencer and must make certain that enough of the sequencer's parts are audible at all times to make possible effective synchronization. In a concert situation, with a complex piece, this may necessitate a separately mixed monitoring system for the performer (or even each performer!) that differs from the sound heard by the audience. In some cases, headphones may be necessary. Their use is generally avoided whenever possible, as they can be uncomfortable (especially the heavier ear-enclosing kind, which are sometimes necessary for sound isolation) and interfere with performance practice. They are also visually less than completely acceptable on stage in certain performance styles (jazz and folk, for example). Small in-ear Walkman-like headphones are more comfortable and less intrusive.

In making a decision about how a sequencer shall be used, the nature of the sequencer part is the critical factor. If it has a readily felt pulse so that the performer can lock into position easily, no separate monitor mix may be necessary. If the piece has a pulse, but one that is well disguised, it may help to emphasize the pulse-implying parts in the monitor mix. Alternatively, if headphones are used, a click track can be superimposed to handle tricky timing problems, even on stage.

However, some pieces have no felt pulse at all. They may have been created at the sequencer without score or pulse conception; they may be extremely rubato versions of pieces with nominally regular metric design; they may be full of irregular accelerandi and decelerandi; or they may be so complexly syncopated that no felt pulse can emerge. In this case the performer must usually try one or more of the following procedures.

First, a score may be used, with the timing of cue points (as displayed on the sequencer during performance) marked in it. Such a score may be supplied by the composer, or it may be constructed using either traditional notation in highlighted form or appropriate graphic symbols by the performer. Where available, large visual count-ins and concurrent score display on computers can be used to make this approach more tractable.

Second, the performer can superimpose a click track pattern on the music and learn the part in relation to it. The click track can be listened to through headphones. This can be effective, but it sometimes seems unnatural and disorienting (especially at first) and requires lots of rehearsal. It is often best used in limited sections, piecemeal.

A third alternative is to use a cueing rather than click track system. Here clicks or other audio or visual cues come in only just as needed to alert the performer to impending required actions. The cues may be part of the music or separately visible or audible only to the performers. This method is versatile and usually to be recommended for cueing the starts and ends of sections or distinctive figures that require coordination between sequencer and performer.

A fourth possibility is simply to the learn the sonic score by heart. This is labor intensive, but not unreasonably so. The performer should, after all, be very familiar with the piece. This approach can be quite comfortable if the performer's part involves a lot of free improvisation so that attention to the mood of the passage is often sufficient to cue correct performance.

The use of audio recorded material and MIDI sequencers can often be combined. If the audio material is not too long, a sampler can do the job. If it is more extended, tape machines and MIDI sequencers can be used in the same setup. If SMPTE (or other) time code reading and writing is available, one track of a multitrack machine can be used for the SMPTE and the remaining tracks for the required audio material. The SMPTE track must be routed to a SMPTE-to-MIDI converter to allow the sequencer to be externally driven by the time code on the tape deck.

Turning Things On and Off

Some special problems occur when turning sequencers on and off. We begin with the "on" problem. If the sequencer is to start first, there is no problem. The performer pushes start and synchronizes by any of the methods described above. If performer and sequencer are to start together, the situation is a little more complex. One approach is simply to put one or two empty bars at the start of the track. The performer then presses start and follows the visual display of beats, or a headphone-monitored click if such display is not available or visible from the performance station, until the performer's own part is due to commence.

However, if more than one performer is involved, visual display may not be possible for all, unless multiple sequencers, some externally synced, are used. In such cases the performer who has the best view can sometimes conduct or cue the entry for all.

The other approach is for the performer to memorize the correct tempo and push start (often via a foot switch) while striking the first chord, preceded by a count-in if other musicians are also playing. This requires a good sense of absolute tempo if the timing relations at the start of the music require high precision, yet in many situations this synchronization is straightforward.

The situation is most tricky if the performer starts before the sequencer. There are two common procedures. In the first, the performer programs empty bars in the sequencer for the duration of the entire introduction and follows the timing of the visual display or headphone click until the sequencer is due to start. This method works best for short pulse-based introductions. It can become tedious and cramping for longer ones and quite impractical for highly rubato passages of any length. It is not particularly practical with some drum machines.

The second method relies on turning the sequencer on at exactly the right time during performance to establish synchronization. The choice of the best spot to do this will depend on the sonic starting relationship between the performer and sequencer parts. If their relationship does not require clear synchrony due to the nature of the music (rubato, unpulsed, freely improvised), any of a number of points may do, and the performer can readily adjust. If, on the other hand, the two are to play synchronized attacks precisely, the sequencer-driven sound may best start at the punch-in point, provided the performer has a body part free (or an assistant) to push the start button or has set up the keyboard interface to trigger the sequencer automatically when some unique musical feature (such as a very high note) is played.

Sometimes a combination of the two approaches is most effective. The player programs in a small number of beats of silence before the start of the sound and turns on the sequencer at a convenient moment near the end of the previous passage, using the intervening silent beats, via headphone click or visual display, to fine tune his or her relation to the sequencer's tempo. Precise rhythmic synchronization can require careful practice.

Turning off the sequencer is less trouble. It can turn itself off by just running out of notes. Drum machines or sequencers in loop mode, however, must usually be shut off. If the sequencer is to be shut off and on a number of times in the piece, using the continue and stop buttons, the points of both stop and continue must be carefully chosen in the way outlined above. To aid improvisation, some drum machines (such as those from E-mu) can loop on one passage until a change is cued by a foot switch.

The actual physical gestures needed to turn the machines off and on are usually handled either from QWERTY keyboard, mouse, foot switch, or sequencer box front panel. Some sequencers and compositional environments allow many of the standard MIDI system common and real-time commands, such as start, stop, continue, and others, to be programmed to be sent from actions at the keyboard, most commonly the depression of indicated keys. This is a useful feature in live performance. For example, the stop key can be set to be a note that is played only in the final chord; the continue key, to a note played only at the start of a new section. These same sequencers commonly allow the performer similarly to turn recording on and off while playing, rewind the sequencer, and hence play along with previously improvised material without hands leaving the keyboard. It is also possible on some machines to switch between different songs as the current song is playing, which can allow a song pastiche technique, for those whose aims encompass sequencer performance art. Some sequencers allow the creation of chains of commands ("macros") that are executed at the touch of a single predefined keystroke. If your computer-based sequencer of choice does not allow this, some "macro-creation" programs can be used.

Performing with Audio Tape

This situation is a commonplace in the recording studio, when the performer is called on to overdub onto a multitrack tape machine. In this case, the considerations for the synthesizer performer are no different than for any other instrument, as described earlier.

A slightly different setup is live stage performance with tape, which occurs primarily in various styles of contemporary art music. The prerecorded parts are stored in 2- or 4-track audio format on tape, which is turned on and off at various points in the piece by the performer or an assistant. The main difference from the studio setup is that no recording is necessarily in progress.

The differences between this case and playing with MIDI sequencers are slight and primarily concern the relatively less sophisticated position- and sound-monitoring possibilities available with traditional tape machines. Traditional tape recorder location numbers cannot be used for precisely dependable cueing, for example, due to tape slippage. Visual display is more limited. A click used for headphone place-keeping on a 4-track analog machine has a slight danger of bleeding through to the audio. Making a separate mix for the performers is not usually possible. These limitations are worth the price when the sounds involved are not easy to synthesize or sample. The advent of digital audio storage and new tape technology like DAT is also removing many of these slight limitations. MIDI Machine Control (MMC) promises to make transport control of audio recorders easier and more reliable for the synthesizer performer.

There is a considerable body of pieces in this format in contemporary art music, and this repertoire far exceeds what we can discuss here since nearly all the pieces are for traditional instrument plus tape and so strictly speaking do not involve synthesizers. For descriptions of representative pieces, the reader should consult Ernst (1977), Schrader (1982), and Manning (1985).

REFERENCES

Dodge, Charles, and Thomas A. Jerse. *Computer Music*. New York: Schirmer Books, 1985.

Ernst, David. *The Evolution of Electronic Music*. New York: Schirmer Books, 1977.

Manning, Peter. *Electronic and Computer Music*. Oxford: Clarendon Press, 1985.

Rowe, Robert. *Interactive Music Systems*. Cambridge, Mass.: MIT Press, 1992.

Schrader, Barry. *Introduction to Electro-Acoustic Music*. Englewood Cliffs, N.J.: Prentice-Hall, 1982.

Vercoe, B., and M. Puckette. "Synthetic Rehearsal: Training the Synthetic Performer." In *Proceedings of the 1985 International Computer Music Conference*, ed. B. Truax. San Francisco: Computer Music Association, 1985.

CHAPTER EIGHT

SOUND AND INSTRUMENT IMITATION

. . . .

In electronic music, we must "constitute" each sound that we mean to use. This is not a question of copying natural sounds—some of them being excessively complex, that synthesis is in practice impossible; furthermore, the very idea of creating an "*ersatz*" natural sound universe is dubious: it will have neither the quality of the original nor the specific characteristics that one has the right to expect from it. This is the sandbank upon which nearly all the specialists have run aground: hybrid, asexual, the electronic instruments have not been capable of posing the real problem of the timbre in this "artificial" realm.

- Pierre Boulez, *Notes of an Apprentice,* trans. Herbert Weinstock (New York: Knopf, 1968), p. 231.

In this chapter we look at the special performance problems encountered in imitating sounds (mimesis). These sounds may be naturally occurring, like the wind, surf, or bird calls; they may be special effects from the machines and artifacts of our civilization; they may be the sounds of traditional instruments. We will survey all these types of sounds but (as usual) will focus on the performance issues. In other words, we will not be describing how to synthesize the individual sound objects, which are in any case increasingly commercially available as samples and presets but how appropriately imitative sound objects should be played. For this reason we will overwhelmingly look at the imitation of human-made instruments and the related issue of imparting realism to electronic sounds.

The process of imitation is a kind of timbral thievery (Robert Moog, personal communication) and depends for its success on both the sonic acuity ("ear") of the musician and his or her detailed practical understanding of the various approaches to synthesis and sampling. The overall process therefore entails "constituting" the sound objects, as Boulez refers to above, designing and implementing the real-time programming, and playing the performance interface with appropriate expression. Successful imitation is also assisted by a knowledge of how the sound source physically produces its sound, what materials it is made of, how the musician physically manipulates the sound source (if it is played), and, in the case of traditional instruments, their traditions of style and repertoire.

The importance of the synthesist's capacity for aural discrimination is convincingly articulated by Wendy Carlos:

> You can put aside any hope of having a machine that will analyze sound for you. There's no such machine I would trust to have the degree of acuity my own ear has when it comes time to synthesize a sound. I think the only way to learn these things is to be a part of the information loop yourself, and refine your own ability until you can hear things that you didn't think were possible. (Milano 1987, p. 36)

It is always best to attempt imitative synthesis or sampling with a good aural referent: a hi-fidelity recording of the sound you want to create or the sound source itself. Use an A/B approach, by which we mean frequent direct comparison, equalizing all other sonic conditions like amplifiers, speakers, volume, reverberation, background noise, and so forth. To avoid desensitization, many synthesists recommend working no more than two hours in a session on any particular sound.

An imitation may succeed to the resolution of human auditory acuity in some ways, but it will inevitably differ from the original in others. The main orientation of the sound imitator must be to focus on the aspects of the sound essential for its intended use(s). In this regard, it is useful to distinguish two kinds of imitation: one that aims for literalness (exact aural identity with the target timbre) and another that is satisfied with functional equivalence. By functional equivalence we mean that the sound is able to achieve the same musical function as its target timbre. This kind of imitation has as much to do with the way the sound is performed as with the way the sound object is synthesized.

Before going on, the questions may be asked: Why imitate? Why not focus on the unique possibilities of the synthesizer rather than make largely inferior copies of instruments that are already at a very sophisticated level of development? In my view these questions are well worth asking but can be answered as follows. First, when good mimesis is available, instrumental sounds can be called on to do things that people can't: execute incredibly fast lines, play an octave below normal sounding range, indulge in inhumanly complex polyrhythms, and so forth. Second, there is a tremendous amount to be learned about the design of engaging sounds by the study of the acoustic signals and methods of control of traditional instruments. New sounds often come from a study of the limitations of old sounds. The sterility of much traditional computer-based music shows the continual need for an examination of not only sound spectra, but the historical processes of control in live performance. Third, the availability of imitative sounds allows new electronic methods of composition, like improvise-and-edit, to be readily used to produce scores for traditional instruments to play, aided by autotranscription programs. To a certain degree, traditional orchestration can be learned with such sounds. Fourth, there are practical cost-saving considerations that make electronic imitation viable for many commercial purposes. In the end, however, it is up to the user to decide on the credibility of this resource for the chosen musical purposes.

GENERAL CONSIDERATIONS IN INSTRUMENT IMITATION

To understand the different kinds of sounds that can come from an instrument, it is useful to begin by looking at the idea of *mode* of sound production. This refers to the method used to cause the object to vibrate. The traditional classification of instruments used by ethnomusicologists runs as follows:

aerophone—sound is produced by a vibrating column of air (e.g., the oboe, tuba, and bull-roarer) *idiophone*—sound is produced by striking, scraping, shaking, rubbing, plucking, or bowing the resonant body of the instrument (e.g., the marimba, guiro, glass harmonica, and jaw's harp)

chordophone—sound is produced by exciting a stretched string (e.g., the guitar, violin, hurdy-gurdy, and Aeolian harp)

membranophone—sound is produced by exciting a stretched membrane by striking, rubbing, or blowing (e.g., the snare drum, quica, kazoo)

electrophone—sound is produced or amplified by electric or electronic means

From this perspective, imitation means that we are trying to use a certain kind of electrophone to mimic the sounds of any of all five categories.

Another important approach to instrumental sound bases itself on the materials making up the various parts of the instrument—particularly the resonator—and those used to set it in motion. Soft wood sounds different from hard wood; wood of any kind sounds different from metal; plastic sounds different from bone; cloth may be packed into the resonator (or mallet) to deaden the sound; and so on. Orchestral percussionists, for example, use a wide variety of mallets with varying head sizes and materials, including heads made of yarn, felt, wood, rubber, various plastics, foam, metal, and even stone. The resourceful synthesist should develop an ear for such distinctions and a route to their imitation with one or more chosen synthesis approaches.

Beyond this, we will assume that the reader has access to synthesized sounds that provide sound objects that are plausible approximations of the target timbres—at least in terms of spectrum and envelope shape. The experience of most programmers, in any case, is that sound building is a continual upgrade process that is rarely if ever completely finished. A strongly effective sound one day will develop more and more chinks in its sonic armor on rehearing the next day. At other times, the process converges fairly rapidly.

In refining such imitations, it is wise to remember that instruments have characteristic *registers*, each of which may have a different *sound ideal.* For example, the clarinet has the dark and rich chalumeau register from written E2 to F#3, the throat register from G3 to Bb3, the clarino resister from B3 to C5, the high register from C#5 to F5, and the shrill extreme high register from F#5 to C6. Note that when instruments are transposing, as in this case, such range descriptions are best given in written rather than sounding pitch. This has the advantage that the register effects will be to a considerable degree transferable to all instruments in the same family, regardless of their sounding range.

Each register may have associated idiomatic playing techniques as well. Lip trills on brass, for example, can be done only between adjacent harmonics, so that trills of a second will be possible only in the instrument's high register. As a second example, the rate of attack and decay is much greater in the treble register of acoustic instruments than it is in the bass. Thus, high notes on decaying envelope instruments like the marimba are by default nonlegato (unless played very fast), and the imitating performer need not worry about playing any specific articulation in this register. Likewise, string and brass instruments may take longer to speak in the low register, due to the longer time it takes to set the instrument in motion in the low part of the frequency spectrum. If the constructed sound reflects this in its design, the performer may need to anticipate notes in that register and avoid fast flurries.

Although all instruments can in principle be used with any repertoire, we will focus here on the typical playing techniques of instruments as used in their better known styles—for example, the drum kit is linked to popular and jazz styles, the violin to classical or bluegrass music, and so forth. This will not be at the expense of discussing creative possibilities, however. We will often need to examine the actual physical technique of the instruments since it is best, whenever possible, to imitate the physical gesture used on the instrument at the synthesizer performance interface to increase naturalness. However, this is not always possible. With practice, almost any performance gesture can come to seem comfortable.

Our focus will be, then, not on the production of the musical note in isolation but on the *idiomatic* production of the note in a musical context. This production will be guided by traditions of interpretation of standard repertoire (in all common styles) and also by historically based sound ideals of the instruments and their idiomatic playing techniques.

It is important to emphasize how context-dependent the success of an imitation can be. Many synthesized strings, for example, are perfectly adequate when functioning as sustaining background pads but would be hopelessly nonrealistic in a passage requiring brisk staccato bowing. A brass imitation sound that works well as a background figure in a popular song would be laughable when used as part of a chamber group like a brass quintet (and perhaps vice versa). The most demanding settings are those that give aural prominence to the imitation of the full expressive capacities of an instrument, as for example chamber music or a prominent improvised solo passage. Sometimes the full versatility of function of traditional instruments can be imitated only by constructing a number of different synthesized or sampled programs and switching rapidly between them.

The tuning systems used by different instruments can also differ. The piano and organ, for example, are stuck with fixed (often stretched) tuning systems. The violin can tune every note differently every time it plays. Sophisticated performers vary this intonation in familiar tonal contexts and sometimes even in contemporary art music repertoire according to the chord, prevailing key center, or perceived voice leading. For example, a C in the key of G will not have the same frequency as the C in the key of D♭ (the second C will be sharper than the first). The details of this process are still being actively researched. It is often claimed that Pythagorean intonation or just intonation, rather than the tempered system used by keyboards, are the norms in many playing situations. The reader interested in these issues should consult Podnos (1981).

The easiest and most natural way to imitate an instrument is to digitally record it and play it back—in other words, use a sampler. For this to be fully effective, a number of velocity-dependent samples must be made across the full range of the instrument and then combined, carefully matching sound, pitch, volume and controllability into an integrated program. Rare is the synthesis technique that can match a good program of samples when it comes to imitating sound objects (although the synthesis techniques of physical modeling and resynthesis hold significant potential for development).

However, there are limitations. In comparison to synthesis, the sampling environment may lack tools for detailed real-time control of the sound object. This means that although the sound objects may be accurate, expressive control may suffer (particularly on sustaining sounds), and the result may be unidiomatic. Sampling is most easily made effective when the instrument being imitated has a limited timbral pallete or a fixed set of invariably pitched sounds. Where a more cybernetically and expressively complex instrument is involved, multiple cross-fades, switching, or both (controlled by velocity or continuous controller) are often necessary to enhance realism. Such features are increasingly available on composite synthesis machines and more recent samplers. If, in contrast, the sound is synthesized from simpler waveforms, more accurate real-time control is usually possible—at the expense of sound object realism.

The difficulty of instrumental imitation is also a function of the number of different modes of production the instrument possesses and particularly of the speed with which the traditional performer can switch between them. For example, the saxophone has normal, subtone, and growl modes. The player can quickly switch between these in the course of a melodic line. Synthetically, they should (if possible) be handled by key velocity or controller-based switching rather than program changes; otherwise, glitches could occur at program change points. Likewise, the imitation of the many subtle bowing possibilities available on the violin is a programming task of daunting complexity. On the other hand, changing the sound on brass instruments with the use of mutes takes several seconds (for their insertion or removal). (One exception to this is the plunger mute, which, after being picked up, is held near the bell of the instrument and used to produce a wah-wah—a filter opening and closing effect—from hand movements.) Hence, synthesis changes representing the addition of a mute can be readily handled by a program change, allowing much simpler programming and performance. Note that here (and in the following discussions) I will assume that line splitting, which circumvents the limitations imposed by rapid program changes, is not an option, since it is not well adapted to real-time performance (as described in chapter 5).

One important resource in designing such expressivity is to use one's own voice to sing the expression in the part. Even if the sound quality is beyond the powers of your (or perhaps anyone's) voice, its time shaping may be imitable. As a general rule, if expressive control can be sung, it will soon be found to be playable.

In discussing the instruments, I will use the common idea of instrumental *families*: groups of instruments of related design, playing technique, and sound. I will look at the general performance techniques used in instrument imitation and describe how they apply to all instruments currently common in the public arenas of music in our culture. (You will find it useful to refer frequently to the two primary performance models of music production given in chapter 5—the sustaining monophonic and decaying polyphonic.) All information necessary to perform a written part on each instrument will be given, including range, use of less common clefs (e.g., alto or tenor), the intervals of transposition for transposing instruments, special performance modes, and other relevant facts required for programming expression. The reader interested in more detail on playing techniques and associated repertoire should consult standard orchestration texts such as Piston (1955), Blatter (1980), Burton (1982) and Adler (1989). Highly recommended for its exploration of the acoustic properties of the full range of contemporary instruments is Murray Campbell and Clive Greated's *The Musician's Guide to Acoustics* (1987). For those interested in instruments off the beaten path, the specialist literature of ethnomusicology, both in written and audio format, should be consulted. The *New Grove Dictionary of Musical Instruments* (1984) remains a tremendous resource in this area.

Ranges, clefs, and transpositions for commonly encountered instruments are summarized in figure 8.1. The normal range for professional performers is indicated by whole notes; additional notes available via special playing techniques or special features found only on some instruments are indicated by stemless black note heads. The ranges, clefs, and transpositions for less common instruments will be mentioned in the discussions below. From the synthesist's standpoint, the given ranges are not hard and fast limitations but rather guidelines for achieving realism.

Instrument	Written Range	Sounding

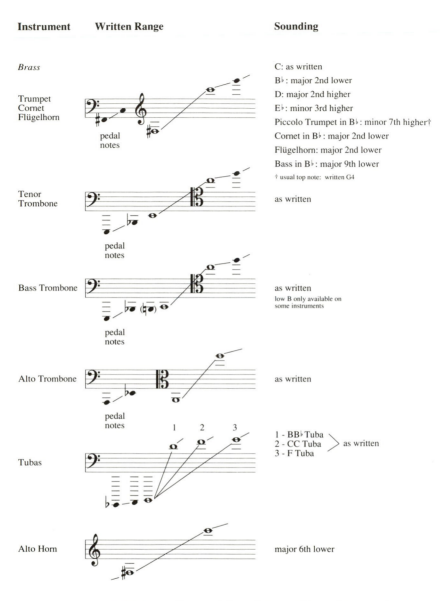

Brass

Trumpet
Cornet
Flügelhorn

pedal notes

C: as written
B♭: major 2nd lower
D: major 2nd higher
E♭: minor 3rd higher
Piccolo Trumpet in B♭: minor 7th higher†
Cornet in B♭: major 2nd lower
Flügelhorn: major 2nd lower
Bass in B♭: major 9th lower

† usual top note: written G4

Tenor
Trombone

pedal notes

as written

Bass Trombone

pedal notes

as written

low B only available on some instruments

Alto Trombone

pedal notes

as written

Tubas

1 - BB♭ Tuba
2 - CC Tuba } as written
3 - F Tuba

Alto Horn

major 6th lower

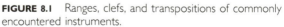

FIGURE 8.1   Ranges, clefs, and transpositions of commonly encountered instruments.

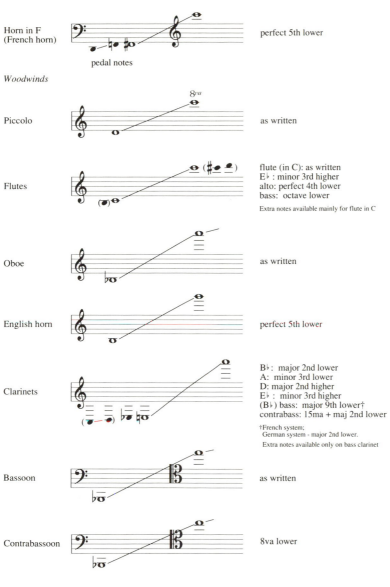

Horn in F (French horn) — perfect 5th lower

pedal notes

Woodwinds

Piccolo — as written

Flutes — flute (in C): as written
E♭ : minor 3rd higher
alto: perfect 4th lower
bass: octave lower
Extra notes available mainly for flute in C

Oboe — as written

English horn — perfect 5th lower

Clarinets — B♭: major 2nd lower
A: minor 3rd lower
D: major 2nd higher
E♭ : minor 3rd higher
(B♭) bass: major 9th lower†
contrabass: 15ma + maj 2nd lower
†French system;
German system - major 2nd lower.
Extra notes available only on bass clarinet

Bassoon — as written

Contrabassoon — 8va lower

FIGURE 8.1 continued.

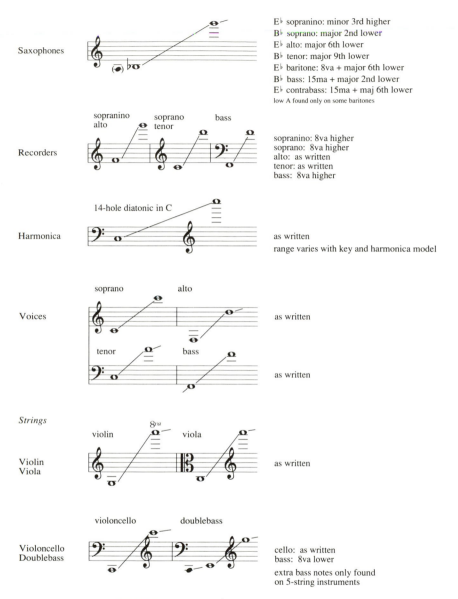

Saxophones

E♭ sopranino: minor 3rd higher
B♭ soprano: major 2nd lower
E♭ alto: major 6th lower
B♭ tenor: major 9th lower
E♭ baritone: 8va + major 6th lower
B♭ bass: 15ma + major 2nd lower
E♭ contrabass: 15ma + maj 6th lower
low A found only on some baritones

Recorders

sopranino
alto
soprano
tenor
bass

sopranino: 8va higher
soprano: 8va higher
alto: as written
tenor: as written
bass: 8va higher

Harmonica

14-hole diatonic in C

as written
range varies with key and harmonica model

Voices

soprano   alto

as written

tenor   bass

as written

Strings

**Violin
Viola**

violin   viola

as written

**Violoncello
Doublebass**

violoncello   doublebass

cello: as written
bass: 8va lower
extra bass notes only found
on 5-string instruments

FIGURE 8.1   continued.

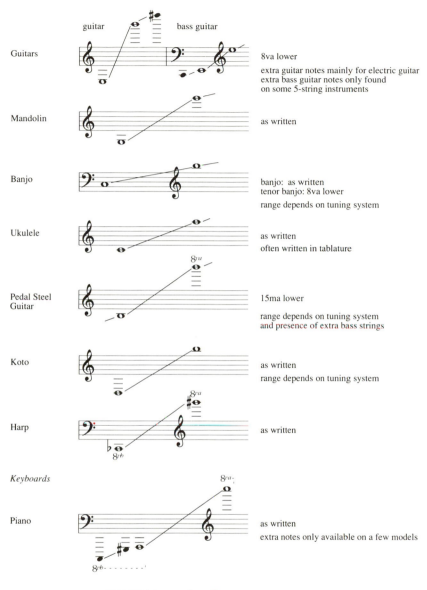

Guitars — 8va lower
extra guitar notes mainly for electric guitar
extra bass guitar notes only found
on some 5-string instruments

Mandolin — as written

Banjo — banjo: as written
tenor banjo: 8va lower
range depends on tuning system

Ukulele — as written
often written in tablature

Pedal Steel Guitar — 15ma lower
range depends on tuning system
and presence of extra bass strings

Koto — as written
range depends on tuning system

Harp — as written

Keyboards

Piano — as written
extra notes only available on a few models

FIGURE 8.1   continued.

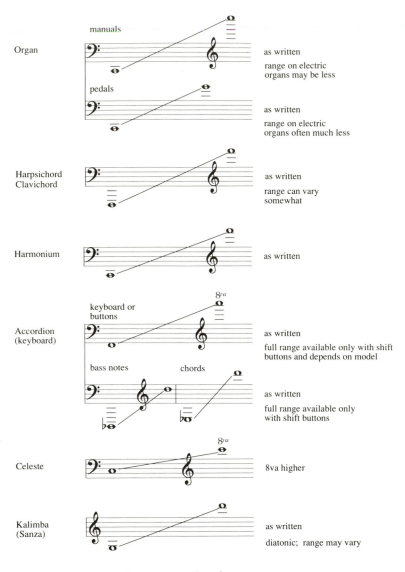

Organ

manuals

as written
range on electric
organs may be less

pedals

as written
range on electric
organs often much less

Harpsichord
Clavichord

as written
range can vary
somewhat

Harmonium

as written

Accordion
(keyboard)

keyboard or
buttons

as written
full range available only with shift
buttons and depends on model

bass notes   chords

as written
full range available only
with shift buttons

Celeste

8va higher

Kalimba
(Sanza)

as written
diatonic; range may vary

FIGURE 8.1   continued.

Percussion

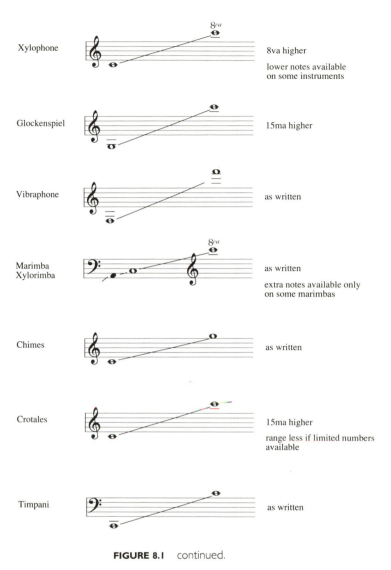

Xylophone — 8va higher / lower notes available on some instruments

Glockenspiel — 15ma higher

Vibraphone — as written

Marimba Xylorimba — as written / extra notes available only on some marimbas

Chimes — as written

Crotales — 15ma higher / range less if limited numbers available

Timpani — as written

FIGURE 8.1   continued.

SUSTAINING BREATH INSTRUMENTS: BRASS AND WINDS

In terms of performance techniques for imitation, brass and woodwinds have many similarities. The instruments of both families are sustaining and monophonic and so can be readily imitated by the sustaining monophonic envelope model of chapter 5.

The primary brass instruments are the various trumpets, the alto, tenor and bass trombones, the French horn, and the various tubas. Their ranges and transpositions are summarized in figure 8.1.

The trumpet is normally in either B♭ (sounding a major second below written pitch) or C (nontransposing). Trumpeters in popular or jazz bands nearly always use the B♭ instrument, whereas orchestral players favor the C instrument. The D trumpet, which sounds a major second above written pitch, and the E♭ trumpet, sounding a minor third above written pitch, are more rarely encountered but have an unmistakably clarion sound. High-pitched piccolo trumpets in A or B♭ also exist, and their characteristic compact sound is most commonly heard to advantage in baroque concerti (e.g., J. S. Bach's *Brandenburg Concerto No. 2*). Closely related in sound is the cornet (in B♭), an instrument associated with brass bands and early jazz, as well as the more mellow flügelhorn, a B♭ instrument favored by jazz players. The bugle is a similar instrument with valveless military associations, although a keyed form does exist. Bass trumpets also occur, in E♭ and B♭; the rarely seen slide trumpet is an F instrument.

The trombones and tubas are all nontransposing instruments. These instruments normally use bass clef but in the high register will often be written in tenor clef. The alto trombone uses alto clef; this is also found for the tenor trombone in a few scores. The tuba family is extensive, and figure 8.1 shows only some of its more common members. The French horn is an F instrument, sounding a perfect fifth below the written part. It is written in either treble or bass clef, as appropriate for its large range. The E♭ alto horn (commonly known as the tenor horn in the United Kingdom and Australia), typically encountered in music for brass band, is a transposing instrument, sounding a major sixth below written pitch.

Less well known than these brass instruments is a host of others that may be rarely encountered. The alphorn is a very long and varyingly transposing instrument. The cornett and serpent are Renaissance instruments with highly flexible intonation; the cornett actually represents a family of instruments with varying ranges. The sackbut is simply an early antecedent of the trombone. These early instruments are all written without transposition in modern transcriptions. The bass horn and ophicleide, popular in the nineteenth century, are called for in a few orchestral scores.

Basic tube resonators are also used as instruments by some musicians, including animal horns (the gemshorn), sea conches and shells, and hollow industrial (usually plastic) tubing. These may have a brass or woodwind style mouthpiece.

The didgeridoo (didjeridu) is an Aboriginal Australian instrument that functions primarily to produce rhythms and coloristic changes, including many animal imitation effects. Its embouchure is closest to that of the tuba, and it is a difficult instrument to play well, as it presupposes circular breathing as one of its most basic techniques.

The primary Western woodwinds are piccolo, the various flutes (bass, alto, C, Eb), oboe, English horn, bassoon and contrabassoon, the various clarinets (contrabass, bass, A, Bb, Eb), the various recorders (bass, tenor, alto, soprano, sopranino), and the various saxophones (contrabass, bass, baritone, tenor, alto, soprano, sopranino). Sonically, these fall into the categories of flutes, single reed, and double reed instruments. Their ranges and transpositions are summarized in figure 8.1.

The Western flutes—piccolo, bass flute, alto flute, C flute, and the rare Eb flute—are nearly always made of metal (in recent times) and are highly agile in the hands of a good player. All these flutes are written in treble clef. Many other types of flutes exist, widely drawn from other cultures, and these sonic resources continue to infiltrate synthesized music. The sounds of flutes are most dependent on their mode of production (endblown or transverse) and material of construction (commonly metal, wood, and bamboo). One of the best-known endblown flutes is the panpipe. Panpipes are found in many cultures, from South America to Southeast Asia to Africa to Oceania, and range from piccolo-like tones to below Western bass flute in pitch. With some endblown flutes the player blows on an edge that splits the air stream, producing a breathy sound of great delicacy and capacity for pitch bend and articulatory nuance, like that of the Turkish nay, or the Japanese shakuhachi. The alternative type of endblown flute uses a whistle-type mouthpiece. These so-called fipple flutes include the recorder, the flageolet, and the slide whistle.

Transverse flutes take their name from the performer's style of blowing perpendicular to the body of the instrument; all the Western metal flutes mentioned, including such things as the fife (a kind of keyless piccolo), are of this type. Notation for the non-Western instruments is not standardized but is usually in concert pitch; some transverse flutes occur in families of different keys (e.g., in India) and are in effect transposing instruments.

The double reed family (best-known members being the oboe, English horn, and bassoon) is united by common timbral features, usually described as piercing in the higher ranges, rich in the region around middle C, and lugubrious in the bass. Older Western double reed instruments include the crumhorn, shawm, rauschpfeife, racket, oboe d'amore, heckelphone, and sarrusophone. The first four of these are written without transposition in modern transcriptions. The oboe d'amore sounds a minor third below the normal oboe, and the heckelphone is a baritone oboe pitched an octave below the standard oboe. The sarrusophone is an entire family of instruments; it is rare but most commonly seen in its contrabass form in C (and in this form has been preferred to the contrabassoon by many French composers). Non-Western double reed instruments (shawms) abound, like the Turkish zurna, the Indian shenai, and the Indian nagaswaram, which can achieve piercing dynamic levels. Some non-Western double reed instruments use circular breathing as a standard practice so that the phrasing concepts of Western wind instruments are inapplicable.

The single reed instruments include as prominent members the clarinet family. All clarinets are commonly written in treble clef, although the bass clarinet has two options: the so-called French system, written in treble clef and sounding a major ninth lower, and the German system, written in bass or treble clef and sounding a whole tone lower. It is a Bb instrument. The A and Bb (soprano) clarinets are the most common members of the clarinet family and sound respectively a minor third and a major second below written pitch. Also encountered are the Eb (sopranino) clarinet, the piccolo clarinet in Ab, and the soprano in C.

The saxophone family includes the Eb contrabass, Bb bass, Eb baritone, Bb tenor, Eb alto, Bb soprano, and Eb sopranino. The saxophones are all written in treble clef. Older related Western instruments include the chalumeau and the basset horn in F, the latter sounding a fifth below written pitch.

The recorders are available in a number of different sizes. Most commonly found are the sopranino, soprano, alto, tenor, and bass instruments.

Other wind instruments commonly encountered include the harmonica, melodica, ocarina, kazoo, slide whistle, nose flute, bagpipes, and sheng.

The harmonica, normally notated without transposition, can be considered a kind of mouth reed organ, and comes in two forms: the diatonic and the chromatic. Blues players play diatonic harmonicas, and classical or jazz harmonica players use the chromatic variety. The range of ten-hole diatonic harmonicas and chromatic harmonicas is usually three octaves, but the fourteen-hole diatonic beast has four octaves, as indicated in figure 8.1. Range also depends on key. Harmonicas are of different timbral types: they may be single reed, "tremolo tuned," or octave tuned. Single reed harmonicas have one reed per note. The harmonicas most commonly used in blues and rock bands are the single reed variety. The tremolo-tuned harmonicas achieve their effect by having two slightly mistuned reeds per note and can be imitated synthetically by detuning two unison sounds. The octave-tuned harmonicas also have two reeds per note, but they are tuned in octaves, which can be readily mimicked synthetically.

The non-classical harmonica usually needs real-time pitch bend to make it realistic.

The melodica is a short plastic keyboard instrument held with both hands. The performer blows on one end in the manner of a fipple flute. It is written at concert pitch. The ocarinas have a limited range of both pitch (about a ninth) and dynamics but are capable of fully chromatic playing. Pitch bend inflections are idiomatic. According to Blatter (1980), the instrument has no standard notation. The kazoo is really a timbrally disguised voice (the performer hums or sings through a buzzy membrane), and the control problems and clefs (if such parts are written out at all) are the same as for the voice. The familiar effect of the slide whistle is based on the exaggerated portamento possible when the slide is used to alter its basically recorder-like sound. Large pitch bend ranges are typically used in synthesized imitation.

The bagpipes are found in many countries, with the Scottish and southern European forms perhaps best known. A lack of dynamic variation, characteristically ornamented lines, and drones characterize it.

Sheng is the Chinese term for an instrument widely distributed in Asia (e.g., in Japan a very similar instrument is called sho); it is a kind of mouth organ with vertical tubes for each note, allowing chords of arbitrary design to be shaped. Its characteristic sound is something like a cross between the harmonica and accordian.

Performance Considerations

The most important attributes for performance imitation of sustaining breath instruments are articulation, dynamics, vibrato, pitch microvariation, use of the breath, and characteristic effects. These will be examined in turn.

Articulation

Each wind or brass instrument has a controllable attack noise component ("chiff" or "spit") used to separate notes and achieve non-legato. This attack noise is produced by interrupting the air stream with the tongue using a consonant sound like "t," "k," or "d." The synthesist must remember that legato is formed with such instruments by the omission of this tonguing attack noise and not by the overlap of adjacent notes as would be normal on a keyboard, as discussed in the sustaining monophonic model of chapter 5. In wind and brass legato passages, the keyboard performer should play at most tenuto if strict realism is to be achieved. However, a slight amount of legato overlap is often acceptable if imitation of the musical function only is to be achieved. Staccato is achieved by leaving space between notes, as usual.

In electronic imitation, the initial noise transient can either be built into one or more components of the sound of one synthesizer or into one synthesizer's contribution to the layered composite sound. Its control will need to be separate from that of overall dynamics. The attack noise component is generally differentiated from the steady-state component by its increased brightness (although there are a number of exceptions to this), along with its more rapid attack and decay envelope times.

It is also possible to achieve legato by using monophonic mode on certain synthesizers. This useful technique is rarely completely satisfactory when it comes to imitating natural timbres, as the control of envelope is too erratic.

Pitch bend legato, as discussed in chapter 5, can usefully supplement the sustaining monophonic model, particularly with sampled sounds (which are often bright and tongued) when sophisticated switching or crossfading is not available. It particularly suits the trombone and slide trumpet but is generally useful.

In general, breath instruments are capable of very subtle and wideranging variation in their attack or, for that matter, in other portions of their envelopes. Where the functions being imitated have certain typecast consistencies in legato, staccato, and tenuto, synthesis is relatively easy. If, on the other hand, the wide-ranging nuances of articulations used on the saxophone in free jazz playing are to be imitated, the synthesist faces a daunting and groundbreaking task in which the ear must be the primary guide and care must be given to the arrangement and design of controller functions.

Dynamics

What is clear for virtually all instruments is that brightness increases with volume, together producing much of what is called call *dynamics.* (As discussed earlier, there will also be envelope effects.) Therefore, key velocity (controlling attack component brightness or volume) and appropriate controllers (controlling sustaining component brightness and volume) should be programmed to allow suitable dynamic variation, as discussed in chapter 5. Appropriate controllers include all continuous controllers, but the quick and characteristic response profile of the breath controller can be especially useful for breath-based instruments like brass and woodwinds. Unfortunately, except for separate wind controllers, this device is only built into some synthesizers made by Yamaha Corporation. (The Synclavier is a very expensive exception to this.) However, it can be used with all synthesizers by renumbering the controller number produced by the breath controller (02) to a controller number used by the sound engine receiving the messages. The procedure is done using a MIDI mapping device. Yamaha makes a separate device, the MCS2 Controller

Workstation, which accepts the breath controller plug and allows it to be routed to any MIDI controller.

Vibrato

This an important feature of realism for all traditional sustaining instruments. Here it is necessary to make a careful distinction between the use of this word in synthesis and its use in instrumental performance, for they are not always the same. The word as used by traditional instrumentalists often includes both frequency and amplitude modulation of the basic sound. The amount of these two forms can vary from instrument to instrument. In the terminology of synthesis, vibrato refers more strictly to frequency modulation by a low frequency source. Hence, in imitation, the synthesist must gauge the nature of the instrumental vibrato required, remembering that too much amplitude modulation can produce an unsuitable tremolo. The flute, for example, seems to have more amplitude modulation than the saxophone. The recorder's "vibrato" is primarily tremolo, and the harmonica's nearly exclusively so. On the other hand, the singing voice's vibrato is dominated by frequency modulation.

For realistic imitation, vibrato must be real-time controllable with regard to depth and onset point and often rate as well. If an LFO is used, it must provide a suitably shaped waveform, normally triangle or sine. Alternatively, pitch bend can be used to achieve vibrato. The discussion in chapter 5 is applicable.

Pitch Microvariation

This term refers to the intentional small "coloristic" changes in pitch used by performers, as discussed earlier. It also refers to the phenomenon whereby, as with most sustaining instruments, brass and winds typically do not hit and hold their pitches with machine-like accuracy. They undershoot (or sometimes overshoot) their target pitch and then quickly adjust, using lip pressure, embouchure, or slide, and don't quite hold things steady thereafter. If the note is very short, adjustment may not happen at all; the note is just out of tune. Such transitory out-of-tuneness is often perceived in timbral terms. These adjustments, when properly controlled, are part of the complex charm of traditional instruments.

Put in more technical terms, these adjustment effects amount to a variable center frequency deviation over the first portion (perhaps 50 to 200 msec) of the note, with less pronounced microtonal variation throughout its "steady" state thereafter. Hence, a discrete amount of pitch envelope shaping at the start of notes may enhance realism, and ideally this should vary in depth or character from note to note; either some randomization or routing of a controller (such as velocity) to the depth of the pitch envelope will be appropriate. The optimal situation is if analogous real-time control (preferably by continuous controller) is available for the sustain portions of the envelope. An intermediate approximation available on some synthesizers is to slightly randomize the steady-state pitch. Likewise, some microtonal pitch randomness in the final portion of each note is frequently useful. However, this degree of programming detail is often not fully available on contemporary synthesizers. In situations of prominent aural exposure, this absence will be clearly heard.

Use of the Breath

It is important to remember that brass and wind instruments are breath instruments; if the synthesist is to imitate the limitations (attributes) of a human performer there must be short pauses or phrase ends to allow air to be taken in. The use of the breath controller can help remind the performer of this. However, in most situations this limitation need not be respected, as the careful listener will rarely be under any illusions about whether a brass or wind sound is synthesized or not. Furthermore, the need to strictly respect this limitation has been weakened by a small but increasing number of woodwind and brass performers capable of circular breathing.

Characteristic Effects

On brass and woodwinds these include the following:

both brass and woodwinds: punch figures, subito dynamic effects, bends, glides, portamento, glissando, falloffs, spills, lifts, rips, plops, the shake, tremolos and trills, ghost notes, use of mutes, open/closed bell, flutter tongue, sing/growl techniques, extended upper register, circular breathing

effects specific to brass: pedal tones, doit, harmonic flip, lip trills, half valving

effects specific to woodwinds: subtone, multiphonics, cross fingerings, key clicks and pops, half keying

Extended techniques for all woodwinds are discussed in Bartolozzi (1962). Extended techniques specific to the flute are given by Howell (1975) and Dick (1975); new directions for the clarinet, by Rehfeldt (1978). The full panoply of trombone special effects is discussed by Dempster (1979).

Punch figures refers to syncopated rhythmic figures with notes of short duration, usually played by brass (and sometimes woodwind) sections. These may be successfully executed under either of the two primary performance models given in chapter 5. The decaying polyphonic model can work (with key velocity controlling dynamics) because of the short note durations; the unsuitable brightness of the steady state will often not be heard. The sustaining envelope model will work because dynamics can be quickly changed by a suitable controller. In this second choice, a controller must be chosen that allows quick movement—breath or foot controllers are best, while aftertouch is in general impractical. Where extremely quick dynamic changes are required, the first model may have some advantages.

Subito dynamic effects refers to very rapid (subito) increases or decreases in dynamics. When the change is from one note to the next, then the existing dynamic control of any kind will be perfectly suitable, provided its range is sufficient. If the effect is within the course of a single held note, then there are two cases: one, where dynamics suddenly drops (e.g., the fortepiano marking *fp*), and another, where dynamics suddenly increases (e.g., the marking *pf* or *pff*). The most versatile programming uses a wheel, foot controller, breath controller, or other continuous controller for quick changes of dynamics in either direction. Fortepiano effects can be handled also by key velocity, and pianoforte effects can be achieved with aftertouch.

Bends and *glides* are categories of terms that are used for bend-like effects in different performance styles. The terms derived from jazz have wide currency and include the bend, glide, smear, and other terms given below. These are obtainable by pitch bend or synthesizer portamento effect. Pitch bend is more generally useful, due to its more powerfully literal control. Portamento, however, can be used to good effect when it can be turned rapidly on and off with a foot switch, especially when its rate can be controlled in real time. It should be kept in mind in either procedure that when bends become larger than a semitone or two, the difference between the effect of a synthesized bend and an acoustic one increases noticeably. The reason for this is that irregularities, noises and resonances are excited in the course of the bend on an acoustic instrument, and the synthesized or sampled sounds lack these characteristic irregularities. Treating the synthesizer's output with a device that enhances or resonates at certain frequencies, such as a graphic EQ with some bands peaked or a very short delay with feedback, can help imitate these irregularitites.

Portamento and *glissando* are used as discussed in chapters 5 and 6. The variation of speed over a controller-played portamento (and, to a lesser extent, a glissando) can be an important expressive feature, particularly with a long slow bend.

Of course, different instruments differ in their ability to achieve these effects. All brass except the slide trombone and slide trumpet can easily achieve a played glissando; only these two instruments can achieve a true portamento. Most instruments can achieve portamento by lipping and the use of half-open keys (woodwinds) or half-valving effects (brass). Also of interest is the harmonic glissando, achievable on brass instruments by rapid change of lip pressure (and air speed). Difficult to imitate at the keyboard, it consists of a glissando of notes up or down the harmonic series of the fundamental of the played note. Related to this is the flip, where the brass player hits the note, flips up to one or more higher harmonics, and then returns to the main note (or goes on to the next).

Falloffs, spills, lifts, rips, plops, and *doits (kisses)* are terms that refer to glissandi or portamento figures that occur before or after and above or below a central note, and that lack either a specified starting or ending pitch. Many of these have been incorporated into recommended synthesizer notation, as given previously in figure 5.1. They are associated with the jazz repertoire but also occur in other styles. One option for the synthesist is direct sampling, and samples of some of these figures are increasingly found as presets in some sound modules. Otherwise, their details must be performed at the synthesizer interface. The kinds of performance issues involved can be highlighted by looking at any one of the effects, such as the falloff. Spills, lifts, rips, plops, and doits are basically executed in line with these same considerations and are left for the reader to develop.

The falloff requires the musician to hit the indicated note and then drop rapidly in pitch by a substantial interval, normally reducing dynamics at the same time. This can be done by lipping, fingering, or a combination of the two, depending on the instrument and the desired interpretation.

The decrescendo part of the synthesized falloff is readily achieved by continuous controller routed to volume and brightness. The pitch part of the synthesized falloff is usually best achieved by a combination of playing techniques. Most important, of course, is pitch bend. If its range is set to a rather large value, say ± 5 to ± 12 semitones or more, pitch bend may be satisfactory by itself. However, since this range is too large for comfortable intermediate goal bending for most performers, this is not always a satisfactory solution for an extended passage. If pitch bend range is set lower, in its customary range of ± 2 to ± 4 semitones, some falloff effect can still be obtained. This becomes more convincing if a fingered falloff is played at the same time, as indicated in figure 8.2. Synthesizer portamento can in principle be similarly used, but it tends to be less versatile and is only viable here if it can be quickly switched on and off (e.g., via footswitch), as otherwise glides will occur both to and from the note in question. Where such portamento control is available, the performer plays the first note, switches glide on, and then plays a lower note chosen to create proper glide range and speed (e.g., in figure 8.2 this might be an octave below the first note).

If the effect of falloff by an entire horn section is desired, it is often useful to put different pitch bend sensitivities on different parts (to sim-

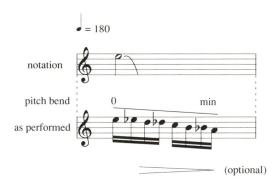

FIGURE 8.2 Executing a falloff.

ulate the lack of strict parallelism in the section bend) and on different sound components of each part (to simulate the pitched roughness that occurs when instruments do not bend quite in unison). This has been called "roughing up" the sound (Kurt Biederwolf, personal communication). There are at least three basic methods. Either the parts and components are given slightly different pitch bend ranges (e.g., pick part and component ranges from ± 11 and ± 12, or from ± 7, ± 8, and ± 9), or some of the voices are set to bend continuously (instrumental portamento) and others are quantized to the nearest semitone (glissando), or a MIDI mapping device or similar processor is used to delay the transmission of pitch bend to some of the parts.

The terms *tremolo* and *trill* are used here in their instrumental sense — namely, to mean the rapid alternation of two notes. To first approximation, tremolos and trills can be simulated easily for woodwind and brass sounds by fingering the corresponding notes on the keyboard. However, in many cases the traditional figures (particularly tremolo) excite instrument resonances or cause other noticeable changes in the sound that this simple procedure will fail to capture. Another source of difficulty is that such figures are nearly always played quite connected on breath (or for that matter, string) instruments, whereas the notes will be reattacked with the same envelope (typically producing nonlegato) if the synthesizer is in traditional polyphonic mode. If the synthesizer is in monophonic mode, there will be a legato-like effect due to the loss of at least the attack portion of the envelope when notes are *played* legato, but this is seldom very convincing as an imitation of a true legato trill (or tremolo) unless the envelope of the sound is very carefully designed and the trill is very carefully executed. The only solution to this in general is to use the sustaining monophonic model and turn up the attack component of the sound only at the start of the trill or tremolo figure, playing with no more than a slight amount of note overlap. This will be successful at imitating fingered trills and tremolos.

However, brass instruments have another possibility known as the lip trill, where the player trills between two notes of the harmonic series by use of the lip. A related effect is the shake, where the player exaggerates the lip trill by physically shaking the instrument, producing a kind of timbral tremolo. When lip trills and shakes are performed on brass instruments, the sound is considerably richer in transients and irregular subtleties than a simple keyboard trill can bring into play. This limitation normally has no solution other than a separate sampling of lip trills and shakes, with suitably timed performance.

The technique of achieving tremolos and trills by using LFOs with quick attack waveforms (e.g., square or pulse waves) to effectively retrigger the sound is generally not convincing in imitating traditional instruments; however, it can produce interesting effects in its own right (see figure 5.15).

Tremolos can in general be *measured* (in strict time) or *unmeasured* (with somewhat variable rate). The synthesist should be sensitive to this difference in certain styles and be able to play both forms.

The term *ghost note* refers to a note much softer than its surrounding notes, with muffled or indefinite pitch. It occurs most often in jazz and popular music. Insofar as it can be imitated, it must be done either by having a controller able to pull the brightness and clarity of pitch from a sound on command (typically by filtering) or having an appropriate ghost note assigned to a specific key that need be used only in this situation. With either method the sound should be played short and at a contextually lower dynamic.

Mutes decrease dynamics and alter the timbre. Sometimes pitch is affected as well—the instrument's intonation is made more irregular, though of course the player will compensate as able. Mutes are primarily used with brass, although they are sometimes called for with woodwinds. The most common mutes are the straight mute, cup mute, plunger mute, mica mute, harmon mute, whispa mute, bucket mute, and solotone mute (the rarest).

Mutes require a moment or two to insert or remove, and so parts incorporating them will have pauses to allow this to be done. In terms of synthesis, this means that there is time to perform a program change and that real-time control within a single patch equivalent to mute insertion is mostly unnecessary. The synthesist must then only be concerned with the imitation of the nuances of the muted sound object, be it harmon, bucket, cup, or other mute. Most of these are readily done (sampling, filtering, and FM seem to be the most successful methods), with such prominent exceptions as the subtle effects of the close-miked harmon mute pioneered so convincingly by trumpeter Miles Davis.

Open/closed bell is accomplished with a muting device, which can be the hand, a hat, or, most commonly, a plunger mute. Real-time controller programming is necessary and should be routed to create a wah-wah-like sound, implemented synthetically by opening and closing a filter or varying the depth of a waveform distortion source such as FM or waveshaping.

Flutter tonguing is a rapid interruption of the air stream driving the instrument, effected by "trilling" with the tongue, and is best imitated in synthesis by strong LFO amplitude modulation using a not too abrupt waveform such as a sine or triangle wave. The speed will need to be in the range of about 15 to 25 Hz; the best way to determine the speed to use is to do a tongue (or lip) trill yourself and match its speed with the LFO. The effect is best turned on or off with a discrete controller. Program changes to and from this sound will sometimes be usable, but flutter tongue requires no audible delay for a wind player to prepare, and so in some situations this will not be suitable. Realism will be enhanced if the speed is varied slightly by the use of a continuous controller. However, synthesis can at best aim at functional imitation; to approach literal imitation, sampling of flutter tonguing is necessary.

Sing/growl techniques refers to the player's singing through the instrument, most commonly at the same pitch the instrument is sounding. Other intervals are also quite usable but are more difficult to hit dependably. The best known uses of this technique in popular and jazz music stick to the same pitch as played, although some contemporary pieces (notably those for trombone) develop the independent vocal line to a high degree.

The effect of unison singing is to create a strong flanging effect, partly caused by the voice and the instrument being slightly out of tune with each other, and partly by cross-resonances between the instrument and vocal cavities. This out-of-tuneness continually changes with time. The growl sound object, therefore, if not available by sampling, may be functionally mimicked by slightly variable unison detuning and increased brightness and roughness. This technique can be brought in and out very quickly on the instrument and so cannot be successfully handled in general by program change, although some cases will allow this. Key velocity can be used as a switch to choose between the normal sound and the growl sound if the notes' durations are not too long; the use of continuous controllers is a better way to accomplish this.

Circular breathing enables the breath performer to play without interruption and changes the nature of phrasing. It is an essential part of some instruments' technique, notably the digeridoo, various Asian and African oboes, and the tenor saxophone as played by Evan Parker. It poses no special synthesis performance problems.

Pedal tones are notes sounding an octave below the normal range of brass instruments. Although available in the trumpet family, they are most effective and usable in the bass register instruments, notably the trombone and bass trombone. Their sound is broad, diffuse, and powerful. They are not capable of very rapid playing or delicate control; therefore there is little to say about their distinctive performance techniques in imitation.

Subtone is a sound largely confined to the saxophone and clarinet families. By playing more softly and making certain changes in the embouchure and the amount of reed taken into the mouth, a distinctly gentler and "sweeter" tone is produced from the instrument. In classical scores, the term *echo* has sometimes been used to indicate this effect. There are no special playing techniques required from the point of view of synthesis; basically, the sound has reduced dynamics and brightness. For a realistic imitation, the synthesist must sample or listen carefully to a saxophone player executing subtone.

A *multiphonic* is a chord played by a single brass or woodwind instrument (nearly always the latter). Multiphonic effects are achieved by careful embouchure control and cross-fingerings and are very diverse. The chords produced typically do not fit in the tempered system. These are very complex sound objects and can really only be approximated by sampling or a tremendous amount of programming. Real-time control is very difficult to imitate with contemporary synthesizers.

Half-keying and *half-valving* are techniques found respectively on woodwind and brass instruments and allow highly variable sounds difficult to imitate other than through sampling.

Key clicks and *key pops* are sounds formed by vigorously slapping the keys of the instruments down. Sampling is readily successful, since they are of very short duration; they can also be imitated on any synthesizer by using an extremely fast decay on the amplifier's envelope. Velocity control of dynamics is necessary for realism.

THE VOICE

True voice synthesis is a specialized and well-researched field, and much progress has been made on imitating both the speaking and singing voice, using such techniques as Linear Predictive Coding and formant analysis. Detailed computer representations of sound have been essential in this process. The options are less extensive for the performing synthesist, who commands a less versatile and powerful system.

I will treat the speaking voice first. Since the voice is our primary means of communication, we are very sensitive to its timbral nuances. Synthesizers are virtually useless here since they are not designed to cope with the special needs of speech; at best, they are good at reproducing only sustained vowel sounds or a few special phonemes like "wow" (via filter sweep). Samplers do allow the phonemes, syllables, words, and phrases of speech to be generally imitated. The limitation here is the familiar one of sampling time, and pronunciation is so context dependent and our lexicon of common sounds and words so vast that all but the largest sampling storage systems are quickly filled up. Real-time processing of speech by samplers is used in performance primarily by popular and "avant-garde" musicians, whose goals often differ markedly.

The familiar vocal singing ranges are summarized in figure 8.1. Imitation of the singing voice separates immediately into two cases: first, where the same speech sound is used for all notes, and second, where the full complexity of speech is to be imitated in the singing tone. The first case is the norm in contemporary work with synthesizers and samplers, since (1) in some vocal functions the use of words is irrelevant (e.g., a vocal pad), (2) synthesizers are not sophisticated enough in the control they offer to convincingly mimic changing vowels and almost all consonants, and (3) as above, the amount of sampling time needed to achieve realism by the second method greatly exceeds that available in all but the most sophisticated systems. Most commercial patches are, for the most part, wordless asexual choirs singing "ooh" or "aah."

Those synthesists who wish to produce voice-like sounds should investigate the use of formant bands for vowel sounds and short noise components for consonants. These formants and noise are largely independent of both the pitch of the note being sung or spoken. To a first approximation, formants occur at intervals of about 1000 Hz, beginning at approximately 400 to 500 Hz. Hence they fall roughly around 500, 1500, 2500, 3500 Hz, etc. (Campbell and Greated 1987; for more detail see Rossing 1990). The first two or three formants are most important. They are achieved physiologically by the speaker changing the positions of the speech articulators: the lips, tongue, velum, and so on. This changes the resonances in the head, and these resonances correspond to the formant areas. Their exact frequency placement depends on gender, age, and throat shape and can be fine-tuned ("formant tuning") by experienced singers.

Apart from phonetics, the most important attributes for performance imitation are very similar to the discussion concerning wind instruments. The reader should consult there the topics of articulation, dynamics, vibrato, pitch microvariation, and use of the breath. Characteristic effects are of course quite different and include head voice, falsetto, ululation, the scream, and various extended vocal techniques like the vocal fry (a raspy type of inhaled or exhaled vocalization) and glottal stop (a sudden cluck-like stopping of the air column with the glottis). These sounds are so distinctive that they are normally accessible only via sampling. The interested reader should consult specialist articles on these techniques and their accompanying tapes. Recommended for this are Kavasch (1980) and Howell and Harvey (1985).

SUSTAINING INSTRUMENTS: BOWED STRINGS

Bowed (arco) strings today include the violin, viola, violoncello, and double bass (contrabass). These instruments are descended from earlier antecedents like the medieval rabab and vielle, the crank-driven hurdy-gurdy, and the viol family (popular in the sixteenth and seventeenth centuries), which are still used by contemporary specialists who wish to duplicate as closely as possible the authentic historical sounds of different musical eras. Many different types of bowed string instruments exist throughout the world, like the Indian sarangi and the Indonesian rebab (a spike fiddle). Their sounds tend to be rougher than that of the modern violin family.

The ranges of the members of the violin family are shown in figure 8.1, and their open string tunings are shown in figure 8.3. The violin uses the treble clef, the viola the alto clef (treble clef in high register), and the cello and double bass the bass clef (tenor clef in high register and treble clef in very high register). All instruments except the doublebass, which sounds an octave below written pitch, are nontransposing. One exception to this is with the use of treble clef in high pre-twentieth century cello parts, which were notated an octave above sounding pitch.

String instruments are primarily monophonic, although more than one note can be played at once (as discussed below). Their sounds are characterized by numerous formants corresponding to resonances of the body of the instrument. For a description of these issues, see the article by Moog in Aikin et al. (1987).

The most important attributes for imitating bowed strings are articulation, dynamics, vibrato, pitch microvariation, and characteristic effects. The issues involved with dynamics, vibrato and pitch microvariation are basically the same as for breath sustaining instruments, and the sustaining monophonic model should be used. Dynamics is thus best handled by an appropriate continuous controller, pitch microvariation by pitch bend device. The use of Pythagorean tuning with string playing is recommended by several sources.

The synthetic design of the vibrato function is in most ways similar to the wind instrument case, even though with string instruments the vibrato is produced by a slight rocking of the the player's fingerboard (normally

FIGURE 8.3 Open tuning for the orchestral strings.

left) hand instead of by embouchure or diaphragm action, as on wind instruments. The main difference is that string instrument vibrato is nearly completely due to pitch (not amplitude) variation; hence in electronic imitation, synthesis tremolo should not be used.

The most basic aspects of articulation (staccato, legato, tenuto, etc.) are also the same as for wind instruments. Bowed strings are an example of a sustaining model sound, with a chiff sound due to bow noise that is a factor in the nonlegato — legato distinction. Even at the basic level, though, differences exist, since strings can play double stops and therefore can make an overlap-type legato. However, this is possible only when successive notes are on different strings and so remains an occasional option that should be used sparingly by the synthesist if a high degree of imitation is required. Significant differences from breath instruments emerge when we look more closely at articulation and characteristic effects, largely due to the use of the bow.

The sound of bowed strings can be very complex. In refined imitation, the problem is not so much in making a proper steady-state spectrum (or even in creating a passable single bow stroke) as in imitating the wide variety of onset shapes and attack spectra the bow makes possible. Up bows sound different from down bows, for example. Notes in slow lyrical passages have different envelopes than notes in quick passages, even if the marked articulation is the same. There is also a host of specialized bowing techniques, such as detaché, louré, spiccato, saltando, jeté, martellato, a punta d'arco, and so forth. It is normally the province of the performer to choose between them, and their detailed description exceeds what can be covered here. Most composers don't specify their scores to this detail anyway but rely on the interpretive know-how of the string instrument performer, giving at most the occasional up or down bow indication, which may or may not be followed by the performer anyway. A synthesist who is not a string player is therefore best advised to use extensive sampling if such distinct gradations are critical for the music under consideration (working in conjunction with an experienced performer), letting the ear be the guide.

Some synthesists address the articulation issue by having separate patches for slow, medium, and fast string passages. This is an improvement that can sometimes work well, but it is not very satisfactory if the string passage changes its character from one type to another in midphrase. A better alternative is for the programming to allow real-time control of onset envelope, volume, and brightness.

Strings may be used solo or in sections, and these alternatives have very different characteristics. The number of strings in a section can vary from two to fifty or more. Two is the most awkward number in live performance because the inevitable small discrepancies in tuning often become painfully apparent. The resultant beating is more noticeable in the higher strings. To create a proper section effect, four instruments are normally preferred as a minimum, although budgetary considerations mean that three are sometimes encountered, and two can be passable for the doublebass. In a full size orchestra, the numbers are more like sixteen first violins, fourteen second violins, twelve violas, ten to twelve violoncellos, and about eight basses. A small orchestra might get by with eight first violins, six second violins, four violas, four violoncellos, and two basses. The effects of such doubling of a line are to broaden and stabilize its pitch, to make more diffuse some of the bow noise, and, due to slight differences in attack points, to change the character of the sound. Many of these qualities can be partially imitated by chorusing and/or flanging a single string sound, using a unison mode with slight detuning, layering different modules, or simply by sampling a section instead of a solo instrument. The amount of added effects can be adjusted in accordance with the number of strings being imitated.

There are a few significant playing differences between the solo and section sounds. Most noticeably, trills and tremolos, which have a clear rhythmic design when played solo, become cloud-like shimmers when played by a section, since the players do not attempt precise rhythmic unison. Consequently, sectional tremolos and trills cannot really be well imitated by a synthesizer soloist through hand action alone; the use of multiple LFOs tuned to different frequencies or even a sample of a section playing tremolo may be needed (although in the case of the sampler, the speed of the tremolo also transposes with pitch). Another difference is that pitch irregularities should be more pronounced on the solo instrument than with the imitated section. If this is handled by real-time control rather than fixed randomness, different playing will be necessary.

Other characteristic differences between keyboard and string writing will force modifications and development in a keyboardist's technique. Most notably, string parts have passages of leaps that are quite large in comparison to the keyboard literature. This comes from the fact that the strings are tuned in fifths, except for the doublebass (tuned in fourths). Sixths and sevenths therefore lie naturally under the hand. When performing single line passages emphasizing these intervals, use two hands wherever possible. If complex articulation changes that require the involvement of the left hand are happening as well, the part will be quite technically demanding (see figure 5.9). In some cases keyboard remapping may be able to make the part more tractable.

Characteristic Effects

Characteristic effects for strings include bends, portamento, harmonics, harmonic glissando, sul ponticello, sul tasto, muting, use of open strings, col legno, special interpretive bowings (as mentioned above, including up bow and down bow), multiple stops, scordatura, tremolo and pizzicato. Some of these effects are very similar to those described above for wind instruments (notably bends and portamento) and will not be discussed separately. Falloffs, spills, and other such figures adapted from jazz writing for brass (found too in many folk music traditions) will also not be discussed separately again. For a look at the many advanced contemporary effects for doublebass and other strings beyond the scope of this book, such as circular bowing, bitones, and the like, the reader should consult Turetzky (1974).

When an open or stopped string is set in motion while being touched at specific spots corresponding to a division of the sounding string length into a small number of equal parts, a *harmonic* is sounded. This is a higher tone derived from the harmonic series for that string. Its tone is purer (more sine wave-like) than in normal playing; its attack, most noticeably in sections, is characteristically gentle. Harmonics may be natural (based on an open string) or artificial (produced from a stopped string). The sound is virtually identical, except that sustaining power on release is somewhat greater for the natural harmonic. A *harmonic glissando* occurs when the performer slides along the string, producing something like an up or down arpeggiation of the overtone series. An interesting variant on this is when the performer uses the artificial harmonic hand position and slides it along the string, producing a seagull-call effect. This is most effective on cello and doublebass.

Notation for harmonics uses either a small circle over the notehead, which sounds as written, or a diamond-shaped note head above the stopped note head, indicating where the player should touch the string to produce a higher note. This second case is the artificial harmonic. The effects of this are shown in figure 8.4; the fourth-based artificial harmonic is the most common. See Warfield (1973/74) for a detailed discussion of notational practices.

These sounds can be synthesized or sampled. Since harmonics may be integrated with conventional playing in a way that makes the use of program changes in playing difficult, it can be necessary to assign separate

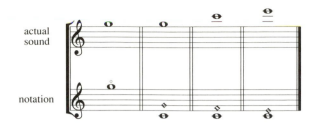

FIGURE 8.4   Notation for string harmonics.

keys on the performance interface to these sounds or access them via velocity switch. If harmonics passages are isolated from other types of passages, then the use of separate programs is the simplest procedure.

The terms *sul ponticello* and *sul tasto* refer to playing at or near the bridge (sul ponticello) or over the fingerboard (sul tasto). Conventional playing position is termed *normale*. The sound of sul ponticello is hard and glassy, with substantial high harmonic components and reduced fundamental; sul tasto playing gives a richer and warmer sound than that of normale bowing, with emphasized lower harmonics. Sometimes these effects are used separately from normal bowing, in which case they can be accessed synthetically in separate programs. Other pieces can require a quick or gradual change from one position to the other. A continuous controller must be used either to cross-fade between two different samples or accentuate high harmonics and decrease amplitude of the fundamental if these effects are to be imitated. No special hand techniques are required.

String players normally interpret sul ponticello as meaning very near the bridge. Some pieces actually call for players to bow the bridge itself, not the string. The sound in this case is quite different and will require sampling.

The string *mute* is a small device that fits behind (or on) the bridge to limit the transfer of the string's vibration to the body through the bridge. It also damps the strings' vibrations. Its primary effect is to reduce spectral brightness; volume is also reduced. It requires several seconds to put on or take off and can therefore from the standpoint of synthesis be handled by program change. Hence, there is no need for distinctive real-time control programming, and there are no features of technique different from ordinary string playing. It is indicated in scores by the instruction *con sordino*.

The *use of open strings* in certain styles, such as bluegrass fiddling or the solo violin sonatas of J. S. Bach, is very idiomatic. This can be best handled synthetically by sampling open and stopped strings separately and using the open samples only on the four open string pitches. An effect of similar function, however, can be created by programming a controller to increase resonance and decay time when an open string is called for.

Open strings are also used to achieve large melodic leaps with an ease the keyboard cannot equal. If the left hand is not otherwise engaged, this ease can be mimicked by the use of two hands. Otherwise the keyboardist will have to practice displacements (or possibly use keyboard remapping).

Col legno refers to performance where the wood of the bow, rather than the horsehair, is used to play the string. The volume and pitch definition of the sound are reduced over that of normal bowing. Often used as a special isolated effect, hence synthetically accessible by program change in performance, it is occasionally found in continuous gradation to and from normal arco playing. There are no differences in required performance techniques for the synthesist. In col legno battuto the wood of the bow strikes and bounces off the string, producing a small brittle sound on a single instrument and a diffuse rustle from an unsynchronized section. This sound requires a little preparation for a string player and transition to it can be achieved by program change.

String instruments can readily sustain two notes or, with some effort, three notes at once (*multiple stops*). There are few differences required in imitative playing techniques. The two (possibly three) notes would normally have a synchronized vibrato. Intonation with multiple stops is more difficult to control for the string player, but the synthesist need not typically imitate this. On the other hand, repeated double stops (bowed tremolo) can present special difficulties to the keyboard performer (as covered below).

Triple and even quadruple stops are written for string instruments, and here the player must quickly arpeggiate across the strings, sustaining either the highest or the lowest one or two notes. The synthesist must be able to imitate this quick arpeggiation successfully. Since the intervals of arpeggiation on strings are typically large, two hands are recommended. If required, three notes (even four in a few cases) can be sustained simultaneously, but this remains difficult.

Scordatura refers to retuning the open strings of the instrument. There are no implications for the performing string synthesist beyond the comments on open strings.

The meaning of the term *tremolo* in string playing is quite different from its meaning in synthesis. Besides the distinction between measured and unmeasured tremolo mentioned above under wind instruments, there are two types of string tremolo: *bowed tremolo,* based on rapid bow alternation across one or two strings with fingers in fixed position—the sonic result being repeated notes; and *fingered tremolo,* which is played

unmeasured
bowed tremolos

measured
bowed tremolos

fingered tremolos

FIGURE 8.5   Bowed and fingered tremolo.

with normal legato bowing but with rapid finger movement between the notes constituting the tremolo—the sonic result being rapid alternation between the tremolo components. (It is possible to combine the two types by fingering and changing bow direction on each note, but this is rare.) The two options are illustrated in figure 8.5. As mentioned above, the effect is also quite different, depending on whether a solo instrument or a section is playing. Both kinds of tremolo raise difficulties in imitation, short of tremolo sampling.

We will look first at solo instrument tremolo. If sampled tremolos are not used, bowed tremolo imitation requires the synthesist to play a rapid repeated single or double stop with a bow onset sound, since the attack part of the waveform is retriggered at each bow change. The string player effectively uses a lighter bow pressure than normal in playing this figure, however, so it may be necessary to adjust the string sound to have less imitation bow noise. Smooth playing of the repeated note figures required by this imitation can be difficult at the keyboard (although not for most other types of controllers) and is most easily done with two hands. It is typically hard to make this sound natural since the back and forth delicacy of the bow stands in contrast to the unidirectional nature of keyboard playing (down motion only). Whenever possible it is preferable to use a unison tuning system so that the figure can be executed more easily as a keyboard tremolo (between up and down bow samples). Sometimes it will be satisfactory to settle for playing a bowed tremolo figure as though it were fingered, making do with functional rather than literal equivalence.

The fingered tremolo is played with only the occasional changes in bow direction required of any sustained note, so it is legato. The performer alternates the two components of the tremolo as though it were a normal keyboard tremolo. This means the synthesist must use a continuous controller adjustment to pull off the attack noise after onset of the figure to promote realism. It can be difficult to achieve a realistic tremolo sound without a separate sample of the appropriate bow action.

With (unmeasured) sectional tremolos, the best hope for the single performer is sampling. Otherwise, if the performer is playing into a sequencer, overlaying a number of different single tremolo tracks with slightly different timings (and possibly tunings) will tend to create the proper effect. Three tracks are a minimum, with four or more preferred. It is important that the different tracks be well balanced. If the performer has two keyboards with the same string sound, the effect can be imitated by one player, where each hand plays the same tremolo figure asynchronously at the same pitch, preferably with a slightly delayed copy of each keyboard's output being created by a digital delay unit.

Pizzicato anticipates the next main section, but it is of course a highly significant playing resource on the orchestral strings. These instruments are played pizzicato by plucking with the fingers. The decay time of pizzicato varies markedly with frequency, so that violin, viola, and higher register cello pizzicati can be shaped in real-time only to a limited degree, whereas lower violoncello and doublebass pizzicati are capable of more audibly complex manipulations (slides, vibrato). Dynamic variation is important in all cases, of course, but there is normally little variation in articulation requiring imitation. Vibrato and pitch bend effects are audible to the extent the instrument sustains the pizzicato, allowing "pizzicato espressivo" (Turetzky 1974). Hence, a standard key-velocity-based dynamic design is the method of choice, with use of pitch bend and modulation devices as necessary. The basic pizzicato sound can be successfully imitated by most synthesis techniques, particularly FM, sampling, and the Karplus-Strong algorithm.

Some variants of this technique do require further explanation. Left-hand pizzicato is usually a lighter sound, played with a strong left-hand finger pluck (or, more rarely, a hammer-on motion, as described below) rather than right arm motion. Snap pizzicato, pioneered by Béla Bartók, entails pulling the string so hard that it strikes the fingerboard on release, causing a pronounced slap sound. It has a short but high amplitude noise component. A pizzicato-like effect is achieved when the string is struck with the bow in a short sharp motion perpendicular to the string. (If the wood of the bow is used, this is called *col legno battuto,* as described earlier.) Pizzicato harmonics are also quite playable, particularly on the lower strings. Chords of up to four notes may be played simultaneously without a bow in hand or with quick up or down arpeggiation (by the left hand) if the bow is also being held. Notations for normal pizzicato, left-hand pizzicato, snap pizzicato, and pizzicato harmonics are shown in figure 8.6.

Some string passages require rather quick changes between arco and pizzicato technique, so rapid that program changes will not be successful. The change will need to be made by rapid controller change, with a switch being the optimum type. If all notes are of fairly short duration, key velocity can be programmed to effect the change. Separate keyboards or cross-fading volume pedals seem to be the only other alternatives.

FIGURE 8.6   Types of pizzicati.

DECAYING INSTRUMENTS: PLUCKED STRINGS

Plucked string instruments come in tremendous variety. Roughly speaking, they can be divided on the basis of physical design, playing technique, and body position into the families of guitars, lutes, zithers, dulcimers, harps, and lyres. Lutes and guitars are distinguished from the others by having frets and differ from each other primarily by the shape of the back—guitars' backs are flat, lutes' are rounded (although there are some exceptions to this). Zithers (also called psalteries) and dulcimers (also called hackbrett) have strings arrayed horizontally in parallel. They are most commonly unfretted, using open strings only, although the popular American three-string dulcimer does have frets. They differ in that zither strings are plucked whereas dulcimer strings are struck with small hammers. The best-known zither in popular Western music is the pedal steel guitar. Harps and lyres use open strings only but differ in terms of the sitting position of the player and size; it is also usual for harps to be plucked with the fingers and lyres to be plucked with a plectrum.

Better known lute and guitar family instruments of specific cultural origin include the mandolin (Italy), bouzouki (Greece), saz (Turkey), ukulele (Hawaii), banjo (USA/Africa), balalaika (Russia), pipa (China), biwa (Japan), oud (Middle East), sitar (India), and surbahar (India). Historical Western instruments in this class encountered in authentic performances of early music are the lute itself, the vihuela, the theorbo, and the chitarrone. Zithers and dulcimers are found in many European and Eastern cultures, with examples that have found their way into twentieth-century scores being the Austrian hackbrett and the Hungarian cimbalom. The Japanese koto has become a familiar sound to most musicians from its use in film music and imitative inclusion in the preset sounds of many Japanese-manufactured synthesis devices. Strictly speaking, the harpsichord is a keyboard controlled zither. Harps and lyres also come in many historical and cultural varieties, such as the West African kora.

In terms of synthesis, all these sounds are of decaying polyphonic character. Their sounds are affected by materials of construction of body and strings, the cavity resonators used, the presence of doubling or resonating strings, the presence or absence of frets, and playing techniques. Performance imitation is most affected by this last factor—in particular, whether the strings are strummed, plucked (with finger or plectrum), struck, or excited by some other method. We will treat plucked string instruments by examining the guitar in considerable depth, followed by comments on a few other selected instruments: harp, mandolin, banjo, ukulele, koto, kora, pedal steel guitar, and pizzicato bass. This survey should address the primary issues found on any string instrument.

The Guitar

In today's musical environment, the guitar has gone beyond being a single type of instrument and instead is a collection of distinct yet overlapping traditions, whether from the standpoints of sound, technique, or repertoire. The acoustic guitar may have steel or nylon or gut strings and may be of classical design or folk design; it may be played with a flat pick, finger picks, bare fingers, fingers plus fingernails, a combination of thumb pick and fingernails, or by hammer-on technique. Strings may be muted and played anywhere along their length, while styles of picking may vary from sharp to oblique (where the pick is dragged at an angle across the string). The left-hand note choices may be made by the fingers or by a mechanical slide controlled by the hand, as on the dobro or slide guitar. In classical guitar playing, different technical approaches have been codified into separate "schools."

The electric guitar may be either hollow body or solid body, with gradations in between. It has its own traditions of lighter strings, enabling easier pitch bends and resulting characteristic figures; sound modifications like fuzz tone, enabling special sound effects, feedback, and increased sustain; the whammy bar, enabling drastic or delicate note or chordal bending; and special playing techniques in addition to those of the acoustic guitar, like two-hand hammer-on technique. Of course, the typical repertoires of the acoustic and electric instruments could not be more different: Andrés Segovia and Eddie Van Halen are virtuosi of very different kinds.

The general guitar sound and performance characteristics are:

decaying envelope, with high frequency components dying out faster than lower ones

longer note duration with lower pitch

highly variable note attack methods

two different types of legato (note overlap and hammer on/pull off)

the importance of the control of vibrato, via depth, rate, and onset point

attack and release portions of the sound have characteristic brightness: a pluck sound at the start and buzz from fret rattle when pressing or releasing the string

The guitar sounds an octave below written pitch and uses treble clef; its range is given in figure 8.1. The highest available notes are found only on electric guitars. Since standard synthesized and sampled guitar-like sounds are becoming increasingly credible, I will focus as usual on real-time programming and largely follow the decaying polyphonic sound model of chapter 5. Real-time programming and performance issues include timbre, articulation, dynamics, vibrato, spacing, and characteristic effects and will be discussed in turn.

Timbre and Articulation

Timbral variability in some styles of electric guitar performance is partly based on the coordinated use of effects devices (e.g., fuzz, chorusing, harmonic excitation, delay) via foot pedals. These can be mimicked by the synthesist directly. But in other electric guitar styles, and for all acoustic styles, the expressive versatility of the guitar melodic line comes from its variable articulation and techniques of sound production. Due to this great variability, the synthesist will be most successful when a particular set of guitar traditions is kept in mind, as only a quite limited number of them will be accessible from any one program.

Since the guitar is a decaying instrument, many aspects of timbre may be linked to dynamics via key velocity. Additional timbral and articulatory nuance can be handled by one or more foot controllers or switches. A breath controller can also be successful but does require a mental readjustment. The most useful control variables are brightness (especially attack brightness) and attack time. Release characteristics can be important as well, especially when notes have considerable sustaining power.

Aside from these timbral subtleties, there are the familiar questions of how one is to execute legato, tenuto, and the like. As usual, the critical issue is how to execute legato. On the guitar there are two possibilities: note overlap and hammering on/hammering off (also called pulling off). Note overlap legato is the same system used by the keyboardist, so this style is directly transferable. However, this option is not always available to the guitarist—notably, when the two notes to be played legato are on the same string. Note overlap legato is also a less prominent effect than on instruments like the piano since most guitar sounds die out fairly rapidly in comparison. In other words, if the note values are long, on the guitar there will be no sound left to overlap.

Since these problems are common occurrences, normal legato is achieved via hammering on or off. In both these techniques it is the left hand—and not the right—that initiates attack of the legato note. Hammering on refers to quickly and firmly stopping a sounding string at a higher fret with a finger of the left hand, without additional right hand pluck. This creates legato by doing away with the usual pluck transient; hence, it is a kind of nonchiff legato, as discussed in chapter 5. In principle, any interval can be so played, but in practice the hammer on is normally not larger than a minor third unless the lower note is an open string or unless the right hand stops the note (without plucking it). In such cases the only interval limitation is the length of the fingerboard.

Hammering off (pulling off) is when, in releasing a string, it is given a slight pull to the side with the finger of the left hand, providing enough energy to stimulate the string at a lower pitch determined by the next lowest stopped position down the fretboard. The effect is similar to hammering on but can have even less attack; its imitation is performed as described for hammering on.

In imitating hammering on and off, the pluck noise (attack brightness) must be therefore separately controllable by ancillary controller. Since finger action or sustain pedal must control the other type of legato (note overlap), the two can be combined or alternated to mimic the versatility of the guitar's approaches to legato.

Pitch bend legato can also be successfully used, both by the guitarist and the imitative synthesist.

As with other sounds, the type of keyboard action (light or heavy) will affect playing style. Some players prefer a light action for quick line passages, as when imitating jazz guitar, and a heavy action for strumming or repeating rock figurations. This is a matter of personal preference.

Dynamics

Control of dynamics should be by key velocity, using the decaying polyphonic envelope model of chapter 5. A foot controller linked to dynamics will also be appropriate for some electric and amplified acoustic guitar styles. Traditions of dynamics in guitar performance vary enormously. Some rock guitarists use a high level of amplification and very little dynamic variation at all, although the potential for dynamic variation is greater on electric guitar than any other. Jazz guitarists have typically made a great point of using accents in improvised solo passages. Classical guitarists use a great deal of dynamic variation within the instrument's somewhat limited dynamic range. The steel string folk guitar is considerably louder than the classical guitar and possesses a somewhat larger dynamic range.

Vibrato

The issues here are mostly the same as for other instruments, and the reader should consult the vibrato section under sustaining breath instruments for a general discussion. However, there are some important differences. Guitar vibrato typically pushes the center of the note slightly sharp, due to the fixed position of the frets, unless the guitar string has already been bent appreciably away from its normal pitch for that fret position, or the whammy bar is used. This means that pitch bend or pitch deflection-type vibrato may be especially effective (even essential) in some guitar styles, although LFO-style vibrato works well in most cases due to the guitar's comparatively short sustaining time. Some styles of guitar playing also distinguish between side-to-side and up-and-down (pressing into the fingerboard) vibrato. The second approach is particularly effective when the space beneath the frets is concave, as with some Ovation guitars. Separate vibrato for each note in the chord is made easier in this way, according to some guitarists. The accurate imitation of separate note vibrato (or bending) requires a polyphonic pressure keyboard with pressure routed to LFO pitch modulation or directly to pitch deflection.

Spacing

If the guitar's pitch layout is to be mimicked, attention must be given to its system of tuning; otherwise, the lines and voicings chosen by the keyboardist may be too pianistically conceived. Standard tuning for the six strings is E1, A1, D2, G2, B2, and E3 (written an octave above this). Melodically, the guitar can accommodate all sorts of leaps and skips. In playing single lines, the improvising synthesist must, in some styles, make an effort to introduce a greater number of larger intervals (fourths, fifths, sixths, sevenths, and in succession) and shifts of register than normal with single lines at the keyboard. Melodic lines that consist largely of diatonic scales may sound too pianistic.

The effect of the guitar's tuning system is perhaps even more noticeable with chordal playing. Standard hand chordal positions often produce characteristic voicings quite different from those used at the keyboard. For example, closed position chords are rare, due to the guitar's tuning in fourths. The best way to gain a practical sense of this style factor is to study the characteristic guitar chord spacings and play transcriptions of guitar music, developing the ability to improvise within the stylistic tendencies of the material. A representative survey of chord voicings in triadic, seventh chord, "contemporary folk," and jazz styles is given in figure 8.7.

Open Position Triads

Seventh Chords

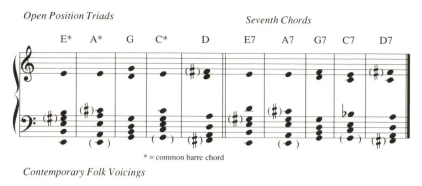

* = common barre chord

Contemporary Folk Voicings

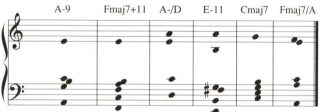

Jazz Voicings

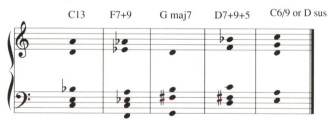

FIGURE 8.7   Representative guitar voicings in several styles.

Characteristic Effects

These include the strum, finger picking, open strings, sul tasto/sul ponticello, idiomatic pitch bending, tremolo, lead playing, muting and damping, different string effects, string slides, harmonics, twelve-string guitar effects, and scordatura.

One of the most difficult effects for the keyboard to imitate is the strum. The reasons for this are several. If the strum is played with a back-and-forth motion, as is typical in flat pick or basic folk or rhythm guitar technique, the two strum directions produce different sounds. A down strum arpeggiates quickly from low pitch to high, while an up strum arpeggiates quickly from high pitch to low. The keyboard, with only one direction of motion of sound production—down—cannot easily duplicate this division into two sounds; nor is it gesturally natural to play down-down-down to achieve a down-up-down effect. The quick up or down arpeggiation figures required of the synthesist typically require special practice, using a technique of "rolling" the hand; the speed of the arpeggiation must be capable of fine control if subtle strumming effects are to be mimicked.

A single keyboard with customary tuning must inevitably leave a gap of silence before reattacking a chord, as well, unless the pedal is used; and this is not true of the guitar strum, which can sustain right up until the next strum. The keyboard pedal, which unlike the guitar permits overlap between notes in successive chords (even allowing the same note to sound twice), must be very carefully handled to create a comparable effect.

Furthermore, the back-and-forth steady strum technique with eighth and sixteenth notes is used naturally on guitar to produce syncopation by striking the strings only on certain rhythmic points or by letting some strings ring on while others are muted by the hand. The kinesthetics of such playing increases rhythmic surety. This must be somehow mimicked by the keyboardist, or playing will not be as comfortable (or as rhythmically well executed).

To achieve back-and-forth strumming on the keyboard, one standard synthesizer technique is to use *unison tuning,* as described in chapter 6. This uses two keyboards, or two different zones of a master keyboard, set up to play at identical pitch. The keyboards may either control two sound modules (usually of the same type) or merge together to a single sound module. The two keyboards or zones should play either the identical sound or two closely related guitar sounds that can act as up and down strokes. A light rather than heavy action is usually preferable. The idea here is then to let each hand function as a strum in one direction only.

But there are limitations. Each strum can encompass only the range of notes playable by one hand, unless you can play across the two zones on one master keyboard, and that is in general not a satisfactory solution. Hence it is not possible with this technique to produce full six-note guitar voicings, even if your hands are large—unless, of course, you retune the notes that are played from the different keys so that voicings you play have a built-in guitar-like spread when closed position is played (as described in chapter 6). This possibility is not available on every synthesizer and requires a lot of preparatory work. In any case each hand has five fingers, and the guitar has six strings. (Oberheim has introduced a device, the Strummer, which translates traditional keyboard playing into guitar-style performance by modifying chordal voicings and introducing slight delays in multiple stops to imitate up and down strums automatically.)

There are other difficulties in synthesized imitation. The strumming guitarist can intermittently mute the guitar's strings and frequently does so to achieve syncopations. On the guitar this can be executed either by damping with the right hand, or releasing pressure from the fretboard with the left hand to mute the strings. This requires a completely different synthesis sound. And where is it to come from? There is no time for a program change in the middle of a strum; therefore, such a timbre change—if imitation is to be taken this far—must be controllable by key velocity or controller switching. Dramatic real-time control of the envelope decay is a natural possibility, as is the switching in of a mute-type sound while playing staccato on the existing sound. Still, this remains a rather complex performance setup.

An alternative approach to strumming is based on sampling actual strummed chords and attaching them to separate notes on the controlling keyboard. This has been described by Jimmerson (1989), and a slight refinement of it runs as follows.

The basic idea is to place a strum of each common chord color under a key of the same name on the keyboard, recording up and down strokes separately. Samples of common major, minor, diminished, and augmented open guitar positions are made. Three or four samples of major chords and minor chords (e.g., E, G, A, C), and at least one sample each of diminished and augmented chords (e.g., B°, C$^+$) are required, in both up and down stroke versions. In general, samples need to be about 1.5 seconds long (or longer). These are then allocated to separate regions as indicated in figure 8.8, where a sixty-one-note keyboard has been assumed. Chords are transposed to cover the entire keyboard as shown. Also recorded are unpitched mute strokes (up and down) and a short open-string stroke that is used as a grace note. These are essential placekeeping strokes. Jimmerson's article indicates how the overall sample time may be kept to a minimum by sampling up strokes for only about 0.5 seconds each and using the later portions of the down strokes to fill out the up strokes to an equivalent 1.5 seconds. Strumming is then accomplished by performing slow tremolos between up and down stroke samples. In the major and minor regions this is achieved by octave tremolos; diminished strums are played as minor thirds, augmented strums as repeated notes (due to lack of keys). Figure 8.9 shows a sample strum pattern using this setup.

This technique can clearly be extended (if sufficient sampling time is available) by sampling more complex chords, such as major sevenths, minor sevenths, chromatic dominants, and chords with higher extensions. Such samples could be arrayed along additional note ranges on a bigger keyboard or put under the same keys indicated, available via velocity switching. (Remember that transposition by too large an interval will

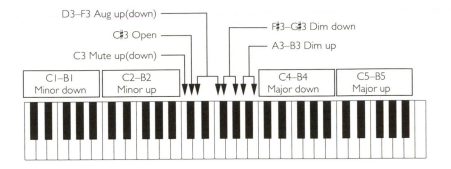

FIGURE 8.8   A keyboard configuration for sampled strumming.

compromise realism.) Completely different stylistic orientations might also be served by this same technique. Jazz chording could be based on minor ninth, major ninth/major 6/9, dominant thirteenth, diminished seventh, and suspended voicings. Complex and dissonant voicings characteristic of contemporary or free guitar playing could be similarly mapped over the keyboard and strummed to useful effect. Other kinds of damping and muting noise could also be recorded.

There are other types of strums that present special problems. The flamenco guitarist's strum, with its complicated onset effects, is virtually unduplicatable without sampling of the actual technique in the sampled sound. And then it loses its characteristic variability, unless a number of samples are used.

Finger picking is another distinctive technique on the guitar. Many such patterns can be readily imitated at the keyboard, provided the performer gives care to voice the chords as they would be played on the guitar. (See above comments on strumming.) For a better understanding, study voicings and transcriptions as used by major acoustic guitarists.

Some finger picking nuances require further attention. One of these is the fact that the guitarist can selectively sustain some notes while others are reattacked without any intervening silence. This means the keyboardist must use the sustain pedal only very discreetly and must cultivate a hyperlegato technique that, even at its best, cannot fully capture the guitar's sustaining capacities. Performance interfaces that have sostenuto pedals can approximate this effect much more readily by sustaining only specific notes, though it does require careful thinking. (As mentioned in chapter 4, the sostenuto pedal functions like the middle pedal on most grand pianos—it sustains notes already depressed but has no effect on notes played after its depression.)

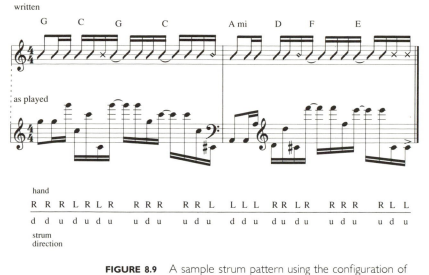

FIGURE 8.9 A sample strum pattern using the configuration of figure 8.8.

For *open strings* see the discussion above under bowed strings. In addition, open strings on a real guitar can be reset by the use of a capo, which transposes all the open strings upwards by a user-selected interval.

The effects *sul tasto* and *sul ponticello* are similar to the same possibilities discussed under bowed strings. The ponticello position is brighter; the tasto position is more resonant and features a more gentle attack. Performers can readily change from one position to the other from normal playing position. These timbral changes are very effective on the electric guitar, particularly where some degree of feedback is used. If this variability is required—and for some styles of contemporary lead guitar, it is essential—real-time control of such things as filtering and frequency modulation or velocity switching of samples will be required.

In chapters 5 and 6, pitch bend was extensively explored. Many of these techniques were pioneered or idiomatically refined in contemporary Western music by guitarists. We therefore here describe primarily how these same effects are achieved on guitar.

There are two methods: finger and whammy bar technique. With finger technique, one or two (and, rarely, more) strings are pressed sideways ("bent"), increasing the pitch. This procedure can only bend up in pitch, so that if a bend down is required, the player must first go to a lower note position, bend the string up to the starting pitch without playing it, then play it and release the applied bend (unless of course the string was already bent). This means that, if a bend down is required, there will typically be at least a short period of silence before the note can be sounded, to allow the silent bend up to take place. The amount of pitch bend possible depends to some degree on the strength of the player's fretboard hand and more on the elasticity of the strings (mainly a function of the gauge and tension of the strings). Lighter strings bend more easily than heavier strings, and lower tension strings bend more easily than higher tension strings. The maximum bend on steel string guitars is often about a major second (acoustic) or minor third (electric), although this can readily be increased with specially light strings to a major third or perfect fourth, or rarely, even larger.

The use of the whammy bar allows pitch bend of all strings at once and allows bends up and especially down by considerably larger intervals than with the finger. It is also the main method allowing concerted vibrato of a whole chord. (The other common one is to shake the entire instrument.) In imitating this technique, pitch bend range should usually be set to at least ± 5 semitones and possibly as much as ± 12. Some performers find it useful to set different upper and lower pitch bend ranges, say $+3/-7$, so that finger bend technique is imitated by positive pitch bend and whammy bar action by negative pitch bend.

Where separate bends for separate strings are required, finger technique is required. The two effects can also be combined. On the synthesizer this corresponds to using the pitch bend wheel or other channel controller routed to pitch bend, with polyphonic pressure also routed to pitch deflection.

For the guitar (and all plucked instruments) the use of a single pick normally suggests that tremolos are played as repeated notes, using the back-and-forth motion known as double picking. Two or more fingers can also alternate to make repeated note tremolo, as in classical technique. Strict imitation requires a repeated note technique at the keyboard, which is more difficult than on the guitar if the keyboard is weighted but fairly comfortable if the keys are unweighted and have sufficient travel before striking the keybed. The technique problems include speed, evenness of execution, and stamina. If the part allows it, two hands can be used in alternation. This is especially helpful on weighted keyboards. Alternatively, such picking can be sampled and played as normal sustained notes. Square wave LFO amplitude modulation can succeed in imitating such effects in certain specialized cases.

When the tremolo is the type consisting of a rapid alternation between two or more notes, the guitarist either uses two fingers of the right hand (commonly 1 and 3) in alternation on two different strings or hammers on and off rapidly on a single string. The sounds of these two procedures are quite distinct, and they may require separate sampling if this type of tremolo (or trill) is to be imitated in its full glory. If the actual tremolo figures are not sampled, both these methods would be imitated by the synthesist not as repeated notes but as keyboard-style tremolos.

Lead Playing

There are too many styles here to allow any detailed comment on the methods of imitation beyond that given in chapters 5 and 6. Most acoustic styles can be handled by playing the requisite lines with sampled or synthesized standard guitar-like note objects. In some highly developed electric guitar styles, there are many nuances of timbral variation, picking, and sound processing that require attention and which must be closely studied. Realism will be aided by selective sampling. Increasingly, many effects in popular and rock styles are available from sound modules and sample players as presets.

Muting or Damping

This has numerous forms, but basically there are two methods. In the first, the heel of the right hand damps the strings near the bridge. In the second, the fingers of the left press down the strings on the fretboard only very lightly, as in the muted strum sound mentioned above. Both methods may be imitated by a rapid decay to zero in the envelope of the electronic sound, manipulable by a real-time controller.

Different String Effects

As with bowed string instruments, the different strings on the guitar have different sounds. The synthesizer can imitate this effect by appropriate timbral gradations across the range of the instrument. This will not be a perfect imitation, since the range of the strings is overlapping; each note except those in the lowest major sixth and high end of the instrument can be played on at least three strings. This timbral variation is not normally available on the synthesizer. If this subtlety is necessary, it can be designed by real-time controller-based timbral control, cross-fading various samples, or assigning different string samples to different keyboard or velocity zones. The first case is perhaps most common, often in the form of brightness control by a non-hand-operated controller, most commonly a foot controller. This controller may be profitably programmed to affect attack envelope also.

String Slides

This refers to sliding along a string between one note position and another, with strings depressed so they continue to sound but without striking the strings with the pick hand. It is often used in moving between barred chords in different transpositions. It is essentially a kind of glissando, but because it adds a considerable amount of fret noise and is variable in nature, it is difficult to emulate without sampling.

Harmonics

Natural (open string) and artificial (stopped string) forms of this are found. The discussion of harmonics under bowed strings should be consulted. Here the effect is pizzicato, so there is a strong but short-lived pluck transient that is not found with bowed strings. These sounds can be sampled or imitated with considerable success by FM and some other types of synthesis. Real-time shaping effects are limited, usually to small amounts of vibrato.

Twelve-String Guitar Effects

To imitate the effect of a twelve-string guitar, it is necessary to know the tuning of the twelve strings. Each string is doubled by a second string that runs on a track very close to it. The lowest four strings— E1, A1, D2, G2—are each doubled by a string an octave higher (E2, A2, D3, G3); the top two strings—B2 and E3—are each doubled by a string at the unison (B2, E3). Figure 8.10 shows the open string tuning. Remember here that we are using synthesizer convention for note naming and that the guitar sounds an octave lower than its customary written notation. Here we are writing the notes at actual pitch, since it is the synthesist who is to play them.

The effect of this is to create a quality of resonance due to sympathetic vibrations between the strings and to change the highest note in the chord, which is now the note found on the G string in most voicings. The second-highest note is normally the note on the top E string but can occasionally be the note fingered on the D string. To derive the standard twelve-string voicings in the four styles listed above (or any style), simply use the voicings of figure 8.7 and add to them the notes created by the extra strings. Figure 8.11 shows several examples of this process.

Customarily, twelve-string guitar imitation is achieved by doubling a guitar sound at the octave or simply by sampling, rather than playing ten-note chords and melodic figures in octaves. Where the first option is used, a very slight time delay between the onsets of the two paired sounds (original and octave) may be programmed in to imitate the sometimes noticeable difference in onset time caused by the plectrum playing across the strings. There will also be a natural difference in onset envelopes due to the different speaking times of the differently tuned strings. The addition of a slight amount of detuning can help mimic the small tuning irregularities that occur due to variable string thickness and other factors. This octave-doubling design will produce in the treble register an effect that differs from that of the twelve-string guitar, but one that is often

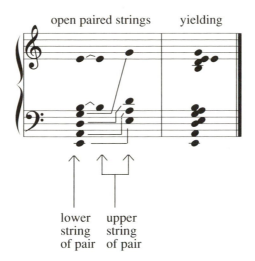

FIGURE 8.10 Twelve-string guitar tuning.

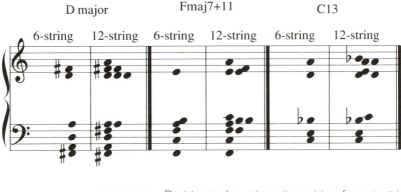

FIGURE 8.11 Devising twelve-string guitar voicings from six-string voicings.

functionally acceptable. It can tend to sound more like a dulcimer than the sound desired, however. Since the transition from unison to octave doubling on the original instrument is not simply a matter of register, but is based on string, it is not possible to imitate the unison string effect very exactly, although there is no reason in principle that this could not be done by a complicated arrangement of controllers and cross-fading. It would, however, require very careful thinking by the performer to execute such a setup, and a simpler solution might be to hire a twelve-string guitarist.

The twelve-string guitar can be retuned so that the strings are not in simple unisons or octaves, and the individual members of the pairs of strings can even be separately plucked by the delicately skillful performer. Ralph Towner's unique guitar style features these devices. To explore the possibilities of such scordatura, the best way is to write out a proposed retuning and then implement it over the appropriate string ranges of the guitar. Use the idea of the six separate string pairs in performing, and try out various possibilities until the new configuration has been mastered. This type of retuning is most easily handled by samplers and those synthesizers that allow note-by-note retuning over the entire keyboard. Then simply put two sounds under each key—one in the normal tempered setup, and the other at a companion pitch corresponding to the desired string doubling. Otherwise, multiple splits and several synthesis sources must be used.

Scordatura

Scordatura means retuning the strings of the instrument, as just described for the twelve-string guitar. For the six-string, there is a very large number of possibilities beyond the standard E1, A1, D2, G2, B2, and E3. Most common perhaps are retunings that tune the low E string down to D or tunings that change the open string configuration into a triad, usually based on open D (retune the low E to D, the G to A, the top E to D) or open E (retune the A to B, the D to E, and possibly the G to G♯). Such things are most commonly done in folk or bluegrass styles. To get the effect of these retunings, proceed as done above with the standard tuning— write out the chord voicings for standard hand positions for the retuned guitar and improvise around them until a style with fluency develops, consulting the written and audio literature for specific musical materials.

The Harp

The standard harp is a diatonic instrument, and passages that seek to imitate the solo harp should use limited chromaticism. Chromatic effects, however, are regularly written in the orchestra by the interlocking use of two or even more harps. As a result, the synthesist may deviate from diatonicism in ensemble use of the harp without any sacrifice in realism. It will be the rare listener who notices the discrepancy.

The harp's diatonic basis must be understood by those wishing to imitate its characteristic effects. It works as follows. There are seven notes per octave but with free enharmonic change. All strings with a given note name may be quickly retuned to natural, sharp, or flat by the use of special pedals located at the base of the instrument. Thus the C may be C♮, C♯, or C♭. For example, all strings can fall in a D harmonic minor scale by the tuning setup C♯, D, E, F, G, A, B♭. A diminished seventh chord may be made by changing the D, F, and A pedals from this previous setup to produce note names C♯, D♭, E, F♭, G, A♯, B♭.

The harpist plays with only the first four fingers of each hand, and therefore chords are customarily limited to eight notes. The characteristic harp glissando can be imitated on keyboards by a keyboard glissando. However, the harp glissando is much more versatile since it can be set up with a great variety of tunings, whereas the normal keyboard only permits white-key or black-key glissandi. To imitate the harp's retunability, the keyboard should be diatonically retuned on synthesizers or samplers that have this feature. Both the individual note retuning and the basic octave approaches (see chapter 6) will be successful in this imitation. Glissandi that have repeated notes in them thanks to retuning particularly require this technique.

Other characteristic harp effects include harmonics, sons étouffés, prés de la table, and bisbigliando. Harmonics require treatment no different from that in the above discussions with guitar. *Sons étouffés* refers to a specially sharp and dry damped pizzicato technique that must be heard to be appreciated. *Prés de la table* means that the string should be plucked near the sound board, producing a thinner tone; this sound is more guitar-like and may be synthesized accordingly. *Bisbigliando* (literally, "whispering") refers to a special harp tremolo technique whereby the fingers cause an arhythmic rustling motion. The best hope of imitating this, outside of sampling, is with a gentle unmeasured tremolo at the keyboard.

The orchestral harp's range is six octaves and a fifth, as indicated in figure 8.1. The many harps found in different cultures around the world generally have a smaller range. Chromatic forms of the harp exist, but these have not won common acceptance.

Mandolin, Banjo, Ukulele, Koto, Kora, and Pedal Steel Guitar

The mandolin has four pairs of strings, tuned in fifths. The tuning system is identical to the violin—G2, D3, A3, E3—and the two strings of each pair are tuned to the same pitch. Written in the treble clef, it most commonly plays single lines, though chords are widely used as well. The mandolin emphasizes the plectrum tremolo effect as a means of sustaining notes.

The banjo normally has five strings, but there also exists a tenor banjo with four, and forms with more than five strings exist. The five-string banjo has many common tunings, characterized by the bottom string having the highest pitch, as in the "C" tuning—from the bottom, G3, C2, G2, B2, D3. The bottom string is often used as a drone. The instrument's taut resonating membrane and the use of metal finger picks in performance contribute to the banjo's characteristic brightness of sound. Complex and variegated finger picking produces the distinctive rhythmic propulsion characteristic of this instrument. The synthesist seeking to duplicate these effects should study banjo transcriptions and write out the voicings that naturally occur with the various common hand positions and tuning systems.

The ukulele has four strings, tuned (from the bottom) either G3, C3, E3, and A3 or D3, F♯3, A3, and B3. It is primarily used to strum chords.

The Japanese koto is a zither with between seven and thirteen strings, usually tuned to one of a number of pentatonic scales—most commonly, modes of C, D, E, G, A; C, D, E♭, G, A♭; or C, D, E♭, G, A. The right hand plucks or strums the strings, while the left hand prominently performs pitch bend, vibrato, and intricate microtonal ornamentations (it can also strum as needed). Serious imitators of this instrument should study these and many other subtle techniques used to set the strings in motion. An approximate range is indicated in figure 8.1, but this depends on tuning to some degree. There are also bass and "soprano" kotos.

The kora, an instrument common in West Africa, is a twenty-one-string harp lute played with the first three fingers of each hand. It uses mainly diatonic tuning systems that include microtonal inflections of what we tend to hear (initially) as major and Lydian scales. Its approximate range is C1 to C4, though this depends on tuning.

The pedal steel guitar is an instrument that is most commonly associated with Hawaiian and country and western music. It is also used in West African pop bands and in mainstream Western popular music. In fact, its stylistic ambit is considerably broader than this. The instrument's range depends upon tuning, with the E9 chromatic and C6 tunings being most common. It also depends on the number of strings: the indicated ten-string form is standard (see figure 8.1 for the corresponding common range), but extra bass strings found on the eleven- or twelve-string varieties will expand the lower register. The pedal steel guitar is played from a tablature notation, and in the hands of an expert it can be very expressive. Its successful imitation requires the selective use of musical portamento, realized via pitch bend, pitch deflection, synthesizer portamento, or a combination of these. The instrument tends to speak slowly, and its attack envelope is variable, best imitated with real-time programming control set for either dynamics or envelope attack time. Furthermore, its vibrato is delicately controllable, and vibrato via pitch bend function rather than LFO may be preferable.

The Pizzicato Bass (Acoustic and Electric)

The bass represents a number of distinct traditions almost as numerous as those of the guitar. The primary distinction, of course, is between the acoustic double bass and the electric bass, though there are hybrids that bridge this distinction to a considerable degree.

The double bass is more difficult to play and to keep in tune than the electric bass, but a good player can play very fast and accurately. It also allows more intonation nuance than the fretted electric bass. The ranges of the two instruments may be compared in figure 8.1. Both sound one octave lower than written and have the same open string tunings. Both are sometimes found with an extra string: On the double bass this is usually a low C, whereas on the electric bass it may be a higher or lower string.

The electric bass may be fretted or fretless, and there is a clear sound distinction between the two. The fretless bass, like the acoustic, can indulge much more readily in microtuning nuance and portamento. Certain players like Jaco Pastorius have also brought distinct traditions of audio processing (phasing, chorusing) to the sound of one instrument or the other.

The basses have several modes of pizzicato production. With the electric bass, as with the guitar, either plectrum or finger technique may be used, with the strong current tendency being toward finger technique. The sounds of the two styles are quite distinct. Slap (pop) technique is also a standard device for both basses, where the string is slapped with either the hand (double bass) or the thumb (electric bass), rather than plucked. Slap and normal technique can be quickly interleaved by the contemporary bassist, particularly on electric bass, where a thumb-to-hand rocking motion is used to expressive effect in funk and pop tunes. The change is too fast, in general, for a program change. Since the slap sound component is short, it can be successfully controlled by the use of key velocity control, which above a certain threshold (switch), or increasingly across a certain velocity range (cross-fade or layer), brings in the slap component of the sound.

Since the actual bass instrument can vary so widely in sound, the sound objects used for synthesized pizzicato bass can be highly variable and still achieve "realism." Bass sounds can succeed whether fat or delicate, muted or buzzy, modulated or pure, with sharp or rounded attack, and so forth. Our main focus will as usual be on how such bass sounds should be played. Since the bass acts to provide critical chordal and time foundations in the contemporary band, it will be useful to describe the fundamental features of its imitative performance in a little detail. In general, successful bass playing has five components:

1. good time
2. good rhythmic design
3. good sound
4. good note choice
5. expressive microstructure (vibrato, bends, articulation)

The bass's critical role in the feel of a popular or jazz ensemble means that the performer must give extra care to point 1. The bass notes must fall in precise relation to the beat: either consistently on, ahead of, or behind the beat. The first possibility is correct for most situations. If, as is common, the bass sounds do not "speak" immediately, this may require the performer to actually strike the keys ahead of the beat. If the delay in speaking varies across the range of the bass sound, compensation will have to be made differently in different ranges—a not infrequent problem in imitative synthesizer performance.

Bass playing can often be done with the best rhythmic precision when two hands are used, to give the placement of notes a better kinesthetic basis. Figure 8.12 shows an example of this. The given bass line could certainly be performed with one hand alone. Yet if two hands are available, it might be more readily executed with the "handing" indicated. Such two-hand technique could also be used with unison tuning, as mentioned in chapter 6. In this last case the split point should be at G3, and the handing should be exactly as indicated, but with the right hand notes played two octaves higher, in the upper zone, which is set to sound two octaves lower than played pitch. Although unison tuning does not have strong advantages in this particular passage, in others, especially those with repeated notes, it can both simplify technique and increase rhythmic surety.

Point 2 is primarily a compositional issue, and so to go fully into this is not appropriate here, but in so far as the performer must improvise around a pattern it is wise to use the edict that "less is more" when playing bass. A common error is to succumb to the technical fluency that is built into the hands with keyboard technique. The bass doesn't usually work that way. Unless it is explicitly playing a solo, its function is supporting—not soloistic. Even when it is functioning melodically, too many notes can spoil the sonic broth. The exception, of course, is in a featured solo section, or where the part has been carefully composed in relation to other parts.

Point 3 is a programming issue; commercially available sounds have become very good in recent years. Point 4 is somewhat style dependent. In general, the bass plays notes with clear chordal and melodic functions in tonal music, unless the style is very progressive.

Point 5 is critical. Most of the commercially available sounds lack well-designed real-time controllability, and the synthesist must add this along the lines of the decaying sound model. The orientation here is the same as for the guitar: Key velocity should affect volume and brightness and attack time, and vibrato should be linked to some continuous controller. "How to" bass texts may be consulted for examples of various styles; often, it is best to transcribe bass parts from recordings since it is in the sonic reproduction that the best source for real-time performance nuance is found.

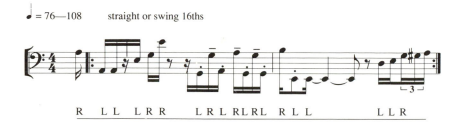

FIGURE 8.12 Alternative executions of a bass line.

KEYBOARDS

The primary keyboard instrument sounds occurring in synthesis work are those of the piano, organ, harpsichord, clavichord, electric piano, kalimba (sanza or thumb piano), celeste, dulcitone, keyboard glockenspiel, clavinet, accordion, melodica, harmonium, and toy piano. The primary technical features of the best known of these instruments were given in chapter 4. Except as mentioned below, they all use the treble and bass clefs and are nontransposing. Their ranges are summarized in figure 8.1.

The imitation of keyboards by keyboard synthesizers and samplers is, not surprisingly, a story of growing success. The primary performance issues are the expressivity of the sound objects, tuning systems, use of pedals, heaviness of action, maximum voice polyphony, keyboard range, and use of multiple keyboards. Several of these can be best discussed for all keyboard instruments; others will be discussed on a case-by-case basis below.

Tuning systems are no more critical for keyboards than for other instruments, but because of keyboards' self-contained polyphony, the issue must sometimes be addressed more systematically. The basic facts have been canvassed in chapters 2 and 6. The general issue of whether *exact* or *stretched* octave tuning will be used, as described in chapter 2, must be particularly addressed in many styles of music.

Heaviness of action and keyboard range can be considered together. Naturally, most players prefer the touch and keyboard range used on the traditional instrument to be coupled with that instrument's sound on the synthesizer. Unless the performer's set-up contains several keyboards, however, compromise in this area is inevitable. If only one heavy touch keyboard is available, organ sounds and others requiring a quick light touch will be more difficult to execute and may consequently sound unnatural. However, many players can adapt to this usage, which does have the advantage that the hands are kept in a more exercised state of strength. If, on the other hand, a light action is used for everything, training in piano technique must be altered, and it may be difficult to make the transition back to the heavier touch of a real piano when this is called for. The solution to this dilemma is a personal matter that will vary from performer to performer. On the other hand, the adaptation to different keyboard ranges is rarely problematical for more than a short transition period.

Maximum voice polyphony problems can occur with all keyboard imitations where the sound engine's voice limit for the program used is ten or less, since at least ten notes can be played by ten fingers. If the number of voices available is on the order of twelve or more, problems essentially occur only in imitating keyboard instruments that have sustain pedals (piano, electric piano, celeste, clavinet), unless the music being played has clusters played by palms or forearms or, in the case of keyboards with very small keys (e.g., melodica, toy piano), the fingers. The problem is most noticeable with the acoustic piano, as many effects of resonance and shading in the real piano will be inevitably lost. In general, when voice limits are exceeded, the musicality of the results will depend on the intelligence of the sound engine's voice-stealing algorithm.

The synthesist may need to fine-tune the provided sound objects for performance. One point worth mentioning here is the attack noise appropriate to the sound. The piano has a woody striking sound, particularly noticeable in its upper octaves; the harpsichord has a less resonant "thunk" sound combined with its basic pluck, whose components can be perceptually separated if the key is depressed sufficiently slowly; the clavichord has a light metallic clank. Key noise is not significant for most organs, but when imitating pipe organs there may be a breathy speaking effect—particularly on lower-pitched pipes.

Piano

The piano's sound is very well known to keyboardists, and its pedal controls have been previously described. A real piano cannot begin to be approximated by any but the most elaborate of pure synthesis methods. Sampling, however, is another matter. Since the control mechanism of the synthesizer keyboard is equivalent cybernetically to that of the piano keyboard, close imitation is possible in principle with regard to the effects of finger action. Samplers and sample players are reaching much higher standards in this regard now. That this will likely never be perfect can be seen by considering the effects of interactive resonance between the strings under one note or between notes held down simultaneously (different effects being obtainable depending on whether finger or pedal sustain is used), the spatial separation of the strings on the real piano, and the limitation of the sustain pedal, which on the piano provides continuous gradation of effect and which on the synthesizer is customarily on/off. (There is nothing in MIDI, however, that requires that such pedals be on/off; this is so far only a convention followed by nearly all manufacturers.) Such problems may well not be insoluble, but they will take some time. In the interim, the loss of these timbral subtleties has no substantial effect in many styles (the styles with which commercial manufacturers are mainly concerned). If your goal is to produce the realistic shadings of a Chopin ballade, however, there may be a substantial wait in store. In the last analysis, a sampled piano can at best only sound like a recording of a piano.

Electric Piano

Many variants of this sound are now available, and no appreciable difference in technique is required between this case and the use of an acoustic piano sound. Characteristic voicings on this instrument differ slightly from those on the traditional piano, mainly in the direction of being more open and having fewer note doublings.

The Organ Family

The organ has many sonic traditions. In basic terms these may be divided into the traditional pipe organ, the reed organs, and electronic organs. The massive sound of a real pipe organ is obtained by the largely vibratoless doubling of notes by many sound components (*stops* or *registers* in organ parlance). The sounds are doubled at the unison and various octaves (the *foundation stops*) and sometimes at the fifth, twelfth, tenth, or other intervals (the so-called *mutation stops*). Mixtures of these sounds can be engaged simultaneously by the use of *mixture stops*. Most such organs allow selections of stops to be arranged (programmed) by the performer and be brought in by the push of a simple button or lever.

A stop is indicated by its pipe length, which is proportional to the inverse of its frequency. The basic octave is that of the $8'$ (8 foot) stop. Hence the $4'$ stop is one octave higher, and the $16'$ stop is one octave lower. Common octave stops are $1'$, $2'$, $4'$, $8'$, $16'$ and $32'$. An example of a mutation stop is *nazard*, whose length is $2\frac{2}{3}'$; its frequency would be $8 \div 2\frac{2}{3} = 3$ times that of the basic $8'$ stop, hence sounding a twelfth higher. Examples of mixture stops include: *rohrflöte* ($10\frac{2}{3}' + 5\frac{1}{3}' + 2\frac{2}{3}'$, adding a twelfth above, fifth above, and fourth below the basic octave) and *septiême* ($4\frac{4}{7}' + 2\frac{2}{7}' + 1\frac{1}{7}'$, adding 15ma + minor seventh, 8va + minor seventh, and minor seventh). The synthesist can mimic such stops by layering.

The pipes making up the church organ are of two kinds: flue pipes, which resemble the whistle flute in design and sound, and reed pipes, which sound more like the timbre of the double reed woodwinds. Smaller organs based on these same design principles include the positive and the even smaller portative organ (or organetto).

Electronic organs come in a wide variety, from single manual band models to massive multiple keyboard installations that have limited synthesizer-like programmability. Two common features not found on the pipe organ are the percussion stop (a percussive click sound at the start of the note, much used by some jazz organists) and the Leslie speaker. In synthesizer imitation of the former, the click's volume is often made velocity dependent. The Leslie speaker typically has a rotating horn and a bass loudspeaker with a rotating baffle. It has two basic speeds of operation, slow and fast, and the effect of changing between speeds accentuates the Doppler effect of the rotating elements. The Leslie speaker effect is now widely imitated as a preset in many audio effects units and can be mimicked by the performer who can change in real time the LFO speed of phasing or chorusing effects. However, anyone who has stood near a real Leslie speaker in operation will appreciate that current electronic imitations of it are far from perfect.

Electronic organs also have many self-accompaniment features: automatic chording, bass line patterns, and drum beats. These have a tradition of suiting the home enthusiast and of producing a grimace of revulsion in many professional musicians.

Organ pedalboards are a keyboard-like collection of foot pedals that vary in range from one flatbed octave on simple electronic organs to two octaves plus a fourth or a fifth (or even more) concave fan shapes on larger electronic instruments and pipe organs. Characteristic parts are designed, where rapidity of execution is necessary, to allow the alternation of feet, since otherwise some passages become very difficult.

In terms of strict organ imitation, the programming of key velocity sensitivity should be highly restricted, notably to key clicks (*a la* percussion stop) for electronic sounds and to the control of pipe onset noise (chiff) on sounds that aim to be that of a direct mechanical tracking pipe organ (as discussed in chapter 4). Reverberation should be cranked up and fine-tuned to imitate the usual environment of the piped instrument. A foot controller should be set up to act as a volume pedal. Additional real-time control (second foot pedal, wheel, pushbuttons, etc.) can act to change the volume of components of the overall sound, imitating the gradual changing of volume via drawbars permitted by most organs.

One major difference between the larger organs and the synthesizer that affects the performer is the presence of multiple manuals (two, three, four, five or even more stacked keyboards) and pedalboard on organs. Many multiple manual organ parts can be imitated on one keyboard, but many cannot—particularly those that overlap large ranges or require the same pitch to be both sustained and also re-attacked. Unison tuning and the discreet use of sustain and sostenuto pedals are important strategies here, but the only general solution is to stack two (or more) keyboards together. The usual vertical distance between synthesizer keyboards stacked in separate levels of keyboard stands can sometimes be inconveniently large for traditional organ technique. It can be preferable to put them directly on top of each other, even if this means covering up the controls on the lower keyboard.

Since there seem to be, as of this writing, no commercially available MIDI foot pedal systems that are the size of that found on a full pipe or large electronic organ, full range pedalboard parts need to be either modified by octave transpositions or played with the hand. Synthesists who want a full organ effect may wish to sequence the pedal part and play the two manuals live. In a band situation, a bass pedalboard can be useful although it will not allow the expressivity of articulation and intonation available on the bass guitar or double bass.

The reed organs are smaller single manual hand-held organs that have only reed pipes (these "free reed" pipes are of a different design and sound than the reed pipes used in pipe organs). They have no pedalboard. In this category are the regal, harmonium, accordion, and concertina (even the harmonica, as mentioned earlier). All these four instruments are similar in having bellows for the air pressure control of reeds. The regal is a small hand-held single keyboard organ. Some forms of the harmonium (e.g., the Indian) are similar in size and layout. The main Western harmonium is a larger instrument (about the size of a piano) that has certain interesting features for the synthesizer performer, including an *expression* stop, which gives heightened timbral and dynamic control via a foot pedal, and a *percussion* stop, whose effect is similar to the stop of the same name found on the modern electronic organ.

The accordian comes in a number of different forms. The *Continental chromatic* version uses buttons for notes, while the *piano accordian* uses a standard musical keyboard for the treble notes. The *free bass* model has an improved range of chromatic buttons for the bass. The concertina is a small type of accordian using buttons rather than keys. The coupling of notes in octaves, or slightly detuned unisons ("tremulant" coupling), is idiomatic, and major and minor triads and seventh chords are readily produced as presets from rows of buttons available on most models. The bellows can produce rapid or delicate shadings of dynamics, including tremolo, which must be mimicked by the synthesist via a real-time controller. The breath controller is a natural choice when this is available.

Harpsichord

The sound of the harpsichord is bright, as befits a plucked string sound. It has important attack and release characteristics—especially the release. (For example, slow release of sounding keys will accentuate the buzziness of the muting.) Brightness must increase at these points for realism. The harpsichord also has no dynamic sensitivity or sustaining pedal, so if true realism is desired these effects should be programmed out. Larger instruments have several ranks of strings that can be used to create octave doublings above and below the main pitch (4', 8', and 16'), and a lute or sordino stop, which mutes the tone. These changes may commonly be achieved by the use of pedals or, in some models, the hand.

Clavichord

The clavichord is the clearest forerunner of the modern synthesizer, with its dynamics-controlling velocity sensitivity and touch sensitivity that can produce vibrato or pitch bend. It has been described in technical terms in chapter 4. Synthetically it must be programmed with key velocity controlling dynamics and aftertouch (polyphonic where available!) controlling pitch bend function with small range (± 1 semitone or even less).

Celeste, Dulcitone, and Keyboard Glockenspiel

The celeste (celesta) sounds an octave higher than written and uses the treble and bass clef system of the piano. It has a sustain pedal, usually at least a four-octave range (written C2 to C6), and its sound is produced by striking metal bars. Its sound is soft and gentle (with few higher partials). Of similar timbre is the dulcitone, where the internal hammers strike tuning forks. The keyboard glockenspiel is simply a glockenspiel with attached keyboard. For more information see below, under percussion instruments.

Kalimba (Sanza or Thumb Piano)

This instrument is African in origin and is found in many sizes, ranges, and tuning systems. It goes under many additional names and is basically diatonic. The range given in figure 8.1 is that of the normal treble models available in the West. Synthetic imitation should have key velocity control of dynamics and should try to duplicate the instrument's distinctive feathery tremolo effect achieved by rapidly fanning the resonator hole with the fingers.

DRUMS AND PERCUSSION

Drums and percussion instruments come in an incredible variety of sizes, shapes, sounds, pitches, and playing techniques. Nearly all these instruments except some of the metal percussion (cymbals, tam-tams, gongs, glockenspiel, etc.) have rapidly decaying envelopes, the rate depending largely on frequency of the sound. This means that the decaying sound model is always the model of choice and that such real-time control as is necessary can be confined to key velocity for dynamics, with other controllers only necessary for timbral gradation (except for the few percussion instruments capable of vibrato). Some types of real-time control are not instrument-specific and can be discussed in general terms.

One such performance technique is muting, most commonly done when the instrument is struck with one hand and its resonating surface depressed (muted) with the other hand. The term is also applied to what is sometimes called a "pressed stroke" or "dead stroke," where stick or hand does not rebound from the playing surface but rather stays pressed in contact (as for example with the conga mute stroke). The effect of either form of this technique is to reduce brightness, resonance, and sustain. In imitation, this is best handled by a controller linked to affect all three factors, or distinct samples on different keys, or distinct samples in different velocity ranges under the same key.

Less generally occurring but still widespread is percussion pitch bending. Although not a feature of basic orchestral or kit drum technique, it is found on the pedal timpani, African talking drums, the Indian bayan drum (part of the tabla set), many other non-Western drums, the waterphone, electronic kit drums, and via special techniques on cymbals, gongs, vibraphone, and traditional Western drums. This can be synthetically mimicked by sampling or real-time use of a pitch bend device or fixed programming of a pitch envelope.

A related factor is the slight dependence of drum pitch and dynamics. If a drum is struck harder, its initial pitch is usually slightly higher (sharp). This effect can be programmed by setting a weak link between velocity and an initial pitch level from a pitch envelope generator, as available.

In this limited chapter it is not feasible to discuss all possible percussion instruments in depth. Fortunately, this is not necessary, since the majority of the instruments are played identically from the keyboard, with no real-time shaping beyond key velocity controlled dynamics. Hence we will just classify the instruments, highlight representative percussion elements, and focus more deeply only on the most common traditions that require performance nuance, notably groove traditions (trap kit and Latin percussion) and the keyboard mallet instruments.

It is convenient to divide the instruments in terms of their contemporary usage as follows:

orchestral percussion
    definite pitch
    indefinite pitch

groove percussion

 drum kit

 Latin percussion

non-Western percussion

Some instruments like the snare drum function in more than one context. Other instruments, like the bass drum, have different forms in orchestral or groove contexts. For extended discussion of the great variety of percussion instruments the reader should consult Brindle (1970), Richards (1972), Burton (1982), and especially Peinkofer and Tannigel (1969).

In terms of synthetic imitation, sampling is the method of choice for all percussion sound objects. Sampled sounds are of course widespread, in CD sample collections, drum machines, sampler libraries, and sample players. Where sufficient sample time is available, velocity switching and multisampling should be implemented. Second choice as a source for percussion-like sounds would very probably be FM synthesis. In any percussion imitation, it is wise to remember the timbral variety that can come from any one instrument via the tremendous variety of possible playing techniques, and the effects of different mallet types.

Orchestral Percussion: Definite Pitch

This includes the timpani, mallet percussion (xylophone, vibraphone, marimba, xylorimba, glockenspiel), tubular bells, handbells, the anvil, and crotales. Other definite pitch instruments that are more limited and only rarely found in the orchestra include almglocken (Swiss cowbells), iron pipes, brake drums and other industrial metal products, slit log drums, steel drums, the musical saw, musical glasses, and the glass harmonica.

The timpani sound as written and use bass clef. The xylophone uses treble clef and sounds an octave higher than written. The glockenspiel (also called orchestral bells) also uses treble clef and sounds two octaves above written pitch. Marimba and vibraphone are nontransposing; both are written in treble clef, with the marimba also using bass clef or even a piano-type double staff as necessary. The crotales, using treble clef, sound two octaves higher than written.

The tubular bells (tubular chimes) are written in treble clef, but there is some dispute about the octave they sound in since the overtones are nonharmonic. Some listeners feel that they sound as written, others that they sound an octave higher. From the standpoint of synthesis, the non-transposing position probably makes more sense.

The mallet instruments are all polyphonic, but to a lesser degree than the keyboard. The limitation here is the number of mallets a performer can hold. The maximum practical limit is about eight, and this is an uncomfortable proposition. Standard technique uses two or four mallets (occasionally three). From the standpoint of synthesis, four is a useful maximum number of voices, with the possible spacings a performer can use in chords determined by two notes (mallets) per hand. The spreads producible tend to be like piano four-part writing for the vibraphone and marimba; for the xylophone and especially the glockenspiel, larger intervals impossible to play at the keyboard are feasible.

Of these instruments, only the vibraphone has a damper pedal. The xylophone and marimba die out so rapidly that one is not necessary anyway. The glockenspiel (orchestral bells), however, has a long sustain—like the orchestral chimes—and damping of individual notes after striking them is common practice by performers of these instruments. This is often best handled on the synthesizer by careful use of the fingers in releasing notes at the keyboard, with as little pedal as possible, unless all notes are to be damped simultaneously. If the original part does not require damping, then the sustain pedal can be left on throughout, provided this does not constrain the voice polyphony of the sound module.

The vibraphone has a motor-produced instrumental "vibrato." It is actually dominated by amplitude modulation and must be imitated by synthesis tremolo. The motor speed can be varied, usually falling in the range of 3 to 8 Hz.

When notes are to be considerably sustained for melodic purposes, the use of single stroke roll technique (repeated note tremolo), characteristic of the marimba, is widely used on mallet percussion. When this is imitated by the playing of repeated notes of sampled sound, the pitch of the tremolo may sound sharp since, as mentioned above, the onset pitch of instruments can be slightly sharper than in the rest of their dynamic envelope. This can be compensated for by lowering the pitch of the sample slightly or by correcting the temporal pitch behavior with the use of a pitch envelope generator. The other common type of mallet instrument tremolo, between two or more notes, can be executed at the keyboard exactly as a tremolo for the piano would be. The pitch problems just described will occur here, but to a lesser degree, and can be handled in the same way.

The fixed synthesis aspects of the imitation of the orchestral mallet instruments, timpani, and tam-tam are discussed in some detail by Wendy Carlos in Milano (1987).

Steel drums, originating in Trinidad, may be found in tuned orchestras of soprano to bass "pans." A typical set of ranges is as follows: bass—C1 to F2; cello—B1 to G3; tenor—F♯2 to A4; alto—G♯2 to C♯5; soprano pan—D3 to F5 (Rossing 1990). Musical glasses are sets of glasses filled with water; they may have a range from about C4 to C6. The glass harmonica has a similar haunting and pure sound, with written and sounding range G2 to

C6. Tuned bottles (tuned again by the addition of water) are sometimes found in sets and are set in motion either by striking or blowing.

Orchestral Percussion: Indefinite Pitch

This great field of possibilities includes the snare drum, orchestral and pedal bass drum, various tom-toms, rototoms and octabans, various cymbals, the triangle, all the Latin percussion used as exotic effects (see below), the sound effects instruments (sleigh bells, sandpaper blocks, lion's roar, whistles, stones, thundersheet, chains, wind machine, whip, ratchet, baby rattles and party noise makers, anvil, siren, automobile horn, police whistle, bird call devices, etc.), bell tree, tambourine, gong and tam-tam, wooden disks, finger cymbals, bowl gongs, flexatone, wind chimes, castanets, temple blocks, wood blocks, waterphone, and others more obscure.

In understanding the imitation of such instruments, it is well to become acquainted with the use of *drum rudiments*. These are the fundamental building blocks of Western drum technique: simple patterns of left- and right-hand strokes that allow a passage of arbitrary complexity to be built up. Some of the best known are the flam, roll, drag, ruff, paradiddle, and ratamacue. The serious drum imitator should consult one of the many standard snare drum texts for a discussion of these rudiments. Orchestral or band snare parts should be studied by the would-be imitator if authenticity is to be most closely approximated. The importance of this approach is that it is applicable to virtually all percussion instruments.

Three common rudiments may give a flavor for the technique. One is the flam, which is a short grace note preceding the main note. Another is the paradiddle, an evenly repeating eight-note pattern sticked R, L, R, R, L, R, L, L. Execute this at the keyboard either by using the middle fingers of the two hands or thumb and middle finger of either hand. Finally, the roll warrants special attention. This occurs primarily in single stroke (R, L, R, L, etc.) and double stroke (R, R, L, L, etc.) forms, though other possibilities, such as the multibounce (buzz) roll, also exist. The speed attainable with stick technique on a surface giving reasonable rebound is well beyond what the keyboardist can normally produce by repeated note technique, so such figures must be achieved by putting the same sound under different keys (by using zones of overlapping pitch range, samples tuned to the same pitch, or fixed-pitch mode). Then rolls can be achieved by trills or tremolos and dynamic variation readily accommodated, as discussed in chapter 5. If fixed-pitch mode is used, a played glissando will produce the roll. Crescendi and decrescendi of percussion rolls and tremolos must be created by controller- or key velocity-based dynamic changes; alternatively, sampled rolls may be used, with aftertouch- or other controller-based dynamics.

In such figures, and in fact in all playing of imitative percussion, the timbre of rapid repeated note figures requires special care. If these are imitated by playing the identical sound in succession, particularly if the sound is sampled, the sound becomes perceptually unrealistic and machine-like since a real drummer naturally adds slight irregularities in any figure, and drum resonance changes the sound when several occur in succession. If this is the sound desired, then no more need be said.

If more realism is desired, this problem can be resolved by having several nearly identical samples of each sound, usually configured adjacently at the keyboard. Often it is sufficient either to transpose the sounds slightly or apply slightly different filtering if separate samples have not been made. Repeated note figures are then played as trills (possibly tremolos), which is a much easier keyboard technique than repeated notes. Flams become, say, small chromatic grace note figures, as discussed in chapter 5. A sample setup that implements this design is given in the section below. This problem exists primarily for sounds that do not decay too quickly. With those that rapidly die out, resonance effects are very limited, and the objectionable quality of repeated notes is reduced.

Cymbals come in many shapes and sizes. If the full variety of sounds available from antique, ride, sizzle, Chinese, suspended crash, hand-held crash, splash (and other) cymbals is to be accessed, considerable sampling will be necessary. Gongs are usually untuned and have many varieties, from the large orchestral tam-tam (Chinese) to the various button gongs (e.g., those of Burma). Sets of tuned gongs also exist. Traditionally, a distinction was made between the untuned tam-tam and the tuned gong, but this naming practice is often not followed.

Muting (damping) of such instruments has considerable gradation of effect. Normal damping causes the sound simply to taper off. In contrast, a sudden rapid damping is called "choking" the instrument, particularly on cymbals. This sound may be captured by separate sampling. An alternative is to allocate a null (silent) sample and the cymbal sample to the same MIDI channel, in monophonic output mode. Striking the silent key after the cymbal key will choke it off (though this choke will have a different quality than a real choke). This sort of cutoff of one sound by another has become standard on drum machine sounds made by open and closed forms of the same instrument, notably with the high hat—a closed high hat drum machine stroke cuts off a sounding open high hat.

Groove Percussion: Kit Drums and Latin Percussion

Although some performers have drastically altered the kit drums, or trap set, by attaching all manner of extra sound sources and paraphernalia to them, it has otherwise remained remarkably standardized in conception since its development in the first third of this century. It consists of a snare drum, pedal bass drum, tom-toms of various sizes, various suspended cymbals, high hat, and perhaps cowbell. Larger sets will have more toms, extra cymbals, perhaps an extra bass drum, perhaps other mounted sets of drums (e.g., bongos, rototoms), and perhaps other mounted Latin instruments.

In imitating trap set percussion, the various sounds must be set up on the keyboard in a way that is natural for the performer. This is a matter for personal preference, as many different designs seem to be used, although the advent of General MIDI (see chapter 3) may bring increased standardization. Figure 8.13 shows one simple possibility, using only bass drum, snare, one tom-tom, high hat, cowbell, and a ride cymbal. Note that each sound is available on more than one key, and a number of drum production methods are sampled: snare roll, sidestick, rim shot, normal strokes, brush hit, brush stir, normal cymbal, cymbal bell, open high hat, closed high hat (the last two both struck with a stick), and closing of high hat (with foot). Each copy of a sound should be slightly different, as mentioned above, whether achieved by transposition through a small interval, separate sampling, filtering, or some combination of these methods. Examples of drum parts using this setup are given in the next section. Other setups may emphasize a greater variety of sound sources by using a greater range or possibly velocity switching.

Latin percussion instruments show a remarkable variety and can be used on their own or with kit and orchestral percussion (for example, the marimba is widely found in Latin America). Besides various types of snare, tom-tom, and small to large bass drums found throughout Latin America, there are specific Latin drums that have become generic: the congas and bongos (both most commonly played with the hand) and the timbales (commonly played with sticks or one stick and one hand). It is on these drums that we will focus in the limited space available. The essential conception here is based on the fact that these drums are African in origin; they not only play a rhythm, they play a registral melody. In other words, the player's hands evoke a set of sounds with different pitches and timbres from the drum, and these create pitch as well as rhythmic contours.

On the conga, these sounds include the tone (T), the bass (B), the mute (M), and the slap (S). The tone is the open ringing sound heard when the drum is struck at the edge; the bass is the open sound heard when the drum is struck in the middle; the mute is the softer sound of playing the drum and not allowing the hand to rebound or deadening the sound with the other hand; the slap is a much louder sound usually created by a special single stoke that slaps and grabs the drum head. Each of these will require a separate sample if realism is to be achieved, although the tone and slap are the most important sounds. Conga drums are often played in sets of two or three, and different samples from different drums (espe-

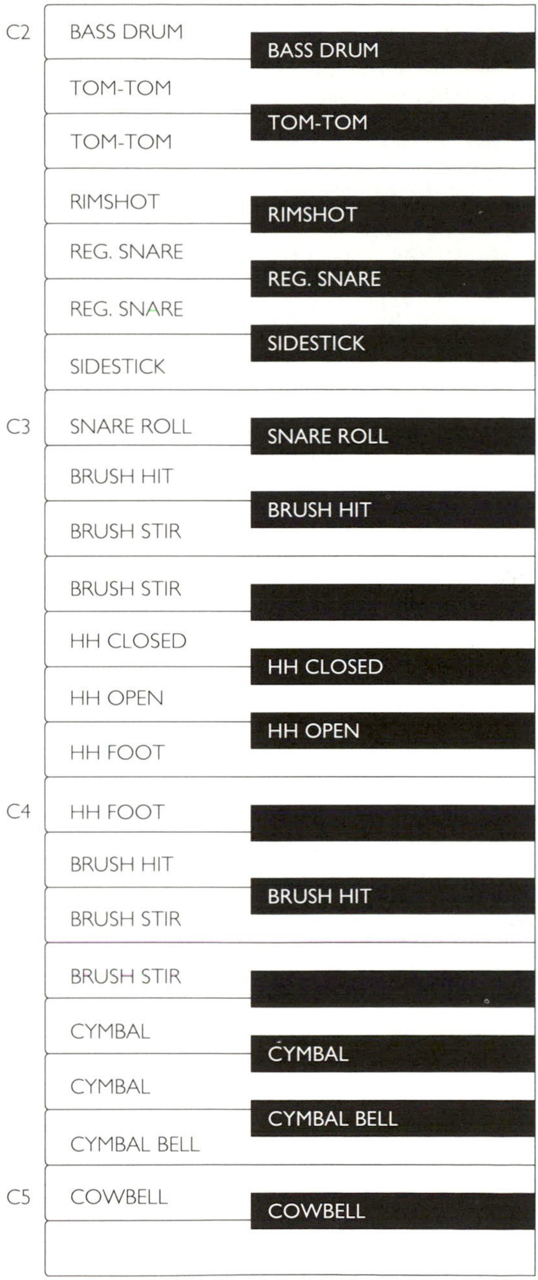

C2	BASS DRUM
	BASS DRUM
	TOM-TOM
	TOM-TOM
	TOM-TOM
	RIMSHOT
	RIMSHOT
	REG. SNARE
	REG. SNARE
	REG. SNARE
	SIDESTICK
	SIDESTICK
C3	SNARE ROLL
	SNARE ROLL
	BRUSH HIT
	BRUSH HIT
	BRUSH STIR
	BRUSH STIR
	HH CLOSED
	HH CLOSED
	HH OPEN
	HH OPEN
	HH FOOT
C4	HH FOOT
	BRUSH HIT
	BRUSH HIT
	BRUSH STIR
	BRUSH STIR
	CYMBAL
	CYMBAL
	CYMBAL
	CYMBAL BELL
	CYMBAL BELL
C5	COWBELL
	COWBELL

FIGURE 8.13   A simple keyboard drum setup.

cially of the tone sound) create the best effect. Alternatively, samples may be transposed. The three common sizes are the tomba (low), conga (medium), and quinto (high). Figure 8.14 shows a notated pattern for two drums, a quinto and a conga.

The same types of strokes apply to the bongos, with the addition that techniques using the separate fingers are also available. Bongos always come in pairs, and each drum should be sampled separately if possible. Both congas and bongos can be played with sticks or with a one-hand one-stick technique of African origin. As far as the synthesist is concerned, this adds some extra sounds (rim shot, stick hitting the middle of the top of the drum or its side, or striking a muted drum). If this sort of realism is required, it is best to work with an expert in such techniques and sample according to the advice he or she gives.

The timbales, which normally come in pairs, are most commonly played with sticks. Strokes here include the open stroke, the muted stroke, and the rim shot. They are commonly mounted on one stand with a cowbell between them, so patterns they play are often best coordinated or played in relation to a bell pattern.

Besides the drums there are many small instruments used in Latin playing: maracas, clavés, guiro, afuche, cabasa, quijada, caxixi, shakers, agogo, cowbell, triangle, quica, pandeira, samba whistle, and others. These small instruments create interlocking and overlaid patterns and must be played with high rhythmic precision to achieve their effect. When using a sequencer, quantization may be appropriate.

Playing Drums or Percussion from the Keyboard

Playing a single percussion line at the keyboard can be done with the fingers of a single hand or with two hands. While both systems can work well, the advantage of the second approach is often increased rhythmic surety, due to closer imitation of the body actions involved in real percussion and greater overall kinesthetic involvement. When several parts are played together, as in a percussion setup of a number of drums, both hands will naturally be used. Here it can be advantageous to use a nontraditional keyboard technique, because the small finger motions characteristic of piano technique do not seem to provide the right type of gestural link to the power and required rhythmic precision of most percussion. Where feasible, a two-arm technique that uses the fingers primarily like the mallets in classical multimallet percussion technique is recommended. Four parts are readily accommodated by using thumb and third finger of each hand.

Figure 8.15 shows some standard types of drum patterns and how they would be executed at the keyboard with the setup of figure 8.13. The parts

FIGURE 8.14 Notation for congas.

are written in drum notation, where most commonly cymbals are on the top line above the staff, snare drum is on the middle line, and bass drum is on the first space below the staff. Tom-toms and other drums are put at a variety of other places in the staff, as indicated. R.S. stands for rim shot. Below the drum staff is the keyboard performance version. Figure 8.15a shows some simple repeating patterns; 8.15b shows basic variation around a jazz-like ride cymbal pattern; and 8.15c shows execution of a fill. For further drum pattern examples see Crigger (1987).

If the performer is playing into a sequencer and the style is basic rock, Latin, popular, and some others, then quantization can successfully remove sloppiness of execution. In many styles, however, such quantization will be inappropriate for it removes rhythmic nuance as well. Furthermore, this option is not normally available to those synthesists playing live.

In playing percussion and drums there are several general approaches for the synthesist:

playing in time, using only fixed or completely scored patterns

playing in time, using a fixed pattern, but with variations (plus fills)

playing in time, but freely varying

playing in free time, emphasizing gesture and timbral variation

Almost all pieces of percussion music may be divided up into sections or layers, each one using one of these approaches.

The first three approaches share common elements and are best discussed together. The starting point in playing drums in good time from the keyboard is the notion of clearly defining the basic pulse. One way this can

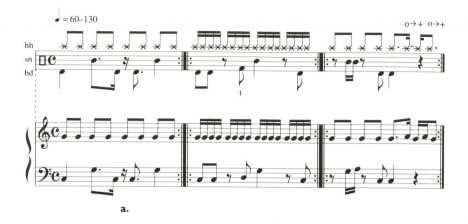

a.

b.

FIGURE 8.15 The execution of some basic drum patterns. The top staff of each example is in drum notation; the lower system (two staves) shows the keyboard execution using the setup of figure 8.13.

be done is by assigning one (possibly more) parts of the sound setup (whether kit or Latin percussion) to play a steady, easily perceived pattern, such as hitting each quarter note or eighth note in the bar or repeating a rhythmic figure of up to a full measure's duration. We will call this special part (or occasionally a composite of several parts) the *time-carrier part*. All other parts of the percussion setup are then played in relation to this part. With the drum kit, the time-carrier part is usually played by the high hat (as an even sixteenth, eighth, or quarter note in most popular, rock, and dance music styles), bass drum (as an even quarter note in some rock styles,

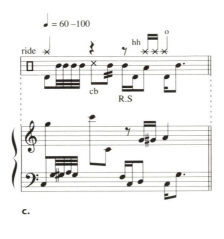

c.

hh	= high hat
sn	= snare
bd	= bass drum
t	= tom-tom
ride	= ride cymbal
cb	= cowbell
R.S.	= rimshot

FIGURE 8.15   continued.

disco, and Swing-era jazz), or ride cymbal (as an even eighth or quarter note in some rock styles; as a dotted and variable figure in modern jazz since bop). In Latin music, the time-carrier part is usually an unvarying syncopated one- or two-bar pattern (sometimes longer) played by agogo, cowbell, clavé, or rattle. The well-known clavé rhythm is the most popular example of this. In African music, this part is called the *time line*.

In a sequencing situation, the time-carrier part should be recorded first, usually in relation to a click track. The click track itself can be used as the time-carrier part (one that will, of course, not be heard in the end product). The time-carrier part may be played in alone or in combination with another important part or parts, depending on the complexity of the music, and the performer's technique and sophistication of musical conception. Remaining parts are then played in, using the time carrier part as reference, possibly also in conjunction with an audible click track. Note that it is quite possible for the time-carrier part to be used as an interim coordination procedure; in other words, the time carrier part may actually not be heard in the final recording or performance.

The overall procedure therefore looks as follows, where each number describes one or more different passes (tracks) of input:

1. Establish basic pulse by inputting the time-carrier part and any other parts as possible, with time carrier most often carried on high hat, ride cymbal, or bass drum (kit); or on agogo, cowbell, shaker, or claves (Latin). Try putting the basic pulse in both the right and left hand (separately) to build versatility. Drummers can do this, and thinking as they do will promote realism.

2. Establish basic feel in relation to this; this is often built on two coordinated parts, such as snare and bass drum.

3. Add additional support layers—highlighting, reinforcing, embellishing, supplementing, or coloring the basic pulse and feel.

4. Add fills (extra material used to fill in gaps at phrase ends or intervals of silence) and support via special accents, with suitable editing.

Use of quantization, where appropriate, is best saved for steadily repeating parts, especially those using the first two approaches to rhythm given previously.

In live performance, if a performing percussionist or drum machine is also in the group, the synthesist should follow the external time-carrier part set by the percussionist or drum machine and play whatever is required from passes 2, 3, and 4. If the synthesist is setting the time-carrier part, then primary attention must be paid to the stability and reliability of that part, with subordinate attention given to any simultaneously played parts that correspond to passes 2, 3, and 4. If a fairly free part is desired, it may be best to distribute the time-carrier function around the percussion setup to avoid too much strict repetition. This is a more advanced technique. If a continually varying (but still pulse-based) time-carrier part is used, as in the cymbal patterns of contemporary jazz, the performer must practice improvisation around basic patterns on each drum kit component.

If the performer has, instead of this time-based goal, the coloristic and gestural orientation listed as approach 4 (p. 367), then there is no intrinsic need for a time carrier. The performer must typically put down the part in one pass if sequencing is used or when playing live. In sequencing, an alternative is to use two passes with a time carrier that is then subsequently deleted, with the time carrier functioning to coordinate larger time groups or certain special accents.

In both the sequencing and live cases, the player will need a very solid technique, precise time sense, complete fluency with trill, repeated note, and tremolo figures, and good finger independence. The player will also need to have programmed the keyboard optimally for performance and have a dependable memory of the key locations of different sounds.

INSTRUMENTAL THIRD-STREAMING

One possibility that emerges from this vast sea of potential sonic imitation is related to the idea of *third-streaming*. This term was coined (as a noun) by American composer and jazz scholar Gunther Schuller to refer to the combination of traditional European music (the first stream) and jazz (the second stream) into a new music (the third stream). The term has since then been generalized by musicians such as Ran Blake (head of the Third Stream Department at the New England Conservatory in Boston) to refer to the combination of any two contrasting musical traditions into a new form or approach. Such syncretism has a long history, from early Islamic influence on chant to the European fetish for Turkish Janissary music in the eighteenth century to Debussy's influence by Javanese gamelan to the "worldbeat" movement of the 1980s. A useful brief history of this has been given by Dery (1990).

In terms of synthesis, there are several possible implications. One is to combine imitated instruments from disparate cultural sources in electronic composition and performance. Since balance is not determined by acoustic factors, instruments of incompatible dynamic ranges can be combined—like clavichord and African drums, for example. Instruments using "incompatible" tunings, such as a piano and a Balinese gamelan, may be synthetically adjusted to increase compatibility. Instruments and sound sources not physically transportable may be brought to the same location by sampling. Performers in different cultures using different notations, natural languages, and musical languages may interact aurally and with computer or MIDI translation. New hypothetical ("virtual") ensembles can be created.

Another approach is to actually synthesize culturally hybrid instruments. This could happen both vertically and linearly. In the first case, a clarinet sound might be layered with a Japanese koto and a Javanese rebab (a spike fiddle). In the second case, a sound might move from the attack of a marimba to the resonance of a sitar and end with the steady-state sound of a South American panpipe. The synthesizer performer should try to gain a sympathetic understanding of the playing techniques of the instruments outside his or her own cultural base to make this succeed.

Yet another approach is based on musical style and function. One may take the function of one instrument in an ensemble and dress it in the sounds appropriate to an instrument of a traditionally completely different function. Or, the style of one instrument may be grafted onto the register of another, the sound of yet another, and the function of yet a third.

There is great scope for imagination here. Such timbral and compositional experiments are already being done by some synthesists (notably

Wendy Carlos). It may pave the way for a genuinely hybrid transcultural international music (besides Western popular and art musics), with all the plusses and minuses that would imply. Music synthesis will have a crucial role in any such process.

ENVIRONMENTAL AND MACHINE SOUNDS

The sounds of the environment are multifarious and open-ended, and no more than the briefest discussion of their imitation will be given for that reason. Furthermore, many of them do not require very developed performance programming (although sympathetic performance will, as always, heighten their effect). Sustaining noise sources can usefully imitate many sounds of the weather, like surf, rain, or wind. Variations in spectrum (via filtering) and volume are the most that is usually necessary in terms of real-time programming. Noise is also useful in imitating rumbles, bangs, crashes, jangles, clatters, and all kinds of collisions of unpitched or nonharmonic overtone objects. Since such sounds are decaying in character, real-time performance with velocity-based control of brightness is usually the most that is necessary. Other more specialized sounds, like the sound of wood cracking, an amplified millipede walking on a leaf, the sound of a mudslide, and so forth, are really too diverse to be profitably discussed in general terms, and so complex that imitation is best done through sampling. See Truax (1978) and Schafer (1980).

Animal sounds are one category that can require real-time performance skill. The sampled bark of a dog, for example, or the high-pitched echoes of a dolphin can be given velocity-based volume and spectral control if something like musical motives or rhythmic patterns are to be developed, although this can readily degenerate into gimmickry. Many bird sounds have a repeating but variable character. Erratic pitch modulation of simple waveforms can imitate some bird calls, and real-time control of the modulation depth can promote the imitation. Other birds, and most single animal sounds, are difficult to imitate well without sampling. On the other hand, the sounds of masses of insects like bees or cicadas have a statistical quality of sameness, so that noisy sources without any real-time control (except perhaps of brightness) can be a useful starting point.

The sounds of machines or the quasi-mechanical sound patterns of workers like carpenters and builders often require no real-time performance programming. FM and noise are common sources for such sounds, particularly those using metal. The more complex and idiosyncratic sounds usually require sampling. Where real-time control is necessary, volume and brightness will often suffice.

REFERENCES

Adler, Samuel. *The Study of Orchestration.* New York: W. W. Norton & Co., 1989.

Aikin, J., C. Anderton, T. Coster, T. Darter, S. De Furia, G. Duke, T. Fryer, P. Gleeson, R. Moog, R. Powell, B. Tomlyn. *Synthesizer Technique.* Milwaukee: Hal Leonard, 1987.

Bartolozzi, B. *New Sounds for Woodwinds.* Oxford: Oxford University Press, 1962.

Blatter, Alfred. *Instrumentation/Orchestration.* New York: Longman, 1980.

Brindle, R. Smith. *Contemporary Percussion.* Oxford: Oxford University Press, 1970.

Burton, S. *Orchestration.* Englewood Cliffs, N.J.: Prentice-Hall, 1982.

Campbell, Murray, and Clive Greated. *The Musician's Guide to Acoustics.* London: J. M. Dent and Sons, 1987.

Crigger, David. *How to Make Your Drum Machine Sound Like a Drummer.* Newbury Park, Calif.: Alexander Publishing, 1987.

Dempster, S. *The Modern Trombone: A Definition of Its Idioms.* Berkeley and Los Angeles: University of California Press, 1979.

Dery, Mark. "The World Pulse." *Keyboard* 16,10 (November 1990) 81–94.

Dick, Robert. *The Other Flute.* New York: Oxford University Press, 1975.

Howell, P., and N. Harvey. "Voice Techniques." In *Musical Structure and Cognition,* ed. P. Howell, I. Cross, and R. West. New York: Academic Press, 1985.

Howell, T. *The Avant Garde Flute.* Berkeley and Los Angeles: University of California Press, 1975.

Jimmerson, Herb. "Just Strummin' Along." *Keyboard* 15,10 (October 1989) 110–111.

Kavasch, Deborah. *An Introduction to Extended Vocal Techniques.* La Jolla, Calif.: Center for Music Experiment, UCSD, 1980.

Milano, Dominic, ed. *Synthesizer Programming.* Milwaukee: Hal Leonard, 1987.

Peinkofer, K., and F. Tannigal. *Handbook of Percussion Instruments.* London: Schott, 1969.

Piston, Walter. *Orchestration.* New York: W.W. Norton & Co., 1955.

Podnos, T. *Intonation for Strings, Winds, and Singers.* Metuchen, N.J.: Scarecrow Press, 1981.

Rehfeldt, P. *New Directions for the Clarinet.* Berkeley and Los Angeles: University of California Press, 1978.

Richards, Emil. *World of Percussion.* Sherman Oaks, Calif.: Gwyn, 1972.

Rossing, T. D. *The Science of Sound.* New York: Addison-Wesley, 1990.

Sadie, Stanley, ed. *The New Grove Dictionary of Musical Instruments.* London: Macmillan and Co., 1984.

Schafer, M. *The Tuning of the World: Toward a Theory of Soundscape Design.* Philadelphia: University of Pennsylvania Press, 1980.

Truax, B., ed. *Handbook for Acoustic Ecology.* Vancouver, Canada: ARC Public, 1978.

Turetzky, Bertram. *The Contemporary Contrabass.* Berkeley and Los Angeles: University of California Press, 1974.

Warfield, Gerald. "The Notation of Harmonics for Bowed String Instruments." *Perspectives of New Music* 12,1-2 (Fall-Winter 1973/Spring-Summer 1974): 331–43.

NONKEYBOARD CONTROLLERS

. . . .

The reasonable man adapts himself to the world; the unreason-
able one persists in trying to adapt the world to himself. Therefore all progress
depends on the unreasonable man.

- George Bernard Shaw

There is no question that keyboards have played a large, even dominant role in the conception of the synthesiser's possibilities in performance since its earliest times. Despite this, many alternatives have existed, from the notably successful Theremin to the band-controlled Hellertion to Hugh Le Caine's electronic sackbut to the Free Music Machines of Percy Grainger and Burnett Cross. Even after the advent of voltage control, a minority of manufacturers, like Donald Buchla, regarded the keyboard as a suspicious source of infection of old performance attitudes and styles. In the 1970s, a number of nonkeyboard controllers such as the Steiner EVI and Lyricon developed increasing refinement, and many of these have now been reborn in MIDI incarnations.

Yet one can point to pro-keyboard bias in the MIDI specification itself—for example, in the area of pitch. Musicians pessimistic about this issue, only partly in jest, have claimed that the specification's real name should be KIDI (Keyboard Instrument Digital Interface). Note selection is based on a fixed number of categories per octave (which, to be sure, can be tuned up to complete arbitrariness, depending on the capacities of the synthesizer), with pitch bend providing a global (as opposed to individual note) facility for microtonal variation and bending. If the part is monophonic, these restrictions are minor, in principle—certainly all traditional Western performance practice is based on a certain number of normative pitch categories per octave, with deviations. Music not so based (e.g., clouds of string glissandi, as in some music by Iannis Xenakis) can be realized using pitch bend and portamento functions, with the overdubbing of monophonic lines. Yet it is not hard to be convinced that, for example, violin or trombone-type interfaces are better designed for such musical conceptions than keyboards. In addition, the continual slight differences in intonation of real brass, string, or woodwind instruments are often awkward to imitate at the keyboard, and even more often completely left out.

Furthermore, if simultaneously sounding notes are to be differently bent (or otherwise continuously controlled), they must be on different MIDI channels or use the only continuous controlling note specific message—Polyphonic Pressure—routed to pitch deflection at the sound module end. Unfortunately, some sound modules still do not respond to this message, and few controllers can send it. It can also readily clog up data transmission when it is used.

Small variations in articulation and the dynamics of sustaining sounds that are second nature to the string or wind player are also difficult to emulate on a keyboard instrument, unless the nature of the sound is very well understood and it has been programmed for appropriate real-time control. Likewise, the acoustic coupling between sequential or simultaneous notes on a traditional instrument is highly dependent on interface type, and this makes it unlikely that MIDI-based keyboard models of note interaction, if developed, will be very applicable to other kinds of sound sources.

At the heart of this discussion, then, is the issue of whether there are irresolvable problems in translating between gestures such as hand pressure and breath or bow actions. The answer to this is not completely clear, in my opinion. MIDI messages like Polyphonic Pressure and Key Velocity are clearly based on a keyboard conception. But this may largely be a question of name, if the same information-carrying variables can be produced with sufficient sensitivity from other kinds of interfaces in a way that is comfortable and convenient for the performer. In many cases, at least, these problems are not likely to prove insurmountable; we are simply at an early point in the development of such controllers with respect to MIDI. The central problems of note tracking and mapping analog performance information (traditional technique) into digital format are being actively pursued by manufacturers, with increasing success.

METHODS FOR CONTROL

A conventional synthesizer keyboard sends a trigger to the sound engine to indicate the start of the note event, along with an associated note number and velocity. These data are combined to produce the Note On message. Nonkeyboard controllers use a variety of methods to define the start of the note. One approach is to use an interface like that of a traditional instrument, with the controller's design based on directly measuring the actions of performers at work on various traditional instruments: the plectrum stroke force and choice of fret and string on the guitar; the bow attack, fingerboard position, and string choice on the violin; the drum pad stroke on percussion; the key positions, breath pressure, and embouchure on wind or brass instruments. Optical, sonar, radio wave, capacitance, resistance, ultrasound, and pressure sensors are all used (on various devices) to determine the actions of the performer's hands, lips, and any other active body parts. From the performer's perspective, a somewhat modified version of traditional technique will be appropriate. Technique will be similar but not identical because the electronic sensors will have different accuracy and nonlinearities than the acoustic coupling of the traditional instrument. Some differences will also be inevitable due to the response programming at the sound engine. Additional controllers on the interface, needed to allow such things as patch change, also change playing requirements.

The other design option for such interfaces is to use a pitch-to-MIDI converter so that the acoustic instrument (or the voice) can be played directly into a microphone (which might be strapped to the body of the instrument) and then converted to MIDI control data. Here again, traditional instrument technique can be relied on to form the basis of needed skills; the better the tracking device becomes, the less change from traditional procedures is needed.

What does this mean for the performer in practice? At the current time, all such controllers (except most percussion controllers, which fundamentally have the same note production method as the keyboard) have characteristic limitations. When played with traditional technique, they sometimes do not respond in sensible ways: Notes are bent that were not so intended; notes are missed or delayed; extra notes are triggered; notes sustain that were to have been damped, and the list goes on. With suitably modified technique such problems are reduced but not completely eliminated. Only time will tell whether these problems can be completely removed, but progress is certainly being made. It is probably best to adopt the point of view that these controllers are not meant to replace the instruments from which they originate but to open up new avenues of control for a wide spectrum of instrumentalists.

In contrast, the controlling device can be based not on a traditional instrument interface but on a completely novel approach such as spatial proximity (the theremin) or acceleration (the Airdrums). This requires the performer to learn a completely new set of performance techniques. This takes a lot of time but can yield results otherwise unattainable. Of course, any successful interface must map gestures onto musical control in ways that are ergonomic and versatile.

Whether the control mechanism uses an existing technique, modifies an existing technique, or proposes a completely new technique, the fundamental point is illuminated by the words of William Hazlitt (ca. 1820): "We never do anything well till we cease to think about the manner of doing it." A new technique takes that much longer to master to make sub- or unself-conscious. Until that stage is reached, real musical expression does not emerge, though any new control configuration will inevitably generate new musical predilections.

PITCH-TO-MIDI CONVERTERS

Pitch-to-MIDI converters lie at the heart of many nonkeyboard controllers and can be used, with a microphone or pick-up, to allow the monophonic input of any instrument or the voice to produce MIDI messages that represent what it is playing. Such devices are also known as pitch trackers or pitch followers (the pre-MIDI terms) and are made by

Fairlight (the Voicetracker, now no longer in production), IVL Technologies (Pitchrider), Roland, and a few other companies. These devices take an input audio signal, digitize it, and analyze it to determine a fundamental frequency that is used to calculate a MIDI note number and an appropriate pitch bend. Most of the devices can use the dynamics of the signal to control a range of synthesis parameters by translating this information for incorporation into assigned MIDI messages like Velocity, Aftertouch, Breath Controller, or Volume (controller 7). A few, like the Voicetracker, can also determine various timbral parameters like brightness, spectral purity, and attack time, using these to produce MIDI messages or control voltages. Some pitch trackers allow chords to be attached to MIDI notes, pitches to be selectively held, octave doubling, and polytimbral output.

Such devices have now entered a more reliable phase, after having been plagued by several persistent problems—primarily the production of erratic or spurious notes and glitches and poor response time (particularly in lower registers). False triggering and spurious notes come about because of the presence of noise (for example pick noise, inadvertent scraping of strings, squeaks, irregular embouchure actions, or other unpitched sounds) and inharmonicities (including short transients), which baffle the fundamental pitch-finding algorithm. On the traditional instruments, these sounds are masked by the primary note events or accepted as part of the sound vocabulary of the instrument. With MIDI tracking, these small irregularities in the performance of traditional instruments may be interpreted as separate very short notes by the pitch-to-MIDI converter; if they are routed to sustaining sounds, these notes may become quite audible. They can also cause bonefide notes to be incorrectly interpreted, either with regard to note onset or pitch.

These small doubled notes or "ghost notes" can be readily seen if pitch-to-MIDI converters are played into sequencers, and may need to be selectively cut out by subsequent editing. In live performance these small notes are typically less noticeable. Even so, on instruments or voice using a pitch-to-MIDI system, the performer must generally play as cleanly and precisely as possible to help out the pitch tracking mechanism, even if this means modifying the playing technique. As the tracking hardware continues to improve, the need for such squeaky-clean technique will probably decrease, but a degree of it will be necessary for the foreseeable future.

The other type of problem—response time—depends on the speed of the processors, the efficiency of the pitch-seeking algorithm, and certain intrinsic limitations in the pitch-to-MIDI conversion process. To understand this let us examine what goes on in pitch tracking. Although it can be applied to any audio signal, the result of pitch extraction will make sense only if the sound consists of discrete frequency peaks—that is, if it is a pure tone, a harmonic spectrum, or an inharmonic spectrum that is not too inharmonic. Formants and noise will just confuse the system.

The processor must analyze the signal to determine a fundamental pitch and a starting time for the MIDI messages. It must see through attack noise and the different time behavior of different harmonics and quick onset changes in intonation characteristic of many instruments. It must then decide on a combination of Note On, Note Off, and Pitch Bend messages that will best portray the audio signal. Some such decisions are fairly complex. For example, in portamento sections the machine must decide when a note is to be bent and when, due to limitations of pitch bend range, a new note attack must be introduced. All this takes a certain amount of time.

There is also a minimum amount of time required to get information from the sound. On most current processors, at least one or two complete wave cycles of all harmonic components must be sampled if accurate tracking is to be possible, though one commercial product as of this writing claims to require only a half cycle, and another only a quarter cycle. One-half or one-quarter or even less of a cycle are in principle enough, but there are practical problems—the required processing time will then be greater, and the errors associated with the analysis of the waveforms mean that the results may be less stable and accurate. When, as is currently the norm, one to two cycles of the fundamental frequency must pass by before the processor can even in principle fully commence its calculation, the frequency-related minimum delays given in table 9.1 are introduced.

Added to this are the delays in processing, which, although steadily decreasing as faster and faster processors become available, are still significant. Since, as we have seen earlier, the onsets of some sounds (e.g., clicks) 1 to 2 msec apart can be readily distinguished, these delays will be quite noticeable in cases where quick attacks are featured and will strongly

MINIMUM SCANNING TIME

Note	One cycle	Two cycles
C1 (65 Hz)	15.3 msec.	30.7 msec.
C2 (130 Hz)	7.7 msec.	15.3 msec.
C3 (261 Hz)	3.9 msec.	7.7 msec.

TABLE 9.1   Minimum possible time response for pitch-to-MIDI conversion of representative pitches. It is assumed here that at least one cycle of the fundamental frequency is required for analysis.

affect the performer's feel. The performer will have to play continuously ahead of the beat, or lead the sound, most noticeably in lower registers. At higher frequencies this problem becomes progressively less important.

Some of these problems can be circumvented by using pitch-to-MIDI data in a different way. Namely, the resulting MIDI note data can be converted (e.g., via MIDI mapping device or keyboard tracking in the sound engine or external device) into Control Change messages, Pitch Bend, and so forth. These messages will be more resistant to minor glitches and may form a quite viable procedure for exotic real-time processing control if routed to things like reverberation level, chorusing, or envelope parameters.

In live performance, the pitch tracker can be easily confused by the sounds of other instruments in the room. For this reason, a contact microphone is strongly preferred when playing with other musicians. The practicalities of using pitch-to-MIDI converters will be discussed further below with different controlling interfaces.

GUITAR AND PLUCKED STRING CONTROLLERS

Plucked string controllers and synthesizers are designed primarily for guitar players, although there is a MIDIfied Stick (called the Grid) and at least one MIDI bass controller. There are also attachable pitch-to-MIDI controllers that are designed for other instruments like the pedal steel guitar that can be readily applied to other string instruments including, in some cases, unamplified instruments without metal strings. The main current manufacturers of guitar controllers, guitar synthesizers, and guitar pitch-to-MIDI trackers (sometimes called retrofit guitar controllers) are Roland, Casio, Zeta Systems, Passac, Yamaha, Korg, Gibson, Quantar, and Audio Optics. Guitar controllers have no built-in MIDI sound engines; guitar synthesizers are self-contained; retrofit guitar controllers are portable from instrument to instrument.

Plucked string controllers operate either by pitch-to-MIDI conversion or by directly sensing finger positions and actions of the hands. One advantage of the first system is that it can be applied to the performer's favored personal instrument when it takes the form of a pitch-to-MIDI attachment (though such attachments can limit the amount of control available from the body of the guitar). Its disadvantages are those of pitch-to-MIDI conversion described above—some spurious notes may be triggered by finger noise, and there are inevitable delays. The first problem can be limited by carefully adjusting the overall and individual triggering sensitivities of the strings and using very clean technique. Delays caused by low register can be circumvented by stringing all strings with high E strings and transposing the results with the controller's circuitry; in this way the delay will be the same for all strings and never more than that associated with the note E2. The disadvantage of this system is that the guitar will now not be normally strung and cannot be played acoustically; bending techniques will also need minor modifications. However, adaptation to these changes is readily accomplished by nearly all players.

Those guitar controllers based on sensing hand position have reduced delay problems since they do not have to perform any real-time frequency analysis. However, they also tend to exhibit spurious note production if anything less than incredibly clean technique is used. Note bending is also severely cramped in some designs that require the performer to keep the string inside a narrow zone on the fretboard. The left-hand position may be determined by a number of methods: infrared sensors, sonar, or the completion of an electrical circuit when the string is depressed onto the fret. The right-hand position may be similarly sensed. In some instruments (e.g., the SynthAxe), a different set of strings is used for both the left hand and the right.

Notes may be sent out over one MIDI channel for all strings (poly mode), or the MIDI channels may be set separately for each string, allowing string-by-string polytimbrality (mono mode). This second procedure is usually more practical and is essential if notes are to be separately bent on different strings. Pitch bend may be turned off, used normally (*nonchromatic pitch bend*), or quantized to the nearest semitone (*chromatic pitch bend*). Pitch bend range of sending and receiving devices will need to be coordinated. Some such machines can send out MIDI real-time commands, store chords in memory, hold certain notes electronically, and select programs from fret position. Software designed to extend the control potentials of guitar (and some other) controllers, such as sYbil, is also increasingly available.

The body of the guitar synthesizer may have additional controls including the vibrato arm (whammy bar) and various switches and knobs; still other controls will be available via foot pedals. In some designs, the guitar synthesizer whammy bar doesn't physically bend the strings, in order to reduce the potential havoc caused to many kinds of sensing devices used to determine pitch and other kinds of bending. In some devices it can act as a controller, with an assignable control number. This is an area of development.

For further information, there is a dedicated publication: *The MIDI Guitarist* magazine.

BOWED STRING CONTROLLERS

Pitch-to-MIDI conversion is the favored method with string controllers and follows in many ways the issues given above. Zeta Music Systems is the primary manufacturer of MIDI electric violins, violas, and cellos (and also pick-up systems for the traditional instruments). As above, each string may be assigned its own MIDI channel and can be finely adjusted (physically and via sensitivity curves) to improve tracking. Selected notes may be held on while the player continues. Bow pressure is sensed and can be routed to affect such things as key velocity, breath control, aftertouch, and MIDI volume (controller 7). If pitch bend is quantized to semitones, or set to zero at the receiving end, the violin will obtain an invisible fretboard. As in other pitch-to-MIDI systems, a very clean technique in playing is essential.

Max Mathews, one of the giants of computer music, has also developed his own electric violin, although this is not marketed commercially.

WIND CONTROLLERS

Pitch-to-MIDI conversion is a viable option here, particularly with higher-pitched instruments. However, the trombone, tuba, and lower saxophones face real limitations as of this writing with such a system. For a variety of reasons, all commercial wind controllers have adopted a finger and mouth sensing system of control.

Brass Model

Few commercial models exist, with the Akai EVI (Electronic Valve Instrument) being the main contender. This is a commercial development of the Steiner EVI, an earlier trumpet-like instrument with built-in synthesis facilities that preceded MIDI and was developed by Nyle Steiner. It has two sets of three "valves" (actually touch-sensitive switches) and a fourth valve to allow certain fingering simplifications. Many of its control features are similar to those of woodwind model wind controllers. Like most of them, it has a seven-octave range, a simplified fingering based on duplicating one octave through the use of separate octave keys, and a number of options for real-time synthesis control. Since the fingering system requires only one hand, however, a trumpet-based wind controller has more versatility for real-time control than do woodwind-based designs.

Also available is the Perkophone, used by Mark Isham, which mounts on an actual trumpet. It has wired valves and uses wind pressure at the mouthpiece for dynamics.

Woodwind Model

Current MIDI-based wind controllers have some important pre-MIDI antecedents, notably the Lyricon (manufactured in the late 1970s), which had a clarinet-like interface and has been used by players like Tom Scott and Sonny Rollins, and Jürgen Schmidt's Variophon (1979), which had a recorder-type control interface.

MIDI-based wind controllers are currently made by several manufacturers, notably Yamaha (WX series), Akai (EWI series), Softwind (the Synthophone), Artisan (MIDIsax), and Casio. The wind controllers are mostly based on a modified Böhm saxophone and flute fingering, which may for example take one standard octave from D to C♯ and duplicate its fingering with additional octave keys, usually played with the left thumb: possibly one, two, or three octaves up and one, two, or three octaves down, for a total range of as much as seven octaves. (A few instruments, such as the some by Casio, use a recorder fingering.) Certain fingering problems are reduced by this modified Böhm scheme, and trills and tremolos can be made much more uniformly accessible over the instrument's range by redefining trill key functions electronically. Extended range fingerings characteristic of altissimo saxophone fingerings are available on the Synthophone, and these can even be customized and ROM-encoded.

The real-time control available from such instruments can basically come from breath pressure or air velocity (that is, how hard the player blows into either a closed or open tube respectively), and from the embouchure. Embouchure control is usually reduced over that available on a traditional instrument, with only pressure of bite having an effect on most models. The instrument's embouchure can typically be fine-tuned to player choice, and lip pressure and breath pressure sent separately to various control parameters on the instrument's attached sound module—commonly at least LFO depth, filtering, and pitch bend. Note velocity information may be read off from breath pressure at the note onset, with subsequent breath pressure information used to determine dynamics, volume, or some other variable. The devices can typically send breath, volume, and aftertouch controller information out via MIDI to other sound sources. Specific messages can often be sent by using special combinations of keys that are not used for note selection.

Selected notes may be sustainable by additional switches on the body of the instrument. Other than this, the instruments are usually monophonic, although the Synthophone can play exactly or diatonically transposable chords. Foot pedals attached to the sound module itself can provide additional real-time control. Ready transposition to common keys—B♭ and E♭ —is usually featured.

Wind controllers suffer from some of the difficulties of other nonkeyboard controllers. The onset of a note is a far more ambiguous event than on a keyboard, and there is a limit to the use of continuous controllers with the hands, as these are already fully occupied selecting notes (although some—notably the Akais—have rollers under the body of the instrument playable by the thumb). Similarly, the keys must be depressed carefully and systematically, and with very accurately coordinated timing, if the proper signal is to be read off the pads. If this is not done, the very brief intervening fingerings will be treated as note-defining, producing annoying sonic glitches and perhaps undesired octave shifts. However, with some practice, the player does adapt to these differences, and eventually (as in every such situation) these "limitations" soon find their own musical uses. The delicate gradations of breath control have compensations, which, in the hands of a seasoned performer, can produce impressive results.

PERCUSSION CONTROLLERS

Percussion controllers have a history that goes back long before MIDI. Performers have long used transducers attached to traditional drums and percussion to trigger synthesizers or even other drums via voltage control. Such devices are still in use: There exist both trigger-to-control voltage devices and trigger-to-MIDI devices.

In many ways percussion controllers are the simplest of all MIDI performance devices, for they most often have in mind a drum stick stroke that imparts a certain amount of force and then rebounds to have no further contact with the drum surface until the next stroke. In such playing, there is no way in which further performed sound shaping can occur or, for that matter, the note can even be manually turned off. In other words, traditional Western drum technique will not enable messages of continuous controller type.

However, many non-Western drum techniques, such as those of African talking drums, do shape the sound after striking, or allow a wide range of timbre to come from one drum by the use of both hands, different beaters, or stick-and-hand combinations. These tendencies are also apparent in extended twentieth-century Western percussion techniques and are found in both fully notated scores and the actions of free improvisers. The potential to have the percussion controller surfaces respond to applied pressure, which is then mapped onto continuous-type MIDI information (pitch bend, aftertouch, control change, etc.), does seem to be gaining some ground (e.g., the KAT DrumKat). Without it, percussion controllers face considerable limitations when using sustaining sounds.

The percussion controllers are based on one or more pads or playing surfaces and model their physical layout either on the drum kit, orchestral mallet percussion, or some novel but symmetrical arrangement of pads on a flat surface. In all cases there are a number of separate objects, pads, or surfaces, each of which may be assigned one or more sounds, one or more MIDI channels, one or more note numbers (even motives in some cases), a program change, velocity specifications (fixed velocity, maximum velocity value, range, or velocity map, depending on the sophistication of the machine), gate time, and possibly other variables. *Gate time* refers to the amount of time the triggered note will be left on: In other words, if gate time is 1.2 seconds, then 1.2 seconds after the pad is struck a MIDI Note Off message will be sent. This can usually be programmed from a few milliseconds to 5 or more seconds and increasingly can be made dependent on key velocity. Where more than one note can be assigned to a given pad, layering, velocity cross-fading, and velocity switching may be available.

These pads are all connected to a central processing unit called the "brain," where signals may be coordinated and converted to MIDI and where sound may be generated and programmed. Programs and setup configurations may be stored and recalled and the properties of individual pads set. Several commercial controllers (e.g., Simmons MTM, DrumKat) allow velocity to pick note number, an effect that can otherwise be obtained with a MIDI mapping device by swapping the data bytes in the Note On command (see chapter 6). Also connected to the brain may be a number of pedals and footswitches, allowing program chaining, sustain on/off, and, on a few machines, the sending of continuous MIDI data such as modulation, panning, and pitch bend.

Drum-kit-type percussion controllers are made by Casio, Yamaha, Roland, Simmons, KAT, ddrum, and other manufacturers. On these devices the performer uses kit technique and usually sets up the pads in the familiar trap set arrangement. Pad layouts that do not rely on the traditional models include the Roland Octapad, the KAT DrumKAT, the Simmons SDX and Portakit. These devices have various design layouts; many of them are not based on a linear sequence, and so the orientation of the steel drum (pan) player can be a useful one. However, naturalness of melodic playing can suffer in some of these arrangements of pads. The SDX, which can be configured like a kit, has different zones on each of its pads, and each of these zones can produce independent sounds.

Orchestral mallet percussion-type controllers include the KAT MIDI Percussion system and the Simmons Silicon Mallet. The former is a one-octave system, expandable to four, while the latter is a three-octave setup, expandable to four or five octaves. These systems have the features described above and, in addition, zones and split points. Despite the fact that their layout is based on that of mallet percussion, there are some technical differences that emerge for traditional players of such instruments. First, since these devices are based on sensing force via resistance, each pad may be struck anywhere on its surface and still produce a clean result. This can mean that a less stringent technique is required; the player can play more reliably and perhaps faster, since it is not necessary to aim for the "sweet spot" of the drum or bar with traditional accuracy. This factor also applies to kit drum setups. Second, bars are most often uniform in size, unlike real marimbas and vibraphones, so that distances are more easily learned and transferred form instrument to instrument. Third, the controllers in this category seem to be made with a rubber-like playing surface. This produces a rebound more nearly like that of a drumhead, and it means that percussionists can use the rebound energy to comfortably execute double stroke rolls and other figures that would be more difficult on a real vibraphone or marimba. This kind of rebounding surface also appears on drum kit controllers (percussionists wouldn't put up with less there).

Acoustic drums and percussion may be used to drive electronic music systems. This is commonly done by attaching force-sensing resistors to the playing surfaces. Two types of devices are most common: trigger-to-MIDI or trigger-to-control voltage. The first type of trigger device has all the advantages of versatility associated with MIDI. However, it also has the liabilities. The delay in conversion from analog to digital format can be up to 10 msec, too long to pass unnoticed with crisp enveloped sounds like a snare drum. The trigger-to-control voltage device, by operating purely in the analog realm, is usually much quicker. Synthesizers with direct control voltage inputs should be triggered this way; unfortunately, such inputs are becoming rarer. The E-mu Emulator and Oberheim Xpander still feature it, however, and some drum machines have direct trigger inputs.

All played notes will only last their preset gate times unless variability is introduced. Some instruments allow this kind of control by assigning velocity to control gate time; in some others frequent patch changes can enable change between preprogrammed gate time options. If the drums are to be used melodically with variable sustain, single stroke roll technique characteristic of the marimba may be used, overriding some of the constraints of gate time. This procedure may cause the sound to become too sharp in pitch if it is sampled since the attack portion of some sounds is sharper than their steady state. This is discussed by Shrieve and Beal (1989) and in chapter 8.

NOVEL INTERFACE CONTROLLERS AND MISCELLANY

Some interfaces adopt only part of the attributes of existing ones. A number of noncommercial devices, for example, have used a guitar design but without strings. These include David Vorhaus's Kaleidophon and Bernard Szajner's Laser Harp. One commercial entry in this field is Dynachord's Rhythm Stick, a stringless guitar-shaped controller designed to control drum sounds.

Other instruments take a completely independent approach. The Theremin, played in free space on the basis of proximity and body capacitance, is the best-known early instrument in this category. A device of comparable conceptual novelty in the post-MIDI era is the Airdrums (Palmtree Instruments). These are two hand-held devices that respond to acceleration, along six different directions each, and are connected to a central processor. These directions are those of aerodynamics: pitch, yaw, and roll. Notes and chords may be assigned to each direction or chosen from an incoming sequence.

Thunder, a MIDI performance interface made by Don Buchla, shows a number of interesting features. It consists of twenty-five variously shaped touch-sensitive pads arrayed in two adjacent semicircles, one lying under each hand. It is distinguished from a standard percussion controller partly by the light touch required to play it properly. The pads sense both pressure and velocity, and the majority of them also sense location; some can be split into two or even three regions. The sensed variables can be mapped to various MIDI messages, cause riffs to trigger, and set off short sequences of commands (delays, repeats, transpositions, logical tests, etc.). The pads can also operate in different modes, whereby Note Ons and Note Offs are selectively controllable, and they can be programmed to modify each other's messages in various ways, creating novel performance possibilities. Lightning, also made by Don Buchla, is played by movement of an infrared-transmitting wand, finger ring, or special drumstick through programmable combinations of eight spatial cells. Movements can be mapped to control a wide range of MIDI variables based upon two-dimensional position in space and velocity. Lightning contains a useful random walk algorithm and a conductor function that sends out MIDI clocks in response to appropriate gestures.

The Radio Drum, a development of computer music pioneer Max Mathews, uses two small percussion mallets with independently tuned short-range radio transmitters in their heads. Their positions are sensed in three dimensions by a radio receiver embedded in a rectangular playing surface. Positions are scanned every millisecond, producing usable velocity data. The mallets can be used to trigger events or send continuous control messages. The triggered events can include strings of notes, whose playback parameters (tempo, transposition) are controlled in real time by the positions and velocities of the mallets.

The Video Harp, a development of inventor Paul McAvinney, is a visually attractive strap-on controller that uses a built-in light source and an array of mirrors to sense the positions of the performer's fingertips on two joined transparent trapezoidal surfaces. The device may be programmed to do such things as produce bowing articulations (using MIDI volume), convert measured distance between the hands into pitch bend, and operate in "conductor mode." This mode, also available on the Radio Drum, allows the performer to control in real time the playback parameters (rhythm, tempo, expressive nuance) of notes previously stored as a sequence.

In general, any type of information can be converted to MIDI, so that all sorts of body actions can be mapped into performance data. A number of researchers have used general spatial position, velocity, and sometimes acceleration measurements to derive MIDI messages (and in the pre-MIDI days, control voltages) from the motions of dancers and performance artists, using such things as video cameras and attched sensors. There is at least one commercial product that does this: EMS's Soundbeam, which uses a system of ultrasonic echoes. Other possibilities in the offing include the MIDI Glove, and the development of virtual reality music technology, where the performer is placed in an invented three-dimensional musical control reality that is both viewed on a monitor and felt.

REFERENCES

Shrieve, M., and D. Beal. "Exploring MIDI Percussion." *Keyboard* 15,7 (July 1989): 102–103 +.

Turkel, Eric. *MIDI Gadgets.* London and New York: Amsco, 1988.

SYNTHESIZER ENSEMBLES AND REPERTOIRE

· ·

The instrument should become part of the player's body. The power and the control should emanate from the core of the consciousness rather than from the surface of the body. The player must live in the sound of the music, . . . involved on a high level of enthusiasm, but without anxiety and overtrying.

▪ Jimmy Giuffre, *Jazz Phrasing and Interpretation* (1969)

Repertoire for any instrument is based upon its typical modes of presentation to listeners. In the case of electronic music, this includes live performance (solo or group, possibly with sequencer/computer assistance or tape playback), studio work, and pure tape pieces. In the case of the synthesizer as instrument, it is this first mode of presentation on which we will focus; to give a major focus to tape pieces would be to turn the chapter into a discography.

What are the specific skills the synthesizer performer should bring to the performance arena? These include:

sight reading: lines, chords, and chord symbols; the ability to interpret synthesizer-specific expression marks, such as pitch bend and modulation, as well as standard articulation and expression marks for winds, brass, guitars, percussion, and strings; also fluency in the five clefs: treble, bass, alto, tenor, and percussion

improvisation: chordal and single-line, and in as many styles as possible

synthesis programming: well-organized access to a considerable library of synthesizer programs and samples, knowledge of the musical potentials of the library, and the ability to modify these on the spot in accordance with the needs of the performing situation

knowledge of style: a wide knowledge of musical styles to allow the player to execute material in a contextually sound manner

technique: on horizontal keyboard, strap-on, and standard ancillary controllers or, on nonkeyboard controller

familiarity with MIDI and audio devices, and computer software: as required for stage or studio work (the degree of knowledge required here varies considerably with the kind of performance work)

THE SYNTHESIZER AND ENSEMBLE PERFORMANCE

Let us look specifically at the ways synthesizers can be used in ensembles. In principle, this is a completely open field, due to the synthesizer's extreme versatility. In fact, it is hard to think of any ensembles in which synthesizers do not already play some role, be it the pop group, jazz band, folk group, traditional "ethnic" ensemble, gospel choir, Renaissance wind band, chamber ensemble, or symphony orchestra. Of course, in some of these, the synthesizer is still a relative novelty, while in others its use is commonplace. Such differences may remain or fade; it is of course the composers and listeners of today and tomorrow who will decide what its ultimate position shall be.

Historically, synthesizer ensembles and ensembles featuring synthesizer came into existence quite early on (many were founded in the 1930s), and a new wave appeared beginning in the late 1950s and 1960s, including such groups as the ONCE Group, the Sonic Arts Union, Intermodulation, Mother Mallard's Portable Masterpiece Company, the Electric Weasel Ensemble, Nuovo Consonanza, FLUXUS, Musica Elettronica Viva, AMM, Teleopa, and others. The post-MIDI era has spawned a fresh crop of ensembles such as the Philip Glass Ensemble. For a comprehensive review of early live avant-garde groups, see Mumma (1975). A slightly later perspective that focuses equally on popular music is that of Ernst (1977). Useful also is the survey by Manning (1985).

Rock music began to become increasingly concerned with the use of synthesizers with the dawn of the voltage-controlled keyboard-based machines in the mid-1960s. Groups and musicians such as Yes, Brian Eno, Emerson Lake and Palmer, Frank Zappa, and Pink Floyd began directions that have become widespread. Jazz musicians like Paul Bley and Jan Hammer have made distinguished contributions, and the use of synthesizers by contemporary jazz keyboardists such as Chick Corea, Herbie Hancock, Joseph Zawinul, and George Duke is now well established, although some jazz artists such as Keith Jarrett and McCoy Tyner have made a point of remaining with traditional keyboards.

We can distinguish several ways in which the synthesizer is used in such groups. It can play according to its own sound traditions in a part specially written for it; it can substitute for a missing instrument in rehearsal or performance of acoustic (or electric) music; or it can be used to completely transform the sound surface of an existing piece for other instruments, as for example the "switched-on" concept popularized by Wendy Carlos. Composers and arrangers writing for synthesizer should either program it themselves, work with an assistant who can help them refine the necessary sounds, or, if no other option is available, describe the required sound in words on the score.

This being said, a number of ensemble configurations involving synthesizer performance can be identified as most common, any of which may involve automated parts via sequencers and drum machines. These are as follows:

Synthesizer Plus Standard Rock, Jazz, or Popular Band

Here the group has a rhythm section, often a front line, possibly one or more singers, and one or possibly two synthesizer/keyboard players. In this case the repertoire of pieces including synthesizer as a component is already considerable. The synthesizer in such groups most commonly functions as a lead line, comping instrument, or bass, or two or three of these at once. Certain large ensembles, like the stage band and jazz orchestra (big band plus strings, horns, and woodwinds), now normally include a synthesizer player or at least a keyboardist who plays synthesizer as needed. Besides synth-specific repertoire, the synthesizer can be readily adapted to play any lead or comping part in normal usage. Where drum machines are used in live performance, they are often programmed and run by the keyboardist or drummer.

Multikeyboard Ensemble

These are like the ensembles mentioned above, but they include three to four synthesizer players so that synthesis and sampling dominate the sound. This sort of ensemble might be purely electronic but would often have singers, drums played live, and possibly a guitar or horn. The distinctive issues here involve synthesizer players working together, being primarily responsible for the sound and feel of the band. This orientation is common among modern "techno-pop" bands. This will require cooperation and will go against some of the conditioning that most keyboard players have experienced since the pianist and organist are used to playing solo or being the only keyboardist in traditional ensembles.

Ensembles of Variable Instrumentation Plus Synthesizer(s)

Compositions ranging over any possible style, drawing on voice, synthesizers, audio processors, computers, visual production, and the full range of orchestral, popular, and ethnic instruments can be found in this catch-all category. Concerts of this orientation must be organized for the specific collection of instruments in the special ensemble.

Some of the sources here are the many works for the older electronic instruments—Ondes Martenot, Trautonium, Theremin, and Synket (in electronic ensembles and combined with acoustic instruments), which may be adapted for contemporary synthesizers; adaptations of traditional acoustic works; and many pieces since the advent of digital synthesizers, with the involvement of the Yamaha DX7 and the Synclavier being especially common.

Some sample pieces are listed below. They vary in format and comprise completely notated traditional scores (notes, articulations, timed sequences of button pushes and controller indications) as well as written descriptions of improvisation attitudes, explicit hardware and software prescriptions, performance checklists functioning as mnemonic aids, and graphic or metaphoric designs. The list also includes some works for solo synthesizer or synthesizer with computer assistance:

Austin, Larry. *Concertante Cybernetica* (1987) for Synclavier.

Boulez, Pierre. *Repons* (1981–) for six soloists (two pianos, harp, cimbalom, xylophone/glockenspiel, vibraphone), chamber orchestra (twenty-four instruments), tape, and computer. This work in progress does not, at last information, directly involve performers on MIDI synthesizers but is significant in its representation of a certain European approach to electroacoustic computer-assisted music performance.

Barroso, Sergio. *La Fiesta* (1989) for synthesizer and tape.

Bresnick, Martin. *Lady Neil's Dumpe* (1987) for MIDI controller and computer.

Cardew, Cornelius. *Volo Solo* (1973) for synthesizer, piano, bassoon, and marimba.

Cary, Tristram. *Trios* (1971) for Synthi VCS-3 and turntables.

Chadabe, Joel. *After Some Songs* (1985)/ *Modalities* (1990); first version for Synclavier, later versions for Macintosh running M.

Dick, Robert. *A Black Lake with a Blue Boat On It* (1990) for flute and MIDI keyboard (playing sampled extended flute techniques).

Eaton, John. *Concert Piece for Synket and Orchestra* (1966) for Synket and orchestra.

Emmerson, Simon. *Pathways* (1989) for sitar, tabla, flute, cello, synthesizer/sampler.

Endrich, Tom. *The Watcher's Orbit* (1986) for four male voices and two DX7 synthesizers.

Erb, Donald. *Reconnaissance* (1967) for Moog synthesizer, Moog polyphonic instrument, violin, bass, piano, and percussion.

Harvey, Jonathan. *Madonna of Winter and Spring* (1986) for orchestra, synthesizers, and electronics.

Hindemith, Paul. *Four Pieces* (1930) for three Trautoniums; *Konzertstück* (1931) for Trautonium and strings.

Honegger, Arthur. *Sortilèges* (1946) for Ondes Martentot.

Jolivet, André. *Ondes Martenot Concerto* (1947) for Ondes Martenot and orchestra.

Kabat, Julie. *The Child and the Moon Tree* (1988) for singer/actor and synthesizer.

Lansky, Paul. *Talkshow* (1989) for voice, pitch-to-MIDI converter, and MIDI synthesizers (single performer).

McClean, Barton. *Earth Music* (1990) for two synthesizers (one performer), processed voice, and tape.

Machover, Tod. *Valis* (1987), opera including KX88, TX816, and intelligent instrument software; *Bug-Mudra* (1990) for KAT mallet controller, percussion, acoustic guitar, electric guitar, conductor wearing EXOS Dexterous Hand Master glove, and hyperinstrument system.

Marshall, Ingram. *De Profundis* (1987) for Synclavier.

Messiaen, Olivier. *Fêtes des belles eaux* (1937) for six Ondes Martentot; *Trois petites liturgies* (1944) for Ondes Martentot; *Turangalîla-symphonie* (1948) for orchestra and Ondes Martenot.

Oliveros, Pauline. *Lion's Eye* (1985) for Synclavier and gamelan; *Lion's Tail* (1990) for synthesizer and Vision or HMSL software for the Macintosh.

Paintal, Printi. *Euroasian Quintet* (1989) for sitar, tabla, flute, cello, Roland D-50.

Pressing, Jeff. *If 19 Were 12* (1982) for synthesizer/electric piano, piano, cello, trombone, flute, percussion; *Cadenza* (1985) for synthesizer/electric piano, piano, trumpet, cello, percussion; *Descent of the Avatar* (1987) for synthesizer, trombone, alto saxophone, and percussion.

Rolnick, Neil. *Real Time* (1983 for Synclavier and fourteen instruments or chamber orchestra, revised 1987 for MIDI); *ElectriCity* (1991) for six instruments, synthesizers, sampling, and digital processing.

Runswick, Darryl. *Dialectic 1* (1990) for sitar, tabla, flute, cello, Roland D-50, tape.

Subotnick, Morton. *The Double Life of Amphibians* (1982) for digital synthesizer, two cellos, two clarinets, two trombones, two percussion, two pianos.

Teitelbaum, Richard. *Golem I* (1988) for two Macintosh controlled MIDI systems. See also subsequent pieces in Teitelbaum's *Golem* series.

Ward-Steinman, David. *Arcturus* (1972) for synthesizer and orchestra; *Chroma* (1984), concerto for four keyboards and chamber orchestra.

See Ernst (1977) and Schrader (1982) for more extensive listings of pre-MIDI scores.

Synthesizer Orchestra

This name is used here, at least partly tongue-in-cheek, as a generic name for the all-synthesizer ensemble. The word *orchestra* can be considered appropriate in the sense that it refers to the widely expanded sound world possible in even very small synthesizer ensembles; the potential addition of sequencers and computer performance environments means also that the term need not be a misnomer in reference to musical complexity. While duo synthesizer groups are quite viable, with or without sequencer/computer assistance, we will focus on ensembles of at least three performers, with no obvious upper size limit.

Small synthesizer ensembles of two to five performers tend to be most practical, but larger ensembles can produce effects otherwise unavailable. Larger ensembles may need a musical director or conductor. In all such cases a wide variety of styles can be accommodated, including the following:

jazz, rock, Latin, pop arrangements

ensemble-specific compositions

adaptations of Western art music of all eras, especially chamber music and chamber orchestra repertoire adaptations, notably of the music of wind ensembles, string quartets, mallet percussion ensembles, and string orchestra (additional non-synth players may need to be added for this)

adaptations of "ethnic" music traditions: for example, African, Middle Eastern, Indian, Indonesian

adaptations of keyboard music (e.g., canons, inventions, fugues, and music for four or six hands)

improvisation (free and otherwise)

In arranging pieces from these varied sources, the arranger may choose to adopt a variety of stances: imitate traditional effects as much as possible; keep the musical substance of the works but change the sonic clothing ("switched-on" style); or completely rearrange the musical materials. Some representative examples in each of these categories will now be discussed.

Jazz, Rock, Latin, Pop Arrangements

The area of rock and popular music is so vast and well exposed that it is impossible to summarize here. Nearly all of the many published commercial arrangements available can be readily adapted for synthesizer ensemble. Adapt these by using one performer or sequencer to perform drums; a second performer or sequencer for bass; another performer or sequencer for rhythm guitar; a performer or sequenced part for pads and backing figures; a performer for significant lead parts; and a live singer or sampled sounds for vocals.

Similar arrangements can be made for Latin American music. Nearly all the Latin small percussion can be well mimicked by most synthesizers, and the metronomic rhythmic character of most Latin music means that the integration with sequencers is relatively straightforward.

Jazz has been synthesized by many people, and again the written literature is vast, with nearly any piece being in principle transferrable to synthesizer ensemble. In practice, swing, the essential jazz rhythmic ingredient, requires considerable care to get right. Likewise, the individuality of sound and nuance of the improvising soloist in jazz is not simple to emulate. The complex syncopations of jazz drum parts are also quite challenging. To develop these aspects of synthesizer playing, the performer should consult the usual jazz sources: landmark jazz recordings, texts, scores, song sheets and transcriptions of improvised solos. A useful general resource is *The Grove Dictionary of Jazz* (Kernfeld 1988). Jazz aids of many kinds are coordinated by suppliers such as Jamie Aebersold, whose continuing series *A New Approach to Jazz Improvisation* (1975–) is a useful examination of the chords and scales approach to jazz soloing. The harmonic materials of jazz are treated by many writers such as Coker (1964) and Haerle (1980). Some of the best analysis of jazz scoring and writing is found in Wright (1982) and Dobbins (1986). Serious jazz research publications are found in the two journals *Annual Review of Jazz Studies* and *Jazz Forschung/Jazz Research*. High quality fake books include those by Sher (1983; 1988).

There is no substitute for the musical development achieved by transcribing music onto paper. This is recommended both for the works of admired artists and the performer's own improvisations, followed by critical analysis of exactly why the music succeeds in having certain effects and may fail to have others.

Ensemble-Specific Compositions

Such scores seem to be only very rarely published. I offer here two of my own: Pressing, Jeff, *Somewhere Northwest of Indonesia* (1986) for three players plus drum machine or four players; *Study Number 1* (1985) for three or four synthesizer players.

Art Music Ensemble Adaptations

The resources here are of course vast and impossible to describe fully in a book on synthesizer performance. Adaptations (transcriptions or arrangements) of traditional art music for electronic instruments will not be to everyone's taste, but they should, in my view, be considered in light of the extensive historical traditions of transcription of music of all types for keyboard and small instrumental ensembles. These traditions go back to the earliest periods of Western music and continue into our own time. Keyboard transcriptions have been particularly wide-spread (in earlier periods they were called intabulations). Noted exponents of transcription include J. S. Bach, Franz Liszt, Anton Webern, and Igor Stravinsky.

In general terms, the sources include scores of music from the early period of monophonic song (called chant or *organum*) to the present day. Early music that survives today is most often vocal or a mixture of vocal and instrumental parts. Any synthesist interested in investigating these sonorities can go back as far as the transcriptions, into modern notation, of the early vocal chant of the first millenium. The earliest pieces are strictly monophonic; later, monophonic sections alternate with others in parallel motion of fourths and fifths, while, increasingly with time, there are poly-phonic tendencies and elaborations, as in so-called *florid organum.* Many special vocal forms came into being, such as the motet, conductus, mad-rigal, rondeau, and chanson. Increasingly, instrumental adaptations of these musics came to be performed by solo organists or small instrumental ensembles. Subsequently, new instrumental forms such as prelude, toc-cata, ricercar, canzona, basse-danse, fugue, chorale prelude, and fantasia developed. While some were based on vocal models, others were for dancing or instrumental display.

In most surviving manuscripts up to the fifteenth and sixteenth centu-ries, and many later scores, there are no indications of what instruments are to play each part; in fact, we do not know in general whether the parts are even to be taken by voices or instruments. It seems both that there were some unwritten interpretive conventions and that it was customary to use whatever resources were available on the concert occasion. Hence, the synthesist playing such music should feel free to voice the sounds in any musically fitting way, even if a close reading of historical procedures may show that some parts in some pieces would probably be preferentially given to one type of instrument or another in practice. Specialist texts in historical musicology are the sources of information to consult for those who wish to develop the notions of faithfulness to the original conceptions of the composer and period ("authenticity"). A vast resource for early music is the *Corpus Mensurabilis Musicae,* a many-volume set of mediae-val and especially Renaissance musics (many of them for unspecified instrumentation) published by the American Institute of Musicology (Ar-men Carapetyan, general editor).

All such adaptations for instrumental ensembles and solo keyboard involved the use of considerable embellishment and improvisation, since instruments have more facility with quick note passages than the voice. Even more important, there was a different spirit afoot than in today's renditions of eighteenth- and nineteenthth-century classical music— namely, professional performers were expected to be able to improvise with fluency. Hence, the synthesizer performer should also feel free to improvise with given material. However, this must be done in a style befitting the materials (of course, the rub lies in the interpretation of "befitting"). Historically, this was usually based on a few general concepts: embellishing a line by adding extra notes; connecting melodic guide points by runs, fills, and figurations; adding extra parts over a repeating or fixed line, the so-called cantus firmus; or theme and variations. The idea of improvising with scales above fixed chordal progressions did not develop until much later; the idea of chord itself does not really stabilize until the early seventeenth century. For a survey of historical improvisation techniques, see Pressing (1984a; 1984b). For a more in-depth look at this the reader should consult the classic works of Ferand (1938; 1961). A survey of the available materials in improvisation in many styles is given in Pressing (1987).

By the baroque period, beginning roughly with the seventeenth century, many instrumental forms were current on which the synthesist can directly draw. In particular, the dance suite, the sonata (both solo and for small ensembles), canzona, sinfonia, and concerto were prominent forms used by small chamber groups and the baroque chamber orchestra.

From this point on, and into so-called classic and romantic periods, the vast body of work now called "standard repertoire" came into being. The standard chamber music ensembles of string quartet, wind quintet, brass quintet, wind trio, piano trio, and so forth can often be adapted for synthesizer ensemble. For the ambitious, concerti and other orchestral works can be adapted, although the complexity of such orchestral works usually means that synthesized realizations are studio rather than live productions. Even if the works are not intended for performance, playing through representative pieces in such an ensemble aids sight reading, knowledge of idiomatic instrumental writing, and understanding of style. The improvisation common in earlier works becomes very restricted in this period. Since this repertoire is so well known and accessible, I will not discuss it further here.

Twentieth-century works are another matter. A vast variety of forms for many specialist groupings of instruments has to a considerable degree supplemented the continuing writings of composers for ensemble groupings inherited from earlier periods. The variety of works here resists easy characterization, but many works can be realized satisfactorily for synthesizers. However, those that depend on extended instrumental techniques tend to be impractical if faithfulness to the sound world of the original is intended, as extensive preparatory sampling of the many different modes of sound production must be undertaken. Providing the requisite degree of real-time control nuance also becomes an involved programming exercise.

Below are listed a number of examples of repertoire readily adaptable to synthesizer orchestra, with typical numbers of performers required. It must be remembered that these are isolated examples from a vast array of possibilities. For a general survey of historical examples of the scores of Western music, the reader may consult Kamien (1990) and Palisca (1988).

Early Music

Anonymous. *De quan qu'on peut* (fourteenth century). Needed: three performers.

Gabrieli, Giovanni. *Canzoni e sonate* (1615). Pieces for any instrumentation, with variable numbers of voices. Number of voices, followed in parentheses by number of pieces for that number of parts, is as follows: four (1), five (1), six (3), seven (3), eight (6), ten (2), twelve (2), fourteen (1), fifteen (1), twenty-two (1). Recommended: two parts per player.

Gesualdo di Venosa. *Sacrae cantiones* (1603–) and *Responsoria* (1611). Six vocal parts. Needed: three to six players.

Marenzio, Luca. *O fere stelle* (1588). Needed: four to five players.

Matteo da Perugia. *Le greygnour bien* (late fourteenth century). Needed: three performers.

Baroque

Bach, Johann Sebastian. *Suite in B Minor* (late 1730s). Needed: five players.

Boccherini, Luigi. *Sinfonia concertante* (1771). 1st and 2nd Vln sections, Va section, Vc solo, Cb/Vc section. Needed: four performers.

Corelli, Arcangelo. *Trio Sonatas* (1681–1694). Needed: three performers.

Locke, Matthew. *Compositions for 2, 3, 4, 5, and 6 Parts* (1650–1665)—especially *Consort of Four Parts.* Needed: two to six players.

Vivaldi, Antonio. *The Four Seasons* (ca. 1725). Solo violin, 1st violins, 2nd violins, Va and Vc sections. Needed: four to five performers.

Classical and Romantic

Chamber and symphonic works (string quartets, quintets, and trios; woodwind quartets and quintets; trios and quartets for variable instrumentation) by Mozart, Haydn, Beethoven, Schumann, Schubert, Brahms, Liszt, Grieg, and many others are all possible here. Of special interest are:

Beethoven, Ludwig van. *Sextet* (1796). Op. 71. Two clarinets, two horns, two bassoons. Needed: three to six players; *Serenade* (1801) Op. 25. Flute, violin, viola. Needed: two to three players.

Brahms, Johannes. *String Quartet* (1873). Op 51, No. 2. Two violins, viola, cello. Needed: four players.

Haydn, Joseph. *String Quartets* Op. 74, 76, 77. (1797–1803). Needed: three to four players.

Mozart, Wolfgang Amadeus. *Quintet in A* (1789). KV 581. Clarinet, two violins, viola, cello. Needed: four to five players.

Twentieth Century

Barber, Samuel. *Capricorn Concerto* (1944). Flute, oboe, trumpet, strings. Needed: five to eight players.

Bartók, Béla. *String Quartet No. 4* (1928); *String Quartet No. 5* (1934). Needed: four players.

Berg, Alban. *Lyric Suite* (1927). String quartet. Needed: four players.

Copland, Aaron. *Fanfare for the Common Man* (1942). Four horns, three B♭ trumpets, two trombones, tuba, timpani, bass drum, tam-tam. Needed: three synthesizer performers and two percussionists.

Feldman, Morton. *Four Instruments* (1965). Violin, cello, chimes, piano. Needed: three to four players.

Françaix, Jean. *Quartet* (1971). Cor anglais, violin, viola, cello. Needed: three to four players.

Hába, Alois. *String Quartets* (1919–1967). Variously in quarter-, fifth- and sixth-tone systems. Needed: four players.

Hovhaness, Alan. *Six Dances for Brass Quintet* (1967). Two trumpets, horn, trombone, tuba. Needed: three to four performers.

Krenek, Ernst. *Serenade* (1919). Clarinet, violin, viola, cello. Needed: three to four players.

Leibowitz, René. *L'explication des métaphors* (1947). Harp, two pianos, percussion, soprano voice. Needed: three synthesizer performers, percussion (or synthesized percussion), and voice.

Ravel, Maurice. *String Quartet in F* (1910). Needed: four performers.

Reich, Steve. *Music for Pieces of Wood* (1973). Five pieces of wood. Needed: three to four performers. *Six Pianos* (1973). Needed: six players.

Stravinsky, Igor. *Pastorale* (1934). Violin and four winds. Needed: four to five performers.

Tippett, Michael. *Sonata for Four Horns* (1955). Needed: four performers.

Zinders, Earl. *Quintet for Brass.* Two trumpets, horn, trombone, tuba. Needed: four to five performers.

"Ethnic" Music Transitions

There is an enormous body of music in this category, but only a very small amount of it has been transcribed in the form of complete pieces in Western notation. Such a procedure has become unfashionable in some circles in ethnomusicology since it downgrades the importance of traditional notation systems that may exist in the indigenous culture and may misrepresent the tuning systems used. This is unfortunate for the keyboard synthesist, who is used to looking at keyboard parts as tablature anyway and can retune the instrument at the push of a button. Here are a few sources offering substantial excerpts or complete pieces in Western notation that can be attempted by the synthesizer orchestra.

Australia: Berndt and Phillips (1973), Moyle (1979).

Bali: Ornstein (1971), McPhee (1966)—notably including *Gending Pelugon* by I. Lotring (1926).

Thailand: Morton (1976).

India: Kaufmann (1968; 1976), Sorrell and Narayan (1980), Daniélou (1968), Wade (1979).

China: Numerous publications for ensembles and piano solo in Western notation can be found, published in China. Some of these are new works and some are transcriptions of traditional pieces into Western notation and for Western instruments. For example: Jiang and Yan (1987—for strings, flute, and mouth organ), Rong et al. (1979—for five stringed instruments). See also Picken (1981) for Tang Dynasty examples.

Mongolia: Haslund-Christensen (1971).

The Middle East: Nettl and Riddle (1974), Signell (1977), Zonis (1973).

Eastern Europe: Bartók (1931).

Africa: Jones (1959), Locke (1979). Numerous short transcriptions of drum patterns and melodies can be found in various articles in the journal *African Music.* For an example see Pressing (1983).

North American Indian: Bierhorst (1979).

Useful as survey sources of notated musical excerpts are Reck (1977) and May (1980) and the continuing series *Selected Reports in Ethnomusicology*, from UCLA, as well as the *Journal for Ethnomusicology.* Issues in performance practice of non-Western music are discussed in Béhague (1984).

Keyboard Adaptations

The solo repertoire, as well as that for four or more hands and two or more pianos, is a rich source. Some examples include:

Bach, Johann Sebastian. *Two and Three-Part Inventions* (1723). Needed: one to three performers. *The Well-Tempered Clavier* (vol. 1, 1722; vol. 2, 1738–1742). Needed: one to five performers.

Bartók, Béla. *Mikrokosmos.* Needed: one to two performers.

Brahms, Johannes. *Sonata for Two Pianos* (1864). Op. 34b. Needed: two to four players.

Ives, Charles. *Three Pieces for Quartertone Pianos* (1923–1924). Needed: two performers, at least one on eighty-eight-note keyboard.

Lutoslawski, Witold. *Miniatures for Two Pianos* (1979). Needed: two performers.

Schönberg, Arnold. *Sechs kleine Klavierstücke* (1911). Op. 19. Needed: one to three performers.

Stravinsky, Igor. *Le sacre du printemps* (The Rite of Spring), four-hand piano version (1913). Needed: two to four performers.

Vishnegradsky (Wyschnegradsky), Ivan. *24 Preludes in Quartertone System* (1934/1975). Needed: two performers.

Improvisation

Besides the many separate style-specific traditions of improvisation, free improvisation is an important context for synthesizer ensembles. It is usually best for each ensemble member to have a certain set of sounds in mind and know how to access them and control them in real time—all the while listening for potential relationships with other members of the group. Improvisation may also be based on novel graphic, text, or framework notations. Composers such as Pauline Oliveros, Karlheinz Stockhausen, Ken Gaburo, Larry Austin, Cornelius Cardew, Earle Brown, and others have played significant roles here. Sample works include (for any number of synthesizer players):

Feldman, Morton. *Intersection I* (1951). Orchestra.

Kagel, Mauricio. *Prima Vista* (1962/64). Slides and undefined sonic sources.

Stockhausen, Karlheinz. *For Times to Come* (1968). Any instruments (text piece). *Aus den sieben Tagen.* (1968). Any instruments (text piece).

The aural traditions here are primary, however. Collections of composed structures promoting free improvisation have been published (Ashley et al. 1972; Gaburo 1976; Byron 1976). A useful tutor in progressive techniques leading to free improvisation is Dean (1989).

DISCOGRAPHICAL SOURCES

Audio recordings of electronic music are extensive, rapidly developing, and stylistically very diverse, and this book does not contain a separate discography. However, a brief bibliography of discographical sources runs as follows.

The most comprehensive catalog of electronic music offerings as of this writing is Kondracki, Stankiewicz, and Weiland (1979), which contains over 2,000 entries. A useful highlight of sources up to the early 1970s that emphasizes avant-garde and art music developments may be found in Manning (1985). More broadly based stylistically is Ernst (1977), which covers up to the same period and is largely devoted to descriptions of specific pieces available on audio disk. Holmes's *Electronic and Experimental Music* (1985) is a useful but not error-free survey of historical developments, with an extensive annotated electronic discography that embraces both rock and avant-garde orientations. A broad survey of recent music that contains a number of sections germane to music synthesis is given by Schaefer (1987). Recordings specifically concerned with microtonality may be found in Wilkinson (1988).

PERFORMANCE PROBLEMS IN ELECTROACOUSTIC ENSEMBLES

When the synthesizer plays with other electric instruments, there is a ready potential for successful blend, based first on the similar colors of the sound sources, audio amplification, and processing, and, second, on the familiar association of these instruments in the widespread rock and popular music of our time. Synthesizers readily mix with other acoustic instruments in a rock, jazz, or popular ensemble for this second reason as well.

When, in contrast, the synthesizer plays with orchestral or unamplified instruments of a different sort, there can be problems with respect to both volume and audio processing. Dynamic range on acoustic instruments is more restricted than on amplified instruments, and it is incumbent on the synthesizer player to match the levels of the unamplified instrument. It is an unfair and unmusical plan to use superior volume to dominate the sound of the ensemble. Restraint and an ear for overall ensemble sound are the guiding principles.

Likewise, audio processing must be given special attention. If the ensemble is to sound unified, it must believably sound as though the members share the same sonic space. In practice this means that reverberation, often used fairly prominently with synthetic sounds to enrich the sound, may need to be reduced to promote blend with the rest of the ensemble. The degree of reduction will depend on the degree of ambient reverberation in the performance space. If there is quite a lot present naturally, it may be best to reduce the electronically generated component to near zero. If the room is very dry there will be a trade-off between adding warmth to the synthesized sounds and promoting blend. Another option might be to add reverberation electronically to the amplified acoustic instruments. Of course, these general guidelines may not pertain to some styles or musical purposes.

Spatial separation also enters into this equation. If the synthesizer has a part written with its spatial potentials in mind, then it may be dispersed in two, four, or even more speakers around the room. Panning effects can be developed and used compositionally with great effectiveness. If, on the other hand, the synthesizer is doubling for an instrument in a traditional ensemble, it may function better with single source localization, in so far as balance and group sound are concerned. In practice this means an amplifier and one speaker box.

In all-synthesizer ensembles, separate localization, either by panning in the mix or separate amplification and speaker systems for each performer or pair of performers, may be useful for several reasons. First of all, it will allow both listeners and performers alike to be sure who is playing what. This promotes audience involvement and also allows the performers to communicate with each other better than they otherwise could. Second, it gives an intrinsically different "sound" to each player, which promotes better hearing of the relation of parts. The practicalities of performance mean this option isn't always possible, but it can be imitated to some degree by putting different sound processing characteristics on different performers in a PA setup, and giving them different stereo images and depths of field. Such things must be fine-tuned in the performance space. Separate speakers for each performer can be very successfully used with performers distributed around the hall.

REFERENCES

Aebersold, J. *A New Approach to Jazz Improvisation*. New Albany, Ind.: Aebersold, 1975–.

Ashley, R., et al. *Scratch Anthology of Compositions*. London: Scratch Orchestra, 1972.

Bartók, Béla. *Hungarian Folk Music*. Westport, Conn.: Hyperion Press, 1931.

Béhague, Gerard. *Performance Practice: Ethnomusicological Perspectives*. Westport, Conn.: Greenwood Press, 1984.

Berndt, R., and E. S. Phillips. *The Australian Aboriginal Heritage*. Sydney: Ure Smith, 1973 (with corresponding records).

Bierhorst, John. *A Cry from the Earth*. New York: Four Winds Press, 1979.

Byron, M. *Pieces*. Vancouver, British Columbia: A.R.C. Publications, 1976.

Carapetyan, Armen (general editor) 1949. *Corpus Mensurabilis Musicae*. Various locations and separate volume editors (many volumes): American Institute of Musicology.

Coker, J. *Improvising Jazz*. Englewood Cliffs, N.J.: Prentice-Hall, 1964.

Daniélou, A. *The Ragas of Northern Indian Music*. London: Barrie Books, 1968.

Dean, Roger. *Creative Improvisation*. London: Open University Press, 1989.

Dobbins, Bill. *Jazz Arranging and Composing: A Linear Approach*. Rottenburg: Advance Music, 1986.

Ernst, David. *The Evolution of Electronic Music*. New York: Schirmer, 1977.

Ferand, Ernst. *Die improvisation in der Musik*. Zurich: Rhein-Verlag, 1938.

———. *Improvisation in Nine Centuries of Western Music*. Cologne: Arno Volk Verlag, Hans Gerig KG, 1961.

Gaburo, K. *Twenty Sensing Compositions*. La Jolla, Calif.: Lingua Press, 1976.

Giuffre, Jimmy. *Jazz Phrasing and Interpretation*. New York: Associated Music Publishers, 1969.

Haerle, D. *The Jazz Language*. Lebanon, Ind.: Studio P/R, 1980.

Haslund-Christensen, Henning. *The Music of the Mongols*. New York: Da Capo, 1971.

Holmes, Thomas. *Electronic and Experimental Music*. New York: Charles Scribner's Sons, 1985.

Jiang Yuan-Lu and Yan Zhu, compilers. *Zhong-guo Si-zhu Yue: Jiang-nan Si-zhu*. Part I. *Scores*. Beijing: The People's Music Publishing House, 1987.

Jones, A. M. *Studies in African Music*. London: Oxford University Press, 1959.

Kamien, R. *The Norton Scores: An Anthology for Listening*. New York: W. W. Norton & Co., 1990.

Kaufmann, W. *The Ragas of North India*. Bloomington: Indiana University Press, 1968.

———. *The Ragas of South India*. Bloomington: Indiana University Press, 1976.

Kernfeld, Barry, ed. *The Grove Dictionary of Jazz*. London: Macmillan and Co., 1988.

Kondracki, M., M. Stankiewicz, and F. Weiland. 1979. *Electronic Music Discography*. London and New York: Schott, 1979.

Locke, D. "The Music of Atsiabeko." Ph.D. diss. Wesleyan University, 1979.

McPhee, C. *Music in Bali*. New Haven: Yale University Press, 1966.

Manning, Peter. *Electronic and Computer Music*. Oxford: Clarendon Press, 1985.

May, Elizabeth, ed. *Musics of Many Cultures*. Berkeley and Los Angeles: University of California Press, 1980.

Morton, D. *The Traditional Music of Thailand*. Berkeley and Los Angeles: University of California Press, 1976.

Moyle, R. *Songs of the Pintupi*. Canberra: Australian Institute of Aboriginal Studies, 1979.

Mumma, G. "Live Electronic Music." In *The Development and Practice of Electronic Music,* eds. J. H. Appleton and R. C. Perera. Englewood Cliffs, N.J.: Prentice-Hall, 1975.

Nettl, B., and R. Riddle. "Taqsim Nahawand: A Study of 16 Performances by Jihad Racy." *Yearbook of the International Folk Music Council* 5 (1974): 11–50.

Ornstein, R. "Gamelan Gong Kebjar: The Development of a Balinese Musical Tradition." Ph.D. diss. UCLA, 1971. (With recordings on Lyrichord LLST 7179.)

Palisca, Claude, ed. *Norton Anthology of Western Music*. New York: W. W. Norton & Co., 1988.

Picken, L., ed. *Music from the Tang Court*. London: Oxford University Press, 1981.

Pressing, J. "Rhythmic Design in the Support Drums of Agbadza." *African Music* 6,3 (1983): 4–15.

———. "A History of Musical Improvisation to 1600." *Keyboard* 10,11 (November 1984a): 64–68.

———. "A History of Musical Improvisation: 1600–1900." *Keyboard* 10,12 (December 1984b): 59–67.

————. "Improvisation: Methods and Models." In *Generative Processes in Music,* ed. J. Sloboda. London: Oxford University Press, 1987.

Reck, David. *Music of the Whole Earth.* New York: Scribner, 1977.

Rong Zhai, et al. *Xian-suo Shi-san Tao.* Beijing: The People's Music Publishing House, 1979.

Schaefer, J. *New Sounds: A Listener's Guide to New Music.* New York: Harper and Row, 1987.

Schrader, Barry. *Introduction to Electro-Acoustic Music.* Englewood Cliffs, N.J.: Prentice-Hall, 1982.

Sher, C. *The World's Greatest Fake Book.* Petaluma, Calif.: Sher Music, 1983.

————. *The New Real Book.* Petaluma, Calif.: Sher Music, 1988.

Signell, Karl. *Makam: Modal Practice in Turkish Art Music.* Seattle: Asian Music Publications, 1977.

Sorrell, N., and R. Narayan. *Indian Music in Performance.* Manchester, UK: Manchester University Press, 1980.

Wade, B. *Music in India: The Classical Traditions.* Englewood Cliffs, N.J.: Prentice-Hall, 1979.

Wright, R. *Inside the Score.* Delevan, New York: Kendor, 1981.

Zonis, E. *Classical Persian Music.* Cambridge, Mass.: Harvard University Press, 1973.

INTELLIGENT AND INTERACTIVE PERFORMANCE SYSTEMS

There is only one condition in which we can imagine managers not needing subordinates, and masters not needing slaves. This condition would be that each inanimate instrument could do its own work, at the word of command or by intelligent anticipation, like the statues of Daedalus or the tripods made by Hephaestus, of which Homer relates that "of their own motion they entered the conclave of Gods on Olympus; as if a shuttle should weave of itself, and a plectrum should do its own harp playing."

▪ Aristotle, *The Politics* (ca. 350 B.C.)

In this final chapter we look at some conceptual extrapolations being carried on by music researchers that seem likely to play a large role in future developments in electronic music performance. The 1980s saw a remarkable growth of activity in what may be called "computer-based interactive music systems." These came about from the explosion of developments in MIDI, personal computers, and synthesis machines of all sorts. Compatible ideas from artificial intelligence research developed in parallel. As a result, the idea of performance has undergone considerable modification. The spectrum of musical activities with "fixed" composition and free improvisation as its two end points has become increasingly densely populated, including activities which have variously been termed "interactive composition" (Chadabe 1984), "composed improvisation" (Chabot, Dannenberg, and Bloch 1986), "extended instruments" (Pressing 1990), "intelligent instruments" (e.g., Polansky, Rosenboom, and Burk 1987), "hyperinstruments" (Tod Machover, personal communication), and "real-time performance synthesis" (David Mash, personal communication). By these terms is meant an arrangement of people, musical instruments, computers, synthesizers, and other hardware designed to produce music whose details are modified in real time by the interaction of distinct parts of the system. The different terms propose different points of view about the activities involved, and these will be explored below, but they typically have in common computers, synthesizers, and MIDI. The issues go beyond music, for MIDI is also being used to control light displays, produce robotic motion and animation, enable musical control by dancers, and many other functions.

In my opinion this will be an area of continuing development for the foreseeable future, and it therefore forms the focus of this last chapter. The approach we will take is to look at the relations between the cybernetics of such systems and the music they can produce. By cybernetics is meant the science of control and communication. Hence, we will be concerned with how different parts of such systems may control and send information to each other and what the musical strengths and limitations of various design choices will be.

AN ANALYTICAL AND HISTORICAL FRAMEWORK

To understand the development of interactive systems, we need to first look at their origins in traditional music making. We begin therefore by looking in detail at the human-instrument interface. Playing an instrument causes the transfer of spatial and temporal information from

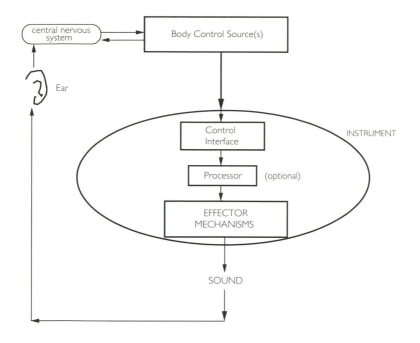

FIGURE 11.1   Cybernetic sketch of a person playing an instrument.

the central nervous system/mind to the system that physically produces the sound. Any such information transfer operates from within complex traditions of culture, musical design, and performance technique, and is shaped by human cognitive and motor capacities as well as personal experience.

A cybernetic sketch of the instrument-playing process is given in figure 11.1. In nearly all instruments, the information transfer from human to instrument depends upon its dynamic encoding in human movement. The parts of the instrument that are directly controlled or manipulated by parts of the body, and to which information is directly transferred, are called the *control interface*. The parts that actually produce the sound are called the *effector mechanism*. Intervening between the control interface and effector mechanism there is often some kind of processor that converts information in control format to effector format (yielding appropriate form, range, and sensitivity). The remaining parts of the instrument (the housing) have decorative or structural functions and most commonly relate to cybernetic issues only peripherally, through their aesthetic or historical associations.

To take an example, consider the piano. Here the directly controlling body parts are hands and feet, the control interface includes the keys and pedals, the processor is the piano action mechanisms, effector mechanisms are the strings and sounding board, and just about everything else is housing.

With such traditional instruments the only "intelligence" of the instrument is that provided by the instrument's designer(s) and builder(s). Since there is traditionally a nearly one-to-one correspondence between actions of the performer and resulting sound, a stimulus—response model fits well. Interaction between person and instrument takes place through the aural feedback loop indicated, but it is only the performer that makes decisions in real time. (This is not to minimize the tremendously sophisticated musical decisions that have been made by instrument makers and built into such instruments' playing mechanisms.)

In comparison, development of even the most sophisticated contemporary electronic instruments is at a comparatively rudimentary phase, and, as Michel Waiswicz has pointed out (Waiswicz 1985), the recent introduction of digital design of synthesizers, with its single editing input device, has in some ways decreased their overall real-time controllability relative to the one knob/one function editing of older analog machines. In compensation, digital electronic design can allow much easier reconfiguration and upgrading of instruments. It can also make more practical the type of interaction and instrument intelligence that is the focus of this chapter. And some digital synthesizers have appeared in the early 1990s that herald a return to one knob/one function design.

But such things are also not without precedent in the worlds of acoustic instruments and analog electronics (Davies 1984a, 1984b; Mumma 1975). Two other performance conceptions besides the traditional "person physically manipulating an instrument" illustrate this. The first of these different conceptualizations relies on using information from the human body not produced by voluntary physical movement; that is, it is either traditionally considered to be involuntary or it doesn't directly involve motion in space. This information is monitored, amplified and/or transduced to be used either as a sound source or a control source for sound production. Examples of the first usage are Pauline Oliveros's *Valentine* (1968) or Merce Cunningham's *Loops* (1971), which are based on the amplified heartbeat. The second usage has most commonly been based on brainwaves (EEG) or myoelectric signals from muscles (EMG). Alvin Lucier's *Music for Solo Performer* (1965), David Rosenboom's *Ecology of the Skin* (1970) and later suggestions (Polansky, Rosenboom, and Burk 1987), and electronic devices in pieces by Richard Teitelbaum have explored brainwave control. Myoelectric control has been outlined, for example, by Gillett, Smith, and Pritchard (1985).

The second type of novel performance model occurs when the human operator directly shapes some external ongoing process (naturally occurring or designed) that is being concurrently amplified or transduced to function as, again, either a sound source or a control source (sometimes the human operator shapes the *effects* of an ongoing process). Shaping can consist of turning on and off, filtering, or using various types of parametric control; a familiar example is the operation of a mixing console at a live concert.

This second type of control is actually very ancient since it includes some of what is usually called sound sculpture, which almost certainly dates to prehistoric times. Some water clocks and musical fountains also belong to this tradition. Yet most such sound sculptures are not people-powered and hence not directly relevant here. However, some sound scultpure *is* meant for human interaction, such as the foot pressure-activated carpet of Horst Gläsker's *Tret-Orgel-Teppich-Objekt,* or Stanley Lunetta's *Moosack Machine* (sensitive to light, temperature, and proximity), or some of Michel Waisvisz's sound machines. Outside of the confines of the term *sound sculpture,* more exotic information sources, sometimes relying on relatively sophisticated scientific sensing devices, have been used. These include electronic disturbances in the ionosphere (Alvin Lucier's *Whistlers,* 1966), the earth's magnetic field, vibrations in the earth, and pulsars (Annea Lockwood's *World Rhythms,* 1975), the radio (John Cage's *Imaginary Landscape No. 4,* 1951), a Geiger counter (Cage's *Variations VII,* 1966), incoming telephone calls to a radio station (Max Neuhaus's *Public Supply,* 1966), voltages from plants (Ed Barnett, Norman Lederman, and Gary Burke's *Stereofernic Orchidstra*), and so forth. Technological developments in the field of interactive multimedia increasingly allow profitable compositional and improvisational interaction between dancers, poets, video artists, dancers, performance artists, and musicians.

These unusual performance models often have strong elements of unpredictability, where musical production is controlled to a considerable degree by neither performer nor composer. The listener is left in some cases to provide the sense of the resultant sounds, without reference to any tradition.

CYBERNETICS OF THE CONTROL INTERFACE

We return now to the traditional instrument design of figure 11.1 and focus on the issues involved in the control interface of the instrument. The performer's body parts interact with the control interface, and information is passed on for further processing. It is not possible to completely disengage this part of the control chain from subsequent parts since an aural feedback loop controls the entire system. But it is possible to list some fundamental issues that must be addressed by anyone designing an interface for human interaction. We consider here the following ten fundamental issues:

1. physical variables carrying the information, as a function of time—position, force (pressure), acceleration, velocity, area (shape)

2. dimensionality of control (degrees of freedom)—one-dimensional, two-dimensional, three-dimensional or greater; strong/weak dimensions

3. multiplicity of control—how many parallel streams of independent information (e.g., musical lines) can be sent simultaneously from a specific controller?

4. Control modality—discrete, continuous, or quantized continuous (meaning that the control interface is physically continuous but it dispatches only a noticeably limited set of discrete values)

5. Control monitoring—one-shot or continuous time; hold last value or return to nominal value; skips out of the continuum possible or continuous output only

6. control distance function—monotonic, nonmonotonic, partially redundant; uni/bipolar

7. literalness of control—one-to-one = WYPIWYG (what you play is what you get), one-to-many, many-to-one, unpredictability (stochastic, chaotic), response delay, time dependence

8. historical foundations—using an existing technique, modifying an existing technique, or creating a new technique

9. design appropriateness—design efficiency, ergonomics, motor and cognitive loads, degree of sensory reinforcement and redundancy, appropriateness of gestures to expression

10. psychological nature of control—perceived naturalness of the link between action and sound response; reflexive—creative continuum; exploratory or goal-oriented

For reasons of space the issues will be explored selectively, initially by looking at two well-known examples.

Consider the violin played arco, issue by issue. The physical variables carrying information are primarily downward bow force (coding for dynamics), horizontal bow velocity (primarily affecting timbre), bow distance from the bridge (affecting timbre), and finger position on the fingerboard (coding for pitch). Hence, there are three or four control dimensions (an alternative term is degrees of freedom) in total for a single melodic line. Control multiplicity is two (in the hands of a first-rate player, two independent lines are possible). Control modality (the spatial nature of control) is continuous, as is control monitoring (this means continuous time readout of what the performer is doing). The distance function is partially redundant (this last term means that each string when stopped is a monotonic pitch controller, but there is more than one place to find each note). Control is traditionally highly literal on the violin, given good technique, with the exceptions of certain types of extended techniques, such as bowing sul ponticello (actually on the bridge) or on the tailpiece. Otherwise, what you play is what you get (WYPIWYG).

The origin of the technique used for the violin was clearly based on existing techniques on previous instruments like the viols (issue 8). Of the design appropriateness of the violin for expressive sound production there can be little doubt (issue 9). Visual feedback of position is clearly quite adequate for the musicality of a seasoned professional; but it is far less than that available on fretted string instruments. The violin's ergonomics can certainly be called into question, as many violinists with stiff necks will readily testify. The violin is seemingly well designed gesturally and can be used profitably with either an exploratory or goal-oriented performance attitude, as can most traditional instruments (issue 10).

We next examine the current crop of synthesizers and synthesizer controllers, which form the essential sound production and control components of nearly all intelligent music systems. Most keyboard synthesizers basically allow two control dimensions per voice (key number, key velocity) plus channel pressure, for a possible total of $2 \times 3 + 1 = 7$ dimensions, if we somewhat arbitrarily say that a performer's two hands at the keyboard can play three parts with complete independence. (This figure obviously can vary with performer and is musically context-dependent; it seems a best compromise value for the rough calculations involved here.) If we add in controller effects (two foot controllers and one breath controller), the number rises to ten.

Keyboards (and other controllers) with polyphonic aftertouch have potential for greater control. Taking three as the nominal number of independent parts, this can yield up to ten dimensions of control from the keyboard alone, a potential that is only currently being explored. If ancillary controllers can be used simultaneously, as in the case of foot and breath controllers, then an additional three dimensions are possible, for a total of thirteen. Specialist keyboard devices (extended instruments) with extra controls can produce up to six dimensions of control per note, as discussed in chapter 6. With three independent note streams and two foot pedal controllers these devices would allow $6 \times 3 + 2 = 20$ dimensions of simultaneous control. That's a lot to think about.

Given these examples let us consider issues 7–10 above more fully. Just what are the optimal ergonomic, philosophical, and psychological principles of electronic instrument design? An attempt to answer this question comprehensively would lead us too far afield, but it is useful to look at a few points of reference.

The desirability of literalness of control is an implicit or explicit design principle in the instruments of every known musical culture. Exceptions are extremely rare until twentieth-century Western culture and are even so a question of degree only (as in some rough-hewn folk instruments like the gut bucket bass). Yet literalness is in another sense more an attitude to music than an absolute factor in musical design, since such unpredictable effects can be readily achieved on all traditional orchestral instruments: col legno or sul ponticello strings, woodwind multiphonics and reed biting, the properly prepared piano, and so on. Electronic instruments can also function this way, by overloading, feedback, or pathological choices of parameter values, as in the "mistreated" oscillator circuits used in compositions by Louis and Bebe Barron since the early 1950s, or Michel Waiswicz's Crackle Box. But I have seen such effects achieved most readily with either lo-tech mechanical or electromechanical conglomerations or extended string instruments, for example, the stringed sound devices of Jon Rose, where multiple and movable bridges (and bizarrely constructed single and multiple bows) mean that the instrument is really continuously evolving under one's hands during performance so that technique must be continuously updated during playing—a joyfully risky form of improvisation at its best.

Another way to look at these issues is from the perspective of transformation of gesture. People act (perform) expressively by way of gesture, by which I mean the integrated production of motion shapes, characterized by parametric control. Cadoz (1988) has discussed these issues with regard to MIDI systems, pointing to a classification of gesture into modulation (parametric or sound object shaping control), selection (picking from a range of discrete values), or exciter (putting energy into the system, e.g., with a violin bow) gestures. Gibet and Florens (1988) have modeled gesture using simple mechanical systems. Azzolini and Sapir (1984) used a gestural system for real-time control of the Digital Processor 4I. Other gestural descriptions can be based on associative kinetic images like *scrape, slide, ruffle, crunch, glide, caress,* and so forth, as used in modern dance instruction. Such ideas have been implemented by some dancers by the use of special costumes or body position monitoring effects (e.g. Gillett, Smith, and Pritchard 1985). Other workers have focused on the idea of a spatial *trajectory.* What is clear is that gesture is a multifaceted phenomenon whose nature is shaped by what it is routed to control.

An Imaginary Superinstrument

The question can also be asked, just how much control is humanly possible? The limitations in principle are apparently both motoric and cognitive. To frame an answer to this we perform a Gedanken experiment by building an imaginary superinstrument. We quantify the control issues in a very rough way by using our idea of dimensionality, with the underlying possibility that an active dimension of control requires something like an active channel of attention or considerable focused preparatory rehearsal to diminish the real-time cognitive load (Pressing 1984). This supposition has its limitations, but it should do for our purposes here.

Discrete switches with a few states will be disregarded in this calculation in comparison to continuous variables or switches with many states (*many* meaning at least a dozen or so—e.g., woodwind fingerings or the keyboard). But one needs also to consider how much sound modification is expressible in the dimension in question. If this is intrinsically limited, either by the nature of the mapping to sound or by the limited resolution of the dimension, we will label that a *weak* control dimension. In making such an evaluation, it is necessary to look at the entire chain of control. For example, one-shot monitored dimensions are often weaker than those based on continuous time. Yet perceptual factors can work against this tendency, notably with regard to the attack portion of envelopes (typically controllable by key velocity directly, or indirectly via the layering of sounds, a one-shot monitoring protocol), which has disproportionate influence over perceived timbre relative to steady-state sound (typically controlled by continuous time monitoring).

As we saw earlier, monophonic traditional instruments have something like two to four dimensions of control, with one of them possibly weak; polyphonic instruments have two to three per independent voice. A historical survey of a wide variety of traditional musical instruments is consistent with this. It is also true of a majority of contemporary instruments based on synthesis.

To see what might be possible, we first note that it is a physical fact that each controlling body part could in principle code six dimensions (three of position, three of orientation). Of course these dimensions are all usable only if each such body part has complete independence, which, for example, the fingers obviously lack. But since traditional instruments have two or three major controlling body parts, twelve to eighteen dimensions total are readily available in principle under this simple design. But let us carry this further. Of what might an imaginary superinstrument be capable?

We may try to estimate the dimensionality of control possible for human beings as follows: Accepting hands as the most sensitive controllers, and focusing on traditional physical variables, we assume that each finger of each hand could in principle act independently (against an external reference frame) over two dimensions of position and a third dimension of pressure, as could each foot; breath pressure could provide one additional control, and perhaps positions of the knees could add one or two dimensions. Hence there is no reason that $(10 + 2) \times 3 + 1 + 2 = 39$ independent dimensions of control could not operate simultaneously, on purely physical grounds. However, as suggested above, all existing forms of music performance (and similarly for dance and sport) use so much less than this capacity that there must be a strong suspicion that cognitive limitations impose far more restrictions than motor control limitations.

A discussion of the cognitive limitations that pertain to performers would be pertinent here, but it would take us too far from our central concerns. The issues are very similar to those encountered in the cognitive modeling of improvisation, and these have been discussed in depth in two recent publications (Pressing 1984; 1988b).

We turn next to a discussion of the implications, illustrating with generic examples, of the concepts of interactive and intelligent instruments.

Interactive and Intelligent Instruments

Interaction means mutual influence. Since there can be no doubt that performers influence instruments, we define an interactive instrument as one that directly and variably influences the production of music by a performer. By "directly" we mean other than through the performer's normal listening process; by "variably" we mean that the instrument's effects on the performer are programmable. In practice this most commonly means that the instrument is acting "intelligently"; conversely, intelligent instruments are nearly always interactive.

We therefore focus on the concept of intelligent instruments, considering the fundamental process to be an interaction between two or more "agents." By agent we mean anything capable of displaying intelligence in the control of music production. This can be a person, non-human living thing, computer program, robot, sequencer, hardware device, or invoked process (naturally occurring or designed). Of course, defining what is meant by intelligence is no simple task, and space does not allow a thorough discussion here. But its crucial components, in this context, seem to be real-time decision making and flexibility of response.

The simplest intelligent music system setup is one with two agents, occurring most commonly where one agent is a human performer and the other is the intelligent instrument. (Larger setups can be readily generalized from this basic case.) A schematic representation of a basic two-agent interactive music system is given in figure 11.2.

In simple terms, sound (S) and performance data (R or T) are produced by the two agents. The agents' choices are shaped by previous output and by a variety of operating constraints including cognitive and motoric limitations, stylistic and formal adherences (score, referent, plan), knowledge of interpretive traditions, and other constraints. The performance data they produce are of two types: Representation (R) and Transformation (T). Representation data describe or represent the musical output of an agent. Transformation data are data produced by one agent and are designed to affect the output of other agents. These are the data that make the system interactive. Sound is either produced directly by manipulation of a musical instrument or with the aid of an intermediary representational form, using some kind of control device. This intermediary representation is most commonly MIDI code, but traditional music notation, computer graphic displays, Music N type event lists and spectral display schemes, as well as the possibilities of integrated multimedia can also be used. The reverse procedure also happens, as indicated in the figure: representations are produced by directly converting sound from the instrument, most commonly via pitch-to-MIDI or amplitude/spectrum-to-control-voltage converters.

The essential interaction process involves transformation data from one agent affecting the output of another agent. The transformation data operate either directly on the sound (via real-time controllable audio processing devices) or on its representation (most commonly via MIDI-based processors). This means that MIDI is the dominant means of control used since there is a strong recent tendency for audio processors and mixers to be MIDI-driven. Work not based on MIDI includes Gordon Mumma's Cybersonic Consoles (Mumma 1975), older "analog" systems with plentiful knob-twiddling possibilities, existing devices using a QWERTY keyboard for real-time input (e.g., the DMX-1000 DSP; cf. Truax 1984), and Morton Subotnick's Ghost Boxes (a series of real-time controllable audio processors). Advances in computer networking and integrated multimedia workstations seem likely to considerably expand the field of possibilities.

A particular configuration of connections, instruments, computers, and processing devices functioning interactively will call for appropriately de- and re-fined technique from the human performer(s). "The problems . . . are those of defining a compositional algorithm and deciding which of its variables are best controlled by a performer and with what device" (Chadabe 1984, p. 26).

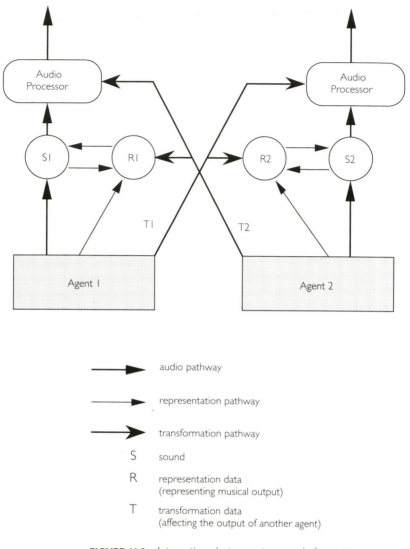

FIGURE 11.2   Interactions between two musical agents.

CYBERNETICS OF INTELLIGENT MIDI SYSTEMS

The idea of instrumental intelligence raises new cybernetic issues that go beyond those raised earlier. This section will survey and discuss these issues and then give generic examples. For a look at specific, practical approaches used by a number of current workers in this field the reader is directed to Roads (1986), Logemann (1987), and Pressing (1988c).

We look at six cybernetic issues, each of which is either unique to intelligent instruments or qualitatively different when applied to them. Each issue is phrased as one or more questions about the nature of the transformations used by one agent to affect another:

1. *Range of operation:* Does the transformation operate on each sent message alone or on groups of messages? Can data bytes of different messages be combined?

The simplest and most common computer transformation effects are those also achievable by MIDI mapping devices, as discussed in chapter 6—single messages can be converted into different single messages. But there is plenty of scope for development. More intelligent environments can consider groups of messages and hence musical issues that operate over longer time spans than that of the single message.

It is impossible to be exhaustive with regard to possible group message transformations, but if we limit our attention to Note On messages, by way of example, typical possibilities can be sketched. In general, a parsing (segmenting) control is needed to define the messages belonging to the group to be transformed. Typical operations on such a group include: permutation of notes; changing notes of the group with specific order numbers; arpeggiation through different octaves; selected transposition or copying and pasting of a subset; time reversal; deleting or adding material; delaying specific notes in the set; various mathematical reordering processes; and "convolution" (e.g., interleaving) with stored material.

2. *Functional conversion:* Is the MIDI status byte (message type) preserved under the transformation or not?

This issue also exists for extended and reconfigured instruments, as discussed earlier. But commercial hardware units have inevitable limitations in scope and versatility in comparison to software-based intelligent instrument environments. Notably, extensive system exclusive synthesis parameter editing can be programmed for direct real-time access from the control interface.

3. *Use of precomposed materials and processes:* Does the transformation incorporate other precomposed or prerecorded material or processes or not? Are the stored musical materials algorithmically defined or entered in by previous or concurrent performance?

There are many ways such ideas can be used. One generic approach calls up stored motives or samples—riffs—on the basis of chosen MIDI note(s), key velocity, controller values, QWERTY keyboard or mouse actions, or combinations of such variables. This is a generalization of the idea of attachment described in chapter 6. The same method can be used to call up stored processes that transform the musical inputs. Another approach uses such variables for real-time control by affecting parameters controlling the stored material. Such parameters include tempo, timbre, envelopes, note velocity, starting point, note density and note order. Some of these features are available in commercial intelligent music software.

Still another approach enables the convolution of played data with stored data, depending on controllable or preprogrammed criteria. In all such approaches, a fundamental distinction for the performer is whether stored materials are entered in prior to or at the time of performance. The first approach tends to create more long-term order, the second more immediacy. Even the most basic storage device, the simple digital delay unit, can produce some powerful effects when configured for sufficiently sophisticated real-time control. Overall, the musical treatment of material here often yields results like motivic liquidation (in the sense of Schönberg) or the production of sonic mosaics.

Where the player is improvising, there can be a qualitative difference between the situations where he or she chooses from among a small number of motives or data lists and situations where many (greater than a dozen or so) motives or lists are involved. This is because most control interfaces except pitch selection interfaces and ribbons have insufficient visual reinforcement to allow individual lists to be called up reliably in the second case. Unless these particular interfaces are used for the selection of stored material, certainty about output diminishes, and from the performer's perspective we approach a situation of unpredictability.

4. *Time independence:* Does the nature of the transformation change from moment to moment, or is it fixed?

Time independence is characteristic of all traditional instruments as well as extended and reconfigured ones. The potentials of time dependence remain relatively undeveloped even with today's intelligent instruments. This is probably because time dependent control poses some difficult (though hardly insurmountable) problems for the performer if the changes in transformation are frequent and substantial, problems such as accurate timing, memory requirements, and conceptualization.

In terms of musical effect, the character of the time dependence is critical. If changes are sudden, the effect will tend to be one of introducing sharp formal boundaries in the music—that is, sectionalization. If changes are gradual, the performer can hear the transformational shifts gradually and adapt, often without the need for extensive rehearsal. This situation can be used to good effect by the improvising performer.

5. *Unpredictability:* Does the transformation contain elements of unpredictability or not?

Unpredictability is not without precedent in conventional acoustic and electronic instruments, but it can be much more powerfully explored within the intelligent instrument framework. Most commonly, unpredictability comes from tapping explicit random processes (designed or naturally occurring), erratic control interface or synthesis engine design, unrememberable complexity, rapid and complex changes in processing by another agent, or interprocess competition between equally matched protagonists. To the performer the source is largely irrelevant. Unpredictability favors the production of music that is more statistical, and less focused or goal-oriented, than that provided by traditional musical development techniques.

6. *Design flexibility:* Is the setup primarily hard-wired, or does it provide a readily reprogrammable environment for refining the control relations in dialogue with musical outcome?

Clearly, only software-based instruments can offer a high degree of flexibility of design. Particularly powerful in this regard is the idea of a multifunctional environment allowing both instrument design and the interaction of definable musically intelligent agents.

SPECIFIC NEW DIRECTIONS

Certain approaches to intelligent music environments have now become generic. These may be illustrated by the following cases.

Variation generators: Here the computer (agent) takes dictation from live instrumental performance and spits back variations. Stochastic or highly nonlinear sources may be used (Pressing 1988a) as well as the explicit programming of the traditional procedures of musical development.

The synthetic accompanist: The computer takes dictation, as above, but produces an algorithmic accompaniment rather than, or as well as, composing variations on the dictated material. This concept has also been used to create a synthetic accompanist that plays a fully notated piece by following the sonic (or MIDI) leadership of the live performer in such matters as tempo and dynamics (e.g., Vercoe and Puckette 1985).

The computer as musical director: Here the computer monitors information put out by the performer(s) and other parts of the system and applies tests, which are used to decide whether to invoke interruptions to ongoing processes, change data transformations, infer the existence of errors and correct them, issue commands to performers, and perform other tasks.

Multifunctional environments: This is where one or more computers and software environments allow instruments to be defined, interactive musically intelligent agents to be created, and a host of additional features that come from generalizations of familiar musical processes and current ideas in artificial intelligence (e.g., learning, parallel processing, neural nets) to be realized. Notable examples of this approach include Lee Boynton's preFORM, HMSL (Hierarchical Music Programming Language; Polansky, Rosenboom, and Burk 1987), and Miller Puckette's and David Zicarelli's Max (Opcode). See Rowe (1992) for a fuller discussion and examples.

Multimedia ensembles: Several streams of work have converged to expand the potential of interactive multimedia ensembles in recent years. The conversion of information between different media has become steadily more sophisticated (e.g., the video-to-MIDI converter, sound-producing costumes, integrated multimedia software such as Max, desktop video, MIDI Show Control). The developments of performance art and nascent virtual reality technology have raised broader aesthetic and practical issues. This has made it possible for practitioners of different art forms to perform with a more intimate sense of communication. On the one hand, musical interfaces can be used in the performance of nonmusical art: For example, MIDI controller performance may be routed to control the shapes and colors of projected visual figures, or may select words from a chosen text that are then read by a narrator, projected on a screen, spoken by robotic voice, and used as an instruction set for dancers. On the other hand, the control and generation of musical statements may be configured to originate from the physical gestures of dancers, drawn shapes, spoken text, and so forth.

THE FUTURE

The procedures here show a tremendous potential. The main hope is for powerful new ways and means of expression; the main danger, that technique outraces musicality. The most profitable path for development may be when the intelligent instrument makers continuously refine their work in consultation with virtuoso performers, particularly those skilled in the many varieties of contemporary improvisation and performance art.

REFERENCES

Azzolini, F., and S. Sapir. "Score and/or Gesture—the System RTI4I for RealTime Control of the Digital Processor 4I." In *Proceedings of the 1984 International Computer Music Conference,* ed., W. Buxton. San Francisco: Computer Music Association, 1984.

Cadoz, C. "Instrumental Gesture and Composition." In *Proceedings of the 1988 International Computer Music Conference,* eds., C. Lischka and J. Fritsch. Köln: Feedback Studio Verlag, 1988.

Chabot, X., R. Dannenberg, and G. Bloch. "A Workstation in Live Performance: Composed Improvisation." In *Proceedings of the 1986 International Computer Music Conference,* ed., P. Berg. San Francisco: Computer Music Association, 1986.

Chadabe, J. "Interactive Composing: An Overview." *Computer Music Journal* 8,1 (Spring 1984): 22–27.

Davies, H. "Sound Sculpture." In *The New Grove Dictionary of Musical Instruments,* ed. Stanley Sadie. London: Macmillan and Co., 1984a.

———. "Electronic Instruments." In *The New Grove Dictionary of Musical Instruments,* ed. Stanley Sadie. London: Macmillan and Co., 1984b.

Gibet, S., and J.-L. Florens. "Instrumental Gesture Modeling by Identification with Time-Varying Mechanical Models." In *Proceedings of the 1988 International Computer Music Conference,* eds., C. Lischka and J. Fritsch. Köln: Feedback Studio Verlag, 1988.

Gillett, R., K. C. Smith, B. Pritchard. "MADDM—Dance-directed Music." In *Proceedings of the 1985 International Computer Music Conference,* ed., B. Truax. San Francisco: Computer Music Association, 1985.

Logemann, G. W. "Report on the Last STEIM Symposium on Interactive Composing in Live Electronic Music." *Computer Music Journal* 11,3 (Winter 1987): 44–47.

Mumma, G. "Live Electronic Music." In *The Development and Practice of Electronic Music,* eds., J. H. Appleton and R. C. Perera. Englewood Cliffs, N.J.: Prentice-Hall, 1975.

Polansky, L., D. Rosenboom, P. Burk, "HMSL: Overview (Version 3.1) and Notes on Intelligent Instrument Design." In *Proceedings of the 1987 International Computer Music Conference,* ed. J. Beauchamp, San Francisco: Computer Music Association, 1987.

Pressing, J. "Cognitive Processes in Improvisation." In *Cognitive Processes in the Perception of Art,* eds. W. R. Crozier and A. J. Chapman. Amsterdam: North Holland, 1984.

————. "Nonlinear Maps as Generators of Musical Design." *Computer Music Journal* 12,2 (Summer 1988a): 35–46.

————. "Improvisation: Methods and Models." In *Generative Processes in Music* ed. J. Sloboda. Oxford: Clarendon Press, 1988b.

————. "Cybernetic Issues in Interactive Performance Systems." *Computer Music Journal* 14,1 (Spring 1990): 12–25.

Roads, C. "The Second STEIM Symposium on Interactive Composition in Live Electronic Music." *Computer Music Journal* 10,2 (Summer 1986): 44–50.

Rowe, Robert. *Interactive Music Systems.* Cambridge, Mass.: MIT Press, 1992.

Truax, B. "Models of Interactive Composition with the DMX-1000 Digital Signal Processor." In *Proceedings of the 1984 International Computer Music Conference,* ed., W. Buxton. San Francisco: Computer Music Association, 1984.

Vercoe, B., and M. Puckette. "Synthetic Rehearsal: Training the Synthetic Performer." In *Proceedings of the 1985 International Computer Music Conference,* ed., B. Truax. San Francisco: Computer Music Association, 1985.

Waiswicz, M. "THE HANDS: A Set of Remote MIDI Controllers." In *Proceedings of the 1985 International Computer Music Conference,* ed., B. Truax. San Francisco: Computer Music Association, 1985.

GENERAL
BIBLIOGRAPHY

. . . .

Included here are selected major references and sources pertaining to electronic music theory, performance, production, and composition. They are grouped under the following categories:

Acoustics and Audio Techniques

Bibliographies and Discographies

Composition and Conceptual Issues

Computer Music

Electronic Music

MIDI

Psychoacoustics

Signal Processing

Synthesizers, Samplers, and MIDI Devices

Tuning and Temperament

In addition, relevant periodicals are listed at the end in a separate category, followed by a few useful addresses. References at the ends of chapters are not included here if they are not of general relevance.

ACOUSTICS AND AUDIO TECHNIQUES

Anderton, Craig. *The Digital Delay Handbook.* New York: American Music Sales Corp, 1990.

Benade, Arthur H. *Fundamentals of Musical Acoustics.* New York: Oxford University Press, 1976.

Beranek, L. *Acoustics.* New York: American Institute of Physics, 1986.

Campbell, Murray, and Clive Greated. *The Musician's Guide to Acoustics.* London: J.M. Dent and Sons, 1987.

Chamberlin, Hal. *Musical Applications of Microprocessors.* Indianapolis, Ind.: Hayden Books, 1985.

Hall, Donald E. *Musical Acoustics.* Belmont, Calif.: Wadsworth Publishing Co., 1980.

Helmholtz, Hermann von. *On the Sensations of Tone.* 1885. Reprint New York: Dover, 1954.

Olson, Harry H. *Music, Physics, and Engineering.* New York: Dover Publications, 1967.

Pierce, John. *The Science of Musical Sound.* New York: Scientific American Books, 1985.

Pohlmann, Ken. *Principles of Digital Audio.* White Plains, N.Y.: Knowledge Industry Publications, 1989.

Rossing, T.D. *The Science of Sound.* New York: Addison-Wesley, 1990.

Strong, William J., and George R. Plitnick. *Music, Speech and High Fidelity.* Provo, Utah: Brigham Young University Press, 1977.

Watkinson, John. *The Art of Digital Audio.* Stoneham, Mass.: Focal Press, 1988.

BIBLIOGRAPHIES AND DISCOGRAPHIES

Battier, Marc. *Musique et informatique: une bibliographie indexee.* Ivry-sur-Seine (France): Elmeratto, Centre National de la Recherche Scientifique, 1978.

Davis, Deta S. *Computer Applications in Music: A Bibliography.* Vol. 4, The Computer Music and Digital Audio Series. Madison, Wisc.: A-R Editions, Inc., 1988.

Kondracki, M., M. Stankiewicz, and F. Weiland. *Electronic Music Discography.* London and New York: Schott, 1979.

Tjepkema, Sandra. *A Bibliography of Computer Music.* Iowa City: University of Iowa Press, 1981.

COMPOSITION AND CONCEPTUAL ISSUES

Busoni, Ferruccio. *Sketch of a New Aesthetic of Music.* New York: Dover, 1987. (Originally published in 1907.)

Cage, John. *Silence.* Middleton, Conn: Wesleyan University Press, 1961.

Dodge, Charles, and Thomas A. Jerse. *Computer Music.* New York: Schirmer Books, 1985.

Emmerson, Simon. *The Language of Electroacoustic Music.* London: Macmillan and Co., 1986.

Erickson, Robert. *Sound Structure in Music.* Berkeley and Los Angeles: University of California Press, 1975.

Heifetz, Robin. *On the Wires of Our Nerves: The Art of Electronic Music.* Cranbury, N.J.: Bucknell Press, 1989.

Hiller, Lejaren. "Music Composed with Computers: An Historical Survey." In *The Computer and Music,* ed. Harry B. Lincoln. Ithaca, N.Y.: Cornell University Press, 1970.

Moore, F. Richard. *Elements of Computer Music.* Englewood Cliffs, N.J.: Prentice-Hall, 1990.

Nyman, Michael. *Experimental Music: Cage and Beyond.* London: Schirmer Books, 1974.

Russolo, Luigi. *The Art of Noise,* trans. Robert Filliou. New York: Something Else Press, 1967. (Originally published in 1913.)

Schaeffer, P. *À la recherche d'une musique concrète.* Paris: Éditions du Seuil, 1952.

———. *Traité des objets musicaux.* Paris: Éditions du Seuil, 1966.

Slawson, Wayne. *Sound Color.* Berkeley and Los Angeles: University of California Press, 1985.

Sloboda, J. *The Musical Mind.* Oxford: Oxford University Press, 1985.

Sloboda, J., ed. *Generative Processes in Music.* Oxford: Clarendon Press, 1988.

Truax, B., ed. *Handbook for Acoustic Ecology.* Vancouver, British Columbia: ARC Publications, 1978.

Xenakis, I. *Formalized Music.* Bloomington: Indiana University Press, 1971.

———. *Arts-Sciences: Alloys.* New York: Pendragon, 1985.

COMPUTER MUSIC

Bateman, Wayne A. *Introduction to Computer Music*. New York: John Wiley and Sons, 1980.

Bigelow, Steven. *Making Music with Personal Computers*. La Jolla, Calif.: Park Row Press, 1987.

De Furia, S., and J. Scacciaferro. *MIDI Programming for the Macintosh*. Redwood City, Calif.: M & T Books, 1988.

Dodge, Charles, and Thomas A. Jerse. *Computer Music*. New York: Schirmer Books, 1985.

Enders, Bernd, and Wolfgang Klemme. *MIDI and Sound Book for the Atari ST*. Redwood City, Calif.: M & T Books, 1989.

Mathews, Max. *The Technology of Computer Music*. Cambridge, Mass.: MIT Press, 1969.

Mathews, Max, and John Pierce, eds. *Current Directions in Computer Music Research*. Cambridge, Mass.: MIT Press, 1990.

Moore, F. Richard. *Elements of Computer Music*. Englewood Cliffs, N.J.: Prentice-Hall, 1990.

Risset, Jean-C. *An Introductory Catalog of Computer Synthesized Sounds*. Murray Hill, N.J.: Bell Telephone Laboratories, 1970.

Roads, Curtis, ed. *Composers and the Computer*. Vol. 2, The Computer Music and Digital Audio Series. Madison, Wisc.: A-R Editions, Inc., 1985. (Originally published Los Altos, Calif.: William Kaufmann.)

Roads, Curtis, and John Strawn, eds. *Foundations of Computer Music*. Cambridge, Mass.: MIT Press, 1985.

——. *Computer Music Tutorial*. Cambridge, Mass: MIT Press, 1984.

Yelton, G. *Music and the Macintosh*. Atlanta, Ga.: MIDI America Inc, 1989.

ELECTRONIC MUSIC

Appleton, Jon, and Ronald Perera, eds. *The Development and Practice of Electronic Music*. Englewood Cliffs, N.J.: Prentice-Hall, 1975.

Darter, T., comp. *The Art of Electronic Music*. New York: Quill and Keyboard, 1984.

Ernst, David. *The Evolution of Electronic Music*. New York: Schirmer Books, 1977.

Griffiths, Paul. *A Guide to Electronic Music.* London: Thames & Hudson, 1979.

Holmes, T.B. *Electronic and Experimental Music.* New York: Scribner's, 1985.

Manning, Peter. *Electronic and Computer Music.* Oxford: Clarendon Press, 1985.

Pellegrino, Ron. *The Electronic Arts of Sound and Lights.* New York: Van Nostrand, Reinhold and Co., 1983.

Russcol, Herbert. *The Liberation of Sound.* Englewood Cliffs, N.J.: Prentice-Hall, 1972.

Schrader, Barry. *Introduction to Electro-Acoustic Music.* Englewood Cliffs, N.J.: Prentice-Hall, 1982.

Schwartz, Elliott. *Electronic Music: A Listener's Guide.* London: Secker and Warburg, 1973.

Wells, Thomas. *The Technique of Electronic Music.* New York: Schirmer Books, 1981.

MIDI

Conger, Jim. *C Programming for MIDI.* Redwood City, Calif.: M & T Books, 1988. (MS-DOS based.)

De Furia, Steve, and Joe Scacciaferro. *MIDI Programming for the Macintosh.* Redwood City, Calif.: M & T Books, 1988.

———. *The MIDI System Exclusive Book.* Milwaukee: Hal Leonard, 1987.

———. *The MIDI Implementation Book.* Milwaukee: Third Earth Publishing, 1987.

———. *MIDI Programmer's Handbook.* Redwood City, Calif.: M & T Books, 1989.

International MIDI Association. *MIDI, Musical Instrument Digital Interface Specification 1.0.* Los Angeles: International MIDI Association, 1983.

Loy, Gareth. "Musicians Make a Standard: The Phenomenon of MIDI." *Computer Music Journal.* 9,4 (Winter 1985): 8–26.

Moore, R. "The Dysfunctions of MIDI." In *Proceedings of the 1987 International Computer Music Conference,* ed. J. Beauchamp, San Francisco: Computer Music Association, 1987.

Rothstein, J. *MIDI: A Comprehensive Introduction.* Vol. 7, The Computer Music and Digital Audio Series. Madison, Wisc.: A-R Editions, Inc., 1992.

PSYCHOACOUSTICS

Deutsch, Diana., ed. *The Psychology of Music.* New York: Academic Press, 1992.

Grey, John. "An Exploration of Musical Timbre." Ph.D. diss., Stanford University, 1975.

Roederer, Juan C. *Introduction to the Physics and Psychophysics of Music.* New York: Springer Verlag, 1979.

Zwicker, E., and H. Fastl. *Psychoacoustics.* New York: Springer Verlag, 1990.

SIGNAL PROCESSING

Blesser, B., and J. M. Kates. "Digital Processing in Audio Signals." In *Applications of Digital Signal Processing,* ed. Alan V. Oppenheim. Englewood Cliffs, N.J.: Prentice-Hall, 1978.

Karl, John. *An Introduction to Digital Signal Processing.* San Diego: Academic Press, 1989.

Strawn, John, ed. *Digital Audio Signal Processing: An Anthology.* Vol. 1, The Computer Music and Digital Audio Series. Madison, Wisc.: A-R Editions, Inc., 1985. (Originally published Los Altos, Calif.: William Kaufmann.)

SYNTHESIZERS, SAMPLERS, AND MIDI DEVICES

Aikin, J., et al. *Synthesizer Technique.* Milwaukee: Hal Leonard, 1987.

Chamberlin, Hal. *Musical Applications of Microprocessors.* Indianapolis, Ind.: Hayden Books, 1985.

Chowning, John, and David Bristow. *FM Theory and Applications.* Milwaukee: Yamaha Foundation/Hal Leonard, 1986.

Darter, T. comp., *The Art of Electronic Music.* New York: Quill and Keyboard, 1984.

Davies, H. "Electronic Instruments." In *The New Grove Dictionary of Musical Instruments,* ed. Stanley Sadie. London: Macmillan and Co., 1984.

Horn, Delton. *Digital Electronic Music Synthesizers.* Blue Ridge Summit, Pa.: Tab Books, 1988.

Milano, Dominic, ed. *Synthesizer Programming.* Milwaukee: Hal Leonard, 1987.

Turkel, Eric. *MIDI Gadgets.* London and New York: Amsco, 1988.

TUNING AND TEMPERAMENT

Barbour, J. Murray. *Tuning and Temperament.* New York: Da Capo Press, 1978. (Originally published in 1951.)

Hába, Alois. *Neue Harmonielehre des diatonischen, chromatischen, viertel-, drittel-, sechstel-, und zwölftel-ton Systems.* Leipzig: F. Kistner and C. F. W. Siegel, 1927.

Blackwood, Easley. *The Structure of Recognizable Diatonic Tunings.* Princeton: Princeton University Press, 1985.

Jorgensen, Owen. *Tuning the Historical Temperaments by Ear.* Marquette, Mich.: The Northern University, 1977.

Lindley, Mark. "Temperament." In *The New Grove Dictionary of Music and Musicians,* ed. S. Sadie. London: Macmillan and Co., 1984.

Lloyd, Llewelyn, and Hugh Boyle. *Intervals, Scales, and Temperaments.* New York: St. Martin's Press, 1978.

Mandelbaum, M. Joel. "Multiple Division of the Octave and the Tonal Resources of 19-Tone Temperament." Ph.D. diss., Indiana University, 1961.

Partch, Harry. *Genesis of a Music.* New York: Da Capo Press, 1974.

Podnos, T. *Intonation for Strings, Winds, and Singers.* Metuchen, N.J.: Scarecrow Press, 1981.

Schneider, Sigrun. *Mikrotöne in der Musik des 20. Jahrhunderts: Untersuchungen zu Theorie und Gestaltungsprinzipien modernen Kompositionen mit Mikrotöne.* Bonn-Bad Godesberg: Verlag für Systematische Musikwissenschaft, 1975.

Wilkinson, Scott. *Tuning In: Microtonality in Electronic Music.* Milwaukee: Hal Leonard, 1988.

Yasser, Joseph. *A Theory of Evolving Tonality.* New York: Da Capo Press, 1975. (Originally published New York: American Library of Musicology, 1932.)

PERIODICALS

The Computer Music Journal (1977–)
Published by the MIT Press, Cambridge, Mass., four times a year. Major journal for new developments in computer music and synthesis.

Contemporary Music Review (1984–)
Harwood Academic Publishers, London. Each issue has a guest editor coordinating a specific theme.

Ear Magazine (1973–)
New York. Reviews and articles on new directions in music.

Electronic Musician (1984–) formerly *Polyphony* (1976–)
Emeryville, California. All aspects of computer and electronic music.

International Computer Music Conference (ICMC) Proceedings. (1976–)
Published yearly by the Computer Music Association, San Francisco.

Interface (1972–)
Swets and Zeitlinger, Amsterdam. Research on new technological and conceptual issues in music.

In Theory Only (1975–)
University of Michigan. Music theory.

Journal of the Audio Engineering Society (1953–)
New York: Audio Engineering Society. Acoustics and audio engineering.

Journal of Music Theory (1957–)
Yale School of Music, New Haven, Connecticut. Music theory.

Keyboard Magazine (1975–)
Cupertino, California. Monthly. Regular articles on keyboards, MIDI, and information on new commercial products and reviews.

Mix Magazine (1977–)
Berkeley, California. The monthly magazine of the recording industry with frequent articles about MIDI and SMPTE products.

Music Technology (1986–) formerly *Electronics and Music Maker* (1981–)
Cambridge, England. Monthly. Articles on all aspects of music technology, including performance reviews, product reviews, and interviews.

Perspectives of New Music (1962–)
Quarterly. Annandale-on-Hudson, New York. Serious investigations of contemporary musical thought and composition.

Source: Music of the Avant-garde (1967–72)
Davis, California. An excellent documentation of avant-garde activities in music during its period of publication.

USEFUL ADDRESSES

Electronic Music Schools

There are many institutions offering instruction in this area. A useful reference for courses in the United States is L. Milano's *Directory of Electronic Music Schools,* GPI Publications, Cupertino, Calif.

International MIDI Association

The body coordinating and publishing the MIDI detailed specification.
>IMA
5316 W. 57th Street
Los Angeles, CA
USA 90056
Internet: MMA@pan.com

Performing Artists Network (PAN)

This is a modem-accessible performing artists network that includes a bulletin board, databases, electronic mail service, a classified ads service, and other features useful to the contemporary synthesist.
>PAN
P.O. Box 162
Skippack, PA
USA 19474
(215) 584--0300

Composer's Desktop Project (CDP)

This group of researchers provides a highly useful set of computer music software products for the Atari computer. Much of the significant mainframe direct digital synthesis material from around the world has been ported to this environment, along with specific new MIDI-based materials.
>CDP
11 Kilburn Road
York YO1 4DF
UK

Other Electronic Bulletin Boards

A range of electronic bulletin boards, such as CompuServe, GEnie, and others, are of relevance to electronic musicians. A useful survey of these is given by Mike Rivers, "Going On Line," *Electronic Musician* 6,11 (June 1990): 20–32.

AN OUTLINE OF DEVELOPMENTS IN ELECTRONIC MUSIC

. . . .

Developments in electronic music have gone hand in hand with innovations in technology and culture, scientific research in acoustics and psychoacoustics, and advances in the techniques of music composition and performance. In the following chronological outline the emphasis is on the performance of electronic music. Related technological, scientific, and cultural events are given in italics.

1759   La Borde invents the electric harpsichord, an early static electricity driven traditional instrument

            1799   Voltaic Pile (battery cell)

1837   Charles Page develops galvanic music using the electric bell principle

            1863   Hermann von Helmholtz's Sensations of Tone is published, a landmark in psychoacoustics

1874   Elisha Gray invents the Musical Telegraph, the first autonomous electrical musical instrument. It is keyboard based

            1878   Thomas Edison invents the phonograph

            1883   Thomas Edison discovers the Edison Effect

            1898   Valdemar Poulsen invents the Telegraphone, the first magnetic (wire) recorder

1899   William Duddell invents the Singing Arc, an instrument that produces whistling sounds from electric arc-lamps

1900–   Thaddeus Cahill demonstrates and develops the Telharmonium (Dynamophone), the first synthesizer (but with limited programmability), the first multimanual electronic instrument, the first touch-sensitive electric keyboard

            1904   Ambrose Fleming invents the diode

            1906   Lee de Forest invents the triode

            1909   The Futurist movement begins, e.g., Filippo Marinetti, Balilla Pratella

            1913–   Luigi Russolo develops his Intonarumori (noise instruments)

            1916   Dada begins: sound poetry, mixed media

1919–   Leo Thérémin invents the Thérémin, the first expressive and commercially viable electronic musical instrument. Clara Rockmore becomes the first virtuoso Théréminist. The Thérémin continues to be used today: e.g., contemporary jazz thereminist Youssef Yancy, Latimer and the Hand People

1920s–   Oskar Vierling, B. F. Miessner, et al. develop the electric piano

            ca. 1925   first electronic amplifiers and loudspeakers

1925–30   Jörg Mager develops the Klaviatursphärophon and Partituro-phone, synthesizers with multiple (3–5) monophonic keyboards

1928   Bruno Helberger and Peter Lertes invent the Hellertion, an
            early multiribbon controller

1928–   Maurice Martenot invents and develops the Ondes Martenot,
            the second commercially viable electronic musical instrument.
            Jeanne Loriod is a major virtuoso on this instrument

1928   Friedrich Trautwein invents the Trautonium, an expressive syn-
            thesizer still played today (in Mixtur-Trautonium model)

1929   Edouard Coupleux and Joseph Givelet invent the Coupleux-
            Givelet synthesizer, the first extensively programmable
            synthesizer. It is a composing, not a performing instrument

> *1930s   Numerous electronic ensembles arise. Composers such
>   as Henry Cowell, Edgard Varèse, George Antheil, and
>   Darius Milhaud use noise sources and electronics*

> *1931   Adolph Rickenbacker develops the first commercially
>   marketed electric guitar*

1933   Richard Ranger invents the Rangertone Organ, the first split
            keyboard polytimbral organ

1935   Laurens Hammond invents the Hammond Organ

> *1935   invention of the Magnetophone, the magnetic tape re-
>   corder, by the Allgemeine Elektrizitäts Gesellschaft*

1937   Harald Bode develops the Warbo Formant-Orgel, a significant
            polyphonic polytimbral electronic keyboard instrument

1938   Harald Bode invents the Melodium, a sophisticated monopho-
            nic touch-sensitive keyboard

1939   Laurens Hammond invents the Novachord, an organ with
            synthesizer-like controls

1944–61   Percy Grainger and Burnett Cross develop their Free Music
            Machines, graphic-notation composing (not performing) ma-
            chines

1947–53   Harald Bode develops the Melochord, a split keyboard instru-
            ment with modular design

> *1947–48 invention of the transistor*

> *1948   debut of the LP record*

1948–   Hugh Le Caine invents and refines the electronic sackbut, a
            highly developed real-time performance synthesizer

1948–   "Classical" studio electronic music develops in the hands of such musicians as Pierre Schaeffer, Pierre Henry, Edgard Varèse, Iannis Xenakis, Karlheinz Stockhausen, Vladimir Ussachevsky, Herbert Eimert, Les Paul, and Mary Ford. Innovations include *musique concrète, elektronische musik,* tape music, the multi-track recorder as a compositional medium

1949–   Friedrich Trautwein and Oskar Sala develop the Mixtur-Trautonium, and Sala becomes a significant performer on this instrument

1950–54   Osmond Kendall develops the Composer-Tron, a composition synthesizer

          late 1950s–60s   proliferation of live electroacoustic ensembles

1955–   Harry F. Olson, Herbert Belar, and Milton Babbitt develop the RCA Synthesizer

1956–   Computer music is developed by many workers, including Lejaren Hiller, Max Mathews, John Chowning, Barry Vercoe, and Jean-Claude Risset

1957–   Max Mathews develops Music N software (direct digital synthesis)

1962–64   Donald Buchla develops voltage-controlled monophonic electronic musical instruments

1963   Paul Ketoff develops the Synket, an early voltage-controlled synthesizer. John Eaton appears as a significant performer on this instrument

1964   Robert Moog invents the Moog synthesizer, the first commercial synthesizer. It is monophonic, modular, and voltage-controlled

ca.1965   Raymond Scott invents the Electronium, a significant interactive/intelligent musical instrument

          1960s–   Multi-media happenings, John Cage, ONCE Festivals, et al.

1960s   Raymond Scott develops the Clavivox, a monophonic instrument with real-time performance synthesis

1968   Wendy Carlos's album *Switched-On Bach* appears

1970–   various commercial monophonic performance keyboard synthesizers appear

1970–   Max Mathews develops GROOVE—an interactive composition system

early 70s   First digital synthesizers

             1972   first microprocessor

1974   first Synthesizer Festival

1975   Jan Hammer makes extensive use of strap-on controller keyboards

1975   David Luce and Robert Moog develop the Polymoog, an early fully polyphonic keyboard synthesizer

1976   New England Digital releases the Synclavier, the first commercially marketed digital synthesizer

1977   Dave Smith (Sequential) develops the Prophet 5, the first microprocessor-based fully programmable polyphonic synthesizer

1979   Fairlight Australia releases the Fairlight CMI, an integrated computer musical instrument (workstation) and early sampling machine

             1980s   microcomputer revolution occurs, enabling extensive development of commercial music software for sequencing, scoring, et al.

1980s   substantial activity in intelligent and interactive live performance systems develops, as in the hands of George Lewis, Michel Waiswicz, and Richard Teitelbaum

1983   MIDI is introduced

1983   the Yamaha DX7 is introduced, the first commercial FM-based synthesizer

1984–   Numerous digital polyphonic multitimbral synthesizers and samplers are released by different manufacturers in Japan, the United States, and Europe

             late 1980s   compact discs and digital audio tape

late 80s   Synthesizer workstations and integrated digital audio workstations develop. Direct to hard disk recording sytems proliferate

REFERENCES

The reader interested in more comprehensive sources should consult Rhea (1972), Mumma (1975), Darter et al. (1984), Davies (1984), and Weidenaar (1988).

NUMBER SYSTEM CONVERSION

· ·

This Appendix provides ready interconversion between decimal, hexadecimal, octal, binary, and 1-starting decimal number systems. Octal numbers have been taken to begin with 1, as is common synthesizer practice. 'A' and 'B' refer to the two banks available on many octal based synthesizers, which allow 128 patch locations to be specified.

Dec.	Binary	Hex.	I-Dec.	Octal	Dec.	Binary	Hex.	I-Dec.	Octal
00	00	00H	01	A11	49	110001	31H	50	72
01	01	01H	02	12	50	110010	32H	51	73
02	10	02H	03	13	51	110011	33H	52	74
03	11	03H	04	14	52	110100	34H	53	75
04	100	04H	05	15	53	110101	35H	54	76
05	101	05H	06	16	54	110110	36H	55	77
06	110	06H	07	17	55	110111	37H	56	78
07	111	07H	08	18	56	111000	38H	57	81
08	1000	08H	09	21	57	111001	39H	58	82
09	1001	09H	10	22	58	111010	3AH	59	83
10	1010	0AH	11	23	59	111011	3BH	60	84
11	1011	0BH	12	24	60	111100	3CH	61	85
12	1100	0CH	13	25	61	111101	3DH	62	86
13	1101	0DH	14	26	62	111110	3EH	63	87
14	1110	0EH	15	27	63	111111	3FH	64	88
15	1111	0FH	16	28	64	1000000	40H	65	B11
16	10000	10H	17	31	65	1000001	41H	66	12
17	10001	11H	18	32	66	1000010	42H	67	13
18	10010	12H	19	33	67	1000011	43H	68	14
19	10011	13H	20	34	68	1000100	44H	69	15
20	10100	14H	21	35	69	1000101	45H	70	16
21	10101	15H	22	36	70	1000110	46H	71	17
22	10110	16H	23	37	71	1000111	47H	72	18
23	10111	17H	24	38	72	1001000	48H	73	21
24	11000	18H	25	41	73	1001001	49H	74	22
25	11001	19H	26	42	74	1001010	4AH	75	23
26	11010	1AH	27	43	75	1001011	4BH	76	24
27	11011	1BH	28	44	76	1001100	4CH	77	25
28	11100	1CH	29	45	77	1001101	4DH	78	26
29	11101	1DH	30	46	78	1001110	4EH	79	27
30	11110	1EH	31	47	79	1001111	4FH	80	28
31	11111	1FH	32	48	80	1010000	50H	81	31
32	100000	20H	33	51	81	1010001	51H	82	32
33	100001	21H	34	52	82	1010010	52H	83	33
34	100010	22H	35	53	83	1010011	53H	84	34
35	100011	23H	36	54	84	1010100	54H	85	35
36	100100	24H	37	55	85	1010101	55H	86	36
37	100101	25H	38	56	86	1010110	56H	87	37
38	100110	26H	39	57	87	1010111	57H	88	38
39	100111	27H	40	58	88	1011000	58H	89	41
40	101000	28H	41	61	89	1011001	59H	90	42
41	101001	29H	42	62	90	1011010	5AH	91	43
42	101010	2AH	43	63	91	1011011	5BH	92	44
43	101011	2BH	44	64	92	1011100	5CH	93	45
44	101100	2CH	45	65	93	1011101	5DH	94	46
45	101101	2DH	46	66	94	1011110	5EH	95	47
46	101110	2EH	47	67	95	1011111	5FH	96	48
47	101111	2FH	48	68	96	1100000	60H	97	51
48	110000	30H	49	71	97	1100001	61H	98	52
					98	1100010	62H	99	53

Dec.	Binary	Hex.	I-Dec.	Octal
99	1100011	63H	100	54
100	1100100	64H	101	55
101	1100101	65H	102	56
102	1100110	66H	103	57
103	1100111	67H	104	58
104	1101000	68H	105	61
105	1101001	69H	106	62
106	1101010	6AH	107	63
107	1101011	6BH	108	64
108	1101100	6CH	109	65
109	1101101	6DH	110	66
110	1101110	6EH	111	67
111	1101111	6FH	112	68
112	1110000	70H	113	71
113	1110001	71H	114	72
114	1110010	72H	115	73
115	1110011	73H	116	74
116	1110100	74H	117	75
117	1110101	75H	118	76
118	1110110	76H	119	77
119	1110111	77H	120	78
120	1111000	78H	121	81
121	1111001	79H	122	82
122	1111010	7AH	123	83
123	1111011	7BH	124	84
124	1111100	7CH	125	85
125	1111101	7DH	126	86
126	1111110	7EH	127	87
127	1111111	7FH	128	88
128	10000000	80H	129	

INDEX

· ·

454   SYNTHESIZER PERFORMANCE